CLASSICS AND CONTEMPORARY THOUGHT

Thomas Habinek, editor

Re-Reading Sappho

Re-Reading Sappho

Reception and Transmission

EDITED BY

Ellen Greene

UNIVERSITY OF CALIFORNIA PRESS

Berkeley   Los Angeles   London

University of California Press
Berkeley and Los Angeles, California

University of California Press, Ltd.
London, England

© 1996 by
The Regents of the University of California

Library of Congress Cataloging-in-Publication Data

Re-reading Sappho : reception and transmission / edited by Ellen Greene.
      p.   cm. — (Classics and contemporary thought : v. 3)
   Includes bibliographical references and index.
   ISBN 0-520-20602-9 (alk. paper) -- ISBN 0-520-20603-7 (pbk. : alk. paper)
   1. Sappho—Criticism and interpretation—History.   2. Love poetry,
Greek—History and criticism—Theory, etc.   3. Literature, Modern—Greek
influences.   4. Sappho—Appreciation—History.   5. Women and literature—
Greece.   6. Lesbians in literature.   7. Transmission of texts.   8. Love in
literature.   9. Sappho—Influence.   I. Greene, Ellen, 1950- .   II. Series :
Classics and contemporary thought : 3.
   PA4409.R47   1996
   884'.01–dc20   96-13701
                                                                              CIP

Printed in the United States of America
9 8 7 6 5 4 3 2 1

To my father and to the memory of my mother

CONTENTS

ACKNOWLEDGMENTS

I wish to thank Tom Habinek, the series editor, and Mary Lamprech, the Classics editor at the University of California Press, for their enthusiastic support of this project. I am grateful to the friends and colleagues who generously offered advice and support, especially Harriette Andreadis, André Lardinois, Yopie Prins, and my colleagues in the Classics Department at the University of Oklahoma, especially my ever-supportive chair, Jack Catlin. I also want to thank Mary Lefkowitz for introducing me to the beauty of Sappho's fragments in a seminar at Berkeley. Finally, I thank Jim Hawthorne for his counsel, his computer expertise, and his love and friendship.

SERIES EDITOR'S FOREWORD

Thomas Habinek

The series *Classics and Contemporary Thought* seeks to encourage dialogue between classical studies and other fields in the arts, humanities, and social sciences. It is based upon the recognition that each generation puts its own questions to the raw material of the past and is grounded in the conviction that the classical past still has much to say to the contemporary world. In contrast to much conventional classical scholarship which seeks ever more sophisticated or detailed answers to questions inherited from earlier scholarship, works selected for publication in this series use the skills of the classicist to address new issues or pose new questions. Because the literature and art of ancient Greece and Rome are distant from our own experience, their interpretation requires the mediation of specialists. But the obligation of such specialists is to the present as much as to the past. It is, in essence, to make the past available to the present.

The essays collected by Ellen Greene in two volumes entitled *Reading Sappho: Contemporary Approaches* and *Re-Reading Sappho: Reception and Transmission* seek to make the poetry of Sappho more readily available to contemporary readers in a variety of disciplines and from a variety of backgrounds. They do not pretend to represent the totality of modern responses to Sappho. Rather, the essays in *Reading Sappho: Contemporary Approaches* focus on the leading interpretations of Sappho, her context, and her achievement advanced by scholars in the field of classical studies in recent years, while the essays in volume two, *Re-Reading Sappho: Reception and Transmission*, examine reactions to Sappho at different stages of history from antiquity to the twentieth century. The juxtaposition of the two volumes provides a useful contrast between contemporary and earlier approaches to the poetry of Sappho, while illustrating the more general claim that each generation makes of the past what it will. Our encounter with the poetry of Sappho today is shaped both by our own experiences and concerns as inhabitants of a late twentieth century post-industrial society and the interests, attitudes, and preconceptions of previous generations of readers, translators, and scholars. By exploring both we can arrive at a richer understanding of Sappho and perhaps even of ourselves.

The essays in the first volume, *Contemporary Approaches*, reflect some of the broader social and intellectual developments that have characterized the last three decades and provide insight into the reconfiguration of classical studies that has accompanied those changes. The increasing empowerment of women, with the resultant interest in women's history, women's writing, and women's "ways of knowing," has accounted for the focus on Sappho as the first female writer in the Western tradition whose works have survived in any quantity. Sappho has become a test case for both the constructivist and the essentialist views of culture and gender, with scholars placing corresponding emphasis on discontinuities and continuities between her era and our own. As proto-queer, Sappho raises comparable issues with respect to sexual orientation: is she the recovered voice of a long-suppressed lesbian consciousness, or does she instead invite us to consider alternative ways of categorizing human sexual behaviors and emotions? Also running through the volume are conflicting views of the importance of institutions and their impact on the creativity of the individual artist. The earlier of the essays, in particular, advocate a direct experience of Sappho's poetry and emphasize the texture of her language and the specificity of her imagery. While later essays never fully abandon such approaches, they pay more attention to Sappho's poetry as a cultural phenomenon, one shaped by and shaping in turn the myths and rituals of the ancient Greek peoples. In this respect, Sappho studies of the past thirty years have followed the trajectory of literary studies more generally, moving toward more deeply historicized and contexualized interpretations.

Underlying the essays in the second volume, *Reception and Transmission*, is a different set of questions concerning the relationship between past and present. For some of the contributors, the vagaries in accounts of Sappho from antiquity through the twentieth century testify to the unrecoverability of past experience or past literature in any but the most attenuated form. In their versions of the reception of Sappho, each generation is seen to create its own Sappho on the basis of its own needs and interests. For other contributors, exploring past versions of Sappho becomes a way of moving closer to a true account of the poet in her original context—like excavating layers of earth at an archaeological site or unwrapping a mummy. For still others, earlier generations' encounters with Sappho become models for our own potentially fruitful relationship with the past. These conflicting views of the task of the critic or historian are not easily reconciled. What unites them, however, is a sense of Sappho as a figure of potential. While the indeterminacy of certain aspects of Sappho's poetry may, as Glenn Most argues, be due to cultural constraints on the expression of female desire in archaic Greece, it is an undeniable source of the interest she continually attracts from disparate readers. Indeed, the fragmentary nature of the surviving texts has only increased their value for succeeding generations. For some, it has meant the opportunity to create whatever Sappho they need. For others, the historical irony implicit in the fragmentary preservation of poems of yearning and separation serves as a reminder of the inevitable incompleteness of human knowledge and affection.

One year before the publication of the earliest of the essays contained in these volumes, Sylvia Plath's poem "Lesbos" appeared in her posthumous collection *Ariel*. While Plath's poem mimics the dialogue style, the temporal compression, and the natural imagery that characterizes Sappho's writing, its speaker places herself, rather than the unnamed addressee, in the position of departing lover. Plath's suicide makes it tempting to associate her with Sappho, whom legend describes as leaping to her death in despair over a failed love relationship, but the testimony of Plath's poetry suggest that she belongs instead to a long line of female writers who have found it necessary to reject the authoritative example of Sappho in order to get on with their creative lives. In her case, the rejection of Sappho marks a more widespread generational resistance to the hegemony of the elite classical tradition, a refusal, in Muriel Rukeyser's words, to enter "the populated cold of drawing rooms." In a sense, Plath (along with Rukeyser and others), by denying Sappho's authority, closed the door on one generation's reading of her poems and their significance. What we have before us, in the two volumes compiled by Ellen Greene, is a report in progress on the present generation's encounter with Sappho—through direct experience of her texts, through contextualized interpretations, and through reflection on her meaning for past readers and re-readers.

INTRODUCTION

Ellen Greene

The greatness of a number of writers from antiquity is so thoroughly unquestioned that they are always granted a place in the annals of literature. Yet none
but Sappho has become a truly *legendary* figure.

JOAN DEJEAN

As poet, as legendary literary figure, Sappho has had an undeniable fascination for readers ever since she composed her poems on the island of
Lesbos at the close of the seventh century B.C.E. From Plato's celebration
of Sappho as the tenth Muse to Robin Morgan's renunciation of Sappho
as literary foremother ("get off my back, Sappho"), the life and lyrics of
Sappho have haunted the Western imagination. Sappho's intense, burning
verses of feminine desire have presided over the Western lyric much the
way Homer's epics have occupied their authoritative position in Western
literature. Sappho comes down to us as a kind of mother goddess of poetry:
imitated, ventriloquized, renounced, worshiped, and feared, as perhaps no
other single poet in the Western tradition.

Why has Sappho come to "inhabit the popular imagination" with so much
intensity? Why have her poetics and her persona engendered centuries
of fantasy, speculation, and mythmaking? Indeed, Joan DeJean points
out that fictions about Sappho started circulating within centuries of her
death. To Socrates and Plato, Sappho is the exemplary Sublime Poetess,
an authority in matters of love. To the writers of late antiquity, Sappho
becomes not only priestess of song but exemplar of the woman who died
for love—reputedly flinging herself off the white cliff of Leukas for the
love of a ferryman. Interest in Sappho, in both the scholarly and literary
traditions, has often reflected a voyeuristic fascination with the "queerness"
of a woman writing poetry in which men are "relegated to a peripheral,
if not an intrusive, role."[1] Curiosity about Sappho over the centuries has
been fueled by the fragmentary condition of her poems, the lack of any
concrete information about her life, and the implications of homoeroticism

---

1. DeJean, "Fictions of Sappho," 790.

1

in her work—implications that all too often have been regarded as sexual "deviance."

Aside from the provocative images of lesbian love that have disturbed many readers through the ages, one of the most compelling aspects of Sappho fiction—making arises from the tendency readers have had to fill in the gaps of Sappho's mutilated texts. Modern scholars have been faced with the problem of how to piece together Sappho's surviving fragments. Nearly all of Sappho's surviving poems have major breaks in the text or are short excerpts from a longer poem. Many of the approximately two hundred fragments attributed to Sappho contain only one or two words. Out of the nine books of her poetry edited by scholars at the great library in Alexandria during the third and second centuries B.C.E., only forty fragments are long enough to be intelligible. Thus, much of the scholarly work on Sappho from the early part of the century to the 1960s focused on textual and philological analysis and reconstruction. Scholarship on the content of Sappho's poetry emphasized efforts to construct her biography—often with the aim of endowing Sappho with "Victorian" respectability. And of course the association of Sappho with female homoeroticism has made her, for many readers, a fascinating yet often problematic subject of speculation and fantasy. In 1913, the classical scholar Wilamowitz declared Sappho to be the official leader of a cult of female worshipers devoted to Aphrodite.[2] The notion of Sappho as the head of a *thiasos* or religious cult for young girls dominated Sappho scholarship and did much to rationalize away the homoerotic aspects of her poetry. As Holt Parker argues in his essay in this volume, "Sappho Schoolmistress," the image of Sappho presiding over a School of Virgins became canonical in early Sappho scholarship, giving rise to a multitude of related speculations about Sappho as music teacher and sex educator for a cultlike circle of young girls.

Edgar Lobel and Denys Page's 1955 commentary on Sappho marked a turning point in Sappho scholarship. Their book, *Poetarum Lesbiorum Fragmenta,* with a complete text and commentary on Sappho's fragments, became the definitive edition of Sappho's poems and, to a large extent, resolved the philological issues of textual reconstruction. Within a decade or so of their commentary, in the late 1960s and early 1970s, an efflorescence of literary and contextual criticism emerged in which scholars began to read Sappho's poetry for its literary content and its relation to literary and mythical tradition. Changes in Sappho criticism, moreover, coincided with general changes in classical scholarship; in the 1970s efforts to assimilate methodologies from other branches of literary and cultural studies began to

---

2. Wilamowitz, *Sappho und Simonides* 17–78.

appear. In addition, feminist scholarship and, more recently, gender theory and criticism have provoked discussions about how Sappho's gender has both shaped her poetic discourse and influenced the social context of her poetry.

The essays collected in this volume reflect not only the burgeoning interest in Sappho over the last thirty years, but a more recent fascination with Sappho's "afterlife"—the seemingly endless permutations wrought upon her life and her work through centuries of literary and scholarly readings and rewritings. The history of Sappho imitations, translations, and scholarship is a history of images and perceptions, fictions and fantasies. As many of these essays show, each age, each generation invents its own Sappho. The authors in this volume examine the ways scholars and writers have read the fragmentary remains of Sappho's poetry and have, to a large extent, created the Sappho they wanted. As Jack Winkler astutely remarked, "Novelists, scholars, and ambitious young literary men (and women), although they knew nothing about Sappho's actual poetry, used her as a Rorschach blot projecting their fantasies and anxieties about sex, gender, and genius."[3] Indeed Sappho's association with female homoeroticism, the fragmentary nature of her work, and the fact that so little is known about her life have generated a multitude of fictions about her—fictions that are themselves fascinating because they reflect the particular cultural attitudes and biases out of which those fictions emerged. "To retrace the development of fictions of Sappho," DeJean writes, "is both to measure the standards imposed on female sexuality at any given period and to provide an index, across the centuries, not only of the received ideas about female same-sex love but also of what it was possible to write about that subject at any given period."[4] Thus, Sappho, as subject of scholarly investigation, translation, and myth, becomes an extraordinary means of access to changing sensibilities and cultural norms about sexuality, gender roles, and notions of female authorship. When we read the history of Sappho scholarship and the numerous translations and imitations of her work, we see how Sappho is, as Yopie Prins points out, "continually transformed and refigured in the process of transmission." Indeed, the study of Sappho reception raises questions about how literary voice may be recuperated through reading and how Sappho becomes both a cause and an effect of literary transmission.[5]

3. Winkler, back cover of DeJean, *Fictions of Sappho*.

4. DeJean, *Fictions of Sappho* 2.

5. See Joan DeJean's exploration of a range of literary imitations of Sappho in *Fictions of Sappho*, which called attention to the intriguing subject of Sappho reception and to Sappho's importance as a literary and cultural figure. As DeJean points out: "The history of Sappho's fictionalization has much to teach us about the evolving discourse of gender, the construction of sexual difference through notions of the feminine and the masculine. All fictions of Sappho

To many male writers, from Catullus and Ovid in antiquity to Swinburne, Tennyson, and Baudelaire in the modern era, Sappho represents access to a woman's voice, the vehicle through which it is possible to "enact a woman's part" and perhaps to escape the boundaries of masculinity. While it is possible to regard imitation of Sappho as praise, it is equally possible to consider the ways male poets have adapted Sappho's lines to their own purposes as an appropriation of the woman's voice, an attempt to master and control feminine desire. For many women poets, on the other hand, Sappho has represented the literary foremother who gave them a poetic tradition of their own. Sappho epitomizes, as Susan Gubar writes, "all the lost women of genius in literary history, especially all the lesbian artists whose work has been destroyed, sanitized, or heterosexualized." For those women poets who identify with Sappho, Sappho's stature in literary history authorizes their own poetic talents and provides them with a precursor to whom they can turn not only for inspiration but also for collaboration. For it is in Sappho's broken fragments that the modern woman poet could reinvent Sappho's verse and thus inscribe feminine desire as part of an empowering literary history of her own.

◆   ◆   ◆

While the number of studies of Sappho's "afterlife" has grown considerably over the last ten years, this book is the first collection of essays that deals exclusively with the topic of Sappho reception and transmission. To be sure, the "afterlife" of Sappho is a huge subject that cannot be addressed in one volume. The essays collected here, however, deal with many of the main themes in afterlife studies of Sappho and are indicative of the wide scope of scholarship in the field.[6] Moreover, these essays are offered as examples of studies of the main historical periods in which Sappho shows up in the literary and scholarly traditions of the West. While the authors in this collection bring diverse critical perspectives to the study of Sappho reception, the selection of recent and new essays included here reflects current scholarly interest in changing discourses of gender at different cultural moments and in a variety of literary and scholarly sources.

---

are fictions of the feminine: they transmit received ideas about female desire, its expression, its plot, its fate" (22).

6. Aside from DeJean's *Fictions of Sappho,* other important "afterlife" studies of Sappho include Robinson, *Sappho and Her Influence;* Mora, *Sappho;* Marks, "Lesbian Intertextuality"; Stein, *The Iconography of Sappho;* Rigolot, "Louise Labé et la rédecouverte de Sapho"; Gubar, "Sapphistries"; Grahn, *The Highest Apple;* DeJean, "Female Voyeurism"; Lipking, "Sappho Descending."

Glenn Most's essay, "Reflecting Sappho," leads off the collection with an overview of the "dramatic changes" Sappho's reputation has undergone over the centuries. As Most points out, Sappho is by no means the only ancient author whose literary fortunes have been drastically altered by generations of mythmaking and literary misunderstanding. But Sappho's fate in the annals of literary history presents an extraordinary disparity between the mutilated remains of her actual poetry and the widespread celebrity of her person in the public imagination. It is the problematic relationship between text and context that Most addresses in his essay. How do literary reputations come about; and in particular, how does Sappho come to exemplify, for example, "insatiable heterosexual promiscuity" in her afterlife in ancient Athens and in the eighteenth century become an emblem of unhappy heterosexual love, evidenced by her desperate passion for Phaon and her suicide from the Leukadian cliff? Most's essay surveys the images of Sappho that have flourished from antiquity through the present in both literary and scholarly sources in an effort to interrogate the complex relation between a literary text and its reception in distant ages and cultural contexts. Most suggests that it is the fleeting, "temporarily fashionable" prejudices about women, sexuality, and poetry in a given culture that have determined the ways in which Sappho's texts were understood, edited, and translated.

Focusing on the theme of translation, Yopie Prins's essay, "Sappho's Afterlife in Translation," traces various English translations of fragment 31 from the seventeenth century to the present in order to focus on the historical and theoretical problems of translating Sappho. While the issue of "reconstituting" Sappho's fragmented voice from her texts is central in the process of translation and transmission, fragment 31 is the only extant poem in which Sappho explicitly dramatizes desire for the beloved through a loss of voice that is associated with a kind of death. In analyzing a number of translations spanning four centuries, Prins examines the representations of Sappho's broken tongue and the various ways translators have tried to "recuperate voice from that break." Her article shows that translation has been one of the most central factors in the transmission of Sappho's texts. The moment of performance during Sappho's own life is replaced by the performativity of translation itself that ensures Sappho's afterlife. Prins reads different translations, not to compare them to the "original" Sappho but to describe how Sappho is continually refigured in the process of translation. Moreover, Prins's analysis of different translations of fragment 31 shows the engendering of Sappho as a "specifically female lyric subject" within a lyric tradition, an emergence that demonstrates the intertwining of gender and genre in the reading of lyric poetry.

Representations of Sappho on Greek vases of the sixth and fifth centuries B.C.E. and brief references to her in Plato, Aristotle, and Menander attest to her reputation in antiquity as a poet of considerable stature. But aside from these references, the earliest evidence for Sappho's direct influence on other poets occurs in the Roman period. Catullus's poem 51, his "translation" of Sappho 31, furnishes a significant opportunity not only to examine the reception of Sappho in Rome but also to investigate the "translation" of a feminine discourse within a Roman male cultural context. A number of important studies have been done comparing Sappho 31 and Catullus 51.[7] Dolores O'Higgins's essay, "Sappho's Splintered Tongue: Silence in Sappho 31 and Catullus 51," considers the image of the "broken tongue" in the two poems, particularly in regard to how that image reflects aspects of oral and literate culture. Sappho's loss of voice in the context of a lyric tradition that is essentially performative threatens to silence her altogether. For Catullus, on the other hand, poetry is written communication—a book, a *libellus*, that is separate from himself. Thus Catullus's "broken tongue" does not to the same degree endanger his ability to "create or communicate his poetry." O'Higgins's essay brings into focus the profound impact "reading" Sappho's poems within written culture has on the interpretation and transmission of Sappho's poems.

One of the main recurrent themes of Sappho's afterlife in both Roman and Renaissance texts is the legend of Sappho's love for a ferryman named Phaon. The famous tale about Sappho and Phaon, which seems to have originated at least two centuries after her life,[8] involves her passionate love for Phaon and her suicidal leap from the White Rock of Leukas (off the west coast of the Greek mainland) into the sea in pursuit of him. The earliest complete version of the legend occurs in the first century C.E. by the Roman poet Ovid in his *Heroides*. In *Heroides* 15, the last in his collection of fictional letters from abandoned heroines, Sappho appears as an abandoned woman writing to her lost lover Phaon. The famous story reappears in sixteenth- and seventeenth-century England, most notably in the poetry of John Donne.

Elizabeth Harvey's essay "Ventriloquizing Sappho, or the Lesbian Muse" and Harriette Andreadis's article "Sappho and Early Modern England: A Study in Sexual Reputation" take up the issue of Sappho's treatment as a literary figure in the Renaissance—a period in which Sappho reemerged from a long period of neglect. The Renaissance authors who dramatize Sappho were acquainted with her mainly through Ovid's depiction in his

---

7. See esp. Paul Allen Miller's article, "Sappho 31 and Catullus 51: The Dialogism of Lyric," for an insightful comparison of the two poems using Mikhail Bakhtin's theories of dialogism. See also Wills, "Sappho 31 and Catullus 51," and Segal, "Otium and Eros."

8. The Sappho-Phaon story first appears in a short fragment from a play by the fourth-century B.C.E. Greek writer Menander called *The Leukadia*. In the play, a speaker avers that Sappho was the first to throw herself off the White Rock of Leukas.

Heroides. As Andreadis and Harvey show, the Renaissance Sappho bears little resemblance to the poet as she is known today.

Elizabeth Harvey's essay traces the reception of Sappho *through* Ovid's Sapphic letter in *Heroides* 15 and analyzes the Sapphic voice enunciated in John Donne's poem "Sappho to Philaenis" and its "Ovidian subtext." In discussing both the Donne and Ovid poems, Harvey focuses on the intertextual problem of what she calls "transvestite ventriloquism," the "male author's appropriation of the feminine voice" and its implications for the silencing of women's speech and writing. Moreover, Harvey links this silencing to the suppression and faulty transmission of Sappho's texts. Thus, Harvey's essay not only provides a study of the images of Sappho perpetuated by Ovid and Donne but also investigates how questions of literary voice and "authorial property" are inextricably linked to gender, to the erasure of a woman's voice altogether.

Harriette Andreadis's article follows by discussing the reception of Sappho in Renaissance England. Using Ovid's "myth" of Sappho as represented in *Heroides* 15 as a starting point, Andreadis examines references to the mythologized reputation of Sappho in sixteenth- and seventeenth-century England in order to explore the public discourse about sexuality in that period. Andreadis's article interrogates the issue of how discourses of female sexuality changed in early modern England, examining the way in which Sappho's literary reputation provided a exemplar for those discourses.

In the late nineteenth and early twentieth centuries, we witness an attempt to explain away Sappho's supposed sexual deviance. Scholars during this period show a tendency to defend Sappho from implied charges of scandal and aberrant behavior.[9] In "Sex and Philology: Sappho and the Rise of German Nationalism," Joan DeJean looks to the origins of this tendency in nineteenth-century German philology, which promoted theories about Sappho's "chastity," and examines its role in facilitating notions of a German national identity. DeJean argues that early German philologists went to great pains to "defend" Sappho from charges of homosexuality, partly as a way to rehabilitate the Greek "national character" as a model for the German nation state, but, perhaps more importantly, also to keep alive the notion of a "purer, masculine eros" that would help inspire German nationalism.

---

9. See Bury, ed., *Greek Literature from the Eighth Century to the Persian Wars;* see also Robinson, *The Influence of Sappho*. Suggestions of scandal and deviance can be detected in Bury's words of caution to readers of Sappho about the need to observe tact and discretion: "Whatever the intimacies of her life may have been—and it may be suggested that there are limits beyond which it is . . . impertinent to inquire into the private lives of eminent people of the past[—] . . . it is clear that in her own day in Lesbos her repute was unblemished" (498).

Likewise, in his article, "Sappho Schoolmistress," Holt Parker argues that the Victorian view of Sappho as the head of a girls' school emerged out of an extreme discomfort with the homoerotic aspects of Sappho's poetry. Parker discusses the myth of Sappho as a schoolmistress as it developed in early "Victorianist" scholarship on Sappho and as it has influenced current views of Sappho and her social context. He challenges the evidence scholars have used to construct images of Sappho as either a "friendly spinster teacher," sex educator, or music teacher. Parker argues that there is no credible evidence that Sappho's poetry was associated with formal, ritual settings or occasions that might link her to a cultlike community of women—a *thiasos,* as it is commonly called. His article calls attention to the difficulties in reconstructing evidence from antiquity and cautions us about the cultural biases scholars often bring to the reconstruction and interpretation of ancient texts and their cultural contexts. Parker is particularly critical of the tendency of critics to assume that Sappho is the older woman in control of younger girls—a tendency Parker attributes to a "disturbing obsession with power and hierarchy" that assimilates Sappho's poetry to a model of male power relations.

As DeJean and Parker point out, much of the criticism on Sappho in the early part of the twentieth century shows an intense discomfort with the homoeroticism in Sappho's poetry. Writers and poets in this period, however, often responded to her quite differently. Many early modernist poets sought to rescue Sappho from the attempts of scholars to cloak Sappho's lesbianism in "modern heterosexual respectability." Erika Rohrbach's essay, "H.D. and Sappho: 'A Precious Inch of Palimpsest,' " discusses the influence of Sappho on the early-twentieth-century American poet Hilda Doolittle (known as H.D.). H.D. so strongly identified with Sappho that she wrote some of her poetry in fragments. For H.D., as for many modernist poets, "rescuing Sappho meant reading Sappho modernly"; that is, reading Sappho with a concern not only for the texts themselves, but for the way they have been read and interpreted through the ages. Rohrbach argues that H.D. turned this palimpsestic reading relationship into a style of writing. Indeed, the modernists' concern for the layers of interpretation enveloping Sappho's fragments may be considered the beginning of "afterlife" studies of Sappho as we now know it.

Susan Gubar's article "Sapphistries" also considers Sappho's influence on H.D. However, it considers that influence in the context of a more general discussion about Sappho's influence on women's writing in the early decades of the twentieth century. Gubar argues that the effort to recover Sappho, for poets like Renée Vivien and H.D., represents an attempt to break away from patriarchal literary tradition and claim a literary inheritance of their own. For both H.D. and Vivien, the recovery of Sappho becomes inextricably associated with the rediscovery of a utopian land and language of female desire. Gubar points out, however, that later women poets, from Amy Lowell to Sylvia Plath and Robin Morgan, often express an ambivalence toward the Sapphic vision. The gulf between Sappho's erotic ideal and the conditions of life for the woman poet in the twentieth century are often regarded as nonnegotiable. As Lawrence Lipking observes, "the genius of Sappho has seldom been easy to live with. Her reputation precedes her and dictates a role. At times she has loomed as a stifling and warning presence: the one acknowledged type of woman poet, who forces every other to take her stamp."[10] While the modern woman poet may at times resist the Sapphic mold, she nonetheless turns and returns to Sappho, linking herself not only with Sappho's poetic brilliance but to a tradition of literary women, that "queer lot, [we] women who write poetry," as Amy Lowell puts it.[11]

While in the last thirty years Sappho scholarship has been a vigorous and growing enterprise, Sappho's afterlife is just beginning to emerge as an important area of study. Joan DeJean's 1989 book on Sappho's literary reception, *Fictions of Sappho,* is among the earliest and most influential works in afterlife studies. DeJean's pioneering book has been largely responsible for the burgeoning interest in this field. As DeJean shows, the fascination with Sappho as a literary figure has a long and tumultuous history. What is most singular about our present moment in this long history, it seems to me, is the turn by literary scholars, like DeJean and the contributors to the present volume, to the Sapphic tradition itself as a touchstone for cultural critique and a source for intimations of the nature of desire and subjectivity throughout development of the Western tradition. I hope that the essays collected here will inspire further inquiry into the Sapphic tradition and into the questions it poses about the enigmatic, multifaceted interrelationship between present and past, gender and culture, text and context.

10. Lipking, *Abandoned Women* 97.

11. See Lowell's poem "The Sisters," which begins, "Taking us by a d large, we're a queer lot / We women who write poetry" (*Complete Poetical Works* 459).

ONE

Reflecting Sappho

Glenn W. Most

As everyone knows, Sappho fell in love with Phaon the very first time she saw him, when he took off almost all his clothes to participate in the wrestling competition in the athletic games at Mytilene. Sappho had read a lot as a child but without ever giving the slightest hint of an inclination toward writing poetry herself; but Phaon's virtually nude body made such an impression upon her that she ran up to him and declaimed an elegant couplet she had spontaneously composed in his honor. His astonishing beauty was the result of a magic unguent that Aphrodite had once given him in gratitude for his having been willing to carry her from Lesbos to Cyprus. Alas, the same goddess was determined to punish Sappho for having once pitied and freed two doves which she was supposed to sacrifice to her. And so, by the pitiless logic typical of pagan divinities, Phaon was beautiful and happily in love with the fair Cleonice, who returned his ardor; but conversely it never even occurred to him to reciprocate the overwhelming passion short, dark, ugly little Sappho felt for him. Phaon sailed off to Sicily on business; Sappho followed him secretly and found lodging in the home of Eutichio, a friend of her father's, where she waited for news of Phaon and whiled away the time discussing philosophty, reading Homer, and writing poetry. Finally, Phaon

Various versions of this paper were delivered as lectures between November 1993 and June 1995 at the Universities of Geneva, Neuchâtel, Lausanne, Zürich, Heidelberg, Freiburg, Columbia, London, and Oxford, as well as at the Internationales Forschungszentrum der Kulturwissenschaften in Vienna and at the 126th Annual Meeting of the American Philological Association in Atlanta, Georgia. I am very grateful both to those who invited me and to those who participated in the lively and helpful discussions. My special thanks also go to Tony Grafton, André Laks, and Katerina Zacharia. A slightly different version of this article appeared in the *Bulletin of the Institute of Classical Studies* (London) 40 (n.s. 2) (1995) 15–38.

turned up; but Eutichio importuned him so insistently that he marry Sappho that, understandably, Phaon preferred to flee in secret. At this point, Sappho finally recognized that she was not going to win Phaon's love. So she decided to follow the advice a witch had given her back in Lesbos: she sailed to the cliff of Leucas and threw herself over the edge into the sea below. Had she only had enough faith in the gods, she would have survived the fall and would have been free of her love; but as it was, she hesitated at the edge, and so was cured of her love in another way—by drowning.

I introduced this edifying story with the words, "As everyone knows." But presumably for most readers it was quite unfamiliar. Nowadays almost everyone with even a minimum degree of familiarity with Western culture has heard of Sappho; but how many know that she loved Phaon in vain and jumped to her death from Leucas? Readers for whom this story is new are not badly educated, but rather well educated—in terms of twentieth-century culture. For that culture, Sappho is first of all the emblem of female homosexuality—indeed, it is in her honor that the terms "sapphic" and "lesbian" are applied to this phenomenon—and secondarily the author of a small number of surviving poems and fragments, some of which, at least in translation, are known even outside of philological circles; in contrast, the supposed details of her biography seem to command little attention outside the occasional historical novel.[1] Two centuries ago matters were exactly reversed. My opening story was a summary of a novel by Alessandro Verri, entitled *Le Avventure di Saffo, poetessa di Mitilene* and first published in 1782.[2] Nowadays it is largely forgotten, but at the time it was an enormous success— it went through at least fifteen editions in Italian and was translated, adapted, and plagiarized into a number of languages.[3] Two hundred years ago, many readers would certainly have been familiar with Verri's narrative—and, what is more, they would have shared Verri's view of Sappho, a view that varies in many details from other contemporary images of Sappho but coincides fully with them in its central emphases. For Verri, and for Verri's century, Sappho was first of all an emblem of unhappy female heterosexual love, as proved by her biography, above all in her hopeless passion for Phaon and her suicide from the cliff of Leucas; in comparison with the alleged events of her life, her poetry was of almost negligible importance. As for the question of her homosexuality, Verri explicitly denies that she preferred women and attributes what he calls this "shameful accusation" to the envious malice of

1. E.g., Green, *The Laughter of Aphrodite*.

2. I cite Verri, *Avventure*, from Alfredo Cottignoli's recent edition. On Verri, see DeJean, *Fictions of Sappho* 169–73, and Tomory, "The Fortunes of Sappho" 124–26.

3. Details in Rüdiger, *Sappho* 136–37.

other poets;[4] most of his contemporaries did not even bother to mention the possibility, so absurd and unlikely did they consider it to be.

The literary fortunes of many ancient authors present remarkable ups and downs and the most astonishing misunderstandings and shifts of emphasis. The esoteric, eclectic, mystical writers of the Roman Imperial period who go under the name of Hermes Trismegistus are now read only by a few scholars; but in the fifteenth century Cosimo de Medici was so convinced that Hermes Trismegistus was far more ancient than Plato and had supplied the Greek philosopher with all his best ideas that, when he fell ill, he ordered Marsilio Ficino to interrupt his translation of Plato and to translate Hermes instead, so that Cosimo would be able to read him before he died.[5]   But Sappho's reception has been more bizarre than perhaps any other classical author's in the striking disparity between the exiguous remains of her actual poetic works and the widespread reputation of her person in the general cultured public, as well as in the dramatic changes the specific nature of that reputation has undergone over the centuries. Between text and context the relation is often problematic; but rarely so much so as here. How is this to be explained?

Since the beginning of the nineteenth century, philologists have tended to explain the development of Sappho's reputation in antiquity by recourse to a hypothesis that no doubt helps account for some of the observed phenomena and has achieved a widespread consensus among scholars[6] —though, as we shall see later, it should certainly be regarded far more skeptically than is currently fashionable. This hypothesis links together two observed facts. The first is that, at least as far as we can tell from the surviving fragments (and there seems no convincing reason to doubt that their testimony is reliable), Sappho's poetry was largely concerned with the expression of her sentiments of affection for the young girls in the circle of her acquaintance: the answers to questions whether those sentiments were primarily sexual or primarily sublimated, and whether that circle was defined primarily by erotic or by pedagogical aims, depend in the end upon the personal taste of the individual philologist.[7] The second is that, again judging from fragments and

---

4. Verri, *Avventure* 3.4, pp. 166–67.

5. See Allen, "Ficino" 39, and Yates, *Giordano Bruno* 12–14.

6. For representative authoritative statements, see Aly, "Sappho," in PW, 2nd ser., 1:2359–65; Dörrie, *Der Brief* 14–18; Wilamowitz, *Sappho und Simonides* 24–36.

7. These issues continue to be hotly debated. For some recent examples, see Burnett, *Three Archaic Poets* 209–28; Gentili, "La veneranda Saffo" 47–50; Greene, "Apostrophe and Women's Erotics"; Lardinois, "Lesbian Sappho," and "Subject and Circumstance" (the latter with a good bibliography, 80–84); Merkelbach, "Sappho und ihr Kreis"; Page, *Sappho and Alcaeus* 140–46; Parker, "Sappho Schoolmistress"; Rösler, "Homoerotik und Initiation"; West, "Burning Sappho" 324–28.

titles, Sappho seems to have been a favorite stage figure throughout most of the history of Athenian comedy, from Old Comedy through Menander—but one who exemplified insatiable heterosexual promiscuity, as instanced in her sexual relations with poets like Archilochus, Hipponax, and Anacreon (some of whom in fact lived several generations earlier or later than she did), in her marriage to a man named Kerkulas ("tail") from the island of Andros ("of man"), in her failure to seduce Phaon, a figure of local mythology on Lesbos who was associated with Aphrodite, and finally in her dive from the cliff of Leucas, traditionally connected with liberation from sexual desire.[8] The scholarly hypothesis attempts to connect these two odd facts with one another by means of the assumption that, within the two centuries that intervened between the death of the poet's body in Lesbos and the beginning of her literary afterlife in Athens, any knowledge of the real circumstances of her life was entirely lost and even familiarity with her poems became rare, so that not much more was known about her than that she was a great poetess from Lesbos. On this view, obscene comic invention rushed to fill in the vacuum of accurate historical knowledge.

We shall return later to the difficulties entailed by this hypothesis. But for the moment, let us focus instead upon the image of Sappho that flourished in antiquity. This image was, to put it mildly, rather complex. The various sources that flowed together to create it credited her with one husband, one daughter, several brothers, numerous female friends and companions (with whom, at least according to certain reports, she had had sexual relations), numerous male lovers, one male who had refused her advances, and a suicidal leap from a cliff. On principle, to be sure, there is no reason why such a richly varied social life could not have been possible—though one might wonder how, between one appointment and another, Sappho could ever have found time to compose her poetry (was this why she preferred to write short poems rather than long ones?). But so much complexity does present a challenge to anyone trying to imagine a coherent picture of Sappho's life, for it requires that potentially divergent elements be brought into plausible relationship with one another. Most fundamentally, the reception of Sappho can be interpreted as a series of attempts to come to terms with the complexity of this set of data.[9] In doing so, authors have tended to apply

8. The titles are conveniently listed as test. 25 and 26 (with n. 1) in Campbell, *Greek Lyric* 1:26–27.

9. For the reception of Sappho, see esp. DeJean, *Fictions of Sappho*, and Rüdiger, *Sappho*. Both books have at least the merit of trying to link the literary and the philological reception of the poetess; but the former is knowledgeable only about French literature and unquestioningly premises the feminist *communis opinio* of the 1980s as the standard by which to measure the past, while the latter is mostly restricted to the German reception and makes the same presupposition concerning the philological *communis opinio* of the 1930s. Robinson, *Sappho and Her Influence* 114–

one or the other of three basic strategies: duplication, narrativization, and condensation.

Most of the ancient scholars who tried to make sense of this mass of information seem to have used the first strategy: they *duplicated* the person of Sappho. Declaring that there were in fact two Sapphos, they assigned some features to the one and the others to the other, in such a way as to create two individuals, both named Sappho, each one internally consistent or at least plausible, but distinguishable by reference to a set of contradictory attributes. After all, this was a favorite technique of Hellenistic scholarship, applied for example to numerous problematic minor characters in the Homeric epics. The usual form this distinction took was the identification of one Sappho as the poetess, the other as a prostitute—this was the approach of the earliest scholar we know of who made this proposal, Nymphodorus, perhaps in the third century B.C.E.[10] The division of labor such a distinction tries to establish is manifest: on the one hand the lyric Sappho retains the connections to family and female friends evidently mentioned in her surviving poems; on the other hand the comic Sappho certainly could not have had so many male lovers if she had not been a professional prostitute. Anyone who thought that the two were the same person would be merely a hapless victim of their inconvenient homonymy: fortunately, an enlightened historical scholarship had discovered their difference and rescued the great poetess from unfair blame.

Such a distinction sounds perfectly clear, yet even in antiquity it seems to have been inherently unstable. Seneca, for example, discussing those philological questions whose answer one should either not know or, if one ever did know it, should forget, lists among the countless books of the scholar Didymus a treatise on Sappho—not on the two Sapphos, but rather on whether the one and only Sappho was a prostitute.[11] And an interesting modification of the two-Sappho theory is found in the eleventh-century Byzantine lexicon, the *Suda*:

> Sappho, daughter of Simon (some say, of Eumenos; others, of Eeriguos; others, of Ecrytos; others, of Semos; others, of Camon; others, of Etarchos; and others, of Scamandronymos); her mother was Cleis. From the island of Lesbos, from the city of Eressos, a lyric poet who was born in the forty-second Olympiad [i.e.,

236, provides many references and citations but little analysis, and does not treat the history of scholarly work on Sappho; conversely, Saake, *Sapphostudien* 13–36, is limited to the latter issue. For more modest studies of particular issues, see also Glei, " 'Sappho die Lesbierin,' " and Tomory, "The Fortunes of Sappho"; a brief survey is provided by Weigall, *Sappho of Lesbos* 310–24.

10. *FGrH* 572.6 = Ath. 13.70, 596e.

11. Sen. *Ep.* 88.37.

612/608 B.C.E., when Alcaeus and Stesichorus and Pittacus were alive too. She also had three brothers, Larichos, Charaxos, and Euruguios. She was married to Kerkylas, a very rich man who came from Andros, and she bore him a daughter, who was named Cleis. She had three companions and friends, Atthis, Telesippa, and Megara; she was also accused of shameful love with them. Her pupils were Anagora of Miletos, Gongula of Colophon, and Euneika of Salamis. She wrote nine books of lyric poems; and she was the first person to invent the plectrum. She also wrote epigrams, elegies, iambs, and monodies.Sappho, from the island of Lesbos, from the city of Mytilene, a harp player. She threw herself into the sea from Leucas because of her love for Phaon of Mytilene. Some have registered that there is lyric poetry by this woman too.[12]

In this passage, one Sappho is still being distinguished from another in terms of erotic interests, profession, and birthplace. But the line dividing them has become blurred by various attempts at compromise. On the one hand, the first, lyric Sappho too has now come under moral suspicion, not as a prostitute but because of her female friendships, and has the husband whose name and whose native island both lend themselves to double entendres; on the other hand, the second, nonlyric Sappho is now no longer a prostitute but a harp player (and therefore is a musician like the lyric Sappho, though perhaps one of a rather lower social and artistic order, closer to that of prostitutes), and what is more, some scholars say that this nonlyric Sappho too was the author of lyric poems. Evidently, already in antiquity it was not so easy to resolve the complexities of Sappho's image by merely duplicating her person; and those Renaissance scholars, like Jacobus Philippus Foresta or Gerard Vossius,[13] who agreed in adopting the same basic strategy, however much they differed from one another in their division of the details, fared no better. The defensive motivation of this first explanatory strategy and the pedantic procedure it deploys are in fact quite transparent; they were already unmasked by Pierre Bayle and Gottfried Olearius at the turn of the eighteenth century.[14]

Few ancient authors seem to have attempted to establish a coherent image of Sappho by simply rejecting some of the stories about her they had encountered. Among them were perhaps certain Neoplatonists and Neopythagoreans, who may have been obliged to dismiss certain reports in order to protect their idealizing view of her, but only a few traces of this

---

12. *Suda*, s.v. Σαπφώ (Σ.107–8 Adler).

13. See Rüdiger, *Sappho* 16, 30.

14. Bayle, "Sappho" 141–42 n. K; on Olearius see Rüdiger, *Sappho* 48–49. Welcker, *Sappho* 124, provides another sharp criticism of such attempts at duplication. Nonetheless, the strategy was reintroduced in 1822 by a French military officer and became widespread in French translations and studies until at least 1937: see DeJean, *Fictions of Sappho* 232–34.

image have survived.[15] If, instead, one wished to retain all the traditional but disparate elements, duplication was not the only way to deal with them: one could also *narrativize* them by distributing them along the single temporal axis of a coherent fiction. After all, Aristotle's law of noncontradiction decrees that two contradictory propositions cannot both be true at the same time: hence, to rescue the truth of both one need only assign them to different times. Actions or tendencies that might seem incompatible, or at least odd, if they were attributed to one and the same person at the same stage of her life can be reconciled by assuming that she had evolved over time in such a way that one phase of her life was characterized by certain features and another, earlier or later one, by certain quite different ones. When I was young I could not stand brussels sprouts; now I like them, especially if they are cooked lightly in olive oil with garlic and ham. So too, the various reports about Sappho's life and interests could be synthesized by inventing a narrative in which all would find their proper place.

The earliest surviving example of this strategy is *Heroides* 15, attributed, perhaps correctly, to Ovid.[16] This poem, in the form of a letter written by Sappho to Phaon, is by far the most influential document in the history of the reception of Sappho: when it was discovered in the early fifteenth century, it was thought to be a genuine letter by Sappho, translated into Latin; and for centuries after, when its author had been identified as Ovid, its elegance, massive availability, and easy comprehensibility ensured that it would dominate over the few, scattered, difficult genuine fragments in establishing the image of the poetess. Indeed, the text Sappho is clutching in Raphael's fresco *Parnassus* in the Stanza della Segnatura at the Vatican is most likely to be this very epistle.[17] Like any letter, the poem focuses upon the particular situation in which it is written—Phaon is absent and Sappho complains to him about his infidelity—but it constantly looks backward and forward to various past and future moments in which other details of Sappho's life are said to take place. For example, Sappho refers to her numerous homosexual affairs as a matter of the past: now that she has fallen in love with Phaon, neither girls nor the poems she had written about them interest her any longer (Ovid [?] *Her.* 15.15–20, 199–204). So too, her family relations belong essentially to her past: her father died when she was seven;

15. Cf. Pliny *NH* 22.9.20, and especially the underground basilica at Porta Maggiore (on which see Dörrie, *Der Brief* 191–201, and Zielinski, "Sappho" 1–2).

16. The standard but not entirely satisfactory treatment of this poem is Dörrie, *Der Brief.* I deliberately avoid taking a firm position here on the controversial question of the authenticity of this poem, as the issue is not germane to my topic; but I will remark that none of the arguments that have been brought against its Ovidian authorship seems to me decisive.

17. See Winner, "Progetti" 286.

her brother and her own child are now only further sources of anxiety for her, not of comfort (61–70). On the other hand, she asserts that she has decided to go to Leucas and is afraid that her leap from the cliff might result in her death (175–80): evidently these events must be assigned to the end of her story, to her future, for otherwise it is hard to see what other events could come after them.

Ovid (or whoever the author of this extraordinary poem is) has been criticized harshly by some modern scholars for having conflated different Sapphos within a single poem.[18] But this strategy of narrativization is extremely effective, and it is not hard to understand why this poem was able to provide not only specific details for enriching the legend of Sappho but also a model for how to organize them within a single fascinating story. For on the one hand it demonstrated that a richly detailed literary image could be obtained not by skeptically rejecting many of the traditional reports but by uncritically accepting as many of them as possible; and on the other it showed that such an image could become quite lively and appealing, since temporalizing the various elements created attractive possibilities for character development, narrative suspense, sentimental reminiscence, and ironic foreshadowing.

Though certain Renaissance scholars, like Domizio Calderini,[19] already experimented with this model, it was not until the end of the seventeenth century in France that it came especially into favor; but thereafter it went on to dominate the (consciously and unconsciously) fictional portrayals of Sappho that flourished throughout the eighteenth century. In 1681, Madame Dacier's brief biographical introduction to her edition of the poet set the pattern: it was the variety of Sappho's heterosexual relationships that was to determine decisively the sequence of the events of her life.[20] Did she die from leaping from Leucas? Then her passion for Phaon must have come late in the story. But how could she have fallen in love with Phaon if she was already married? Then her husband must already have died. What about the reports of her many male lovers? Yet these were not lovers but suitors, attracted by the widow's wit and intelligence. But then how could Phaon endure to reject her? Evidently because by this time she was not only small and ugly, but also middle-aged. It was Mme Dacier (anticipated by Domizio Calderini)[21] who introduced the image of an older, disappointed Sappho that was to become dominant for well over a century and to define for that period the genre

---

18. Cf. Dörrie, *Der Brief* 226.

19. On Calderini see Dunston, "Studies in Calderini," and Rüdiger, *Sappho* 19.

20. Dacier, "La vie," in *Les Poésies d'Anacréon et de Sapho* 233–41. On Mme Dacier's Sappho, see DeJean, *Fictions of Sappho* 57–58, 121, 123; Rüdiger, *Sappho* 37–39.

21. See Rüdiger, *Sappho* 19.

of Sapphic novels and dramas like Jean Du Castre d'Auvigné's *L'Histoire et les amours de Sapho de Mytilène* (1724) or Alessandro Verri's *Le Avventure di Saffo, poetessa di Mitilene*,[22] as narrative explorations of the casuistics of unhappy heterosexual love. By contrast, the question of Sappho's homosexuality was evidently secondary in this period. Mme Dacier herself wanted Sappho to be morally blameless (no doubt in part as a projection of herself, in part as a reaction against the licentious version propagated several decades earlier by her own father, Tanneguy Le Fèvre),[23] so she dismissed the accusations of homosexual relations as vicious rumors circulated by the poet's envious enemies; and in this she was followed by most eighteenth-century novelists, who either rejected the reports, as Verri did with the same arguments, or did not even bother to mention them. Yet a minority refused to discredit the rumors, most notably Pierre Bayle in his article on Sappho in his *Dictionnaire historique et critique* (1695), in which he pointed out that it was hard to read some of Sappho's transmitted poetry about her feelings for girls without finding expressed in it what he called "l'Amour de concupiscence."[24] Nevertheless, Bayle wholeheartedly adopted Mme Dacier's heterosexual determination of the plot structure of Sappho's life: like Ovid's Sappho, Bayle's was cured of her homosexuality by falling in love with Phaon; like Mme Dacier's Sappho, his too became a middle-aged widow—only his was far more lubricious than hers and may have survived her leap from Leucas.

Whatever its narrative virtues, this second strategy, so typical of the eighteenth century, had at least one fundamental defect. On the one hand it defined Sappho essentially as a woman in love, for whom poetry was at best incidental; but on the other hand it had to tacitly presuppose Sappho's fame as a poet in order to suggest that what had happened to her had any claim upon our attention. No matter how skillfully the actual fragments of Sappho's poems were interwoven into the erotic narrative as evidence for its various episodes, in the end her poetry remained secondary, and inevitably the story became the banal account of one more woman's loves and losses. For the strategy of duplication, Sappho had been at least 50 percent a lyric poet; but in the eighteenth century she came to seem much less so. Verri's Sappho is not a natural poet and derives her inspiration entirely from her passion for Phaon; she composes her most famous poems during a pause of the action, while she waits for Phaon to arrive in Sicily,

22. Verri also uses the duplication strategy: *Avventure* 3.4, p. 167. See in general on the literary representations of Sappho during this period DeJean, *Fictions of Sappho* 116–97.

23. Le Fèvre, *Les poètes grecs* 21–24.

24. Bayle, "Sappho" 139 n. F. On Bayle's Sappho see DeJean, *Fictions of Sappho* 124–25, and Rüdiger, *Sappho* 40–43.

and these poems have absolutely no influence upon the further development of the plot.[25]

It was the Romantics who experimented most successfully with a third strategy designed to restore to the image of Sappho the centrality of its poetic function.[26] By *condensing* into a single person the many contradictions with which the tradition had furnished Sappho, they invented an intensely para-doxical figure: a poet, and therefore someone uniquely capable of combining disparate qualities with one another in a way that would destroy any ordinary person; desperately unhappy but capable of achieving superhuman happi-ness; deeply committed to her poetry but aware of its limits. The Romantic Sappho is the first one who is essentially a poet—but a Romantic poet, one dissatisfied with banal reality and striving to achieve a spiritual perfection incompatible with this life and attainable only at the cost of death. Thus the Romantic Sappho, like her eighteenth-century aunt, plunges to her death from Leucas: but whereas for the narrative strategy that suicide had served as one terminus of a temporal axis along which all the other episodes could be distributed, for the Romantic strategy of condensation it provides the only possible resolution of contradictions that define the essence of the poetess's character.

The earliest clear formulation of this Romantic view seems to have been provided by Friedrich von Schlegel in his essay "Über die Grenzen des Schönen" (1794).[27] Here he invites the reader to imagine what life would be like for someone who possessed what he calls (in his not very felicitous terminology) only a minimal receptivity (*Empfänglichkeit*) but an infinite capacity for being stimulated (*Reizbarkeit*):

> That person's existence would be a constant oscillation, like the stormy wave—just now it seemed to touch the eternal stars, and already it has fallen into the terrifying abyss of the sea. The urn of life assigned to this spirit the highest and the lowest lot of mankind; though it is most intimately unified, it is nonetheless entirely divided, and in the superfluity of harmony infinitely torn apart. Think of Sappho in this way, and all the contradictions in the reports about this greatest of all Greek women are explained.[28]

Here, perhaps for the very first time ever, no attempt is being made to rationalize the various traditions about Sappho. Instead of applying a preconceived idea of what an ordinary person might be capable of toward analyzing and sifting the disparate legends, Schlegel accepts them all as

25. Verri, *Avventure* 3.4, pp. 163–68.
26. Tomory, "The Fortunes of Sappho," provides a brief survey of Sappho in the art and literature of this period.
27. On Friedrich von Schlegel's Sappho, see Rüdiger, *Sappho* 90–96.
28. F. Schlegel, *Studien* 43.

components in an unstable mixture that makes Sappho unique. The very complexity of the traditional reports, which hitherto had always been felt as a difficulty to be resolved, now becomes a badge of honor: deploying the traditional vocabulary of the Longinian sublime,[29] Schlegel assigns Sappho a privileged position above and beyond ordinary human experience. In their critical writings, Friedrich von Schlegel himself and his brother August Wilhelm went on to lay the foundation for the modern philological view of Sappho.[30] But it was in a number of poetic works in the decades after Schlegel's essay that this Romantic conception found its most convincing expression. I shall briefly consider three of them, all composed within a few years of one another: Alphonse de Lamartine's "Sapho: Élégie antique" (1815), Franz Grillparzer's *Sappho: Trauerspiel in fünf Aufzügen* (1817), and Giacomo Leopardi's "Ultimo Canto di Saffo" (1822).

For Lamartine, the constitutive contradiction that determines Sappho's fate is the tension between her identity as a lover and her identity as a poet. His poem takes the form of a dramatic monologue delivered by the poetess to the girls of Lesbos just before her leap from the cliff at Leucas; it is framed by a few lines at the beginning and end in which Lamartine sets the scene. The poetess's compositions had enchanted all of Greece but had failed to seduce Phaon. During her life she had tried to reconcile the contrast between poetry and love by making her poetic gifts instrumental to the attempt to win over Phaon, but in vain: she remained a poetic success but an erotic failure. Hence her decision, if not to resolve that contrast, then to dissolve it by destroying the lyre that did not help her in love. But, since her identity as a poet is no less essential to her existence than her identity as a lover is, this means that she must simultaneously kill herself, indeed must attempt to efface any trace of that existence.[31] The poem she is now declaiming is itself her final poetic triumph, magnificently conceived and expressed, and it culminates in a vision of Phaon whom it has persuaded to return to her. But the vision is only a hallucination, in which erotic desire and poetic imagination conspire to create a product that cannot exist in the reality of this world, and when she recognizes this she has no choice but to abandon it.

Superficially, Grillparzer's tragedy dramatizes the same contradiction between poetry and love, but in fact it makes use of this tension in order to explore a more fundamental one, between the individual's need for isolation and self-determination on the one hand and for the society of other people on

29. Cf. [Longinus] *Subl.* 10.5 (and cf. also 33.5). Not by chance, a nearby passage of this same treatise cites and praises Sappho's most celebrated poem; see 10.1–3.

30. For example, for the role of Greek comedy in creating Sappho's later image, see F. Schlegel, *Studien* 96, 379, and A. W. Schlegel, *Vorlesungen* 670–71.

31. Lamartine, "Sapho" 121–36, in *Œuvres* 116–17.

the other.[32] Grillparzer exaggerates Sappho's poetic triumph by introducing her as just having returned to Lesbos from victory in the Olympic games over all the other poets of Greece. She is a higher, sublime being, one to whom ordinary mortals can only look up in reverent awe; yet she herself seems not to feel entirely comfortable in the splendid isolation of poetic triumph. Her overwhelming need for other people is manifested not only relatively innocuously in her desire to be integrated among her fellow citizens of Lesbos (who are perfectly willing to revere her but will never be able to accept her as being merely one of them) but above all—and this is her tragedy—in her passion for the good-looking but ultimately rather mediocre Phaon, who is supposed to bring her back down to earth.[33] But Phaon will turn out to be incapable of making the leap up to Sappho's level, instead returning to his true identity by falling in love with her pubescent slave Melitta; while Sappho will discover that what is right for her after all is not the love of ordinary humans but the veneration due to the gods:

> Den Menschen Liebe und den Göttern Ehrfurcht!
> Genießet, was euch blüht, und denket mein!
> So zahle ich die letzte Schuld des Lebens!
> Ihr Götter, segnet sie und nehmt mich auf![34]

> For humans, love; and for the gods, reverence!
> Enjoy what blooms for you, and think of me!
> This is how I repay the last debt of life!
> You gods, bless them and accept me!

These are her last words, spoken to Phaon and Melitta, but also to all humanity, as she stands above the other characters and the audience on an elevation; then she hurls herself down—but only so that she can rise up as a pure spirit to her authentic home among the gods. In the play's very last words, her servant points not downward to where she has fallen but upward and declares, "Es war auf Erden ihre Heimat nicht— / Sie ist zurückgekehret zu den Ihren!" (Her home was not on the earth— / She has returned to those to whom she belongs!).[35]

In Leopardi's ode, Sappho's fundamental contradiction is that between her spirit and her body. Her soul is noble and loves beauty; but alas, it has been packaged in a body that is ugly and thus itself lacks beauty. Her love for Phaon is part of her soul's desire to unite itself with all that is beautiful;

---

32. On Grillparzer's Sappho, see DeJean, *Fictions of Sappho* 193–96, and Rüdiger, *Sappho* 126–32.

33. Grillparzer, *Sappho* 1.2, ll. 88–99, in *Werke* 1:720.

34. Grillparzer, *Sappho* 5.6, ll. 2025–28, in *Werke* 1:787.

35. Grillparzer, *Sappho* 5.6, ll. 2040–41, in *Werke* 1:788.

but because God has given dominion among mankind only to beautiful appearances, Phaon can only reject her. Sappho is torn between, on the one hand, her own love for beautiful appearances, like Phaon's and nature's, and her contempt for whatever is ugly, including her own body, and, on the other hand, her hatred for mere appearances and her desire for the truth of a beauty beyond appearances. Her poetic sensibility, sharpened by erotic disappointment, brings her finally to the recognition that her problem lies neither in beautiful appearances nor in ugly ones, but in appearances themselves—in her life in this world, the life of the body, whose radical deficiency is manifested not only in ugliness and disappointment but in sickness, old age, death, and the very passage of time. Thus her suicide is the expression not so much of disappointed passion for Phaon (for her, this too by now has passed) as rather of an almost Neoplatonic philosophical desire to free her pure soul from this world of appearances and to restore it to whatever it is that lies beyond.[36]

Leopardi's decision to take on a feminine voice in this poem is deeply significant, even more so than it was for Lamartine and Grillparzer: for whereas Lamartine's Sappho is an essentially literary figure for the tension between poetry and love, and Grillparzer's functions as a means for him to meditate upon the difficult but not embarrassing question of the relation between his work, his life, and his Viennese audience,[37] Leopardi's is a way for him to address in public, in disguise, a profoundly intimate issue that, as we know from his contemporary letters and notebooks, was a source of great private anguish for him: his own ugliness and lack of erotic success.[38] By entrusting his meditation to a woman's voice, Leopardi may be implying that he shares the traditional view that it is less dignified for a man to complain publicly about his lack of beauty than for a woman to do so (since such issues were long considered to be more central to woman's life than to man's); but at the same time he is certainly also demonstrating his own capacity to empathize with the misfortune of an ugly person—precisely what no one had been willing to do for Sappho or, *mutatis mutandis*, for Leopardi himself. As a man who redeems Sappho, he not only compensates Phaon's cruelty but also invites his own readers, by empathizing with his Sappho, to empathize with him. By reversing the genders and putting Sappho into his own place, he allows her to mediate his redemption as no male voice could.

36. Leopardi, "Ultimo Canto di Saffo" 55–72, in *Opere* 1:15.

37. On this aspect of the play cf. DeJean, *Fictions of Sappho* 195.

38. In his commentary on the poem, *Opere* 1:1426, Binni refers to Leopardi's letter of 26 April 1819 to Pietro Giordani (*Opere* 1:1076) and to *Zibaldone* 718–20 of 5 March 1821 (*Opere* 2:219–20), and also to a prose preface to the poem, which Leopardi suppressed (*Opere* 1:76).

In none of these Romantic texts is Sappho's morality an issue: for all, she is the paradigm of poetry and womanhood, what August Wilhelm von Schlegel called "a wonder of nature, the prophetess of the divine in feminine form"[39]; only as such can her sufferings exceed the limits of her personal fate and cast light upon the basic nature of all human experience. So too, most eighteenth-century authors had either ignored or dismissed the question of Sappho's homosexuality so that they could concentrate upon the heterosexual liaisons that determined their narratives. Hence it is at first sight rather surprising that the founding text in the modern philological study of Sappho, Friedrich Gottlieb Welcker's *Sappho von einem herrschenden Vorurtheil befreyt* (1816), which was likewise published in these very same years, should have been programmatically devoted to liberating her from the charge of homosexuality—a charge that had hardly figured prominently in views of the poetess for well over a century.[40] Of course, philologists are almost always out of date; and only the very fewest, like Nietzsche in his *Untimely Observations*, try to be so. Any interpretation of Welcker's essay that tries to understand it as a contribution to a heated ongoing discussion of Sappho's homosexuality will fail for the simple reason that hardly any traces of such a contemporary controversy can be found.[41] But this does not mean that we should reduce the essay to being a simple expression of Welcker's own psychological needs.[42] Rather, Welcker's goal is to secure the legitimate status of the young German science of philology by establishing as its peculiar object an emphatically pedagogical vision of Sappho; and to justify this vision he must discredit older alternative accounts, largely Latin and Romance ones, which depicted Sappho as a libertine (whether heterosexual or homosexual). His chivalry[43] is designed both to rescue her reputation—and to safeguard that of those who study her (as well as her male, often pederastic colleagues in Greek poetry and philosophy). Methodologically, Welcker seeks to attains this goal by deploying two strategies, one of them quite new and pathbreaking, the other extremely ancient. Welcker's newer strategy is *Quellenforschung*, the analytical

39. A. W. Schlegel, *Vorlesungen* 669. On his Sappho see Rüdiger, *Sappho* 96–99.

40. On Welcker's Sappho see Calder, "Welcker's *Sapphobild*"; DeJean, *Fictions of Sappho* 207–11; and Rüdiger, *Sappho* 102–9.

41. Welcker, *Sappho* 81, refers to frequent and recent attacks on Sappho's character but names not a single author or title. The anomaly is pointed out by DeJean, *Fictions of Sappho* 207–8. In his chapter on Welcker's philological predecessors, Rüdiger, *Sappho* 82–90, actually succeeds, despite his declarations, in identifying no plausible candidate except for Friedrich August Wolf's lectures (85); yet these were not published until 1839, twenty-three years after Welcker's essay.

42. So implicitly Calder, "Welcker's *Sapphobild*" 155–56.

43. Welcker, *Sappho* 127, refers to his essay as "der ritterliche Schriftstellerversuch" (the chivalric authorial attempt).

method by which, following up an intuition of Vossius and the Schlegels[44] and applying the most up-to-date technique of Old Testament, New Testament, and Homeric studies, he traces back the multiplicity of legends concerning Sappho to what he takes to be their various sources, either in Sappho's own poetry or in Attic comedy.[45] But then Welcker applies the second, older strategy, one we have seen philologists favoring since antiquity: he *duplicates* Sappho by distinguishing rigorously between what he declares to have been two separate Sapphos—the real one, the poetess from Lesbos, and a fictional one, the creation of Attic comedy. Like his ancient predecessors, Welcker distributes all the features tradition had associated with the poetess between these two characters; the only difference is that this time one of the two is declared to have been fictional.

It is one of the ironies of the history of classical scholarship that the method Welcker devised to support his view of Sappho ultimately quite destroyed its credibility. For Welcker, Sappho's feelings for her girls were entirely idealistic and nonsensual: as was only appropriate for a figure modern schoolteachers were authorized to study, she was herself a pedagogue, instructing her female pupils in the arts and graces, and it was only natural that she should have felt strong feelings of friendship for them.[46] But Welcker's dismissal of the comic tradition and his insistence upon Sappho's own poems as the only reliable basis for understanding her character[47] inevitably led people to focus upon those texts; and their message would seem to be unequivocal. Consider the famous ode in which Sappho describes the intensity of her feelings:

φαίνεταί μοι κῆνος ἴσος θέοισιν
ἔμμεν' ὤνηρ, ὄττις ἐνάντιός τοι
ἰσδάνει καὶ πλάσιον ἆδυ φωνείσας ὐπακούει

καὶ γελαίσας ἰμέροεν, τό μ' ἦ μὰν
καρδίαν ἐν στήθεσιν ἐπτόαισεν·
ὡς γὰρ ⟨ἔς⟩ σ' ἴδω βρόχέ ὤς με φώνη-
σ' οὐδὲν ἔτ' εἴκει,

ἀλλὰ †καμ† μὲν γλῶσσα †ἔαγε†, λέπτον
δ' αὔτικα χρῶι πῦρ ὐπαδεδρόμακεν,

---

44. For Vossius, see Rüdiger, *Sappho* 30. Welcker himself refers to A. W. Schlegel at *Sappho* 110 and n. 53; on Welcker's debt to him see Rüdiger, *Sappho* 104. But the debt goes deeper than sometimes seems to be recognized: the kernel of Welcker's whole essay is contained in a few sentences of A. W. Schlegel, *Vorlesungen* 670.

45. Cf. Calder, "Welcker's *Sapphobild*" 141. Welcker himself uses the metaphor of the "Quelle" at *Sappho* 122.

46. See Welcker, *Sappho* 96–98.

47. He was anticipated in this by such eighteenth-century figures as Wilhelm Heinse and Johann Heinrich Just Köppen: cf. Rüdiger, *Sappho* 72 and 88, respectively.

ὀππάτεσσι δ' οὐδὲν ὄρημμ', ἐπιβρό-
μεισι δ' ἄκουαι,

†ἔκαδε† μ' ἴδρως κακχέεται, τρόμος δὲ
παῖσαν ἄγρει, χλωροτέρα δὲ ποίας
ἔμμι, τεθνάκην δ' ὀλίγω 'πιδεύης
φαίνομ' ἔμ' αὔται.

ἀλλὰ πὰν τόλματον, ἐπεὶ †καὶ πένητα†
(Sappho fr. 31 Voigt [V.])[48]

Astonishingly, in his text Welcker almost succeeds in passing over this poem in silence.[49] For him its main point seems to be its (lost) conclusion, about which he writes a two-page footnote interpreting τόλματον as meaning not "one must dare" but "one must endure."[50] In his view the poem describes the poetess not as abandoning herself to her strong feelings for her pupil, but rather as doing everything in her power to control them (and hence, by implication, to teach us to control ours); thus in the end he can claim that he is not at all denying "that what the poetess felt for her friends was true love and tenderness, but rather only that this love was immoral or even vulgarly sensual and criminal."[51] Yet the text itself speaks strongly against such a reading. Nowhere in the surviving part of the poem does Sappho give the slightest hint that her feelings were not sensual, and the missing conclusion is hardly adequate evidence for reversing the poem's apparent meaning. So too all Welcker's followers have had enormous trouble dealing with this poem. Karl Ottfried Müller suggested that Sappho was describing "nothing but a friendly affection for a young girl"[52]—but in that case one wonders what language Sappho would have used to describe her feelings if they had been ones of sexual excitement. And Ulrich von Wilamowitz-Moellendorff even thought that Sappho was praising the beauty of the bride at a wedding ceremony— to which Denys Page sensibly replied, "With what pleasure will they listen, 'father and wedding guests,' to this revelation of Sappho's uncontrollable ecstasy...? There was never such a wedding-song in the history of

48. For a translation, see Anne Carson's version in "The Justice of Aphrodite."
49. Welcker, *Sappho* 99.
50. Ibid., 99–101 n. 45.
51. Ibid., 101.
52. Müller, *Geschichte der griechischen Literatur* 321, whose sentence in its entirety suggests that he is not unaware of the difficulties of such an interpretation: "So und mit noch stärkeren Zügen schildert die Dichterin nichts als eine freundliche Zuneigung zu einem jüngern Mädchen, die indeß bei der großen Reizbarkeit aller Gefühle den Ton der glühendsten Leidenschaft annimmt."

society; and there should never have been such a theory in the history of scholarship."[53]

One would think that the briefest unprejudiced inspection of this poem must suffice to convince anyone that Sappho was passionately attached to the woman in question and that in this attachment sexual excitement was a dominant component. And so it has come about that Welcker's dismissal of the comic traditions concerning Sappho and his concentration upon her surviving poems have ended up providing evidence not for the idealized fondness for these women that he sought to demonstrate, but rather for a sexual attraction to them on her part that he tried vigorously to refute. And as a result of the tendency, widespread since the nineteenth century, to classify kinds of people on the basis of what are taken to be their fundamental sexual preferences,[54] "sapphic" and "lesbian" have become convenient labels for a female sexual orientation directed exclusively towards other women. By a common circularity, Sappho's poems could then be read in this light as documents of early lesbianism; as such, they have been of enormous importance to many women writers, who have found in their Sappho a precedent, a model, and a justification (and have forgotten, or did not know, that the impulse toward this classification derived entirely from considerations of male sexuality.[55] If it seems self-evident to us to suppose that Sappho was a female homosexual, we should remember that such a view of her was never widespread before our century—indeed, that the very notion that people are either homosexual or heterosexual is a modern invention. Sappho herself would have had no idea what people mean when they call her nowadays a homosexual. Sappho was a Lesbian only in her place of birth.[56]

Just now, I wrote that "one would think that the briefest unprejudiced inspection of this poem must suffice" to exclude certain interpretations of it. And yet this has obviously not been the case. That is strange. Philologists may well tend to ask the wrong questions, but all the same most of them are not just stupid; and Welcker, Müller, and Wilamowitz in particular were among the most intelligent Hellenists of the past two centuries. How could they possibly have been so wrong about this poem? Our perplexity becomes even greater when we note how the poem was usually read before Welcker.

53. Page, *Sappho* 33. See Wilamowitz, *Sappho und Simonides* 58; Snell, "Sapphos Gedicht" shares this view, though he cannot quite conceal his discomfort with it (see 83 n. 1).

54. See in general on this development Foucault, *La volonté*, and Halperin, *One Hundred Years of Homosexuality*.

55. A very helpful survey is provided by Gubar, "Sapphistries." On the classification as resting on a male model, see Irigaray, *This Sex*.

56. See the sensible remarks in Lardinois, "Lesbian Sappho," esp. 30.

For Verri, it expresses Sappho's love for Phaon, and he translates it accordingly, appending a discussion in which he argues that it is a mistake to think it was addressed to a girl;[57] so too, Lamartine adopts its language to describe Sappho's feelings when she first saw Phaon.[58] In both cases, we can easily see that the unusual aorist subjunctive in line 7, ἴδω,[59] has been mistakenly interpreted as though it were an aorist indicative, so that the meaning becomes not, as it should be, "as soon as I see you," but rather "as soon as I saw you," and the statement can be erroneously referred to the very first time that Sappho saw someone (a crucial moment for all love stories). But more important, how could it even occur to Verri, Lamartine, and many other writers to apply the poem to Sappho's feelings not for a woman, but for a man?

Let us consider this poem more closely. Sappho begins by describing a scene that she observes, a man and a woman engaged in intimate and pleasurable conversation; she then goes on to describe the way she herself feels, a volcano of intense and conflicting sensations, most of them not very pleasurable at all. What is the relation between these two parts of the poem? More concretely, just what is Sappho responding to? Is she expressing sexual passion for the woman, or sexual jealousy at the man's relation to the woman, or admiration for the woman's beauty, or admiration at the man's fortitude in enduring the woman's beauty, or some mixture of these, or something else?[60] Sappho herself explicitly provides a link between the two parts of the poem by means of the neuter pronoun τό, "that," in line 5: "*that* has made my heart tremble within my breast." But what does this pronoun refer to? If it were feminine, we could easily refer it to the woman in question, or, if it were masculine, just as easily to the man. But it is neuter: what is the grammatical antecedent, that is, the precise cause, for Sappho's remarkable emotional state?[61]

---

57. Verri, *Avventure* 3.4, pp. 165–66.

58. Lamartine, "Sapho" ll. 29–34, in *Œuvres* 114.

59. On the grammatical oddity see, e.g., Page, *Sappho and Alcaeus* 22, and Privitera, "Ambiguità antitesi" 55–56.

60. All these positions have been maintained by scholars. Though there is a clear drift in the last decades toward interpreting the poem as an expression of homoerotic passion for the woman concerned, no clear consensus has emerged. Representative recent discussions include Beattie, "Sappho Fr. 31"; Bremmer, "Reaction to Tsagarakis"; Burnett, *Three Archaic Poets* 230–43; Devereux, "The Nature of Sappho's Seizure"; Evans, "Remarks" 1021–22; Glei, "'Sappho die Lesbierin'" 151–57; Koniaris, "On Sappho Fr. 31"; Latacz, "Realität und Imagination" 74–93; Lefkowitz, "Critical Stereotypes" 120–22; Marcovich, "Sappho Fr. 31" 19–27; Page, *Sappho and Alcaeus* 19–33; Privitera, "Ambiguità antitesi"; Rösler, "Realitätsbezug und Imagination"; and Tsagarakis, *Self-Expression in Early Greek Lyric* 182–87, "Aspects of Love," and "Broken Hearts."

61. Emmet Robbins, "'Every Time I Look at You,'" provides a subtle analysis of the difficulties connected with this pronoun and a helpful bibliography.

Let us suppose for a moment that the poem ended with the end of line 6, and that we had no other information with which to answer these questions than that supplied by lines 1–6. If that were the case, the reference of τό would be strictly undecidable. It could well refer to the nearest possible antecedent, the woman's laughter, picking up the adjective applied to that laughter, ἱμέροεν (lovely). If so the poem would most likely be expressing sexual passion for her; the man at the beginning would play a merely subsidiary role, to contrast either by his superhuman happiness Sappho's own mortal misery or by his superhuman strength her all-too-human weakness. But by the laws of Greek grammar the τό could refer just as well not to the woman's laughter alone but to the whole preceding scene, involving both the man and the woman, as observed by Sappho;[62] in that case, since the symptoms Sappho describes are not very agreeable ones, it is unlikely that she is intending to express her joy at the sight, and instead we shall think it more probable that she is expressing violent jealousy at the harmonious conversation she is witnessing. But, on this hypothesis, just what is she jealous of? Scholars almost always seem to assume as self-evident that she is upset because the man might steal the woman from her, and this is certainly not impossible—after all, Sappho does describe the attractiveness of the woman's voice and laughter, and it is to her that the poem is addressed. But by the same token it is by no means impossible to think that what is upsetting her is instead the possibility that the woman might steal the man—does she not begin the poem by saying that he seems to her to be the equal of the gods, and might the reference to the woman's sweet voice and desire-instilling laughter be describing not so much lovely sources of attraction for Sappho, as rather dangerous sources of seduction for the man?[63] Indeed, if we limit ourselves to this first part of the poem we can perhaps not even exclude the possibility that the principal referent of the pronoun is the *man* in this scene: for could not Sappho have written, "That man seems to me the equal of the gods, the one that listens to you—what makes my heart tremble. For as soon as I see him, I fall to pieces...."[64] If the poem ended here, we would be forced to conclude that Sappho had not specified the precise link between its two parts and thereby had left underdetermined the source of her emotional upset.

If you want readers to look at line 7 of a poem, the best way is to suggest to them that they pretend that it stops at line 6. By now the reader has

62. Cf. Page, *Sappho and Alcaeus* 21–22.
63. So Beattie, "Sappho Fr. 31" 110–11.
64. Indeed, one might even suggest yet another possibility: that what is bothering Sappho is not this particular man nor this particular woman nor their specific relation with one another, but the very sight of any other people happily in love with one another.

surely examined line 7 and discovered that this line seems to provide an unambiguous answer to the questions I have just been posing. Does not Sappho here explain her preceding sentence with a γάρ (for) and specify that she becomes upset when she looks even briefly "at you," that is, at the woman (ἔς σ' ἴδω)? Does not this sentence make it obvious that what Sappho is responding to is exclusively the woman and hence that her poem is not a statement of jealousy, be it homoerotic or heteroerotic, but rather of straightforward homoerotic sexual passion?[65] Why have I been raising all these difficulties if Sappho herself is clear and simple? But matters are in fact much more complicated. The pointed brackets around the letters ἔς mean that they are not transmitted but are the result of scholarly emendation. In fact, the sole evidence upon which the text of this part of the poem rests, the oldest manuscript of Pseudo-Longinus's treatise on the sublime, the tenth-century Parisinus graecus 2036, has a different reading at this point: not ὡς γὰρ ἔς σ' ἴδω, but ὡς γὰρ σἴδω. This reading is metrically defective, as it is missing a syllable: the meter required is — ∪ — ∪ —, but the line as transmitted only contains four syllables. The text of the poem printed above, taken from Voigt's edition, is identical at this point to that of all other modern standard critical editions: it repairs the meter by adding the preposition ἔς (to) and by interpreting the transmitted σἴδω as σ' ἴδω (I see you).[66] It is only on the basis of this emendation that it can seem obvious that Sappho's upset is a response to seeing the woman. Yet this emendation is not the only one possible, nor even the best one.[67] From the point of view of paleography, it is much likelier that the letters that fell out were not epsilon-sigma but instead epsilon-iota—especially in uncials, the similarity of epsilon to sigma is such that a scribe could easily have omitted epsilon-iota before the following sigma-iota by haplography;[68] and once this had happened the accentuation of the remaining letters, as we find it in the Paris manuscript, would have been inevitable. If, as Gottfried Hermann already suggested in 1816, the very same year in which Welcker's book was published, we restore these two

---

65. So, e.g., Robbins, " 'Every Time I Look at You' " 257.

66. Voigt ad loc. attributes the emendation to Edmonds, *Lyra Graeca*.

67. Bolling, "Textual Notes" 163, raises a grammatical objection to Edmonds's conjecture. Other difficulties in the standard printed text of this line are examined with great care by Lidov, "Second Stanza" 517–25; but his own suggestion—ὡς γὰρ ⟨εἶδον⟩, ὠ⟨ς⟩ βροχέως—leaves the manuscript transmission too far behind and presupposes too complicated a mechanism of corruption to command assent. Other suggested emendations include the following: ὡς ἴδον σε (Stephanus), ὥστε γάρ σ' ἴδω (Neue), ὡς γὰρ ἐσϝίδω (Hiller-Crusius), ὥς σε γὰρ ϝίδω (Ahrens, Wilamowitz, Pisani), ὥς σε γὰρ ἴδω (Diehl, Bowra), ὡς γὰρ εὔιδον (Bergk), ἃς γὰρ εἰς σ' ἴδω (Milne), and ὡς γὰρ ἐς σ' ἴδω (Gallavotti, Schubart).

68. Roberts, *Longinus* 169, provides examples for errors by haplography in Par. gr. 2036.

letters, then we read in line 7 ὡς γὰρ εἰσίδω[69] and translate it "for when I behold"—what? Now the object of the verb is no longer specified as "you" but is left unexpressed, as often happens,[70] and can easily be supplied from the context: what Sappho beholds is τό, "it," the very same neuter pronoun that so perplexed us in our discussion of line 5.

The only reason to prefer the reading printed in the standard editions is the assumption that Sappho must have wanted to specify the reason why she is so upset.[71] Yet if she had wanted to do that, she could already have done so in line 5.[72] If she chose not to designate it unambiguously in line 5, there is no reason to think that she would have changed her mind in line 7. To be sure, Catullus, in his translation of the poem, and Plutarch, in his discussion of it, both seem to understand Sappho to be expressing love for the woman in it and to focus upon the sight of her;[73] but these interpretations are not to be taken as evidence for what both authors actually read in their editions at line 7, but rather only as two readers' simplifications of the deliberate ambiguity of this passage.[74] No modern edition of Sappho mentions Hermann's conjecture, either in its text or in its apparatus or in its commentary. Yet, methodologically, this emendation has the decided advantage of leaving open what Sappho seems to have wanted to leave open and of not creating a false impression of specificity that is not supported by the rest of the poem. The violence performed upon Sappho by reading ἔς σ' ἴδω in line 7, as English editors and those who have followed them have done throughout this century, is certainly less massive than that perpetrated by Mme Dacier, Verri, Grillparzer, and her many literary admirers—but it is far more insidious.

---

69. Hermann, *Elementa doctrina metrica* 679. The same conjecture is proposed independently by Beattie, "Sappho Fr. 31" 111, and Gallavotti, *Saffo*; it is supported by Bolling, "Textual Notes" 163, and considered by Robbins, "'Every Time I Look at You'" 258 n. 12. The same verb recurs in Sappho at fr. 23.3 V.

70. As W. Burkert points out to me, the direct object is very frequently elided in the familiar ὡς ... ὡς construction that begins with Homer and continues through Greek and Latin poetry; on this construction cf. Gow, ed., *Theocritus* 2:51–52 on Theoc. *Id.* 2.82; Page, *Sappho and Alcaeus* 22–23; and especially Timpanaro, "*Ut vidi, ut perii*." The verb εἰσοράω frequently appears without an expressed direct object in Greek literary texts.

71. Indeed, Koniaris, "On Sappho Fr. 31" 176; Marzullo, *Frammenti* 54; and Privitera, "Ambiguità antitesi" 40, reject Hermann's conjecture for just this reason: in Privitera's words, it "esclude l'oggetto atteso."

72. West, "Burning Sappho" 315, notes how important a feature of this poem is its refusal to specify matters too precisely; and cf. Kirkwood, *Early Greek Monody* 122: "Neither the man nor the girl really matters much in the poem."

73. See Catull. 51.6–7 and Plut. *Amat.* 763a. Cf. Marcovich, "Sappho Fr. 31" 22.

74. See Lidov, "Second Stanza" 522 n. 48. It might be noted that Catullus uses Sappho's poem as a model for a heterosexual poem.

With regard to Sappho, it is not my intention to suggest that all the peculiarities that characterize her literary fortunes have been due to false texts or mistaken translations. On the contrary, it has been contingent and temporarily fashionable prejudices—about the nature of women, of sexuality, of poetry, and so on—that have determined the contexts of expectations concerning what is reasonable or probable, which editors, poets, and other readers have brought to the surviving poems and reports; and it has been these contexts that have played a decisive role in determining how these texts and stories were to be understood, edited, and translated. The tiny and apparently purely technical problem of filling out the defective meter in a single line of one of Sappho's surviving poems turns out to have been closely linked with larger prejudices of which the philologists, intent on their editorial tasks, may not even have been entirely conscious. Matters have always been this way, and they always will: becoming aware of the hidden links between texts and contexts does not guarantee that we shall be able to escape from their traps, but it does teach sympathy for other readers, past and present, and caution for ourselves.

The most curious feature of Sappho's literary fortunes has been the contrast between the certainty attaching to the fact of her passion and the uncertainty attaching to the objects of that passion. At least since Welcker, this has usually been explained as due to the fraud perpetrated by Attic comedy upon posterity's image of the poetess. But this explanation can hardly be entirely adequate. It presupposes that any authentic knowledge of Sappho's real poetry and circumstances must have vanished, so that the comic playwrights could fill the vacuum with invention. But we know for a fact that at least some of Sappho's poems continued to be sung enthusiastically in symposia and studied carefully in schools, in Athens and elsewhere in Greece, from the fifth century B.C.E. until the end of antiquity.[75] Aristophanes himself alludes to Aeolic poetry as being well known in Athens.[76] If Sappho's poems, at least some of which were familiar to Athenian audiences, had directly contradicted the comedians' image of her, we might expect someone to have protested. If no one did, if instead the lubricious heterosexual Sappho was a stock figure of comedy, then at least

---

75. The most important evidence for Sappho's importance in fifth-century Athenian symposia comes from vase paintings; cf. Wilamowitz, *Sappho und Simonides* 40–42. A list of portraits of Sappho is provided by G. M. A. Richter, *Portraits* 1:70–72. For Sappho at much later symposia, see Plut. *Quaest. conv.* 622c, 711d; Gell. *NA* 19.9.3 f. For Philodemus, the proof of an Oscan girl's foreignness is that she cannot sing Sappho's poems: *AP* 5.132.7.

76. See Ar. *Ves.* 1232–33 (= Alc. fr. 141 V.), 1236–37 (= inc. auc. 25 C V.).

those of her poems that were most familiar must have been at least partially compatible with such a view.[77]

This does not mean that Sappho really wrote poems about someone's love for a man named Phaon or her desire to leap from Leucas, though the fragmentary nature of our evidence does not permit us categorically to exclude such a possibility.[78] But it does mean that Sappho's poetry could lend itself to such a distortion precisely because Sappho herself tended to focus in her poems more upon her own feelings than upon the specific object to which they were directed. Fragment 31 is an extreme case in this regard; but other, similar examples can be found among Sappho's surviving works. Here I name only two examples. First, the prayer to Aphrodite (fr. 1): the goddess asks Sappho pointblank who her lover is, but Sappho conceals this information so successfully that, by a freak of the transmission, even the answer to the question whether the lover is male or female depends upon a single, badly transmitted letter.[79] Second, the beginning of fragment 16: Sappho declares that what is most beautiful upon the black earth is whatever one loves—once again, as in fragment 31, avoiding both the masculine pronoun ("whatever man one loves") and the feminine pronoun ("whatever woman one loves") in favor of the neuter ("whatever one loves"). Partly by concentrating so much on her own feelings, partly by generalizing beyond any single object, Sappho succeeds in making her poetry not less personal

77. The portrayal of Socrates in Aristophanes' *Clouds* may provide a parallel. We tend to think of Socrates as having been interested only in moral and political philosophy, not in natural science, and this is indeed how he was often viewed by later ancient philosophers (see especially Cic. *Tusc.* 5.4.10); hence Aristophanes' portrayal of a Socrates interested in meteorology and entomology has bothered many modern scholars. Yet we know at least from Plato *Phd.* 96a ff. that at one time Socrates did indeed have a very strong interest in a variety of natural sciences. Aristophanes' portrayal may well be a one-sided distortion, but it is not likely to be entirely without foundation. The parallel between the comic Socrates and the comic Sappho is noted by Welcker, *Sappho* 109—but of course in a different sense from the one suggested here.

78. See Lardinois, "Lesbian Sappho" 22–23, and "Subject and Circumstance" 60 and n. 14 (who refers to frs. 140a, 211 V.); Müller, *Geschichte* 314–15; Wilamowitz, *Sappho und Simonides* 40 n. 1; and Zielinski, "Sappho" 17–19.

79. Only MS F of Dion. Hal. *Comp.* gives κωυ κεθέλουσα, referring to Sappho's lover and identifying her as a woman; the other witnesses refer the lack of desire to Sappho herself (MS P of Dion. Hal. *Comp.*: κ' ώυ κ' ἐθέλοις; the MSS of the epitome: κώ εἰ καὶ θέλεις or similar readings. The text printed in modern editions goes back to Bergk, *Poetae Lyrici Graeci* 599, Sappho 1.24. See on this passage Calder, "Welckers *Sapphobild*" 146 and nn. 82, 83; DeJean, *Fictions of Sappho* 306–7; Degani and Burzacchini, *Lirici greci* 131; and Zielinski, "Sappho" 10–11. A pleasant vagueness in the whole poem is noted by West, "Burning Sappho" 308. Of course I am not suggesting that Sappho intended that there be uncertainty on this score (she could not foresee how her texts would be corrupted), but only that her reticence was such that this odd result could come about.

(very little poetry survives from antiquity that is more personal than hers) but less bound to specific and unrepeatable occasions. This certainly suggests a transition from a first performance within a small group, where all the allusions would presumably have been immediately understood by those who needed to, to a wider form of publication among later, unknown audiences, for whom the texts would have become ambiguous and underdetermined (and not for that reason any less attractive);[80] it may also be a sign of the emancipation of a written mode from originally oral circumstances.[81] In addition, it is likely that considerations of gender also played a role in determining the way Sappho chose to express herself. Male Greek love poets are far less nonspecific and abstract than Sappho is: they use masculines, not neuters.[82] Presumably the constraints upon the public expression of male desire in Greece differed from those that applied to women.[83]

Sappho's poems are both intensely passionate and resolutely abstract.[84] Whether intended or not, this feature certainly helped ensure Sappho's popularity for later generations, for it meant that, with little or no change, her poems could be reused in completely different social—and sexual—circumstances.[85] Indeed, we may even be able to distinguish in this regard between those poems of Sappho's that were read in schools and widely disseminated in ancient culture (and which are therefore transmitted as citations in the manuscripts of rhetoricians) and those that circulated only or primarily within collected editions of her works for a highly literate and specialized audience (and which have only survived on papyri): for the former class seems to be somewhat less closely tied to a specific referent, and hence to be easier to recycle, than the latter class.[86]

80. Shakespeare's sonnets seem to furnish a close parallel in this regard.

81. Along these lines, but focusing on other features of Sappho's poetry, cf. Rösler, "Über Deixis" and "Realitätsbezug und Imagination."

82. Sappho's erotic language is soberly discussed by Lanata, "Sul linguaggio amoroso." Stigers [Stehle], "Sappho's Private World," discusses other differences between Sappho and the male Greek erotic poets. West, "Burning Sappho" 322–24, points out some similarities between Sappho's erotic language and that of male poets. Of course, males often wrote not for a named boy but rather for an anonymous ὦ παῖ, like the vase painters who wrote ὁ παῖς καλός: cf. West 309. But they do not generalize as much as Sappho does, nor do they employ neuters as often.

83. See in general Winkler, *The Constraints of Desire*.

84. At Plato *Phdr.* 235c Socrates may be suggesting that Sappho had taught him about philosophical eros; if so, perhaps he was thinking of this feature of her poetry.

85. West, "Burning Sappho" 309, makes a similar connection between the anonymity of the love poet's or vase painter's praise of male beauty and the poem's or vase's ability to be recycled by later users.

86. Fr. 16 is only an apparent exception: it is transmitted directly (*POxy* 1231) rather than by citation, but it begins with the generalizing neuter—yet it goes on to praise the specific girl

Sappho's literary fortunes have certainly been, at least in part, a onesided distortion of what we modern philologists seem to be able to perceive in her poetry; yet no part of her reception can safely be dismissed as simply false. Even the Sappho of Attic comedy is probably not a groundless invention, in the way that many philologists since Welcker have thought, but rather a response—mistaken and exaggerated to be sure, but a response nonetheless—to perceivable features in her poetry. How can we understand the relation between a poet's actual intentions, as documented in her texts, and the reception of those texts in distant ages and countries? The literary fortune of an author is always full of the most absurd errors, at least measured against what seems to us philologists to have been the truth of the matter. Of course, the creative power of stupidity and misinformation should never be underestimated. But I would suggest that in many cases even the errors in the reception of a poet can be traced back to genuine features of her texts.

Perhaps we should think of the relation between a text and its reception on the model of the relation between the intention of any human action and its proximate and ultimate consequences. Whatever we do sets off causal chains that sooner or later go beyond our intention and our expectation. But where does our responsibility stop? When an action or a text is inserted into the world, contingencies and unforeseen misunderstandings always distort the plenitude with which the original intention can be realized. A purist might want to defend at all costs the purity of that original intention and feel obliged to reject the later consequences as unintended and hence false. But an important component of most successful intentions is some degree of awareness of the complexity of the world, an understanding of the necessity to factor in just this tendency toward distortion and error in planning the realization of one's intentions. In action, we call such an understanding practical judgment and experience; in poetry, literary skill. If we choose to attribute literary skill to Sappho, as I think we must, then we must suppose that even in the most intense fire of her passion, she remained lucid enough not to forget that one day she would feel the same way for some other person too, male or female.

"Burning Sappho," yes: but also "Reflecting Sappho."[87] And within the space opened up by Sappho's own reflections, the reflections upon Sappho that her literary reception was to construct could come to reside.

Anactoria. West, "Burning Sappho" 318–20, suggests that in those poems in which Sappho identifies the lover and the beloved either the erotic involvement belongs to the past or Sappho's attitude to it is hostile.

87. Cf. Kirkwood, *Early Greek Monody* 148–49. Byron's famous lines, "The Isles of Greece, the Isles of Greece! / Where burning Sappho loved and sung" (*Don Juan* 3.86.1), supplied the title for West's important article.

TWO

Sappho's Afterlife in Translation

Yopie Prins

Σαπφῶιαι δὲ μένουσι φίλης ἔτι καὶ μενέουσιν
ὠιδῆς αἱ λευκαὶ φθεγγόμεναι σελίδες.

"But the pages of Sappho's lovely song remain and will remain, white pages speaking out loud."[1] This Hellenistic verse proclaims the afterlife of Sappho, four hundred years after she lived and died. No longer bound to the time and place of oral performance, Sappho's songs are transformed into lyrics within a written tradition, and the voice of Sappho lives on in a displacement of her "lovely song" onto "pages speaking out loud." The pages speak in place of Sappho: we read past her name in the nominative (Σαπφῶιαι) at the beginning of the first line, and her song in the genitive (ὠιδῆς) at the beginning of the second line, in order to discover the grammatical subject φθεγγόμεναι σελίδες, the vocal pages of Sappho's song, twice removed from Sappho. Where then, does the voice originate: from Sappho or Sappho's song or the pages of Sappho's song? In a simultaneous conversion of voice into text and text into voice, what remains is pure "white" pages that are not mere transcriptions of song but the inscription of an idealized voice that leaves no textual trace. The afterlife of Sappho is predicated on the death of a living voice: Sapphic song "will remain" precisely because the songs themselves do not remain.

Sappho thus emerges as figure for voice in a lyric tradition that marks the loss of song. This, at least, is the Hellenistic reincorporation of Sappho's poetry into a body of writing that memorializes lyric voice and immortalizes Sappho as "the tenth Muse." Collected into nine books at the Alexandrian library, canonized as one of the nine Greek lyric poets, and ranked alongside

1. From the epigram on Doricha by Posidippus, quoted by Campbell, *Greek Lyric* 1:17. I am grateful to members of the audience at Duke University, the Boston University Translation Seminar, and the 1993 Modern Language Association convention for listening and responding to earlier versions of this essay.

the nine Muses, Sappho is read as the very embodiment of lyric as a genre: an exemplary lyric figure, despite the increasing fragmentation of her texts over the centuries. Indeed the reclamation of Sappho's voice increasingly depends on the scattering of these fragments. The "white pages speaking out" to Hellenistic readers no longer speak to the twelfth-century Byzantine scholar Tzetzes, who laments the literal and figurative dismemberment of the Sapphic corpus: "Both Sappho (ἡ Σαπφώ) and Sappho's works (τὰ Σαπφοῦς) have been destroyed by time."[2]   And yet, in this sentence she is named twice as a poet to be remembered: the name survives in a long tradition of recollecting her scattered fragments. The mediation between corpse and corpus in the remembering of Sappho defines her afterlife and has become the subject of *Nachleben* studies. In surveying the history of Sappho's reception in a wide range of historical contexts, such studies demonstrate the continual transformation of Sappho in the process of transmission. Through multiple reconstructions and translations, versions and revisions, speculations and reinterpretations, Sappho proves to be an imitation for which there is no original. Thus, as Joan DeJean has argued, "fictions of Sappho" are a function of their own historical moment and no longer to be measured against—except perhaps to measure their distance from—the time of Sappho.[3]

My own focus is more specifically on English translations of Sappho, using translation not only as a mode of reception but as a theoretical model for the problem of reading Sappho. Rather than reclaiming Sappho's "original" voice, I approach the Sapphic fragments as simultaneous cause and effect of translation. The moment of oral performance during Sappho's lifetime is therefore replaced by another kind of performativity: it is the performance of translation itself that ensures Sappho's afterlife.[4]   Here I follow Walter Benjamin's reflections on translation as *überleben*, as a form of survival or "living on" within an original text that is only made manifest in its translations. "A translation issues from the original—not so much from its life

---

2. Tzetzes, quoted by Campbell, *Greek Lyric* 1:51.

3. DeJean's *Fictions of Sappho* is the most recent of several books surveying the reception of Sappho, including Robinson, *Sappho and Her Influence*; Rüdiger, *Sappho*; Saake, *Sapphostudien*. See also duBois, *Sappho Is Burning*; Williamson, *Sappho's Immortal Daughters*; and Prins, *Victorian Sappho* (forthcoming).

4. My analysis of Sapphic voice within a textual tradition differs in emphasis from recent scholarship that interrogates the construction of Sapphic voice in, and through, oral performance. For various approaches to the performative function of Greek archaic lyric within its own cultural context see Segal, "Eros and Incantation"; Calame, *Les chœurs*; Gentili, *Poetry and Its Public;* Nagy, *Pindar's Homer*; Kurke, "The Politics of ἀβροσύνη"; and Eva Stehle, whose work on Sappho elaborates the "pragmatics of performance" in order to interpret the lyric "I" as performative utterance.

as from its afterlife," he writes in "The Task of the Translator." Benjamin's essay defines translating as an *Aufgabe*, an impossible task that recognizes its own failure in recreating the original, yet also creates a possibility for the original to be changed: "For in its afterlife—which could not be called that if it were not a transformation and a renewal of something living— the original undergoes a change."[5] The relationship between *übersetzen* and *überleben* is exemplified in Sappho's *Nachleben*, to the extent that Sappho *lives on* in translation and *only in* translation.

What makes Sappho perpetually translatable? Her translatability, I would like to suggest, is the manifestation of a question about voice in Sappho's fragments, as they simultaneously provoke and resist voicing. More than an accident of textual transmission, the fragmentation of Sapphic voice is implicit within the texts themselves. No poem demonstrates this more dramatically than fragment 31, where Sappho seems to speaks through and out of apparent death in an already posthumous voice. "Tongue is broken," we read in line 9. Here a conspicuous metrical break performs a linguistic disarticulation precisely when a speaking subject is expected to emerge. In my reading of fragment 31, I develop the implication of Sappho's broken tongue in order to demonstrate how this text anatomizes the figure of voice. Next I argue that this "voice" becomes gendered through its interruption: the textual break in fragment 31 necessitates the translation or "transport" of Sappho through lyric reading, as performed by Longinus in his treatise on the sublime. Finally, turning to several English versions of fragment 31, I analyze and historicize different strategies for the constitution of Sappho as lyric subject within an English lyric tradition. The attempt to reclaim female subjectivity and feminine voice through Sappho, I conclude, inevitably repeats the break inscribed and indeed *pre*scribed within Sappho's fragment. Thus through Sappho's afterlife it is possible to trace the gendering of lyric as a genre simultaneously feminine and dead.

FRAGMENT 31: TONGUE IS BROKEN

Placed at the origin of lyric poetry—or what Eric Gans has called "naissance du moi lyrique"[6] —Sappho seems to give birth to the lyric "I": the conception of a singular self that also speaks as generalized lyric subject. Page duBois describes the historical emergence of this particular kind of first-person utterance: "Sappho and the poets who are her near contemporaries are the first to speak in the first-person singular, to use the word 'I' to anchor their poetic speech, to hollow out for their listeners and readers the cultural

---

5. Benjamin, *Illuminations* 71, 73.
6. Gans describes the birth of the lyric "I" in "Naissance du moi lyrique."

space for a creating subjectivity."[7] The interesting implication here is that subjectivity is a fictional space hollowed out rather than occupied by Sappho. In fragment 31, for instance, the birth of the lyric "I" seems to coincide with the moment of its own death. Where, then, shall we locate a "creating subjectivity" or a "speaker"? Is it even possible to locate a grammatical subject in the Greek text of fragment 31?

φαίνεταί μοι κῆνος ἴσος θέοισιν
ἔμμεν' ὤνηρ, ὄττις ἐνάντιος τοι
ἰσδάνει καὶ πλάσιον ἆδυ φωνείσας ὑπακούει

καὶ γελαίσας ἰμέροεν, τό μ' ἦ μαν
καρδίαν ἐν στήθεσσιν ἐπτόαισεν·
ὡς γὰρ ἔς σ'ἴδω βρόχέ, ὥς με φώναι-
σ'οὐδ' ἒν ἔτ' ἔικει,

ἀλλὰ κὰμ μὲν γλῶσσα ⟨μ'⟩ ἔαγε, λέπτον
δ' αὔτικα χρῶι πῦρ ὑπαδεδρόμηκεν,
ὀππάτεσσι δ' οὐδ' ἒν ὄρημμ', ἐπιρρόμ-
βεισι δ' ἄκουαι,

κὰδ' δέ μ' ἴδρως κακχέεται, τρόμος δὲ
παῖσαν ἄγρει, χλωροτέρα δὲ ποίας
ἔμμι, τεθνάκην δ' ὀλίγω 'πιδεύης
φαίνομ' ἔμ' αὔτ[αι.[8]

There is no "I" to "anchor" poetic speech in this poem, if we read it grammatically: the first-person pronouns appear as indirect object (the dative μοι) and direct object (the accusative με), and in the reflexive ἔμ' αὔται, but never in the position of subject (the nominative ἐγώ). The effect of subjectivity depends, rather, on a sequence of first-person verbs that proceed from seeing (in stanza 2) and not seeing (in stanza 3) to the assertion "I am" (in stanza 4). In this stanza a gendered being finally emerges in the form of two feminine adjectives (παῖσαν and χλωροτέρα), followed by the first-person indicative ἔμμι. But this moment of self-assertion is immediately qualified by "I seem," creating a highly specularized subject that invites speculation about its own claim to subjectivity. "It is a strangely theatrical poem, as brightly lit as a stage set and much concerned with the problem of seeming," Anne Carson therefore comments on fragment 31. Her translation presents this

---

7. DuBois, introduction to *Love Songs of Sappho*, trans. Roche, 113. See also her "Fragmentary Introduction" in *Sappho Is Burning* 5.

8. I follow Campbell's reconstruction of the text. For discussion of textual difficulties see Page, *Sappho and Alcaeus*; for an assessment of variant readings see Wills, "Sappho 31 and Catullus 51," and Lidov, "Second Stanza."

strange theatricality as a complex linguistic event, by closely following the word order in Greek:

> He seems to me equal to the gods that man
> whoever he is who opposite you
> sits and listens close
> to your sweet speaking
>
> and lovely laughing—oh it
> puts the heart in my chest on wings
> for when I look at you, a moment, then no speaking
> is left in me
>
> no: tongue breaks, and thin
> fire is racing under skin and in eyes no sight and drumming
> fills ears
>
> and cold sweat holds me and shaking
> grips me all, greener than grass
> I am and dead—or almost
> I seem to me.[9]

There is some evidence that the text continues past stanza 4 to recuperate Sappho from death (l. 17: ἀλλὰ πᾶν τόλματον, ἐπεὶ ‍ὺ‍ καὶ πένητα, "but all must be endured, since even a poor woman ..."); however, fragment 31 has been assimilated into a lyric tradition that keeps Sappho suspended at the moment of dying. In her translation of the fragment, Carson follows the decision of most translators and many scholars to read it as four stanzas framed by the verb φαίνομαι: "he seems to me" (φαίνεταί μοι in l. 1) and "I seem to me" (φαίνομ' ἔμ' αὖτ[αι in l. 16).

What happens between these two verbs of seeming? Once fragment 31 is taken out of context, what emerges as its "phenomenon"? Is it, as Carson reads the poem, Sappho herself? "The action of the poem is in a true sense spectacular," she writes: "We see the modes of perception reduced to dysfunction one by one; we see the objects of outer senses disappear, and on the brightly lit stage at the center of her being we see Sappho recognize herself: *emmi*, 'I am,' she asserts at verse 15."[10] And yet what we "see" in Carson's translation, spectacular in its own way, is the *de* centering of Sappho "at the center of her being." In Greek, as in Carson's English, the syntax shows a lack of personal agency: "no speaking is left in me," "tongue breaks," "fire is racing under skin," "in eyes no sight," "drumming fills ears,"

---

9. Carson, "Just for the Thrill" 149. A slightly different translation of fragment 31 appears in *Eros the Bittersweet* 12–13, where Carson also uses a theatrical metaphor to introduce her reading: "The poem floats toward us on a stage set. But we have no program. The actors go in and out of focus anonymously. The action has no location."

10. Carson, "Just for the Thrill" 150.

"cold sweat holds me and shaking grips me." These oddly impersonal constructions present "Sappho" as object rather than subject of bodily sensation, and the grammatical split between subject and object persists in φαίνομ' ἔμ' αὔται, doubling self reflexively back on itself: "*I* seem to *me*." Although Carson's reading centers on "I am" in the preceding line, her translation demonstrates how the Greek text proceeds to decenter this self-assertion: ἐμμι is immediately followed by τεθνάκην, reversing being into its own negation. Carson translates this final sequence into her own series of reversals, rendering the status of "I" increasingly ambiguous: "I am" is juxtaposed with "and dead" and followed by "—or almost" and qualified by "I seem." What emerges as "I" is neither subject nor object, but somewhere in between, perhaps—alive and almost dead, dead and almost alive, neither dead nor alive, both dead and alive. Can this be personified as "Sappho"?

The performance of subjectivity, then, is less the central assertion of fragment 31 than its central problem. Instead of presenting Sappho as its phenomenalized subject, the poem would seem to be, as it were, an inquiry into the phenomenology of its own seeming. What Carson calls the "mise-en-scène" of the poem is more like a mise-en-abyme, as this text is an infinitely regressive structure, an exercise in referential circularity that leaves readers groping for a stabilizing referent. For example, the poem has often been referred back to "that man" in line 1 as one possible point of reference: he may be a real man at a wedding, or a rhetorical convention.[11] However, after the demonstrative (κῆνος) the man rapidly fades out of sight (in the contraction of definite article and noun in ὤνηρ), and he loses definition altogether in the indefinite relative pronoun (ὄττις): "that man whoever he is who ..." He is, in the words of Burnett, "a faceless hypothesis."[12] He appears at the beginning of the poem only to disappear, much as the appearance of "I" at the end of the poem is predicated on its own disappearance. Despite an apparent contrast between seeming immortal and seeming mortal, the deeper question pertaining to both "he" and "I" is how to refer *seeming* to *being* at all—it is the illusion of reference itself, staged as the "spectacular action" of fragment 31.

This question about referentiality is enacted even more dramatically by the Greek relative pronoun τό in line 5, introducing a relative clause. The

11. See for example Snell's "wedding hypothesis" to create a "real" dramatic context for fr. 31 ("Sapphos Gedicht"), or Winkler's suggestion that Sappho is reworking the Homeric "makarismos" convention ("Double Consciousness"). Attempts to create a narrative context for, or a coherent narrative within, fr. 31 are too numerous to summarize here—indeed, such a summary would amount to a history of Sappho's scholarly reception. My point here is not that such interpretations are right or wrong, but that they are symptomatic of the desire for a stable referent.

12. Burnett, *Three Archaic Poets* 229–43.

antecedent of τό has been the focus of much debate among scholars: what is it in stanza 1 that sets the heart in commotion in stanza 2, and thus sets the poem in motion? "Translators and commentators must all face the problem of the τό in line 5," Emmet Robbins remarks in a survey of various scholarly responses to this problem.[13] He observes a tension between grammatical and rhetorical readings of fragment 31: while the "speaking" and "laughing" of the girl in lines 3–5 can be read grammatically as the immediate antecedent of τό, rhetorically this reading creates an abrupt transition from sound to sight in line 7. By repunctuating fragment 31 Robbins attempts to restore continuity, but in doing so he overlooks the implications of his own analysis, insofar as it points to an important anacoluthon that interrupts the referential function of language in fragment 31. What τό means is less significant than how it functions in the poem: it marks a decisive break that reduces "he" and "you" in stanza 1 to mere pretext, and produces the remaining text as a discontinuous utterance that cannot be referred back to "I" without interruption.[14]

Carson's translation conveys this interruption with a dash and a dramatic enjambment: "—oh it / puts the heart in my chest on wings." Suspended at the end of the line, "it" retains the ambiguity of τό, although the anacoluthon also eases into an apostrophe: the interjection of "oh" translates the break into a spoken utterance that implies the continuity of a speaker and allows the poem to be read as the representation of speech. One way to "face the problem of the τό" (as Robbins puts it, perhaps punningly) is to give face to it—by projecting voice into the text and thus assuming a speaking persona as well. The creation of such a persona for Sappho has been the primary critical strategy in recent interpretations of fragment 31: as a monologue in which we may "refer to the *persona loquens* as Sappho," or as a dramatized dialogue that creates Sappho as dramatic speaker, or as an internal dialogue in which Sappho speaks as "the face behind the mask."[15] But what, we might ask, is *behind* the face behind the mask? How can we personify the speaker of a poem in which face is a figure that depends on the fiction of a voice and voice is a fiction that arises from the figure of face? Indeed, if we follow recent speculation that Sappho was a stock persona in archaic poetry rather than a living person, to what degree is Sappho a "speaker" at all?[16]

13. Emmet Robbins, " 'Every Time I Look at You' " 256.

14. Privitera, "Ambiguità antitesi," also argues against the attempt to find a clear antecedent for τό, although his appeal to its "intentional ambiguity" transfers the problem of reference to the inference of authorial intention, thus supplying a cause where there is only an effect.

15. For these positions see respectively Koniaris, "On Sappho Fr. 31" 173; Lidov, "Second Stanza" 530; and McEvilley, "The Face behind the Mask."

16. Lardinois, "Subject and Circumstance" 62–63, suggests Sappho may have been "a poetic construct rather than a real life figure in sixth-century Lesbos," yet his interpretation of

Facing the problem of the τό means not only to notice the problem of reference but to notice, more fundamentally, the complex relation between face and voice in fragment 31. The act of seeing and hearing the girl in stanza 1 leads, by means of a chiastic reversal, to the loss of hearing and sight in the following stanzas. Likewise the assertion of voice leads to its negation: the "sweet speaking" of the girl leads to "no speaking is left in me," and the parallel placement of φωνείσας and φώναισ' (both enjambed in ll. 3–4 and 7–8) further emphasizes the mutual implication of speaking and not speaking in this poem. The anacoluthon thus opens a space for personification and depersonification, producing *prosopopoeia* as the figure that gives face by conferring speech upon a voiceless entity, yet in doing so also defaces it. Paul de Man defines prosopopoeia etymologically: "Voice assumes mouth, eye, and finally face, a chain that is manifest in the etymology of the trope's name, *prosopon poien*, to confer a mask or face (*prosopon*)."[17] In translating the name of the trope, de Man both describes and enacts the relationship between defacement and the giving of face in prosopopoeia: he decomposes the word into component parts, thus simultaneously "giving face" to this figure and "defacing" it as a mask. Likewise fragment 31 performs its own figuration as an act of disfiguration: the face is systematically disfigured, broken down into component parts—tongue, skin, eyes, and ears—that do not function together. Thus the prosopopoeia in fragment 31, rendering face faceless and voice voiceless, points to its own anthropomorphism as a deadly trope. What seems dead yet "speaks"—what speaks of its death—is language itself, as a mechanism for simultaneous articulation and disarticulation.

The most striking instance of this linguistic disarticulation is the "lingual" break in line 9: γλῶσσα ἔαγε, "tongue is broken." Instead of voice, we discover a broken organ of speech alienated from its speaker: γλῶσσα displaces φωνή, the word that usually designates voice in the Sapphic fragments, as in the compound adjectives "clear-voiced" (λιγύφωνος; fr. 30), "soft-voiced" (μελλιχόφων; fr. 71), "sweet-voiced" (ἀδύφωνον; fr. 153), and "honey-voiced" (μελίφωνοι; fr. 185). Furthermore, the hiatus between γλῶσσα and ἔαγε creates a break in the meter that leaves the tongue literally and figuratively broken. How shall we interpret this metrical break? Some scholars avoid the metrical difficulty through textual emendation. Campbell's reconstruction of fragment 31, for example, follows Sitzler in interpolating ⟨μ'⟩ as an elided

---

the Sapphic fragments still depends on constructing Sappho as "the speaker, although not necessarily the performer"; my own argument interrogates the need for such an interpretive strategy.

17. De Man, "Autobiography as De-Facement" 76. For further discussion of defacement and the giving of face in prosopopoeia see also Chase, "Giving a Face to a Name," in *Decomposing Figures* 82–112.

first-person pronoun: γλῶσσα ⟨μ'⟩ ἔαγε. The interpolation prevents hiatus and restores apparent continuity to the utterance, but as hypothetical rein-scription of a speaking subject it also raises questions about where to place this speaker, grammatically and rhetorically. Do we read the emendation as the dative μοι ("my tongue is broken") or as the accusative με ("tongue has broken me")? Either way, the subject is still the tongue and not "I." Another emendation proposed by West would change the verb ἔαγε from third to first person: γλῶσσαν ἔαγα, to be translated as "I have broken my tongue." By turning the tongue into grammatical object, West therefore attempts to recuperate a speaking subject but "without implying intent or contributory activity."[18] But here again, the implied speaker lacks personal agency, since the action of the verb cannot be referred back to an intentional subject.

Yet another way to make the break pronounceable is to assume a digamma, a lost letter from the primitive Greek alphabet that often accounts for metrical hiatus in Homeric epic. Parry has argued that the digamma also left its trace in the Lesbian dialect of Sappho's time, although it was no longer pronounced.[19] The presence of a digamma in γλῶσσα ⟨ϝ⟩ ἔαγε would make the vowels α and ε, otherwise elided, pronounceable. The hiatus would then mark the trace of a letter that existed within an oral tradition, allowing fragment 31 to be construed as a spoken utterance and Sappho to be inferred as its speaker. The appeal to a lost digamma for the restoration of voice is odd, however, since the hiatus functions equivocally to mark both the absence and presence of a letter that used to be voiced: the digamma is a non-sound, a voiceless consonant representing something written or read but *not* heard. Indeed, the digamma is displaced in the text by two gammas (in Γλῶσσα and ἔαϝε), enclosing the hiatus like two glottal stops around a gap in sound. How, then, can the digamma resolve the question about voice in fragment 31? Instead of reading the poem as representation of speech, we might look at the hiatus as the unsolvable crux in a text that points to the problem of its own voicing.

Gregory Nagy therefore reads the meter mimetically, as performance of the very break that γλῶσσα ἔαγε describes: "The expression γλῶσσα ἔαγε displays a hiatus otherwise intolerable in this Lesbian genre. The ἔαγε should not be deemed corrupt on that account. Rather, hiatus is the very factor that creates the special effect, namely, that the form is arranged in such a way that it symbolizes what it means."[20] One consequence of a

18. West, "Burning Sappho" 311.

19. Parry, "Traces of the Digamma" 401. While Lobel refused to restore the digamma in his edition of Sappho, most scholars now agree with Parry's conclusions; see also Heitsch, "Sappho 2,8 und 31,9 L-P" 284–85.

20. Nagy, *Comparative Studies* 45.

mimetic interpretation of the meter, however, is that it reads voice into the break in order to reclaim the voice of Sappho prior to that moment in the text—a tautological solution that hypothesizes voice in order to confirm it, even (or especially) in the absence of a speaking subject. Thus the "special effect" described by Nagy is recuperated by Dolores O'Higgins in terms of authorial intention, to suggest that the metrical irregularity in the hiatus is "deliberate, intended audially to reproduce the 'catch' in the poet's voice; Sappho dramatically represents herself as being almost at the point she describes—losing her voice altogether."[21] While O'Higgins understands speech to be the central question in fragment 31, she does not call into question the status of Sappho as its speaker; to the contrary, her account of fragment 31 as representation of "the poet's own voicelessness" uses the silence of Sappho to reinstate her as speaking subject within an unequivocally oral tradition.

Jesper Svenbro proposes, instead, that we read Sappho as the subject of writing, or rather as a subject displaced by writing. He situates fragment 31 in the context of emerging literacy around the time of Sappho and suggests that the break in γλῶσσα ἔαγε reflects on the conversion of her voice into writing: "Sappho understands that, as a consequence of writing, she will be absent, even dead. For although her poem takes the form of a transcription of a living voice, that voice 'breaks' (line 9) even as she transcribes it. She loses her voice as she writes the poem."[22] In this reading of fragment 31, Sappho is still present in the written speech act of her poem, but soon to be separated from what she has written; hence she is "almost dead"—but not quite yet, or not for long, since the poem is triangulated in such a way that Sappho may be revived by the voice of a reader, who lives in a future when she will be dead. Thus Sappho's "death by writing" is also the birth of reading: Sappho speaks as "I" (in the first person) in order to predict how the reader ("that man" in the third person) will read her poem (addressed as "you" in the second person). What is unusual about this configuration, according to Svenbro, is the personification of the written utterance as "you," in contrast to archaic inscriptions in which the inscribed object refers to itself in the first person, names its writer in the third person, and addresses the reader (directly or indirectly) in the second person. Fragment 31 is unique in allowing both writer and reader to address the poem as "you," with the effect of animating the writing itself, giving it face and voice.

This prosopopoeia becomes increasingly complex, however, in the rhetorical triangle described by Svenbro. In order to allegorize how Sappho "loses her voice" in writing, he assumes an originary voice that exists prior to

21. O'Higgins, "Sappho's Splintered Tongue" 71.
22. Svenbro, "Death by Writing," in *Phrasikleia* 152.

writing and may be recuperated by the reader. Indeed, he confidently invokes what "Sappho understands . . . as a consequence of writing" without acknowledging that personification as a consequence of his own reading. But did "Sappho" ever own the voice that she "loses"? Where, in the continual rotation of speakers, shall we locate a first-person utterance? The position of a first-person speaker keeps shifting (the girl speaking to the man, "Sappho" speaking to the girl, "the reader" speaking to the poem) and in each case what the address to "you" conceals is an objectified utterance that is already dead, or rather was never alive to begin with: instead, it is personified by means of a second-person address. Indeed, what happens when the reader who "voices" the poem in the first-person singular encounters the break in line 9 and repeats its broken tongue? Isn't the reader, like Sappho, already an effect of that break? The prosopopoeia of fragment 31 therefore produces a speaker whose utterance points to the impossibility of a speaker, and so introduces another triangle where this logic repeats itself.

To stabilize this infinite regress, Svenbro's allegorical reading of fragment 31 conjures up the figure of a "Reader" to take the place of the writer. The disappearance of Sappho as the "mortal" writer guarantees the appearance of an "immortal" reader, each fixed in seemingly symmetrical relation to the other through the personification of the poem as "you." But can such a "Reader" offer, or be, the final answer to a poem in which first-, second-, and third-person positions are asymmetrical and self-dislocating? Does the lyric triangle stop here, or will reading fragment 31 exceed every attempt to achieve the position of the first-person "I"? By virtue of its own prosopopoeia, fragment 31 does not lead to the discovery of the poem as "you," but rather, to the discovery that "you" is the personification of an "it" that remains mute. What we discover, in other words, is neither the death of Sappho as speaker nor the death of speaking voice as such, but dead letters that cannot be read as voice: hence, tongue is broken. How is "Sappho" to be recuperated from that break—except, perhaps, as a name for it?

THE SAPPHIC RIDDLE

Reading fragment 31 proves to be a form of riddling: the text is a lyrical provocation that provokes, time and time again, an attempt to phenomenalize voice by means of the prosopopoeia it sets into motion. Yet as we have seen, a reading that locates Sappho as rhetorical subject is complicated by a reading that dislocates the grammatical subject, and in the disjunction between rhetorical and grammatical reading the phenomenon we call Sappho is even more literally grammaticized—through letters or grammata that ask to, yet cannot, be voiced. In this respect fragment 31 is not a lyric but a nonlyric that makes lyric reading possible, in a movement that Jonathan

Culler calls "lyrical translation"—it is a "materiality on which meaning is imposed by lyrical translation."[23] How does Sappho emerge as lyric subject through the transport, transfer, or metaphor of such reading? Or, to put the question differently, why does Sappho in particular emerge as the female embodiment of that textual exchange?

This is the riddle of Sappho, inviting the reader's answer, and it is wonderfully dramatized in the fragment of a fourth-century comedy by Antiphanes. Sappho appears as a character in his play *Sappho* and poses a question:

> There is a female being that hides in her womb unborn children,
> And although the infants are voiceless (ἄφωνα) they call out
> Across the waves of the sea and over the whole earth to whomever
> they wish, and people who are not present
> And even deaf people are able to hear them.

What kind of female creature is it that carries such children? What kind of infant is voiceless yet vocal? What kind of voice can be heard by the deaf? The "answer," says "Sappho," is a letter:

> The female being is a letter (ἡ ἐπιστολή),
> And the infants she carries are the letters of the alphabet (τὰ γράμματα): Although they are
> voiceless (ἄφωνα) they can speak to people far away,
> To whomever they wish; and if some other person happens to be
> Standing near the one who is reading, he will not hear them.[24]

The riddle revolves around ἡ ἐπιστολή as a feminine noun: the female creature is an epistle, containing inside of itself letters of the alphabet that will speak to the reader who voices them. These letters are figured as infants born into speech, and the letter bearing them (in all senses of the word) as a female body about to give birth.

The Sapphic riddle allegorizes the invention of silent reading between the time of Sappho and the time of Antiphanes: the letters of the Greek phonetic alphabet no longer need to be spoken aloud, but speak in silence to the reader. Silent reading presents the reader with a literal contradiction, however, since letters become vocal through their voicelessness. Separated from their source of utterance and crossing great distance, these letters are necessarily voiceless: ἄφωνα γράμματα can only be "heard" by the reader, and emphatically not by anyone standing nearby. But if reading substitutes absence of voice for its originary presence, the riddle allows the female body to be read as the container of this absence, as an "epistle" that reinscribes

---

23. Culler, "Reading Lyric" 105.
24. Antiphanes *Sappho* fr. 196 (Kock).

the utterance by means of the letters it now contains. Thus the body of the text is made to speak in place of the author, according to an allegory of reading that also allegorizes more specifically the logic by which Sappho comes to be read as the personification of her own texts. Posing the riddle, both the question and the answer, Sappho is its very embodiment: she too is a letter composed of voiceless letters, a text that becomes vocal through the transportation of reading. Following this logic, Svenbro quotes the Sapphic riddle in order to confirm his reading of fragment 31: both revolve around the possibility of hearing voiceless letters, figured as the offspring of their author and acquiring voice when they are delivered to, and by, the reader.[25]

But can the Sapphic riddle be solved in this way, or is it a trick question? By attributing the answer to Sappho—allowing her to name the answer, and her name to be the answer—the riddle complicates the question rather than solving it. What is literal and what is figurative in the riddle, the female body literalized as letter or the female letter figured as body? And how shall we read a letter simultaneously containing letters yet also contained by them? What the Sapphic riddle leaves unresolved—what it poses as its circular conundrum—is the simultaneous existence of two different conceptions of text: the text as figural body that contains voice, and the text as literal vehicle for the transport of written letters. The transportation of ἄφωνα γράμματα is mechanical, yet somehow in being transported they seem to become articulate beings with a life of their own. This movement of transport turns out to be the precondition for the animation of letters, for the riddle emphasizes they speak to people "far away." Greater distance requires more motion and so increases the effect of animation. The same is true of Sappho's fragments, as inanimate structures that are increasingly animated through transportation over time. In the transmission of fragment 31 in particular, readers discover life in its ἄφωνα γράμματα by voicing them *as if* they were alive. Sappho is therefore made to speak only at a distance.

This is the lyrical translation performed by Longinus, whose reading of fragment 31 proves influential for the reception of Sappho not only because we owe the transmission of the text itself to his rhetorical treatise *On the Sublime*, but because he introduces it into a tradition of lyric reading that discovers Sappho as ideal medium for sublime transport. The Longinian sublime is an effect of transferential reading that produces ἔκστασις, an ecstatic moment that dislocates the reader in the encounter with "high" language (ὕψος). For Longinus this is by definition a linguistic encounter, initially overwhelming and then uplifting the reader: a powerful utterance strikes us down like "a flash of lightning or a thunderbolt," but immediately

25. Svenbro, "Death by Writing" 159.

fills us "with a sense of proud possession ... as if we had ourselves produced the very thing we heard."[26]   The exchange between author and reader through a sublime text redefines Sappho's transport to the reader across great distance (a horizontal movement in space and time, according to the Sapphic riddle) in terms of the reader's transport up to the "height" of Sappho—a vertical movement that occurs at the instant of lyric reading and presents Sappho as the instantiation of this reading. Indeed Longinus turns to fragment 31 as a central example in his treatise on the sublime because it replicates—that is, figures—the experience of expropriation and reappropriation that characterizes sublime reading.

When Longinus quotes fragment 31 as example of sublime writing, Sappho's sublimity therefore becomes an effect of his own reading and Longinus hears a voice he has himself produced. He reverses the terms of the Sapphic riddle, by converting Sappho's text into a figural body and then discovering its voice. "Are you not amazed," he asks,

> how at one and the same moment she seeks out soul, body, hearing, tongue, sight, complexion as though they had all left her and were external, and how in contradiction she both freezes and burns, is irrational and sane, is afraid and nearly dead, so that we observe in her not one single emotion but a concourse of emotions? All this of course happens to people in love; but as I said, it is her selection of the most important details and her combination of them into a single whole that have produced the excellence of the poem.[27]

The Longinian reading of Sappho hinges on the transition from the first to the second sentence in his commentary, enacting on the level of syntax what Neil Hertz has called "the shift from Sappho-as-victimized-body to Sappho-as-poetic-force."[28] The first sentence names the scattering of Sappho in "a concourse of emotions" and the second sentence begins with a phrase that collects these scattered parts and identifies a single cause: "All this of course happens to people in love." Through this unifying phrase Longinus is able to shift his analysis from content to form: rather than simply enumerating erotic symptoms, the poem excels in the "selection" and "combination" of details into "a single whole."

Paraphrasing the poem as a rhetorical question, Longinus performs the Sapphic riddle in reverse. He begins by quoting ἄφωνα γράμματα and then organizes these letters into a textual body that speaks paradoxically ("as I said," Longinus inserts) in an organically unified form. Through such personification Longinus is able to conflate poem and poet: Sappho *is*

---

26. [Longinus] *Subl.* 12.4, 7.2; trans. Fyfe, *On the Sublime* 165, 139.
27. [Longinus] *Subl.* 10.3; trans. Campbell, *Greek Lyric* 1:80–81.
28. Hertz, "A Reading of Longinus" 7.

fragment 31, simultaneously losing composure and composing herself, falling apart in the poem and coming together as a poem. Thus fragment 31 comes to exemplify the movement of disintegration and figurative reconstitution that Hertz describes as the sublime turn throughout the Longinian treatise. Sappho's body is reincorporated into the body of the poem, confirming the doctrine of organic unity that asserts that a poem must be organized like a living organism in order to speak. Yet as Hertz points out, Longinus considers fragment 31 sublime because it demonstrates this doctrine precisely when the body appears most threatened: "It is clear that Longinus admires the poem because when it becomes 'like a living creature' and 'finds its voice,' it speaks of a moment of self-estrangement in language that captures the disorganized quality of the experience."[29]

It would seem, then, that the Longinian sublime falls short of reconstituting a unified subject, and thus Sappho is used to locate the persistence of an ecstatic or self-dislocating moment that inheres in the sublime and cannot be recuperated in terms of a self. Instead of asserting Sappho as sublime subject, fragment 31 stages a scene of subjection that produces Sappho as its feminized object. Here Hertz underestimates, or avoids articulating, the necessary implication of gender in any account of the sublime, even one as rigorously rhetorical as that offered by Longinus. It is striking, on the face of it, that Longinus turns to Sappho—the only woman poet quoted in his treatise—precisely when he wishes to "embody" his argument for organic unity. But since it is not the "face" of Sappho that speaks in fragment 31 as much as its defacement, the very possibility of reading Sappho as woman poet is a rhetorical problem. Rather than assuming that Sappho exists as a female body *prior* to the argument on the sublime, we might consider how this body becomes gendered *through* the Longinian reading of Sappho: not as an organic figure but as the simulacrum of a living body, a posthumous figure that renders Sappho as an already dismembered remembering. For in the Longinian twist on the Sapphic riddle, fragment 31 proves to be a speaking corpse: a body pregnant with dead letters, giving birth to its own death. Thus Longinus performs an ironic autopsy on Sappho, anatomizing the parts of her poem by means of a rhetorical reading that in its very rigor produces the pathos of a "feminine" Sappho.

While Hertz is still willing to personify this pathos in his appeal to "Sappho-as-victimized-body," and feminist critics responding to Hertz have attempted to recuperate a Sapphic body no longer victimized by the

---

29. Ibid., 5. Hertz's reading of Longinus is further elaborated by Guerlac, who discerns "a more radical force at work in the Longinian sublime, one which threatens the very notion of the subjective, or the unified self-identity of the subject" ("Longinus and the Subject of the Sublime" 275).

sublime,[30] what becomes increasingly evident in a tradition of Longinian reading is how such a feminine subject emerges through the reader's affect. It is not the identity of Sappho's body—as if her body were the literal "ground" for analysis rather than its deeply ironic figure—that produces a gendered reading of fragment 31, but the reader's identification with that figure: Sappho is identified, in other words, with the figurative feminization of a reader whose "affect" is an effect of the sublime. The transference of such reading is presented throughout the Longinian treatise in terms of the subjection of the reader, "mastered" by the sublime in a scenario that implies masculine domination and feminine submission. "Such passages exercise an irresistible power of mastery and get the upper hand with every member of the audience," Longinus writes, describing the sublime as a violent power that "scatters everything before it."[31] Here the reader's ravishment sets up an implicit comparison with the violent self-scattering dramatized in fragment 31. Longinus strategically quotes this Sapphic fragment in order to set the scene for an exchange between the "body" of the text and the "body" of the reader, and in this exchange Sappho is feminized not as a female body per se but as a symptom of the very structure of transference.

A reading of fragment 31 as a sublime text therefore depends on the *figure* of the body of Sappho, in a movement of sublimation described more generally by Elisabeth Bronfen in *Over Her Dead Body: Death, Femininity and the Aesthetic.* Bronfen demonstrates how often a dead woman serves as medium for aesthetic articulation, and how a feminine corpse seems to materialize as the consequence of such aesthetics. Quoting "The Philosophy of Composition" by Edgar Allan Poe, she interprets his infamous words as a tautological proposition: "The death of a beautiful woman is, unquestionably, the most poetical topic in the world." What Poe here asserts "unquestionably" is the very question posed by the Sapphic riddle, understood now as the morbid repetition of a lyric reading that kills the very thing it would bring to life, producing more and more dead women and therefore also the most feminine death. Poe's "Philosophy of Composition" thus rearticulates the Longinian sublime, insofar as both depend on an implicit analogy between aesthetic form and the composition of a female body. About the death of this beautiful woman, Bronfen writes: "Because her dying figures as an analogy to the creation of an art work, and the depicted death serves as a double of its formal condition, the 'death of a beautiful woman' marks the *mise en abyme* of a text, the moment of self-reflexivity, where the text seems to comment

---

30. Recent feminist responses to Longinus include Battersby, "Unblocking the Oedipal," and Freeman, *The Feminine Sublime.*

31. [Longinus] *Subl.* 1.4; trans. Fyfe, *On the Sublime* 125.

on itself and its own process of composition, and so decomposes itself."[32] The style of rhetorical reading introduced by Longinus in his treatise *On the Sublime* works according to this logic, allowing Sappho to be aestheticized as a beautiful woman whose decomposition is the "formal condition" of fragment 31. Insofar as Sappho speaks at the moment of dying, her death proves to be "the most poetical topic"—presented by Longinus not only as central example of the sublime but as exemplary medium for lyrical translation.

In addition to preserving the fragment that we now read as the text of Sappho, the treatise on the sublime therefore serves to demonstrate how this fragment has been and will be read, repeatedly, as a movement that Longinus calls sublime transport, or that the Sapphic riddle calls the transportation of letters, or that we may call translation. In this way the Longinian reading of fragment 31 reveals the afterlife of Sappho, who neither lives nor dies in fragment 31 but "lives on" as a function of both literal and figurative translation. What is revealed, in other words, is a structure of survival within the text itself, as a formal principle that exceeds biological life and death and is best understood in Walter Benjamin's sense of a *Nachleben*: the "renewal of something living" that is beyond Sappho as the "original" author of the "original" text. In this respect "The Task of the Translator" should be read in conjunction with Benjamin's essay "On Language as Such and on the Language of Man," as an attempt to "found the concept of translation at the deepest level of linguistic theory."[33] For what is at stake in translating Sappho is not "her" language but simply the linguistic being of language itself: it is in her name that this law of language appears.

In his meditations on Benjamin, Derrida therefore points out that the task of the translator is not to "engage in relation to a hypothetical subject-author of the original text—dead or mortal, the dead man, or 'dummy' of the text—but to something else that represents the formal law in the immanence of the original text."[34] If in the case of fragment 31 the "dummy of the text" survives, still, as a dead woman, it is precisely through the interruption of Sapphic voice that it becomes gendered as feminine: the "something else" is a feminized difference (or Derridean *différance*) that is predicated on and performed through the break in γλῶσσα ἔαγε. Thus, when translators attempt to make Sappho speak, what they engage is the formal law of fragment 31: the literal *lingua* of its broken tongue, a lingualism or literality that Benjamin would define as "pure language" (*reine Sprache*) because it points to the internal disjunction—the γλῶσσα ἔαγε—within

32. Bronfen, *Over Her Dead Body* 71; Poe, "The Philosophy of Composition" 425.

33. Benjamin, *Illuminations* 325. For a more detailed discussion of Benjamin's radically linguistic approach to translation see Jacobs, "The Monstrosity of Translation."

34. Derrida, "Des Tours de Babel" 182.

every language. Translations of Sappho confront and repeat this literal break in the broken tongue of yet another language—which is another way of saying that each translator answers the Sapphic riddle by asking it again.

SAPPHO IN TRANSLATION

Since fragment 31 opens itself to perpetual translation—the breaking of a tongue in different tongues—Sappho survives as something simultaneously translating itself and being translated, as both the active principle "in" translation and the product "of" translation. This point about the double valence of prepositions like "in" and "of," which mark "a vacillation between two modes, active and passive, transitive and intransitive, on either side of the relation they splice," is made by Philip Lewis in his essay "The Measure of Translation Effects." Sappho, too, is a translation effect: her sublimity is a function of her translatability, to be measured not only in terms of a movement from "original" to "translated" text but also in terms of the reverse effect of translation on the original. Following Benjamin (or a Derridean "translation" of Benjamin), Lewis argues that the task of the translator is to produce difference rather than identical meaning, to "abuse" a text in the etymological sense of ab-use: as the preposition "ab" indicates, translation swerves away from the uses of the original text, departing from this origin in order to expose its already self-differing structure. Insofar as this abusiveness also implies a violation of meaning, it is not a random act of textual violence but directed at a specific place in the text to be translated: "a decisive textual knot that will be recognized by dint of its own abusive features." Thus, Lewis concludes, the translator will "rearticulate analogically the abuse that occurs in the original text," by actively reproducing that original abuse and reactively transforming it.[35]

To extend this theoretical model into the historical practice of translation, I would like to notice how γλῶσσα ἔαγε is a "decisive textual knot" in fragment 31—which we have already recognized "by dint of its own abusive features," as a poem anatomizing the figure of prosopopoeia—that forces translators into abuse or excess of the original. And indeed it is through such abuse that Sappho increasingly emerges as a feminine figure within a tradition that presents the female lyric subject—and the woman poet—in terms of a violent disjunction between body and voice. Sappho enters into the tradition of English lyric through the example of fragment 31 in particular, and English translations of the fragment furthermore contribute to the formation of that lyric tradition, as Lawrence Lipking points

35. Lewis, "The Measure of Translation Effects" 32, 42–43.

out: "A history of lyric poetry could be written by following the ways that later poets have adapted her lines to their own purposes."[36] Lipking surveys numerous translations and imitations of fragment 31 from Catullus onward, in order to describe Sappho "descending" from the past and toward the present. Alongside Lipking's critical survey, contemporary translators and poets have also aligned themselves with a history of Sapphic translation: Willis Barnstone illustrates a poetics of translation by comparing several versions of fragment 31 including his own, and Rosanna Warren reflects on her experience of translating Sappho as "a small instance of lyric lineage, a type of model for poetry's perpetual re-engendering of itself."[37]

My purpose here is not to reconstruct the entire history of fragment 31 in translation, although such a project is certainly worth undertaking in further detail. Rather, I want to construct an argument about the engendering of Sappho as a specifically female lyric subject through translations of fragment 31, in order to demonstrate the mutual implication of gender and genre in lyric reading. In analyzing several translations spanning the past four centuries, I am particularly interested in the representation of Sappho's broken tongue and the various ways in which translators attempt to recuperate voice from that break. Each translation goes beyond the Greek text of fragment 31 in order to rearticulate in English what is missing from it: namely, Sappho's "voice," which can only be constituted as a variable effect of various translations. Sappho emerges as female lyric subject at the precise moment when the tongue breaks, and this moment has different implications in different historical contexts. Thus Sappho survives as figure for translation, not as an allegorical or ahistorical principle but in the actual practice of translating itself.

I begin with John Hall, who is not the first to imitate Sappho in English but does offer the first version of fragment 31 taken directly from Greek, as part of his translation of Longinus: *Peri Hypsous or Dionysius Longinus of the Height of Eloquence rendered out of the Original*, published in 1652. Translating Sappho within the context of the Longinian sublime, Hall introduces her into the tradition of English lyric as an apparently self-recuperating lyric subject:

> He that sits next to thee now and hears
> Thy charming voyce, to me appears
> Beauteous as any Deity
>   That rules the skie.

36. Lipking, *Abandoned Women* 58.
37. Barnstone, *The Poetics of Translation* 98–105; Warren, "Translation as Elegy" 200.

How did his pleasing glances dart
Sweet languors to my ravish'd heart
At the first sight though so prevailed
    That my voyce fail'd.

I'me speechless, feavrish, fires assail
My fainting flesh, my sight doth fail
Whilst to my restless mind my ears
    Still hum new fears.

Cold sweats and tremblings so invade
That like a wither'd flower I fade
So that my life being almost lost,
    I seem a Ghost.

Yet since I'me wretched must I dare ... [38]

Hall preserves the first line of the fifth stanza and recuperates Sappho from the moment of death, so that she may live on past the ellipses. Indeed, Hall's Sappho seems to "quicken" in every sense: although her life is "almost lost" and she might "seem a Ghost," in the rapid stanzas of this translation her mind is "restless," her ears "still hum" and she speaks emphatically "now" in the present tense.

Only momentarily does Hall's translation lapse into the past tense, in describing how "voyce fail'd" in stanza 2. The failure of voice is therefore projected into the past while stanza 3 immediately shifts back to the present: "I'me speechless." In this temporal transition it is difficult to locate the exact moment when the tongue breaks: the sequence of the Greek (where "no speaking is left in me" is followed by "tongue is broken") seems to be reversed in the English (where "my voyce fail'd" is followed by "I'm speechless"), so that voice seems to fail *before* rather than *after* the inability to speak. The implication here is that voice can still be recovered through speech, even if the speaker is temporarily speechless, and this recovery of voice is already implied at the beginning of Hall's poem, where the Greek phrase "sweet speaking" is translated, proleptically, into "charming voyce." If Hall's Sappho has lost her tongue in this poem, it is never quite as literally as the tongue breaking in fragment 31. Nowhere, in fact, does the word "tongue" appear in this English translation, which insists on the persistence of voice without leaving much room for the linguistic break in Greek—except perhaps in the break between stanzas 2 and 3. This stanzaic break creates an empty space, a silent interruption, in a poem that otherwise flows with effortless rhymes; here, in the breaking of Sappho's tongue between two stanzas and its disappearance into that break, we rediscover the hiatus

38. Hall, *Peri Hypsous.*

of γλῶσσα ἔαγε. The death of Sappho haunts the white spaces between stanzas, as the spectral emanation or afterlife of the Greek text: "I seem a Ghost."

What do we make of this ghostly manifestation of Sappho's broken tongue? If Hall seems to bring Sappho back to life, it is to inscribe her death into the margins of this English translation after all—not only in the stanzaic break but in the final line: "Yet since I'me wretched must I dare ... " The ellipsis here opens the possibility for various interpretations and allows the utterance to be recontextualized. When fragment 31 is placed within the larger context of Sappho's Renaissance reception, a reader might speculate about another, more familiar, ending to Hall's translation: perhaps, like Ovid's Sappho, she is "wretched" in her unrequited love for Phaon and therefore "must dare" to perform her suicide—the infamous leap from the Leucadian cliff into the waters of posterity, as described by Ovid in "Sappho to Phaon." Throughout the Renaissance Sappho is primarily known by the Ovidian narrative, which transforms Sappho of Lesbos into a woman love-struck by a man. This heterosexual reading of Sappho explains, as well, the change of pronouns in Hall's translation of fragment 31: no longer addressed to a girl, it describes "How did *his* pleasing glances dart / Sweet languors to my ravish'd heart." Hall exploits the ambiguous anacoluthon in Greek to suggest it is not the girl but the man (Phaon?) who leaves Sappho "ravish'd" in stanza 2, and erotically deflowered in stanza 4: "Cold sweats and tremblings so invade / That like a wither'd flower I fade." Pierced by his "pleasing glances," Sappho acquires lyric subjectivity through subjection to a man whose presence is more central in Hall's translation than he ever was in the Greek.

Indeed the presence of the man proves to be a rhetorical necessity in Hall's translation, which is mediated not only by Longinus and Ovid but also by the conventions of Renaissance love lyric. The ravishing of Sappho by a male gaze allows fragment 31 to be read as another version of Petrarchanism, described by Nancy Vickers in terms of the obsessive dismembering and remembering of the female body by male poets. Vickers argues that the scattering of Laura's body in Petrarch's scattered rhymes allows his voice to emerge while her speech is silenced—or rather, reified as another one of the many body parts enumerated but never unified by Petrarch. Hall's Sappho therefore "speaks" from the position of Petrarch's Laura, through a Petrarchan legacy of fragmentation that, according to Vickers, leaves "bodies fetishized by a poetic voice" and poetic voice fetishized as one of the "exquisitely reified parts" of the body.[39] Here the logic of Petrarchan lyric

---

39. Vickers, "Scattered Woman and Scattered Rhyme" 107.

converges with the Longinian reading of fragment 31, to produce Sappho as a paradoxical lyric subject: she is made to speak as "woman poet," but only by dying. Predicated on the opposition between masculine subject and feminine object, Hall's translation thus reflects seventeenth-century assumptions about lyric as an already implicitly gendered genre.

In the proliferation of eighteenth-century translations and editions of Sappho, fragment 31 begins to influence as well as reflect newly emerging ideas about lyric. In 1711 Sappho is introduced to the readers of the *Spectator* by Addison, who invokes her as alternative to the Petrarchan poets of the previous century and mistakenly (or perhaps strategically) presents Ambrose Philips as the first translator of fragment 31 into English. Sappho is "extreamly difficult to render into another Tongue," according to Addison, who nevertheless praises the Philips version because it is "written in the very Spirit of Sappho, and as near the Greek as our Language will possibly suffer."[40] Here the rendering of Sappho's broken tongue "into another Tongue" implies the rending of "our Language" as well, as a form of estrangement that the English tongue must "suffer" in order to create new possibilities for expression.

Thus the translation by Ambrose Philips, published in 1711, looks quite different from Hall's version:

Bles't as th'Immortal Gods is he,
The Youth who fondly sits by thee,
And hears and sees thee all the while
Softly speak and sweetly smile.

'Twas this depriv'd my Soul of Rest,
And rais'd such Tumults in my Breast;
For while I gaz'd, in Transport tost,
My Breath was gone, my Voice was lost;

My Bosom glow'd; the subtle Flame
Ran quick thro' all my vital Frame;
O'er my dim Eyes a Darkness hung;
My Ears with hollow Murmurs rung:

In dewy Damps my Limbs were chill'd;
My Blood with gentle Horrours thrill'd;
My feeble Pulse forgot to play;
I fainted, sunk, and dy'd away.[41]

In this translation, the break in γλῶσσα ἔαγε is conveyed by the comma between "My Breath was gone, my Voice was lost." The lack of a conjunction

40. *The Spectator* No. 229 (22 November 1711).
41. Philips, *Odes of Anacreon and Sappho* 74–75.

suggests the disjunction in Sappho's voice, which can only be recovered as posthumous utterance: Philips shifts from present to past tense in stanza 2, as in Hall's translation, but without reverting back to the present. The effect of this shift, as Lipking points out, is that Sappho seems to speak "from the other side of the grave."[42] Unlike Hall, Philips ends his poem with Sappho definitively dead and fallen into silence in the final line: "I fainted, sunk, and dy'd away."

And yet it is the inspiration of this translation by Philips, "written in the very Spirit of Sappho," to figure her death as loss of breath. What Addison admires about Philips is the enthusiasm with which he reenacts Sappho's rapture and even names it as sublime within the poem itself: in line 7, Sappho is "in Transport tost." This inspirational moment exceeds the loss of breath in the next line and presents Sapphic inspiration as a poetic power that lives on past the death of the poet: hence the vivid description of Sappho's "vital Frame" in stanza 3. Philips therefore animates the poem and infuses it with the "spirit" of Sappho, by translating fragment 31 into a highly artificial body, or "most artificial Union." According to Philips, fragment 31 is "the most inimitable Example of the most artificial Union, or rather Combat, of all the Passions, and of all the moving Circumstances that can enliven a piece."[43] He in turn attempts to "enliven" Sappho, by recreating her "vital Frame" through an elaborate framing of words—the division of stanzas into two rhyming couplets, the division of couplets into two lines, the division of lines into two balanced phrases, the division of phrases into four syllables each, the division of syllables into phonemes, the division of phonemes into letters. In this way the formal mechanism of his verse converts the "moving Circumstances" of the original poem into the movement of language itself, "in Transport tost."

In his attempt to breathe life into the pieces of Sappho's poem, if not Sappho herself, Philips anticipates eighteenth-century debates about whether language is "natural" or "artificial" and whether the body is "spiritual" or "mechanical." Indeed, his translation proves influential throughout the century because his Sappho is a point of convergence for both sides of the debate, and a medium for the conversion of each into the other. When Addison introduces Philips as the definitive translator of Sappho, he articulates the same contradiction. In *Spectator* No. 229 he proclaims the "natural Beauty" of Sappho, but also describes her as the fragmented simulacrum of a body: she is one of the "famous Pieces of Antiquity," to be compared to "the Trunc of a Statue which has lost the Arms, Legs, and Head." Recalling how Michelangelo learned "his whole Art" from a "maimed Statue," Addison

---

42. Lipking, *Abandoned Women* 82.
43. Philips, *Odes of Anacreon and Sappho* 69–70.

finds beauty in this dismemberment and urges English readers to find the same in Sappho's "mutilated Figure." In this account, Sappho becomes a maimed and truncated statue that may be recomposed according to the logic of the Longinian sublime, but without an appeal to organic unity: Addison's emphasis is more on a literalizing disintegration than a figurative reconstitution. And, increasingly, the figure for such "literal" disintegration is feminine, as Sappho "herself" is read as a fragmentary female body.

The Longinian reading of fragment 31 is important for Sappho's reception throughout the eighteenth and nineteenth centuries, preoccupied as they are with theories of the sublime. Insofar as such theories are structured around a gendered opposition between "masculine" sublimity and "feminine" beauty, the example of Sappho contributes to a gradual "feminization" of the sublime that makes it possible for women poets to imitate Sappho as well. Their Sapphic imitations, however, appear to be a mockery of the sublime by the time of Byron, who writes:

> I don't think Sappho's Ode a good example,
> Although Longinus tells us there is no hymn
> Where the Sublime soars forth on wings more ample.[44]

Sappho's name has become synonymous with sentimental lyric and "women's poetry," where (in Byron's pun) "no hymn" is also "no him." Ambrose Philips, whose translation of fragment 31 is widely anthologized in nineteenth-century collections of women's verse, acquires the reputation of "Namby-Pamby"—an emasculated poet, whose effeminacy is an effect of a lyric tradition that assimilates Sappho's seventeenth-century association with Petrarchanism and her eighteenth-century association with the sublime into a nineteenth-century rhetoric of the sentimental suffering body. Fragment 31 becomes the vehicle for this new engendering of lyric by women poets, or so it seems to Byron when he asks, "Is not Philips' translation of it in the mouths of all your women?"[45]

Byron's tongue-in-cheek question has serious implications, however. How do all those women speak, with Sappho's broken tongue in their mouths? How do they revive a lyric voice that is predicated on its own death? While the translation of fragment 31 by Philips is reputed to be "as near the Greek as the Genius of our Language will possibly suffer," women poets tend to anatomize the assumption of Sapphic voice itself as a form of bodily suffering. In their appeal to Sappho, what emerges increasingly is the "woman poet" as a *figure* that embodies the problem of speech: here lyric voice is gendered as feminine precisely because it doesn't speak. Nineteenth-century female

44. Byron, *Don Juan* 1.42.
45. Byron quoted by Robinson, *Sappho and Her Influence* 199–200.

authorship is therefore constructed through Sappho, as the proper name for the "Poetess"—invoked by British and American women writers as the "original" woman poet, yet figured in their poetry as nonoriginary voice.[46]

Consider, for example, how fragment 31 is translated by Mary Hewitt and published in 1845 by Poe as editor of *The Broadway Journal*. We might read her "Translation of an Ode of Sappho" as an ironic reincorporation of Sappho's translation by Ambrose Philips:

> *Translation of an Ode of Sappho*
>
> Blest as the immortal gods is he
> On whom each day thy glances shine;
> Who hears thy voice of melody,
> And meets thy smile so all divine.
>
> Oh, when I list thine accents low
> How thrills my breast with tender pain—
> Fire seems through every vein to glow,
> And strange confusion whelms my brain.
>
> My sight grows dim beneath the glance
> Whose ardent rays I may not meet,
> While swift and wild my pulses dance,
> Then cease all suddenly to beat.
>
> And o'er my cheek with rapid gush,
> I feel the burning life-tide dart;
> Then backward like a torrent rush
> All icy cold upon my heart.
>
> And I am motionless and pale,
> And silent as an unstrung lyre;
> And feel, while thus each sense doth fail,
> Doomed in thy presence to expire.

While Philips recuperates the possibility of Sapphic inspiration after death by translating fragment 31 in the past tense, Hewitt translates it into the present tense to suggest that Sapphic voice suffers death at the very moment of speaking: the "vital Frame" of the Philips poem becomes the "unstrung lyre" of a body about "to expire." This phrase refigures "my Breath was gone" (in the Philips translation) as a loss of inspiration, in an infinitive that locates this loss in the perpetual present. Hewitt thus postpones her translation of γλῶσσα ἔαγε until the end of the poem, yet anticipates Sappho's broken tongue throughout the previous stanzas as the very condition of speaking.

---

46. For further discussion of Sappho's influence on nineteenth-century women poets, see, e.g., Leighton, *Victorian Women Poets*; Gubar, "Sapphistries"; Brown, "A Victorian Sappho"; Prins, "Sappho Doubled"; and M. Reynolds, "Sappho's Last Song."

For what "speaks" in the previous stanzas instead of voice is the body itself, through an intensification of "tender pain" that eroticizes death and may even make it seem desirable. Thus Hewitt translates fragment 31 into an anatomy of the lyric subject, as she proceeds to anatomize the suffering body with pseudo-medical objectivity—enumerating its symptoms in stanza 2, testing its pulse in stanza 3, taking its temperature in stanza 4. Contrasting "thy voice of melody" in the first stanza with the decomposing body of the following stanzas, Hewitt presents Sappho to the reader as a corpse for ironic dissection.

It is no coincidence, then, that Hewitt's translation is printed in the same issue of *The Broadway Journal* that also features (prominently on the front page) "The Premature Burial" by Edgar Allan Poe. As editor of the journal, Poe publishes Hewitt in conjunction with his own lurid tale, allowing fragment 31 to be read as its epilogue. In Poe's account of "living inhumation," he describes a man "seemingly dead" who survived his own burial and "in broken sentences spoke of his agonies in the grave"; he describes how another man "pronounced *dead* by his physicians" also revived and "then—spoke," much to everyone's "rapturous astonishment"; finally, he describes his own "authentic" experience of death: "I grew sick, and numb, and chilly, and dizzy, and so fell prostrate at once," and when buried, "I endeavored to shriek ... but no voice issued." As Poe turns his increasingly extravagant report of "authenticated instances" into a fiction that comically exposes its own assumption of "authentic voice" ("I read ... no bugaboo tales—*such as this* "), he anticipates Hewitt's ironic assumption of Sapphic voice as well. For Poe's description of speaking corpses are all reminiscent of fragment 31, setting the reader up for Hewitt's Sappho translation as yet another case of "living inhumation"—the premature burial of Sappho, perhaps?

In this context, Poe's gothic tale serves not only as parody of journal reportage but as a reflection on lyric reading that is predicated on voice: neither dead nor alive, how is such a voice to be authenticated? And why does this equivocation produce the posthumous figure of Sappho as feminine speaker? Her death proves to be "unquestionably, the most poetical topic in the world" because it bodies forth the persistence of such questions. Sappho has become the rhetorical embodiment of this disjunction between body and voice, a nineteenth-century topos for the "most poetical topic." Hewitt returns to this poetical topos in a later version of fragment 31, more loosely paraphrased in a poem entitled "Imitation of Sappho" (1853). This translation is not only an imitation "of" Sappho but addressed "to" Sappho as well, enabling Hewitt to reflect on her previous attempt to reincorporate Sapphic voice:

Imitation of Sappho

If to repeat thy name when none may hear me,
  To find thy thought with all my thoughts inwove;
To languish where thou'rt not—to sigh when near thee—
  Oh! if this be to love thee, I do love!

If when thou utterest low words of greeting,
  To feel through every vein the torrent pour;
Then back again the hot tide swift retreating,
  Leave me all powerless, silent as before—

If to list breathless to thine accents falling,
  Almost to pain, upon my eager ear;
And fondly when alone to be recalling
  The words that I would die again to hear—

If at thy glance my heart all strength forsaking,
  Pant in my breast as pants the frighted dove;
If to think on thee ever, sleeping—waking—
  Oh! if this be to love thee, I do love![47]

As in Hewitt's 1845 translation of fragment 31, this love lyric also anatomizes its own lyric subject. For the repetition of "thy name when none may hear me" produces loss of voice, leaving "me all powerless, silent as before—" and "breathless." The dash here renders the hiatus in γλῶσσα ἔαγε, exchanging breath or inspiration for the panting of the heart "in my breast," and defining voice no longer as a function of speech but as an utterance inscribed on the body, suffering "almost to pain." Yet by invoking "words that I would die again to hear" Hewitt's poem provokes this infinitely repeatable death, and inscribes it on the written body of her own poem. Thus Hewitt incorporates the Sapphic corpus into her own body of writing, figuring lyric voice as the reiteration of Sappho's name in a body that cannot speak: a reinscription of Sappho's broken tongue that refuses, or at least resists, sublimation into voice. For the entire poem is conscious of itself as nonoriginal imitation, predicated on an "if" at the beginning of each stanza that renders the utterance entirely conditional and mediates its claim to "feminine" voice. Hewitt's "Imitation of Sappho" therefore poses the very question of female authorship that critics often take for granted in their reading of Mary Hewitt as woman poet.

Here we can understand a critical tendency to conflate body and voice in women's writing as symptomatic of an idealization of feminine voice that must itself be historicized as a nineteenth-century legacy, and theorized as a problem raised rather than solved by the example of Sappho. Lipking's reading of Mary Hewitt, for example, assumes that she turns to Sappho to identify herself as woman poet: "like Sappho, she has a body," he writes in

47. Hewitt, *Poems* 56.

response to Hewitt's "Imitation of Sappho."[48] In quoting the poem, however, he omits the first stanza that sets up the complex mediation between Hewitt and Sappho. This enables him to identify one with the other ("like Sappho, she"), and so assert an identity for the woman poet that in the poem itself can only be discovered as an effect of repetition. In this respect the lively survey of Sapphic imitations in his book, and especially his discussion of nineteenth-century women poets in whom he discovers echoes of Sappho, reflects the historical gendering of lyric itself as a feminine genre. For as the title of Lipking's book suggests, *Abandoned Women and Poetic Tradition* presents us with the contradiction of a poetic tradition predicated on the recuperation of an always already abandoned woman poet, an originary loss figured most often in Sappho.

The identification of women poets with Sappho is a legacy that persists into our own century as well, as we see in the example of Mary Barnard's *Sappho: A New Translation*, published in 1958. These translations are still in wide circulation, and indeed Barnard's Sappho is often read as if it *is* Sappho, taught in the classroom either as representative of "women's voices" in antiquity or as representation of a timeless "feminine voice" in poetry. Barnard herself also makes claim to such a voice through "Sappho's Greek," as she writes in her memoir: "I found in Sappho's Greek the style I had been groping toward, or perhaps merely hungering for: spare but musical, it had the sound of the speaking voice making a simply but emotionally loaded statement. It is resonant although unmistakably in the female register."[49] The final phrase, "although unmistakably in the female register," is an interesting qualification of Barnard's claim to "the sound of the speaking voice," however, for it points to the persistence of a break in Sapphic voice, no matter how "resonant." This break is "in the female register" not because it was once spoken by a woman, or is now translated by a woman, but because it manifests a lyric voice that is gendered *through* a tradition of reading and translating fragment 31. The fact that Barnard discovers in Sappho a voice she had been "groping toward" or "hungering for" only serves to emphasize, in tautological fashion, the construction of "feminine voice" on the model of Sappho. In other words, when Barnard turns to the Sapphic fragments, what she discovers is the textual reconstruction of a voice, and within its resonance there is a silence corresponding to the lack or absence of a voice that Barnard would call her own.

Barnard's translation of fragment 31 is poised between the continuity of a speaking voice and the discontinuity of a fragmentary text:

48. Lipking, *Abandoned Women* 103.
49. Barnard, *Assault on Mount Helicon* 282.

He is a god in my eyes—
the man who is allowed
to sit beside you—he

who listens intimately
to the sweet murmur of
your voice, the enticing

laughter that makes my own
heart beat fast. If I meet
you suddenly, I can't

speak—my tongue is broken;
a thin flame runs under
my skin; seeing nothing,

hearing only my own ears
drumming, I drip with sweat;
trembling shakes my body

and I turn paler than
dry grass. At such times
death isn't far from me[50]

Barnard creates an effect of discontinuity through her use of enjambments, interrupting dashes, and no punctuation at the end of the final line. The most deliberately discontinuous effect is, of course, the stanzaic enjambment in "I can't / speak—my tongue is broken." Here the verb for speaking is split in two, and the dash between "speak" and "my tongue" performs the hiatus between γλῶσσα and ἔαγε in Greek. This representation of Sappho's broken tongue is primarily visual, however. While presenting the image of a fragment on the page, Barnard also represents it as a continuous first-person utterance. Despite the short lines and the shortened stanzas, despite the spare diction and the fragmentary ending, her poem implies the continuity of a speaking voice: in "the sweet murmur of / your voice," we see a gap but we hear a continuous murmur; in "hearing only my own ears / drumming" the hearing persists into the next line; and in "death isn't far from me" we see the line has ended, but without a period its cadence continues.

Barnard therefore translates fragment 31 into a broken image of unbroken speech, a text from which the "sound of the speaking voice" or "that underlying cadence" may still be recuperated: "Underlying the stanzaic form there is, I swear (in the teeth of those who have said otherwise) a cadence that belongs to the speaking voice. That underlying cadence is what I tried to find an equivalent for, because so far as I knew, no English translation had yet conveyed it."[51] Following Pound's modernist edict to

---

50. Barnard, *Sappho* 39.
51. Barnard, *Assault on Mount Helicon* 284.

"make it new," her purpose in *Sappho: A New Translation* is to reconstruct Sappho in a modern idiom "equivalent" to speech. This reclamation of Sapphic voice is an implicit rejection of earlier translators, whose language seems too antiquarian and antiquated to bring Sappho back to life. She writes in her poem "Static":

> I wanted to hear
>
> Sappho's laughter
> and the speech of
> her stringed steel.
>
> What I heard was
> whiskered mumble-
> ment of grammarians:
>
> Greek pterodactyls
> and Victorian dodos.[52]

Like Pound, who parodies the stuttering of "φαίνε-τ-τ-τ-τττ-αί μοι" by fusty classical scholars who lose voice in their attempt "to scan φαίνεταί μοι,"[53] Barnard wants to restore continuity to Sappho's broken tongue, in a language pared down to essential images and purified into essential voice rather than obscured by the "mumblement of grammarians."

Indeed, when she assimilates Pound's modernism into her translation of fragment 31, Barnard appeals to an aesthetic that is already derived from the early imagist reading of Sappho, in whom Pound discovered the prototype for and ideal of imagist poetry. The discovery of new Sapphic fragments on papyri in Egypt at the turn of the century had produced a flurry of new reconstructions, translations, and imitations of Sappho, and Pound seized the historical moment to introduce new poetry by H.D. as if he had discovered yet another Sapphic fragment: "It is in the laconic speech of the Imagistes. Objective—no slither; direct—no excess of adjectives, no metaphors that won't permit examination. It's straight talk—straight as the Greek"[54] Pound's high praise of H.D. is what Barnard seems to aspire to in her own translations of Sappho, several decades later. Her English version of fragment 31 refuses the "slither" of Victorian translations, preferring active verbs and concrete description to an "excess of adjectives." Thus like Pound and H.D., Barnard discovers the possibility for "straight talk—straight as the Greek" in Sappho. Yet this rediscovery of lyric voice is predicated on ancient Greek as a dead language that is no longer spoken, and what haunts Barnard's translations is the unspoken awareness that Sappho is nothing but

---

52. Barnard, *Collected Poems* 64.
53. Pound, "Canto LXXIV," in *Cantos* 458–59.
54. Pound, *Letters* 11.

text—a mere fragment, a piece of writing deciphered with difficulty, a strip of Egyptian papyrus wrapped around a silent corpse.

In his correspondence with Barnard, Pound therefore observes a curious disjunction of "living" voice and "dead" text in her translation: "you mix two languages, the LIVE . . . and the dead." His advice to Barnard is "to get the LIVE language AND the prosody simultaneously," so that her prosody may achieve "articulation of the total sound of a poem (not bits of certain shapes gummed together)." At the same time, Pound also urges Barnard to produce more discontinuity in her translations, allowing the "total sound" to be interrupted by "abruptness." "What is the maximum abruptness you can get it TO?" he asks in another letter.[55] Barnard's solution to this double imperative is, on the one hand, to give continuity to her translations by filling in textual gaps, supplying titles that point to an implicit narrative, and using colloquial language to create the effect of a living speaker. On the other hand, the fragmentary appearance of the texts on the page, their broken lineation and multiple enjambments, creates an effect of "abruptness," an interruption of the very voice that she wishes to produce. Barnard's Sappho is a contradictory figure, in the literal sense: she speaks in different ways, and ultimately not at all.

Nevertheless Mary Barnard is read as the modern reincarnation of Sappho, as Dudley Fitts writes in his preface to *Sappho: A New Translation*: "This, one thinks, is what Sappho must have been like."[56] This may be understood not only as a comment on the apparent fluency of her translations, but as an idealization of Sapphic voice that characterizes the history of translating fragment 31 and allows women poets in particular to be conflated with the figure of Sappho. I have argued, however, that fragment 31 cannot be read as the simple assertion of Sappho's voice, or feminine voice, or a transcendent lyric voice. For what we have seen in a brief survey of translations is the difficulty of such a recuperation: Hall introduces Sappho as a lyric subject within a legacy of Petrarchan fragmentation, Philips translates Sappho into the past tense as a posthumous lyric subject, Hewitt inscribes Sappho onto a suffering body that does not speak, and Barnard locates Sappho's voice in the moment of its interruption. Sappho survives as a text never quite sublimated into voice: a corpus used for, and ab-used by, translation.

In her recent book *Art and Lies* (as much a prose poem as a novel), Jeanette Winterson offers yet another translation of Sappho that reflects on this tradition as a history of abuse. She creates a fictional persona

---

55. Barnard quotes the letters from Pound in *Assault on Mount Helicon* 282–83.

56. For further discussion of Fitts responding to the "transparency" of Barnard's Sappho translations, in contrast to Pound's interest in a more "heterogeneous discourse," see Venuti, *The Translator's Invisibility* 211–13.

for Sappho, who wonders about the violence directed against the Sapphic corpus:

> I have a lot of questions, not least, WHAT HAVE YOU DONE WITH MY POEMS? When I turn the pages of my manuscripts my fingers crumble the paper, the paper breaks up in burnt folds, the paper colours my palms yellow. I look like a nicotine junkie. I can no longer read my own writing. It isn't surprising that so many of you have chosen to read between the lines when the lines themselves have become more mutilated than a Saturday night whore.[57]

This vision of Sappho burning up in the pages of her own poetry—smoked like a sublime cigarette, down to its ashes—leaves her unable "to read my own writing." Thus in another repetition of the Sapphic riddle, Winterson's Sappho asks: "What have you done with my poems?" Here Sappho embodies yet again the fate of fragment 31, mutilated beyond recognition through the history of its transmission. For in the long tradition of translating fragment 31, Sappho is defaced in the very attempt to give face and voice to this text. If translators wish to recuperate Sapphic voice, they have no choice but to "read between the lines"—and between the letters—of fragment 31, yet in doing so they (or "you," or we, or I) repeat the break inscribed in γλῶσσα ἔαγε: a broken tongue that speaks, through violent disjunction, of Sappho's afterlife in translation.

57. Winterson, *Art and Lies* 51.

THREE

🎵

Sappho's Splintered Tongue:
Silence in Sappho 31 and Catullus 51

Dolores O'Higgins

Sappho 31 concerns poetry as much as love or jealousy, like Catullus's "response" in 51, a poem which addresses Sappho's poetic claims and poetic stance at least as much as Lesbia's beauty.[1] This study considers the impact of the beloved on each of the two poets, focusing especially on the disturbing and memorable image of the "broken" tongue in Sappho's poem, and the relative seriousness of Sappho's "fracture" and Catullus's sluggish tongue.

The Greek poem's first line introduces what appears to be a highly charged emotional situation, whose "literary" implications appear only later. Sappho (as I shall designate the speaker) supposes a man who sits—or any man might sit—opposite the girl she loves.[2]

φαίνεταί μοι κῆνος ἴσος θέοισιν

This essay was originally published in slightly different form as "Sappho's Splintered Tongue: Silence in Sappho 31 and Catullus 51," *American Journal of Philology* 111 (1990) 156–67.

1. For bibliography on this and other poems of Sappho, see Gerber's two "Studies in Greek Lyric Poetry." For bibliography on Catullus 51, see Holoka, *Gaius Valerius Catullus* 195–97. For summary of earlier treatments of the poem's *cruces* and insightful comment, see Kirkwood, *Early Greek Monody* 255–60. Him. *Or.* 28.2 significantly says that Sappho made a girl's beauty and graces a pretext (πρόφασις) for her songs. Lefkowitz, "Critical Stereotypes," shows how Sappho's work has been seen as the artless outpouring of a woman whose emotional energies have been diverted from the "normal" channel—i.e., child raising. For the artistry of Sappho 31, see Segal, "Eros and Incantation." This issue of rationality and poetic control is related to the question of poetic persona. My position resembles that of W. R. Johnson in *The Idea of Lyric*: the singer is "partly herself perhaps, the woman Sappho; partly an ideal, universal fiction: their fusion in imagination" (40–41).

2. I agree with Winkler, "Gardens of Nymphs," that the expression "that man whosoever" is "a rhetorical cliche, not an actor in the imagined scene" (74).

Before she identifies the subject of the very *phainetai*, Sappho introduces the pronoun *moi*, the indirect object of the verb and perceiver or interpreter of the scene. The line might translate "It seems to me that he is like the gods. . . ."[3] The verb reappears at line 16, where Sappho "seems to *herself*." Thus, most of the extant poem is contained within a framework or "ring" of authorial memory, perception, imagination, or opinion. Although the poet dramatizes herself as an alien figure, looking wistfully at the unattainable, she is not altogether an outsider. *Phainetai moi* marks the boundary of a world contained within Sappho. By contrast, Catullus begins his poem, *and* its second line, with the third-person pronoun *ille*, a change which shifts the emphasis from perceiver to perceived. Catullus's naming of his beloved—Lesbia—also grants her a specific identify and a more substantial independent existence than Sappho's anonymous girl.

Lesbia's audience responds to both her visual and her verbal charm; the man watches and listens to ("spectat et audit"; 4) the seductress, who laughs sweetly. In Sappho the man only listens (*hupakouei*; 4), but the girl's aural charms are double; she speaks sweetly (*hadu phōneisas*; 3–4) and laughs caressingly (*gelaisas himeroen*; 5). Thus in Sappho's opening scene the girl's seductiveness is emphatically vocal. The subsequent expression "whenever I see you—even for a short time . . ." in 7 may suggest that the girl's beauty was such that it could be felt in the briefest glimpse, yet the passage seems at least as concerned with Sappho's extraordinary susceptibility to her beloved's presence as with the girl's appearance.

> The thing makes the heart in my breast tremble.
> For when I see you even for a short time
> I can no longer speak . . .
>
> (7–8)

The poet's heart is shaken by "this thing,"[4] i.e., by the girl's voice, the man's reaction to the girl, her own sense of mortality, in fact by the complete "moment and its beauty and anguish," as Ralph Johnson has put it.[5] The verb *eptoaisen* (causes to tremble), describing the scene's shattering effect on Sappho, connotes more than a *frisson* of sexual excitement; she feels the debilitating fear that precedes lethal encounters on the

---

3. The verb is not used impersonally at this early date—but my translation preserves the order in which the pronouns appear. Catullus's poem reverses that order.

4. The antecedent of *to* has been the subject of much debate. For recent discussion and bibliography, see Emmet Robbins, "'Every Time I Look at You.'" Whether or not the ambiguity of the relative pronoun in l. 5 is deliberate, it cannot be argued into clarity; *to* glances cursorily back at all that precedes it—the entire series of images, impressions, and opinions.

5. W. R. Johnson, *The Idea of Lyric* 39.

battlefield.[6] The poem gradually unravels the signs and implications of her terror/excitement.

The man faces the girl, listening closely, and seems "like the gods" in his felicity or perhaps his hardihood.[7] Although the immediate context allows either reading, the tone and imagery of the remainder of the poem point in the direction of hardihood. The man, in his divine invulnerability, may dally in the girl's destructive ambiance, but Sappho fears even a momentary and relatively long-range encounter.

Sappho is a battered "veteran" whose previous encounters with the girl have always had the same outcome.[8] First she is struck dumb. Then a subtle fever (9–10) is succeeded by blindness, humming in her ears, cold sweat, a grasslike pallor—and finally (15–16), "I seem to myself to be little short of dying." It has been observed that details of this disintegration echo Homeric descriptions of dying or mortally threatened warriors—for example the pallor, blindness (or faintness), and sweat.[9] I wish to focus on another aspect of Sappho's reaction, however.

Symptoms that do *not* characterize the beleaguered warrior include the humming, fever, and silence.[10] Of these the silence—the first in Sappho's catalog—is perhaps the most interesting. Silence does not generally afflict Homeric warriors, even desperate ones. More significantly, it does *not* afflict the one Homeric poet who is threatened with mortal danger. Phemius pleads

---

6. For discussion of the meaning of *ptoieō*, see Rissman, *Love as War* 110 n. 22. For comparable uses of the verb in an amatory context, see Mimnermus 5.1–3 West [W.]; Alc. 283.3–4; Anac. 60.11–12. Wills, "Sappho 31 and Catullus 51" 186–87, takes *eptoaisen* as hypothetical (*ken* being understood) but the aorist makes better sense, and the indicative mood is accepted by most scholars (see Koniaris, "On Sappho Fr. 31" 184–85).

7. Robbins, " 'Every Time I Look at You' " 260, takes the expression as capable of referring both to strength and happiness; I also prefer an inclusive reading. See Koniaris, "On Sappho Fr. 31" 181–82, for discussions of *isos theoisin*.

8. See Markovich, "Sappho Fr. 31" 21, who notes—citing Kuhner and Gerth 2:449—that the subjunctive *idō* in line 7 "denotes the repetition of this chain reaction." See also Wills, "Sappho 31 and Catullus 51" 170, and Koniaris, "On Sappho Fr. 31" 184.

9. See Rissman, *Love as War* 72–90. Rissman studies the expressions *eptoaisen, tromos . . . agrei, khlōrotera . . . poias, isos theoisin*, etc. in the context of certain Homeric passages. See also Svenbro, "La tragédie de l'amour" 66–72. Svenbro remarks that several of Sappho's "symptoms"—trembling, blindness, sweat, pallor—resemble those of wounded, struggling, or fearful warriors.

10. See Svenbro, "La tragédie de l'amour" 69, for discussion of the humming and fever, both of which are without parallel in Homer. See also Page, *Sappho and Alcaeus* 29, for (rare) parallels of these erotic symptoms in Greek and Roman poets. Page cites several Homeric passages where silence afflicts someone who is shocked or afraid. Antilochus's inability to speak at his discovery of Patroclus's death (*Il.* 17.695–96) is not, as Svenbro claims, a symptom comparable to the trembling, sweat, etc., of an embattled warrior. As in the case of Eurylochus (*Od.* 10.244–46), Antilochus is temporarily too shocked to communicate terrible news.

eloquently—and successfully—for his life at *Odyssey* 22.344–53. Yet, just as
Sappho evokes the girl with a double description of her voice—speaking
and laughing—so Sappho's reaction begins with a double account of the
poet's own voicelessness, a double wound to correspond to the double blow.
Sappho is no longer permitted to say anything; instead, her tongue has been
shattered into silence.

ἀλλ' ἄκαν μὲν γλῶσσα †ἔαγε† . . .

(9)

The hiatus in line 9 has placed the reading *eage* in doubt. I believe with Nagy,
however, that it is deliberate, intended audially to reproduce the "catch" in
the poet's voice; Sappho dramatically represents herself as being almost at
the point she describes—losing her voice altogether.[11] It is a critical loss
for an oral poet, and a paradoxical and dramatic beginning to the poet's
response.

I do not maintain that Sappho was an oral poet in the sense that Homer has
been described by Parry and Lord; but, as Ruth Finnegan has shown, oral and
written literature form a continuum rather than entirely separate traditions.[12]
Sappho inherits an ancient lyric tradition which sees and describes itself as
essentially performative, and communicated, if not created, with the voice.[13]
Pindar for example uses the word *glōssa* (tongue) and its compounds—
"straight-tongued," "tongueless"—to describe poets and poetry.[14] Although
she was almost certainly literate, Sappho's references to tongue and voice
reflect a lingering concept of poetry as an oral medium.[15]

---

11. See Page, *Sappho and Alcaeus* 24–25. Nagy, *Comparative Studies* 45, defends the hiatus as
Sappho's conscious effort to reproduce the sense ("my tongue is shattered") in the sound. See
also West, "Burning Sappho" 311. West also defends the MS reading, which seems to have
been the one with which Lucretius was familiar ("infringi linguam" at *DRN* 3.155 seems also to
have been a unique metaphorical use).

12. See Finnegan, *Oral Poetry* 272. Finnegan rejects Lord's definition of oral poetry as too
narrow. She observes, "If a piece is orally performed—still more if it is mainly known to
people through actualization in performance—it must be regarded as in that sense an 'oral
poem'" (22).

13. See Segal, "Eros and Incantation," for the importance of the oral tradition for understanding Sappho's work. See also Merkelbach, "Sappho und ihr Kreis."

14. See *Pyth.* 2.86 where Pindar talks about the *euthuglōssos* man and his responsibility to
speak out within various political systems. The passage immediately succeeds one in which
Pindar speaks of himself and his own function as a poet in society. *Aglōssos* (tongueless) at
Nem. 8.24 signifies (among other things) the man who lacks a poet to speak for him. The word
glōssa is used of the poet's tongue and the process of poetry making at *Ol.* 6.82, 9.42, 11.9, 13.12;
Pyth. 1.86, 3.2; *Nem.* 4.8, 4.86, 7.72; *Isth.* 5.47; *Pa.* 6.59.

15. For other references by Sappho to the voice and its seductive power see frs. 118, 153,
185 Lobel-Page (L.-P). Of course, like all ancient poets, Sappho is known to us only through

By contrast, in the aftermath of the Hellenistic revolution, Catullus occupies a point nearer the other extreme of the oral/literary spectrum. Thus for Catullus, being "tongue-tied" does not to the same extent threaten his ability to create or communicate his poetry. His poetry is a *libellus*, separable from himself and transmitted as a gift to a friend. For Catullus, poetry exists on paper or tablets, and indeed, destruction of the material may mean the end of the poem. At 68.45–46 the paper containing Catullus's poems is imagined as an old woman, transmitting its message:

> Sed dicam vobis (i.e., Musis, deis), vos porro dicite multis
> milibus et facite haec charta loquatur anus.

> But I will tell you (i.e., Muses, gods), tell the tale to many
> thousands, and let the paper speak this in its old age.

Poem 36 opens and closes with the famous reference to the *cacata charta* of Volusius's *Annales*. This poem also includes a drama between Catullus and his beloved, who has been injured by angry iambics. She wants to burn the poems, but Catullus deliberately misinterprets and consigns Volusius to the flames instead. Burning may be a symbolic gesture of destruction, but in the case of a single copy, burning will end the poems' existence.

In Catullus, poetry may be lost, burned, stolen, but it is not necessarily imperiled by a silenced poet. Poems are comically—but significantly—endowed with independent life and moral responsibility; "little verses" may be wicked while their creator is still unsullied in 16. They are newborn infants in 65. Poems take part as third characters in the little dramas taking place between himself and their recipients; hendecasyllables are sent out to dun for missing tablets in 42. Their effect may be felt in the absence of their creator. In 35, merely *reading* Caecilius's poem on the Magna Mater has caused a girl (who is described as more learned than Sappho's Muse) to fall passionately in love with him.

For Sappho, however, the poet's voice is the instrument of seduction. Sappho's verb *eage* (shattered; 9) describing her tongue metaphorically associates this "symptom" also with a warrior's death on the battlefield. Just as the Homeric warrior defines, defends, and justifies himself with a sword, so the poet with a tongue. Sappho is disarmed, her voice a splintered weapon, like the sword or spear of a doomed warrior who has encountered an immortal or immortally aided foe. After only a glimpse, *before* she can engage in

---

the printed page. Ath. 13.596c–d quotes Posidippus: Σαπφῷαι δὲ μένουσι φίλης ἔτι καὶ μενέουσιν / ᾠδῆς αἱ λευκαὶ φθεγγόμεναι σελίδες. Fr. 157d, an epigram probably of Hellenistic date, ascribed to Sappho, announces that even though she is *aphōnos* she will speak, because she has a tireless voice (*phōnan akamatan*) set at her feet—i.e., a stone inscription.

"combat," Sappho's weapon—the tongue—is destroyed. One might compare *Iliad* 16.786 ff., where Apollo knocks off Patroclus's helmet and destroys his corselet and spear directly before Patroclus is killed by Hector.

At the end of the fourth stanza Sappho marks a break with what precedes with a repetition of the verb *phainom'* (I seem to myself) in 16, which completes the "ring" of the perceptual, imaginary world of the poem's first four stanzas and begins a new phase in the drama. It is followed by a one-line fragment of what I take to be the poem's final stanza, as the poem—hitherto an account of the narrator as vulnerable audience—turns to consider its own audience.

ἀλλὰ πὰν τόλματον ἐπεὶ † καὶ πένητα †

The expression *pan tolmaton* is not simply an exhortation to endure, although connotations of endurance are present.[16] In this martial context *pan tolmaton* may be translated "all can be dared." It is a call to arms providing a dramatic peripeteia within the poem itself. The poem, which ironically records the poet's own near-death, repeated in the past and again imminent, now reveals itself as a lethal weapon. Whether it was the girl's voice or appearance (or both) that seduced Sappho, it is her own voice with which she plans to attack in her turn, uncannily recreating her fractured weapon. The rout will become a duel, indeed perhaps an upset victory. In fact *pan tolmaton* marks a "counteroffensive" *already* launched—a song, divinely seductive as the Sirens'. Sappho seduces in her turn, by daring to approach her audience and perform it. The poem's various audiences— including the girl—experience the dangerous felicity of listening and coming under its spell.

Sappho probably concluded her poem with a gnomic statement of fortune's reversal. "Even the poor man may become rich—and the rich man poor."[17] Martin West cites as parallel Theognis 657, which exhorts the addressee to maintain a calm spirit in good fortune and adversity, for reversals of fortune are commonplace. I agree with West that Sappho here speaks of fortune's reversal—for good and ill. It does not follow, however, that she takes the same attitude as Theognis, seeing fortune's vagaries as uncontrollable, simply to be endured. As her hymn to Aphrodite suggests, a reversal in the

---

16. The line is usually translated "But all can be endured." Fränkel, *Early Greek Poetry* 199 n. 16, draws a distinction between the endings *-tos* and *-teos* in the verbal adjective. *-tos* (the ending of *tolmaton* in l. 17) indicates possibility, not necessity. See Smyth 358. I differ from Fränkel and those who translate "may be endured." See Pucci, *Odysseus Polutropos* 47, where he remarks with reference to *Il.* 10.231 that the verb *tolman* (as distinct from its cognate, *tlēnai*) usually means to dare rather than to endure, and that is does not appear to be used in the sense of "endure" in the *Iliad*. Given the martial tone of Sappho 31, valor rather than endurance seems particularly appropriate.

17. See West, "Burning Sappho" 312–13.

fortunes of love can be deliberately achieved: by the lover who enlists the help of Aphrodite. This poem (1 L.-P.) consists of a prayer—and a corresponding promise from the goddess—not, as we might expect, to unite Sappho in bliss with her beloved but to reverse the situation, to inflict on the girl who has wounded Sappho an equal agony. She will give presents instead of receiving them: she will chase instead of fleeing.

It has long been recognized that Sappho's hymn to Aphrodite resembles in tone and diction the lethally vengeful prayer of Diomedes to Athena at *Iliad* 5.115–20.[18] Sappho's "borrowing" of the Homeric situation establishes a complex, reciprocal literary relationship, many of whose ironies have been well discussed.[19]

Homer's battlefield afforded little opportunity for relationships between enemies (the exchange between Glaukos and Diomedes in *Il.* 6 being a famous exception). The only permanence or stability lay in the shared *kleos* of death, the poetic fame that united victor and vanquished, incorporating the victim into his conqueror's song of triumph. Similarly on Love's battlefield in the hymn to Aphrodite a reciprocal relationship seems impossible; there is only unequal battle: pursuit or flight.[20] For the speaker of Sappho 31 also, Love's battleground seems tense, unstable, and lethal, with the additional threat of oblivion, since love's imperiled "warrior" is also the singer. This "warrior's" death, far from earning an expensive glory for the hero from the poet or poetic tradition, will necessarily silence the singer.

Sappho's "myriad-mindedness" makes her battlefield less bleak than Homer's, however. Whereas in Homer the victor and victim seem to be clearly distinguished from one another, Sappho incorporates both roles in herself within her poem as she moves from victim of love to conqueror/seducer. Further, for all the grimness of these metaphorical battles, there is also a sense of the generative excitement of the lethal dialogue between lover and beloved, a sense of irony, delight, and of exhilarating—and divine—energy. The expression "paler than grass," for example, even as it evokes unconsciousness and death, also suggests tender growth and

18. See Svenbro, "La tragédie de l'amour" 57–63, and Page, *Sappho and Alcaeus* 17.

19. See especially Winkler, "Public and Private" 65–71. For example, Winkler shows how, in the hymn to Aphrodite, Sappho encompasses within herself both the role of expelled female (like Aphrodite in *Il.* 5) and that of aggressive male who seeks the help of a female goddess (Diomedes and Athena in *Il.* 5). Thus Sappho shows how she responds, as a subtle and many-minded female reader, to the "male" text of the *Iliad*. Far from being excluded from the warrior's world, like Homer's Aphrodite, she contains many aspects of it within her single persona.

20. But Stigers [Stehle], "Sappho's Private World" 45–61, argues that Sappho's description of love exhibits a mutuality characteristic of women, rather than the desire for domination more typical of men. Stigers does not discuss this poem.

life.[21] Moreover, Sappho in a sense achieves the enviable divinity that she attributes to another. It is not merely a question of survival, of enduring recurrent brushes with death or approaches to death; as far as the poem is concerned, death is a threat that is never fully realized. But the terrible silence, which threatens both the poet's existence as a poet and the existence of this or any poem of Sappho, actually and repeatedly assails her. The act of *poiēsis* resists the obliteration that passion threatens, and the existence of the *poiēma* proclaims a permanent triumph over the recurrent threat of poetic nonbeing. Indeed, to an extent, the act of making a poem *replaces* the passion, just as epic may be said to replace the mortal organism with a divine artifact.[22]

Sappho's poem, in its final stanza, dramatically wills itself into existence despite the silencing nature of its subject. Catullus's final stanza, however, shifts in a different direction. His poem details a disintegration both similar to and subtly different from Sappho's. Sappho records a heart-stopping fear or shock, which she then explains in terms of a recurrent series of past catastrophic symptoms, beginning with loss of her voice and ending in a state near death. Catullus summarizes his entire reaction at the outset. He does not, like Sappho, explain a present sense of fear with reference to repeated past experience; this particular (vicariously experienced) encounter with Lesbia affects him precisely as all other encounters. All his senses are snatched away ("misero quod omnis / eripit sensus mihi ... "; 5–6). Whereas Sappho's poem may be located in the moment of fear between the vision of her beloved and the physical breakdown which usually results from such an encounter, Catullus leaves no distance between his vision of Lesbia and his reaction. He sees her and loses all his senses. Catullus's anticipatory summary has the effect of placing on an equal footing all of the symptoms he subsequently lists. Loss of all the senses is unconsciousness, of which loss of speech is merely one aspect. The following catalog of individual symptoms only spells out what has already been said.

Catullus's "lingua sed torpet" achieves roughly the same sense as *glōssa eage*, but lacks the hiatus, the violence, and the military connotations of Sappho's expression.[23] A tender flame ("tenuis ... flamma") answers Sappho's

---

21. For *khlōros* see Irwin, *Colour Terms in Greek Poetry* 31–78.

22. See Nagy, *The Best of the Achaeans* 144 ff., for this question of the living organism replaced by or opposed to inorganic *kleos*.

23. The final lines of Catull. 11 show a similar "softening" of a Sapphic image; his love is like a flower which has been brushed by the plow and falls. It is not—as K. Quinn points out in his commentary ad loc.—actually plowed under, merely fatally bruised. Sappho fr. 105c L.-P. depicts a hyacinth trampled underfoot by shepherds.

lepton pur; the humming in the ears also reappears. But in Catullus un-consciousness ("gemina teguntur / lumina nocte"; 11–12) apparently inter-rupts the poet before he himself can describe his own approach to the edge of death. Catullus depends on his audience's familiarity with the Sapphic poem to create this sense of interruption. His poem enacts the final unconsciousness of which Sappho stops short before he moves to an entirely different plane of reality, stepping abruptly aside from the obvi-ous impossibility of saying anything further within his current dramatic framework.

In place of Sappho's reversing "resolution" (*pan tolmaton*), Catullus's final stanza moves to self-reproach. The disputed meaning of *otium* in Catullus's fi-nal stanza lies at the heart of the poem's notorious interpretive difficulties.[24] My treatment is very brief, its purpose merely to suggest how I feel Catullus's final stanza may comment on Sappho's poem and on the question of orality and literariness and the poet's silence.

For the Roman Neoteric poets *otium* was a symbol—the antithesis of *ne-gotium*, a responsible citizen's official "activity," forensic, military, mercantile, or political. It was an attitude as much as the state of leisure, and it could be considered the very soil which nourished elaborate, personal poetry.[25] Catullus 50, for example, records a day in which Catullus and a friend composed verse "in a leisurely way" (*otiosi*). Significantly he uses the word *scribens* (writing) to describe this process; even though each man had a ready audience in the other, they apparently required *tabellae* to facilitate the pro-cess of composition and exchange. Even the most light-hearted and casual symposium requires writing implements. In poem 50 *otium* facilitates the leisured process of *writing* poetry.

In poem 51 the effect of *otium* on Catullus himself apparently is analogous to its destructive effect on "kings" and "wealthy ... cities."[26] *Otium* can mean a state of peace, in contrast to the rigors of war, a state which allows the growth of moral degeneration and renders cities vulnerable to attack.[27] By this reading, the word *otium* responds to Sappho's military imagery of love. Catullus has not been "fighting" in Love's wars, and his idleness has

---

24. For *otium* in Latin literature, see Andre, *L'Otium dans la vie morale*; Laidlaw, *"Otium."*

25. For discussion of the elegiac poets on *otium*, see Andre, *L'Otium dans la vie morale* 403 ff.; Laidlaw, *"Otium"* 47–48; Alfonsi, *Otium e vita d'amore.*

26. Lattimore, "Sappho 2 and Catullus 51" 184–87, cites similar lines in Theognis 1103–4, where hubris is said to have destroyed famous cities like Colophon and Smyrna. Troy also comes to mind, with its proverbial wealth, the luxurious peace shattered by the Greek expedition. Passerini, "La τρυφή" 52 ff., links Catullus's *otium* with *truphē*.

27. For *otium* as peace as opposed to war, see, e.g., Sall. *Cat.* 10.1, *Iug.* 41.1; Livy 1.19.4, 1.22.2, 6.36.1; Sen. *Ep.* 51.6.

made him unfit for close "combat" with Lesbia—the sort of literary/amatory "confrontation" that Sappho's poem seems to indicate.[28]

Yet although Catullus seems to rebuke himself for succumbing to *otium*, he does *not* indicate that he intends to abandon or resist it. It is significant that, unlike Sappho (with her *pan tolmaton*), Catullus does not express intention or desires for the future, although it is possible to *infer* that the poem develops out of the poet's resistance to *otium*. Thus, to a greater extent than Sappho's, Catullus's poem presents itself as rooted in the poet's present, which is colored by persistent indulgence in *otium*. I suggest that *otium* is not inactivity—literary or amatory—so much as a reluctance or failure to *confront* in one or more areas of life.[29] Poems are created and love is expressed—in private. *Otium*, which I define as a withdrawn and leisurely indulgence in a lover's sensibilities, forms the background of Catullus's poem. The poem can address Lesbia in the absence of its creator, who can thus reproach himself for his *otium*—a "disengagement" both literary and emotional.

In conclusion, Catullus depicts total breakdown as the direct and immediate result of his vision of Lesbia. He narrates his collapse as an accomplished thing rather than a threatening possibility. Thus his poem does not, like Sappho's, claim to be situated in a terrifying moment of suspense and anticipation. His narrative of disintegration, rather like Horace's ironic description of his own transformation into a swan in *Odes* 2.20, bespeaks a certain detachment. Thus Catullus clearly establishes the poem's existence as separate from the dramatic situation that it describes and independent of the precarious articulateness of its poet. Catullus's final stanza, with its thrice-intoned *otium*, formalizes this emotional and literary distance between himself and his subject.

Sappho's poem, in contrast, appears delicately balanced between the inspiring/destructive girl and Sappho's daring/enduring response, and between the anticipatory fear or excitement produced by this particular "occasion" and the familiar series of debilitating reactions which such an encounter

---

28. For discussion of the final stanza of Catullus's poem, and its possible relationship with the Sapphic poem, see Wills, "Sappho 31 and Catullus 31." Wills argues (196) that Catullus is talking about "a lover's code—one that embraces suffering and condemns desertion under trial. . . . Love is his negotium, and he must be fit for all its encounters." Wills's interpretation of *otium* is persuasive, although there is no "must," no exhortation to abandon *otium*—which constitutes a major difference between Catullus's poem and Sappho's.

29. Segal, "Catullan Otiosi" 25–31, argues that, for Catullus in poems 50 and 51, the concept of *otium* links love and the writing of poetry. "50 deals primarily with the literary or 'poetic' side of otium; 51 with the amatory side; but the two strands of otium are intertwined" (31). I agree that there is a literary and an amatory aspect to otium, but I prefer not to divide its twin aspects between the two poems. Itzkowitz, "On the Last Stanza of Catullus 51," also argued that *otium* has twin aspects—*otium-amor* and *otium-poesis*.

generally produces. Her fear or tension exists because she expects these reactions, but although they are imminent, they are not yet fully realized. The
poem breathlessly describes such an imminent breakdown, beginning with
a critical failure of her tongue, the instrument of self-expression. Her tongue
"breaks" and seems to doom her, as a fractured spear often dooms a warrior
in Homer—before he can harm his opponent.

Sappho's poem is conditioned by the oral culture in which it was created. It is not only a vividly enacted drama of seduction; the poem actually
dramatizes its dependence on the vulnerable living organism who must perform it. Of course, as has often been observed, its very existence testifies
to a considerable degree of emotional and literary control, but the poem
presents itself as suspended in a state of tension between past silences and
a future, imminent silence. The song exists in the threat of its own ex-
tinction, a threat which is formally confronted and triumphantly survived
only at the end, where, in a dramatic peripeteia, Sappho reveals that she
has replied to unanswerable enchantment with her own song of seduction.
Ultimately Aphrodite proves to be the mother of Persuasion and not the
death of the poet.[30]

30. Fr. 200 L.-P. (a scholiast on Hes. *Op.*) says that Sappho made Aphrodite the mother
of *Peithō*.

FOUR

Ventriloquizing Sappho, or the Lesbian Muse

Elizabeth D. Harvey

I'll tell thee now (dear love) what thou shalt do
To anger destiny, as she doth us,
How I shall stay, though she esloign me thus,
And how posterity shall know it too;
How thine may out-endure
Sibyl's glory, and obscure
Her who from Pindar could allure,
And her, through whose help Lucan is not lame,
And her, whose book (they say) Homer did find, and name.

JOHN DONNE

When in John Donne's "Valediction: of the Book" the male speaker urges his mistress to compose the "annals" of their love, he also implicitly interrogates both the status and viability of female authorship.[1] He advises the beloved to chronicle their passion so that she might achieve fame as an author and "outendure / Sybil's glory," casting into obscurity even those women he cites as paradigmatic examples of feminine literary preeminence: "Her who from Pindar could allure, / And her, through whose help Lucan is not lame, / And her, whose book (they say) Homer did find, and name" (7–9). Although the speaker ostensibly praises these three women, suggesting that their talents either surpassed or helped to shape the poetic genius of Pindar, Lucan, and Homer, his rhetoric ironically deflates the encomium. He describes the women periphrastically but declines to name them, substituting instead the names of the men whose reputations have supplanted theirs. This elision

---

This essay was originally published in slightly different form as "Ventriloquizing Sappho, or the Lesbian Muse," in *Ventriloquized Voices: Feminist Theory and English Renaissance Texts*, 116–39 (London: Routledge, 1992).

1. All quotations from Donne's poetry, unless otherwise noted, are from Grierson's edition.

of the proper name within the poem mimetically reproduces the historical effacement of the women's identities, underlining and reenacting the mechanism through which their accomplishments were originally eclipsed. The speaker initially seems to be asserting that Homer plagiarized his poems, but the qualification "they say" introduces an element of indeterminacy, and the acts of "finding" and "naming" blur the distinctions of poetic property and effectively neutralize the implicit censure of Homer's alleged appropriation. The speaker's complicity in the erasure of the women's identities is furthered by his treatment of his mistress, for he suggests that she could overshadow only female authors whose literary reputations have already been forgotten and buried: the Theban poet, Corinna, who putatively beat Pindar in a literary competition; Lucan's wife, Polla Argentaria, who was supposed to have helped him complete (and versify) the *Pharsalia*; and, perhaps most egregious of all, Phantasia, the woman who was reputed to have composed both the *Iliad* and the *Odyssey* and from whom Homer allegedly plagiarized them.[2] That the poem is framed by a series of imperatives to write underscores the irony that informs the situation; what the speaker exhorts of his mistress he has already accomplished. His instructions function, then, as a proleptic completion of the act he invites his addressee to undertake. His persistent emphasis on the permanence of the book that will record their love ("as long lived as the elements") is also ironically undercut both by his references to actual threats (the Vandals and Goths, as well as the elements themselves) and by the material instability of Donne's poem itself, with its multiple variants and textual inconsistencies. While he seems to promise his mistress a status that would rescue her from the oblivion to which Corinna, Polla Argentaria, and Phantasia have been relegated, the act of offering firmly resituates her on the margins of discourse, where she is confined as the nameless, faceless handmaiden to poetic accomplishment.

Donne alludes to these connections between the politics of gender and the poetics of plagiarism in "A Valediction: of the Book," but he makes them his central subject in the poem enunciated in the Sapphic voice, "Sappho to Philaenis."[3] This neglected text has disturbed and offended

---

2. Gardner, *John Donne* 192–93.

3. "Sappho to Philaenis" is not the only instance of his assumption of the feminine voice, of course; such poems as "Woman's Constancy" and "Confined Love" see the question of fidelity from a feminine perspective, and in "Break of Day" it is a woman who speaks the aubade, translating the sun's voyeuristic gaze into words (for "light hath no tongue"), just as Donne in turn gives voice to the woman. In Holy Sonnet No. 14, the speaker occupies the position of the Petrarchan lady who is besieged by the lover. Although the lover is in this case God, the ultimate union is imaged in paradoxically erotic terms; unless "enthral[ed]," the speaker never will be free nor ever chaste unless "ravish[ed]" by God. The erotic conquering that the speaker so ardently desires entails an entering, possessing, and radical refashioning that has

critics and editors, and until very recently they have by turns ignored it, questioned its authenticity, and censured its subject matter.[4] Herbert Grierson, for example, the first editor to identify its genre as a heroical epistle, called it "passionate and eloquent in its own not altogether admirable way," while Helen Gardner consigned it to the *Dubia*, for she judged it "too uncharacteristic of Donne in theme, treatment, and style to be accepted as unquestionably his," and furthermore, she found it difficult to imagine him "wishing to assume the love-sickness of Lesbian Sappho."[5] As the language of these judgments makes clear, its exclusion from the canon of Donne's poetry appears to have been based more on moral objections than textual evidence, since its presence in numerous manuscripts that purport to be collections of his poetry and in the first edition of Donne's poems (1633) would seem to support its authenticity.[6] If we are to take the manuscript evidence seriously and consider "Sappho to Philaenis" as Donne's, how can we account for its different style and for the uncharacteristic submersion of his own distinctive poetic "voice" and unabashedly "masculine expression"[7] in the accents of a Greek lesbian woman poet? Given the male poet's clear recognition of the female author's ultimate invisibility in "A Valediction: of the Book," why should Donne choose to speak in the feminine voice, thus risking both the neglect accorded to women writer in general and the censorship associated with Sappho in particular?[8]

---

in Western culture tended to be the prerogative of the male. In both of these poems, Donne is writing within well-established conventions, and the employment of the feminine perspective as central inverts and remakes tradition, establishing Donne as master rather than slave of inherited forms. The male poet's use of the feminine voice in these cases would thus seem to afford a means of countering a received poetic tradition whose authority always threatens to overwhelm the poet's singular identity.

4. John Carey, who calls it "the first female homosexual love poem in English," discusses the poem as it thematically replicates Donne's obsession with union and merging (*John Donne* 270–71). G. R. Wilson has included it in his discussion of mirror imagery in Donne's poetry ("The Interplay of Perception" 107–21), and F. Verducci refers to it in her analysis of Ovid's Sapphic epistle (*Ovid's Toyshop of the Heart*). The most sustained and important essay on "Sappho to Philaenis" is Holstun, " 'Will You Rent.' "

5. Grierson, *The Poems of John Donne* 2:91; Gardner *John Donne* xlvi.

6. Gardner, *John Donne* xlv–xlvi.

7. The phrase is, of course, from Thomas Carew's *Elegie*, which has generated a tradition of Donne as a typically "masculine" poet, one whose style is marked by force (even violence, according to Samuel Johnson's famous definition of metaphysical wit) and an apparent disregard for the sweetness and regularity of conventional verse. Ben Jonson provides a characteristic example of this categorization of style according to gender in *Timber* (395–96).

8. Much recent feminist work on Sappho has focused on her power as a female precursor for women figures, as the originary figure in a matrilineal poetic genealogy. See Gubar, "Sapphistries," and DeJean, "Sappho's Leap" and "Fictions of Sappho."

I will suggest some answers to these questions by analyzing both Donne's poem and the various subtexts with which it is filiated. Because all of the texts I treat are marked by their emphasis on feminine speaking and their ambiguous or unknown authorship, I also focus on the intertextual problem of transvestite ventriloquism; in this case, the male author's appropriation of the feminine voice. I argue that the issue of ventriloquistic speech informs all of these texts and is not incidental to the debates about their attribution, since the questions of literary voice and authorial property are closely related to gender, to the historical possibility of women's speech and writing. This problem is complicated and intensified by the texts' linkage to Sappho on one hand and to their history of suppression and faulty transmission on the other, for the representation of lesbianism in Western literature is also a history of censorship. Indeed, James Holstun has recently alluded to the absence of references to lesbianism not only in literary sources but also in legal records and philosophical tracts as a phenomenon of "voicelessness,"[9] an epithet that precisely describes the strategies of silencing I will be investigating.

Donne's poem is a verse letter, written, the title tells us, by Sappho to another woman, Philaenis. The letter describes the erotic union of the women, and the ideal world created by their love explicitly excludes men (and by extension the male author). Further, the poem's form and the Sapphic voice turn out not to be Donne's invention at all, but are instead borrowed from Ovid's fifteenth epistle in the *Heroides*. Like Donne's poem, the attribution of Ovid's Sapphic letter was uncertain until quite recently; the question of authorship was complicated because the epistle became separated from the rest of the *Heroides* and was not rediscovered until the fifteenth century.[10] But the difficulties in assigning an author to the voice

9. Holstun, " 'Will You Rent' " 836. He cites J. Brown's study, *Immodest Acts*, which has noted the paucity of references in legal, literary, and philosophical records to lesbianism (a nineteenth-century term; 835–36). Even assuming that one could overcome the "conceptual distortions" incumbent on a reconstruction of lesbianism in the early modern period, Holstun argues, unless the mechanism of its "voicelessness" is revealed and unless "we take care not to perpetuate the exclusion of lesbianism" by taking the isolated cases as "ignorable oddities" (836), we risk complicity in the larger structure of censorship. My own argument about Ovid and Donne sees the treatment of Sappho by subsequent poets (and some critics) as a heightened version of a general suppression of the female voice, a project of cultural silencing which would, of course, be especially threatened by the preeminence of Sappho's reputation and by the erotic self-sufficiency of lesbian love. See also Faderman, *Surpassing the Love of Men*, who, in writing a history of lesbian love, seeks both to break the silence surrounding lesbianism and to analyze its changing representations.

10. The manuscript history of the Sapphic epistle was separate from that of the *Heroides*; besides excerpts from it in the twelfth-century *Florilegium Gallicum*, the letter appears in only one medieval source in conjunction with the other fourteen Ovidian epistles, and the evidence suggests that it was copied from a different source. From 1420 onward, it is to be found in

that speaks do not stop here; the Ovidian epistle, it could be argued, is about the very questions that have surrounded the poem's transmission and attribution throughout its history. The issues of poetic property and authorial signature are inscribed within the text, in the citations from the historical Sappho's poetry that are woven into Ovid's letter, in its purported status as autobiography, and in its thematizing of voice. Thus, although my argument is structured like a traditional source study in its investigation of Donne's primary subtexts, Ovid's *Heroides* 15 and Lucian's *Amores*, it is fundamentally intertextual in Barbara Johnson's sense of that distinction: source studies, she asserts, tend to speak "in terms of a transfer of property ('borrowing')," while intertextuality tends to speak "in terms of misreading or infiltration, that is, of violations of property."[11] In these texts, the issue of literary property is further complicated both by the ventriloquistic cross-dressing of the speakers and by the representation of intertextual violation as erotic.

I

It is a commonplace of Donne criticism that his mastery of the persona is a result of scrutinizing Ovid's complex manipulation of narrative voices.[12] I want to examine this assertion with specific reference to Donne's "Sappho to Philaenis" and to its Ovidian subtext,[13] for both poems are, in a sense, about their own borrowed voices and the problematized status of poetic property. Sappho's epistle to Phaon is situated at the end of the single *Heroides*, Ovid's collection of verse complaints supposedly written by mythological heroines to the lovers who have abandoned them. It differs from the preceding fourteen, however, for whereas Ovid insinuates in the other epistles that he has liberated the heroines from the tyrannical bonds of the narratives that had confined and defined them (as Dido's letter differentiates itself from the Virgilian account in the *Aeneid* on which it depends), ostensibly allowing them to assume control over their own representations through their manipulation

---

some 200 manuscripts, all derived from a common source. Daniel Heinsius established its order in the *Heroides* by placing it in the fifteenth position in his edition of 1629. See Reynolds, *Texts and Transmissions* 268–72, for a detailed history; Baca, "Ovid's Epistle from Sappho to Phaon" 29–38, and Jacobson, *Ovid's Heroides*, for the arguments about its transmission.

11. B. Johnson, "Les fleurs du mal" 264.

12. For more extensive treatments of Donne's Ovidianism, see Leishman, *The Monarch of Wit*; Gill, "*Musa Iocosa Mea*"; and Armstrong, "The Apprenticeship of John Donne."

13. Jacobson, *Ovid's Heroides* 277–99, has focused on the poetic relationship between Ovid and Sappho, and his discussion of the Sapphic echoes in Ovid's letter is invaluable. Kauffman, *Discourses of Desire* 50–61, explores the poem as a travestied expression of female desire, and Verducci, *Ovid's Toyshop of the Heart*, provides a detailed analysis of the epistle in relation to the other Heroidean letters.

of language, Sappho's case is unique. She alone among these famous women is a poet in her own right, one so preeminent that Plato called her the tenth Muse, Longinus praised her for the sublimity of her style, Horace admired her poetry, and Catullus translated her.[14] Only in Sappho's letter does Ovid make use of the speaker's own writings, because only here do the roles of fictional and actual author coalesce. Ovid knew Sappho's poetry and his epistle is full of its echoes, but whereas "echo" suggests a disembodied voice capable only of repetition, Ovid's radical reinscription of Sappho bears the marks of sexual mastery and theft. His ventriloquistic appropriation of her voice subordinates Sapphic meter to the demands of his own elegiac lines, and the portrait that he presents provided an indelible legacy that displaced the authority of her own words, blurring the boundaries between "authentic" and constructed discourse.

Ovid's epistle played a central role in perpetuating an image of Sappho that was probably originally fashioned by the Middle and New Comedy.[15] The candor and passion of her poetry became an object of ridicule for these playwrights, who made her into a caricature of love longing and sowed the seeds for the reputation of immorality and licentiousness that was still attached to her name in the Renaissance.[16] It is in these parodic portraits that Sappho is first connected with Phaon, the ferryman upon whom Venus bestowed preternatural beauty; made desperate by her unrequited desire for him, Sappho reportedly threw herself off the Leucadian cliff. The story was retold by poets of the New Comedy, but Ovid's version of Sappho's story is the one that has survived, bequeathing a detailed account that carries the weight of authenticity through its pseudo-autobiographical narratorial voice. Ovid's Sappho conforms to the Heroidean paradigm of the abandoned woman, and she displays an intense, indeed humiliating, erotic yearning, given the context of Phaon's disdain. The dynamic of power within the poem relies on a sexual subjugation that entails poetic submission, and we must read Ovid's concern with the question of poetic ownership, then, as relating partly to the potency of the reputation he seeks to subordinate to his own in his desire to establish himself as a love poet. His use of the feminine voice allowed him to challenge the epic and patriarchal ethos of Augustan Rome (just as eroticism undermines the stability of epic in the

14. Jacobson, *Ovid's Heroides* 281–82; Stigers [Stehle], "Retreat from the Male."

15. Jacobson, *Ovid's Heroides* 281.

16. With the exception of a few metrical experiments (Ben Jonson's lines from *The Sad Shepherd* 45, "But best the dear, good angel of the spring, / The nightingale," and Sidney's translation of Sappho's ode into anacreontics in the Second Eclogues of the *Arcadia*), it appears that most Renaissance poets knew Sappho only as she was mediated by the portrait of her in Ovid's epistle. Lyly's *Sapho and Phao*, for instance, depends heavily on the biographical details that Ovid supplies.

Metamorphoses),[17] but the constructed voice in *Heroides* 15 must assert itself against the real Sappho's poetic voice, which continually threatens to usurp Ovid's mastery.

Sappho's initial response to Phaon's abandonment of her is a frozen grief that admits no expression, neither tears nor words ("[L]acrimae deerant oculis et verba palato, / adstrictum gelido frigore pectus erat," 111–12; "My eyes had no tears, my tongue no words, a clear chill gripped my heart").[18] Even though Sappho does speak and eloquently describe her own suffering, it is not in her habitual discourse that she does so. Her voice, as she continually reminds us, is silenced:

> Nunc vellem facunda forem dolor artibus obstat,
> ingeniumque meis substitit omne malis.
> non mihi respondent veteres in carmina vires;
> plectra dolore tacent, muta dolore lyra est.
>
> (195–98)

> I wish I were eloquent now! Sorrow checks my art
> and all my genius is halted by my grief.
> My old power for poetry will not come at my call;
> my plectrum is sorrowing and silent, sorrow has hushed my lyre.

Even while she laments the diminishment of verbal power that psychic pain has imposed upon her, she recalls the poetic skill that she once possessed, expressing the pride that she takes in her lyric gift in fiercely competitive terms: not even Alcaeus, her contemporary and countryman, garnered greater praise. Although nature has denied her physical beauty, making her short ("brevis") and dark-complexioned ("non candida"), her corporeal deficiencies were nevertheless compensated for by her poetic ability. Her poetry had the capacity to mold and shape perceptions, so that, while she lacked conventional beauty, she appeared alluring to Phaon when she sang to him. Indeed, she speaks of her poetry as an aphrodisiac; she remembers singing her lyrics to Phaon, and, while she sang, he stole kisses. Sappho tells us that she excelled at this amorous play:

> tunc te plus solito lascivia nostra iuvabat,
> crebraque mobilitas aptaque verba ioco,
> et quod, ubi amborum fuerat confusa voluptas,
> plurimus in lasso corpore languor erat.
>
> (47–50)

---

17. This is an argument familiar from Lanham, *The Motives of Eloquence* 48–64, which recognized Ovid's challenge to the legitimating stability of Virgil's *Aeneid*, a subversion that is apparent in Ovid's intercalation of erotic incidents in his retelling of Aeneas's adventures in the *Metamorphoses*.

18. All citations from *Heroides* 15 are from Verducci's text and translation.

> Then, more than ever, my wanton play delighted you,
> my constant motion, my observances of delight,
> and, with the body's exhaustion, that languor beyond languor
> in us both, after that final, fine confusion of our desire.

Her regard for her own erotic skill is matched by her awareness of the lyric power that was hers, for her descriptions of passion incited and fed the desire of her listeners, allowing her to transform herself and her audience, literally to enchant them.

Ovid, however, divests Sappho of this potent metamorphic gift and borrows it for himself, making her subject to the power that was once hers. His poem transforms the direction of Sappho's affections, leading her to disdain not only the formerly enticing Lesbian girls for the unattainable Phaon but also to chastise her previous lesbian affections in favor of a heterosexual attachment. That Ovid converts the object of Sappho's passion from the girls she addresses in her own songs (Anactorie, Cydro, Atthis) to a man who scorns her suggests a subjugation that is at once sexual (made all the more demeaning, given her praise of her sexual abilities) and poetic. Sappho's songs are silenced within the poem's fiction by Phaon and literally by Ovid; in this way Ovid aligns himself with Phaon, since Sappho must yield to his poetic authority in the same way that she succumbed to Phaon's erotic mastery. Ovid thus provides a narrative logic for Sappho's switch from song to elegy, for, though she herself claims to be better suited to the lyric mode, her sorrow makes her prefer elegy ("elegiae flebile carmen," 7; "elegy is the music for pain"). Ovid superinscribes a new metrical style over her silence, which, while uncharacteristic of the historical Sappho, is nevertheless appropriate to the occasion he has fashioned for her speaking.

Fittingly, then, the epistle opens with a reference to poetic signatures: Sappho's first words are a question to her lover as to whether her style is instantly recognizable. The query, posed as it is by Ovid speaking through Sappho, has a pungent irony since Sappho's fame as a lyric poet depended at least in part on the verse form that carries her name, the Sapphic stanza. Ovid's witty remark calls attention to his suppression of Sapphic meter in favor of his own elegiac couplets, to the translation from Greek to Latin, and to the transformation of gender from female to male poet. In the process, it points to the question that subtends the poem: who is speaking and to whom does the speaking belong? Clearly, the poet is neither Sappho, despite the echoes of her verse and despite the speaker's identification of herself as Sappho; nor is it Ovid, despite the poem's conforming to the demands of his newly invented genre of the mythological complaint and to the elegiac meter that characterizes the other letters in the collection. In a sense, Sapphic and Ovidian signatures are superimposed on one another in a palimpsestic transparency, and the usurpation that has made Ovid's ventriloquized speech possible is thus thematized in the text.

The textural violation that has occurred, the splicing together of the Greek lyric fragments in this new context, is figured, appropriately, in a buried allusion to the Philomela myth, for in both cases sexual seduction or rape becomes a prelude to the theft or literal extirpation of the tongue, a kind of linguistic rape.[19] Indeed, Sappho claims that in this landscape of abandonment no birds warble their sweet complaints:

> sola virum non ulta pie maestissima mater
> concinit Ismarium Daulias ales Ityn.
> ales Ityn, Sappho desertos cantat amores—
> hactenus; ut media cetera nocte silent.
>
> (153–56)

> Only the nightingale, only Philomel, whose terrible grief took vengeance
> most terrible against her husband, laments for Itys her son.
> The nightingale sings of Itys, her abandoned love is Sappho's song:
> Only that; all else is as silent as the dead of night.

Ovid's lines actually refer to Procne (the most mournful mother), and Verducci's mistranslation thus transposes the "terrible grief" and the subsequent revenge to Philomela. Verducci's rendering confuses the family lineage by making Itys Philomela's son, yet her translation does nevertheless make visible (and audible) what Ovid's lines elide, namely, the rape and mutilation (of Philomela) that provoked Procne's horrific vengeance. In a sense, Ovid's focus on Procne reenacts the silencing of Philomela: the tongueless sister stands as a mute but powerful presence in the poem, in the same way that Sappho herself appears as a silenced voice within the epistle.

Ovid has in one sense perpetrated a corresponding theft of Sappho's tongue; her letter is as much a lament for her extinguished voice as it is a complaint about Phaon's abandonment. Yet, even while the Ovidian allusion carries the traces of silencing, it also focuses insistently on Procne's mourning of Itys, a grief suffused with the memory of maternal savagery. Procne's murder of her child becomes an act of vengeance that links the organ of speech (the tongue) with the organ of eating; the revenge for Philomela's rape and muting was, of course, to kill the son, who resembled his father, and to have the father unknowingly consume the child. This act of cannibalization, the

---

19. Joplin's analysis of the Philomela myth in "The Voice of the Shuttle" reveals the crucial role that gender and power play in the story, elements that she claims were elided in Hartman's reading (*Beyond Formalism*), which tends to mystify rather than expose the violence that subtends the myth. She argues persuasively that the Philomela story is about the exchange of woman, an issue that makes it particularly pertinent to the issue of literary property I am discussing.

father's literal ingestion of the child's body, offers a trope for intertextuality. While the Daulian bird laments the death of Itys, the dismembered body that Sappho now mourns is the corpus of her poems that has been cut and scattered, only to be remembered in a different, Ovidian shape. The reference to Itys alludes not only to the myth of Procne and Philomela, then, but perhaps even more powerfully, to Sappho's use of the myth in her own poetry ("oh, Irana / why . . . me? / daughter of Pandion / swallow?");[20] Ovid thus invokes a myth of silencing and cannibalization at the very moment that he reenacts it by echoing or incorporating her verse.[21] The violence that lies at the heart of these intertextual maneuvers is thus recorded in a self-reflexive gesture, as if Ovid recognized his own complicity in the suppression of the Sapphic voice. The doubleness of his elegy acknowledges his own competitive, masterful silencing, even as it registers Sappho's lament and the mournful voices of the other muted or transformed women in the poem.

Ovid speaks from "the place of the silenced woman" through the figure of woman,[22] but the voice remains hermaphroditic, denying the possibility of "authentic" female speech through its distorted, travestied expression of feminine desire. Having subordinated Sappho's voice to his own and used her to demonstrate his poetic mastery, Ovid has no further use for the querulous caricature of longing that he has created. The genre of the erotic complaint, a form initially defined but ultimately undone by its repetitive, formulaic character, eventually offers itself to precisely this kind of parody. With a form unable to sustain the escalating intensity it generates except by inscribing the very caricature it invites, Ovid must have realized the limits of the genre he claimed to have created, and whatever risks he incurred are shifted on to the ventriloquized feminine voice, particularly Sappho's, whose own poetic gifts are held up to comic scrutiny. Ovid has his Sappho vow to dedicate her lyre to Apollo before she jumps off the Leucadian rock, a fittingly hyperbolic symbol both of his own departure from the genre of erotic complaint and of his neutralization of the threat that Sappho's reputation represents. Sappho leaves behind the epitaph she wrote for posterity, in which she bequeaths her lyre to Apollo. As Paul de Man has argued, prosopopeia is the dominant figure of epitaphic discourse, for it creates the fiction of "the voice-from-beyond the grave," conferring a mask or face (*prosōpon poiein*) that makes

---

20. Sappho, *The Poems of Sappho* 83.

21. DeJean, *Fictions of Sappho* viii, cites an ancient commentator on Lucian who compares Sappho to a nightingale: "As far as Sappho's body went, she was exceedingly disgusting to behold, being short and of dark complexion—resembling a nightingale whose tiny form was enshrouded in shapeless wings."

22. B. Johnson, "Les fleurs du mal" 280.

one's name "as intelligible and memorable as a face."[23] Here, however, the Sapphic voice that speaks registers only its resolution not to speak, so that the trope of prosopopeia (which is also the figure of voice) offers an empty mask, a name without a referent. The inscription carries the authoritative weight of Sappho's final words, a memorial that engraves a place and an instrument for a later poet to inhabit and use, petrifying her relinquishment of her own poetic gift in perpetuity.

II

Although John Donne can no more speak for—or in the place of—Sappho than Ovid can, since both poets' ability to represent her voice depends upon her silence, Donne appears to challenge the erotic subjugation perpetrated by Ovid, acting out his rivalry with his predecessor in the art of love poetry upon the body (or in the voice) of Sappho. Donne's subversion of Ovidian authority begins with the filiation of his poem with Ovid's through their genre, but this similitude serves merely to accentuate the difference within. "Sappho to Philaenis" masquerades as a recuperation of the original Sappho, since, inverting Ovid's distortion of her sexual preference, it represents her as lesbian. Donne's Sapphic epistle is, then, addressed to Philaenis, an obscure Greek writer from the island of Leucas, and, although it reproduces the situation of the Ovidian letter through its apostrophe to an absent lover, the beloved is now a woman. Apart from the tenuous geographical link between Sappho and Philaenis (Leucas), there appears to be little historical or poetic reason for this choice of companion, since neither Sappho nor Ovid mention Philaenis, and antiquity furnishes us with only a few references to her lost writings.

Who is Philaenis and why should Donne pair her with Sappho? Since only one critic who has discussed this poem has attempted to identify her, I want first to suggest a source for her and then to offer an explanation for the appropriateness of that context.[24] Most of what little we do know about

23. De Man, "Autobiography as De-Facement" 76, 77.

24. D. Allen's learned note on Philaenis ("Donne's Sappho" 188–91) offers three plausible sources, one of which is the *Greek Anthology*. He suggests that Donne may also have found her in Martial's epigram (7.66), which describes her as "play[ing] handball and lift[ing] weights in the dusty palaestra and whose supra-masculine drinking and eating were exceeded by her perverted lust for young girls of whom she devoured eleven at a sitting" (190). Calderinus's commentary on Martial (which Donne almost certainly knew) connects Sappho and this athletic Philaenis and refers indirectly to a second Philaenis, the author of erotic poetry. Allen argues that these two figures, as well as the chaste and defamed Philaenis of the *Greek Anthology*, combined in Donne's mind to form his Philaenis. Although Allen does not mention it, there is a second reference to Philaenis in Martial's epigrams (7.70), where she appears as a tribade;

Philaenis can be gleaned from two epigrams in the *Greek Anthology*, where she figures, significantly, at the center of a debate on disputed authorship. The first (345), ascribed to Aeschrion, is articulated in her voice; it situates her tomb on a headland, overlooking the sea, and, from beyond the grave, she addresses passing sailors, exhorting them not to insult or mock her. She swears that she was neither lascivious nor a "public woman," and she attributes the writings (the subject matter of which she professes not to know) associated with her name to Polycrates, an Athenian possessed of an evil tongue. The second epigram (450), composed by Dioscorides, is also enunciated by Philaenis and again protests against the slander that attached itself to her name. She denies that she authored an obscene treatise that was "offensive to ladies," and, after swearing to her chaste and modest nature, pronounces a hypothetical malediction on the writer who may have composed the work to shame her and ruin her reputation. Apparently, the work with which her name is connected is a kind of erotic guidebook that furnished its readers with explicit information about diverse sexual practices and positions. It is not clear, however, that Philaenis ever had a historical existence; the name may have stood simply for the prototypical harlot, and it may have been affixed to the pornographic work as a pseudonym.[25] Nevertheless, the similarities between this "constructed" Philaenis and Sappho are instructive: both women wrote erotic works, both women were therefore presumed to be immoral and licentious, and, in both cases, their alleged sexual notoriety made the identity of the author and the attribution of the work questionable. (In Sappho's case, it was posited that there were actually two women of this name from Lesbos, one a courtesan and one a poet, a dualism whose sustained life has haunted criticism of Sappho's poetry.)[26]

---

in the epigram just preceding (7.69), which praises the taste and learning of Theophila as transcending that of her sex, there is a reference to Sappho. Sappho herself would have praised Theophila's verses, we are told, but Theophila was more chaste than Sappho. The proximity of Sappho and Philaenis in these two epigrams, together with the idea of praising (or loving) another woman poet, provides another conjunction that may have influenced Donne's choice of Philaenis.

25. Vessey, "Philaenis" 79–81.

26. Aelian provides one of the earliest references to the "double" Sappho in his *Varia Historia*. In the words of Abraham Fleming's English translation of 1576, "*Plato* the sonne of *Aristo*, numbreth *Sapho* the Versifyer, and the daughter of *Scamandronymous* amonge such as were wise, lerned and skilful. I heare also, that there was another *Sapho* in *Lesbus*; which was a stronge whore, and an arrant strumpet" (quoted in *Works of John Lyly* 2:365). Twentieth-century critics, such as Robinson, *Sappho and Her Influence*, have expressed their disbelief that anyone as licentious as Sappho was reputed to have been could have written such exquisite poetry.

Although Philaenis is vehement in her denial of sexual misconduct, her references to heterosexual relationships only has led at least one critic to suppose that her silence elides a greater sin: that she was a lover of women. This supposition is supported by a depiction of her supplied in the pseudo Lucianic dialogue, the *Amores or Affairs of the Heart*.[27] A debate on the virtue of heterosexual love for men as opposed to pederasty, the dialogue has at its center a brief digression on lesbianism in which Charicles defends the right of women to love each other:

> if males find intercourse with males acceptable, henceforth let women too love each other. Come now, epoch of the future, legislator of strange pleasures, devise fresh paths for male lusts, but bestow the same privilege on women, and let them have intercourse with each other just as men do. Let them strap to themselves cunningly contrived instruments of lechery, those mysterious monstrosities devoid of seed, and let woman lie with woman as does a man. Let wanton Lesbianism—that word seldom heard, which I feel ashamed even to utter—freely parade itself, and let our women's chambers emulate Philaenis, disgracing themselves with Sapphic amours. (Lucian *Affairs* 8.195, trans. MacLeod)

The passage is important most obviously because it provides a linkage between Sappho and Philaenis within an explicitly lesbian context, one which may have furnished Donne directly or indirectly with the subject and treatment of his poem. Even more interesting, however, are the implications of this defense, in which women appear to achieve sexual autonomy through their employment of the dildo as a pseudo-phallus and are not only thus freed from their dependence upon the capriciousness of male desire but are compensated for their anatomical lack and apparently also accorded some of the symbolic power associated with the phallus. (This representation also encodes the common supposition that heterosexual intercourse is the only form of pleasure, and that lesbian love is thus an inferior copy of the original).[28] Charicles subverts his magnanimous gesture, however, through the strong moral censure that modifies his description, infiltrated as it is with terms of outrage ("monstrosities," "wanton," "ashamed," "disgracing"). His suggestion of sexual independence for women turns out to be doubly ironic: first, in his "conferring" independence on women and, second, by making that autonomy a ludicrous example of the social depravity male homosexuality might foster were it to replace conjugal love as the dominant mode of sexual relations.

---

27. Foucault, *The History of Sexuality* vol. 3, examines this dialogue in some detail. He does not comment on the discussion of lesbianism, however, but focuses instead on the opposition between heterosexual love and male homosexuality.

28. Butler, "Imitation and Gender"; Faderman, *Surpassing the Love of Men* 31–37.

Charicles is nevertheless praised by his audience for his impassioned rhetoric in defense of women, and the terms of their approbation are significant: Callicratidas claims that, if the political and legal spheres were open to women, they would have elected Charicles as their champion for his rhetorical zeal. Not even those women considered outstanding for wisdom and verbal power, not even "Sappho, the honey-sweet pride of Lesbos" herself (Lucian *Affairs* 8.197), could have pleaded their case with such vehemence. Indeed, Callicratidas argues that Charicles' passion gives him the right—even the duty—to speak on behalf of women, for, after all, he can do it more forcefully than they can themselves. Clearly, there is an analogy between women who become men by means of a mechanical device that duplicates the phallus and men who speak on behalf of women (or in ventriloquized feminine voices, which is the logical extension of this surrogacy). In each case, the difference between sexes is collapsed into a reconstruction of self as other, and, while it looks as if both men and women might gain independence through this process, it short-circuits the possibility of genuine difference. That women's sexual independence as it is constructed by these male speakers depends on their mimicry of the male anatomy points to the dangers of having men speak on behalf of or in the place of women; if women are excluded from legal and civic contexts and by extension exiled from the text, who is to ensure that their representatives can or will genuinely argue for their interests? What is at issue is not only whether it is possible to speak on behalf of or in the place of another, for advocacy is clearly a cornerstone of many political and legal systems, but also the ethical implications of assuming this power.

Donne's "Sappho to Philaenis" seems to depict an idyllic version of lesbian love in which the women do not attempt simply to replicate heterosexual relations and take on male characteristics, as they do in the pseudo-Lucianic dialogue, but rather evolve a specifically feminine mode of erotic union within a utopian world that excludes men and which seeks to invent a language that will reflect its new ideology. As an address to the absent beloved, Philaenis, the poem employs apostrophe, what Jonathan Culler has called the figure of voicing.[29] Apostrophe conventionally signals spontaneously adopted passion, the "turning away" from description or narration to direct address, and it is thus an appropriate figure in a reconstruction of the Sapphic voice. More importantly, apostrophe confers animicity or presence upon an inanimate object or absent addressee, transforming, in effect, object into subject; it functions, then, as a dialogue between subject and the implied new subject that is constructed by the apostrophe. The vocative of apostrophe enables the

---

29. Culler, "Changes in the Study of Lyric" 40.

speaker to fashion a relationship with an object that in turn helps to constitute the identity of the speaker as poet, for the figure of voice dramatizes both its own speaking and its power to invest the inanimate or absent with life and presence.[30] Yet this vitalizing force is ultimately illusory, since as Culler argues, "this figure which seems to establish relations between the self and the other can in fact be read as an act of radical interiorization and solipsism."[31]

"Sappho to Philaenis" follows a similar trajectory, moving from its opening, which reproduces the Ovidian complaint in its mourning for Philaenis's absence; to Sappho's conversion of that absence into presence, with the celebration of poetic language that this reanimation entails; and finally to a dramatization of the radical solipsism and narcissism of this recovery, in which the other turns out to be the self. What is enacted within the poem (between Sappho and Philaenis) points to an analogous relationship between author and speaker, where what appears to be Donne's generous bestowing of language and independence on Sappho, in direct contrast to Ovid's violations of her, turns out to be an act of colonization,[32] an act that is perhaps most clearly visible in the metaphor central to Elegy 19, where the mistress's body and the New World become versions of each other ("O my America, my new found land"). As this apostrophic formulation suggests, both mistress and land are mastered by man's exploration and possession of them. The "O" of apostrophe points not just to "undifferentiated voicing," nor to its emptying of "semantic reference,"[33] then, but also to the cipher of the uncolonized land and to woman's "centric part." In a similar way in "Sappho to Philaenis," the otherness of a classical text (Ovid's) and the otherness of woman (Sappho) are domesticated and reshaped into an image of the self, a process that is mediated both by ventriloquism and by voyeurism.

"Sappho to Philaenis" opens with a lament not only for the beloved's absence but also for the dwindling potency of poetic language in general. Like the Ovidian Sappho, this Sapphic voice wonders whether that "enchanting force" is "decayed," since, although verse can with Orphic power move or "draw" "Nature's work" against the laws of nature, it nevertheless cannot restore Philaenis. But an alternate reading of these lines suggests in addition the reciprocal attraction between an original in nature and its representation or copy "drawn" in verse, an interpretation that is supported by Sappho's

30. Culler, *The Pursuit of Signs* 138–42.

31. Ibid., 146.

32. Docherty, *John Donne* 51–87, has a perceptive discussion of women in Donne's poetry in terms of the metaphor of colonization, an idea that has been compellingly articulated by Cixous in "The Laugh of the Medusa" 47, where she suggested that woman has been constructed as the "dark continent."

33. Culler, *The Pusuit of Signs* 142–43.

later satisfaction with the poetic image of Philaenis that she fashions. She initially worries that the wax image of Philaenis that she carries in her heart will be destroyed in this crucible of desire, but it is instead radically reconfigured. The recreation of the absent beloved takes place as Sappho gazes in a mirror. Caressing her own body, she remarks on the similarity between herself and Philaenis, who are as alike, in fact, as the two halves of a single body:

> My two lips, eyes, thighs, differ from thy two,
> But so, as thine from one another do;
> And, oh, no more, the likeness being such,
> Why should they not alike in all parts touch?
> hand to strange hand, lip to lip none denies;
> Why should they breast to breast, or thighs to thighs?
> Likeness begets such strange self-flattery,
> That touching myself, all seems done to thee.
> Myself I embrace, and mine own hands I kiss,
> And amorously thank myself for this.
> Me, in my glass, I call thee; but alas,
> When I would kiss, tears dim mine eyes, and glass.
>
> (45–56)

The identification between a body and its reflection or between an image and a copy marks in this passage a dissolution of boundaries, a blurring of difference, in which Sappho comes to master both Philaenis and herself through the objectifying, controlling power of the gaze. Although the passage is full of tactile imagery, in furnishing a comic rewriting of Ovid's description of Narcissus in the *Metamorphoses*, and thus making the mirror central to Sappho's fantasy, the poem invokes the power of vision to construct the other. That is, Sappho's entrance into the scopic economy simultaneously displaces male desire, since she now assumes the normally male position of looker (with its ability to shape what it sees—"to make blind men see, / What things gods are, I say they are like to thee"; 17–18), and makes her subject to it, for she is now also the recipient of that gaze (as the reflection of Philaenis).

This doubleness, which is made possible by the physical correspondence between self and other, leads Sappho to discover the body's bilateral symmetry, the perfect equivalence between its right and left halves. Symmetry gives rise to a new language that Sappho coins to describe Philaenis, for, as she implicitly argues, the most available idiom, Petrarchism, is no longer a sufficient or even accurate mode of praise. The Petrarchan blazon that itemizes the mistress's body parts through a catalogue of extravagant comparison cannot function without borrowing its terms from the external world; the blush of the mistress's cheek must be described with reference to the canonical roses and lilies. Rather than being "soft," "clear," "straight," or "fair" as "stars, cedars, and lilies are," then, Sappho claims that Philaenis is already perfect, sufficient unto herself. The language that Sappho employs is thus corre-spondingly symmetrical, a tautological idiom whose referent has already been named: Philaenis is beautiful not because she possesses the attributes of stars and flowers but because she is perfectly balanced, one half mimicking the other: "thy right hand, and cheek, and eye, only, / Are like thy other hand, and cheek, and eye" (23–24).

The specular symmetry of this lesbian world stands in sharp contradis-tinction to that of the Ovidian epistle in which the boundaries between self and other were more clearly delineated, boundaries continually transgressed by acts of penetration, in which Ovid stole from Sappho's poetry, in which women are violated and savagely silenced. Ovidian eroticism carries with it a poetics based on an analogous ideology of violence and possession, and it is precisely against this ideology that Donne's poem seems to protest. Sappho's revision of the rhetoric of Petrarchan praise implicitly suggests a remedy to these intersexual rivalries through its fashioning of a world dominated by an unfamiliar erotic ethos. She praises love between women as a utopian union in which it is possible to love without possessing and to take pleasure without violating. The intrusion of men into this world is figured in terms of agriculture and theft, appropriations designed for self-gain. Lesbian love, on the other hand, is commendable precisely because it leaves no traces and en-tails no ownership: "of our dalliance no more signs there are, / Than fishes leave in streams, or birds in air" (41–42).[34] Sappho proclaims Philaenis's body to be a natural paradise that already contains perfection, an image of the Golden Age in which the earth produced abundant food without culti-vation and people lived in harmony without the need for laws to protects their rights and property. Why, then, should she admit the "tillage" of a "harsh rough man"?—an intrusion that signals simultaneously the agricul-tural appropriation of the earth and also points toward the sexual "tilling" of the female body that subtends the patriarchal order. The sense of prop-erty implicit in this heterosexual union is imaged as an indelible sign: for "men leave behind them that which their sin shows, / And are as thieves traced that rob when it snows" (39–40). The metaphor is so suggestive of literary borrowing that Dryden used it to describe Ben Jonson's pillaging of his classical sources, asserting that Jonson's thefts could be tracked in the

---

34. Docherty, *John Donne* 236, refers to a passage in *Measure for Measure*, where fish become a metaphor for female genitals, and this sense may underwrite the erotic fantasy of "The Bait," where the fish amorously swim to the woman, happier to catch her than she them. Donne uses a similar image in a verse epistle to Sir Henry Wotton, where he recommends that Wotton behave "as / Fishes glide, leaving no print where they pass, / Nor making sound" (Milgate, *John Donne* 56–57).

snows of the ancients.[35] Donne's ventriloquistic borrowing of Sappho's voice allows him to create an intertextuality that appears to be different from the Ovidian rivalry, in which poets steal from one another's work and where such plagiarism can be traced.

Yet the collapse of other into self, registered in Sappho's narcissistic absorption of Philaenis, also describes Donne's relationship to Ovid and Sappho, for they are both ultimately assimilated into a poem of his making. We might read the lines "Likeness begets such strange self-flattery, / That touching myself, all seems done to thee" (51–52), then, as a slippage between ventriloquized and authorial voices, in which Donne's characteristic pun on his name functions as a signature, transforming the "thee" to Donne. (It then becomes tempting—if sexually complicated—to read "restore / Me to me; thee, my half, my all, my more" as referring to Ann More.) This dislocation of voice reveals both the ventriloquist and the voyeur, the first producing speech that appears to emanate from a source other than the real speaker, and the other deriving pleasure from a looking that requires no participation (as Donne watches Sappho watching—and touching—herself). Both scopophilia and the borrowing of voices are mediated activities that necessitate no direct involvement; just as voyeurism is the wish to see without being seen, a mastery and form of possession of the object through the gaze, so is ventriloquistic appropriation of the feminine voice a mastery of the other, a censorship of its difference. Donne borrows the feminine voice as a way of acting out his rivalry with Ovid, but he controls its dangerous plenitude by domesticating its alterity and ultimately turning it into a version of himself.

That all of these texts are in various ways censored points to a crucial aspect of the feminine voice in general and of Sappho's reputation in particular: the suppression of actual feminine speaking enables and authorizes the fictional reconstruction of the (other) feminine voice, and ventriloquism thus functions as a poetic enactment of the mechanism of censorship at work within the broader cultural context. It is not in spite of the destruction of Sappho's verse, then, but partly because of it that she was so frequently acclaimed and imitated by subsequent poets (male and female), for it is upon her absence and silence (broken only by the surviving fragments of poems) that subsequent accounts of her could be and were inscribed.

Feminine speech and its literary representation in Western culture have historically depended on a long and potent tradition, reflected, on the one hand, by the invectives against woman's irrepressible garrulity and, on the other, by the Pauline injunctions for feminine silence. Because

---

35. Dryden, *An Essay on Dramatic Poesy* 333. Grierson, *The Poems of John Donne* 2:91, notes that "Sappho to Philaenis" is very probably the source of Dryden's metaphor.

woman's voice metonymically figures both her essential nature and her sexuality in this tradition, silence comes to stand for sexual continence, the closing of the double "mouths" of the feminine body.[36] That the connection between silence and chastity was an active nexus in the English Renaissance is evidenced not only by the wealth of pamphlet material on the subject but also by the copious references to and moral pronouncements on woman's speaking in literary contexts.[37] We might compare the description of Cordelia's voice in *King Lear* ("Her voice was ever soft, / Gentle and low, an excellent thing in a woman"; 5.3.271–72), for instance, with that of Milton's Dalila in *Samson Agonistes*, who is likened to a hyena, the putatively bisexual beast whose ability to mimic the human voice lured men to their destruction (l. 748).[38] Cordelia's linguistic restraint, registered not only in her decorous and pleasing voice when she does speak but also by her unwillingness to "heave [her] heart into [her] mouth" (1.1.90) in the first place, stands for a constellation of particularly feminine virtues: filial loyalty, modesty, chastity, the capacity to endure suffering, humility, and patience.[39] Dalila, conversely, is notoriously unfaithful, and her political treachery is intimately allied to her (presumably limitless) sexual promiscuity. Yet her seductively dangerous ability to counterfeit voices (registered in her parodically distorted reproductions of Samson's arguments) aligns her voice with Milton's own, for the feminine voice represents the rhetorical plenitude and versatility coveted by the poet. For a male author to assume the feminine voice is thus necessarily to confront in complex ways the "issue" of female sexuality, since the source of feminine verbal facility was thought to be coextensive with her erotic nature.

The imbrication of woman's putatively insatiable sexual desire and her uncontrollable urge to speak renders the appropriation of her voice a dangerous business for the male author, for it threatens to relegate him to the

---

36. Patterson, " 'For the Wyves,' " has explored this linkage in relation to Chaucer's Wife of Bath, a discussion to which my own formulation is indebted. For a more extended treatment, see Parker's analysis of the anatomical and rhetorical aspects of dilation (*Literary Fat Ladies*).

37. See especially Swetnam's comments on speech and sexuality (*The Arraignment*), Woodbridge's analysis of the pamphlet literature (*Women and the English Renaissance*), Henderson and McManus's treatment of the gender controversy (*Half Humankind*), and Jardine's examination of the specific ligature of eroticism and female speech in her chapter on the figure of the shrew (*Still Harping on Daughters* 103–40).

38. Gloss of the Geneva Bible to Eccles. 13.18; quoted in Milton, *Complete Poems* 569. Tobin, "A Note on Dalila" 89–90, refers to the hyena's traditional attributes of bisexuality, capacity for mimicry, and uncleanness, as well as its association with Circean enchantment.

39. Maclean, *Renaissance Notion of Women*, provides a detailed summary of the tradition that associates women with these qualities. He locates one origin for the tradition in Aristotle's *Nichomachean Ethics*, where these particular virtues appear to be regarded as involuntary and hence "imperfect," effectively "exclud[ing] [women] from Aristotle's moral universe" (51).

position of voyeur, unable either to satisfy her limitless desire or to control the voice he has borrowed. This threat is especially evident in male borrowings of the Sapphic voice, because the poet must face not only the otherness of her gender and sexual preference but also the legendary power of her reputation. His capacity to insert himself into her discursive space is dependent on the strategies he develops to mute or refashion her original voice, an intertextual rivalry which although similar to the competition between male poets and their precursors, both in its homage to her power and its complicity in her silencing, manifests itself as well in intersexual politics. Lesbianism complicates transvestite ventriloquism, since its presence in Western culture has, of course, been heavily censored. Ovid makes Sappho heterosexual so that she will be vulnerable to his erotic and poetic mastery, whereas Donne marginalizes her within a utopian world that—despite its allusion to the fertility of the Golden Age—is narcissistically sterile. Although love between women leaves no "signs," Sappho's poetry is also without signature and without poetic "offspring." Indeed, male borrowings of the feminine voice seem to provide an intensified version of intertextuality, for, where a system of diachronic textual echoes and citations continually subverts the ontological security of a text, its discrete historical boundaries, and its status as self-contained property, the phenomenon of transvestite ventriloquism provides in addition a powerful critique of phonocentrism.[40] That is, while all textual "voices" are constructions, tenuously connected with their referents and ambiguously tethered to the authorial presence that supposedly stands behind them, critical discourse has traditionally relied on the implicit presence of a stable author who manipulates these personae or voices. Ventriloquistic crossdressing, particularly when the borrowed voice belongs to an actual poet, transgresses the laws of gender, propriety, and property by undermining in a fundamental way the conventional relationship between author and voice, making visible in the process the radical contingency of poetic and authorial identity.

Why use the feminine voice for this interchange between male poets? Luce Irigaray, in her feminist rewriting of Lévi-Strauss, has argued that Western patriarchal culture is organized and subtended by the exchange of women, who function as commodities to be passed between men. Within the social context, women have value only as they facilitate relations among men; the sociocultural endogamy "excludes the participation of that order, so foreign to the social order: woman. . . . Men make commerce of them, but they do not enter into any exchanges *with* them."[41] Thus, although the poet purports to defer to the feminine voices that speak his texts (including the

40. See Goldberg, *Voice Terminal Echo*, for a theoretical meditation on the problematic of voice in Renaissance texts.

41. Irigaray, *This Sex* 172.

most potent of all, the voice of the muse), she is mastered within the economy of representation, and embodying the potential for signification as she does, she becomes the perfect medium of exchange. This is perhaps nowhere as clearly apparent as in Donne's verse letters, where the muse forms the basis of poetic transaction between the author and his (male) correspondents. In a letter to Roland Woodward, for instance, communication is effected through the voice of the muse:

> Zealously my Muse doth salute all thee,
> Enquiring of that mistique trinitee
> Wherof thou' and all to whom the heavens do infuse
> Like fyer, are made; they body, mind, and Muse.
> Does thou recover sicknes, or prevent?
> Or is thy Mind travail'd with discontent?
> Or art thou parted from the world and mee
> In a good skorn of the worlds vanitee?
> Or is thy devout Muse retyr'd to sing
> Upon her tender Elegiaque string?
> Our Minds part not, joyne then thy Muse with myne,
> For myne is barren thus devorc'd from thyne.[42]

Natural reproduction is here appropriated to the symbolic order, where the relations between the muses reenacts the heterosexual economy of which it is a reflection, providing poetic offspring through their disembodied commerce. Just as woman's reproductive value is subsumed under the monopolization of the proper name in order to insure the property and stability of the patriarchal order, so, too, are the transactions within the poetic order bounded and informed by an attention to property and ownership. Chastity is the keystone of Renaissance patriarchal culture, since sexual propriety alone determines the identity of the child as property of the father (Jonson's praise of Lady Sidney's chastity in "To Penshurst" provides a reminder of this fundamental organizing principle: "Thy lady's noble, fruitful, chaste withal. / His children thy great lord may call his own: / A fortune in his age, but rarely known"; 90–92). Commerce between the muses is also governed by laws of sexual propriety, which provides a context within which we might begin to understand the strange conceit used in a letter to Donne, written by "T.W.," presumably Thomas Woodward:

> Have mercy on me my sinfull Muse
> Wc rub'd tickled wth thyne could not chuse
> But spend some of her pithe yeild to bee
> One in yt chaste mistique tribadree.
> Bassaes adultery no fruit did leaue,

---

42. Milgate, *John Donne* 62.

Nor theirs wc their swolne thighs did nimbly weaue,
And wt new armes mouthes embrace kis
Though they had issue was not like to this.
They Muse, Oh strange holy Lecheree
Beeing a Mayd still, gott this Song on mee.[43]

Woodward compliments not only the powers of inspiration Donne's muse possesses but her chastity as well. Disdaining the base fruit that adultery (transgressive heterosexual congress) yields, the muses engage instead in tribadism, a lesbian exchange that merely simulates heterosexual intercourse; as a parodic version of the virgin birth, Donne's muse begets the verse poem on Woodward without ever impeaching her own virtue or threatening to transgress the boundaries of property/propriety. In a heterosexual economy, sexual exchange that does not involve the phallus does not "count," is excluded from the circuit, and so cannot threaten the integrity of feminine virtue.[44] What is appropriated is the figure of the muse, whose reputation for chastity and fertility the (male) poets guard, since her capacity inspires the poet with words, with voice. Just as the muse provides inspiration in a figure distanced from the poet and over whom he purports to exert only partial control, so too is the feminine voice a distanced figure, an image of surrogacy, whose viability depends finally upon the silence of actual women.

III

I have argued that Donne's "Sappho to Philaenis" seems to present an idyllic world of lesbian congress, but that this utopian vision is a male construction of lesbianism. Not only does the poem encode a portrait of Sappho as slightly ridiculous in her lonely passion and finally enclosed within a symmetrical, almost tautological sterility, but it also uses a lesbian erotic ethics as an implicit strategy for overcoming a male poetic rival. Nevertheless, there are

43. Ibid., 212. I am indebted to Gordon Braden for calling my attention to this verse letter.

44. In "Fiction and Friction" Stephen Greenblatt analyzes two instances of transvestism and supposed lesbianism in France. In the first instance, an incident reported by Montaigne, a woman dresses as a man, marries a woman, but is then discovered to be a transvestite. Condemned for using "illicit devices to supply her 'defect in sex'" (66), she is convicted and executed. In the second case, a servant dressed as a woman claims to be a man, but the sex of the man is disputed. The couple is accused of sodomy, and the "man" is charged with being a "tribade," who has "abused" his female lover with his unnaturally enlarged clitoris (73–74). In both cases, the supposed lesbianism seems to have been condemned because prosthetic devices were employed. In T.W.'s letter, however, the lesbian union seems to be chaste precisely because its eroticism involves "tickling" and "rubbing" (the etymology of "tribade" is, of course, from the Gk. *tribas*, "rubbing"), rather than penetration.

elements within the poem that strikingly anticipate recent feminist theory. My interpretation of Donne's poem as a voyeuristic illusion depends upon my supposition of a Renaissance context and a male author. Yet the epistle's fascination with the relationship between eroticism and language, its desire to abolish an exchange system that relies on women even as it renders them invisible, and its emphasis on touching as a source both of erotic pleasure and epistemological understanding links it to a feminist text to which it bears an uncanny resemblance, Luce Irigaray's "When Our Lips Speak Together." Just as Donne's Sappho laments the bankruptcy of language, its lack of resources for expressing an erotic passion that differs from or surpasses the heterosexual, so does Irigaray begin her lyrical apostrophe by condemning the poverty of language. Yet where Donne's Sappho envisions a paradise of homology and symmetry that is based on a celebration of the sameness of the female bodies, Irigaray makes sameness the principle of patriarchal domination, what Jane Gallop calls the "unicity of phallomorphic logic": "all round us, men and women sound just the same. The same discussions, the same arguments, the same scenes. The same attractions and separations. The same difficulties, the same impossibility of making connections. The same ... Same ... Always the same."[45]

To continue to speak in the sameness would be to fail, for words would pass above "our bodies," and they would remain enveloped "in proper skins, but not our own" (205). "When Our Lips Speak Together" alternates between the intimacy of direct address ("Don't you think so? Listen." "How can I touch you if you're not here?") and the encompassing plural that collapses boundaries between women ("If we keep on speaking sameness, if we speak to each other as men have been doing for centuries, as we have been taught to speak, we'll miss each other"; 205). Irigaray's new feminine speaking relies, of course, on the relationship between the lips that speak and the lips of the female genitals (labia minora and labia majora), for this conjunction ensures that woman's voice will no longer be similar to and indistinguishable from man's voice, but that it will be rechanneled through the female body, a specifically sexualized female body.[46] As Irigaray continually reminds us, such a speaking is always a reversal ("So let's try to take back some part of our mouth to speak with"; 208), a strategy of mimicry, that playful assumption of the role assigned to women by patriarchy. In this case, the double mouths of the feminine body, the site in the Renaissance of the control both of female

45. Irigaray, *This Sex* 205 (further citations will be given in parentheses in the text); Gallop, *Thinking through the Body* 94.

46. Gallop, *Thinking through the Body* 98, argues that in French, *lèvres* always refers (also) to the mouth, and that the application of *lèvres* to the vulva (*les lèvres de la vulve*) is necessarily figurative.

sexuality and also of female speaking, are occupied subversively by Irigaray. They become the basis not only of a new sexuality, one that bypasses the Freudian binarism of clitoris and vagina and the unicity of the penis, but also of a new linguistic and significatory economy.

This economy is, according to Irigaray, based on principles of contiguity and association rather than on the notions of sacrifice and substitution that figure so prominently for Lacan. Thus, rather than having the son-father relationship that organizes the Oedipal complex, which is based on renunciation and metaphoric substitution, the mother-daughter bond would be founded on metonymic identification, what is contiguous, associative, or combinatory.[47] Irigaray's juxtaposition of white and red blood crystallizes this distinction: white blood (*sang blanc*), which is a pun on *semblant* (the "other of the same"), stands for paternal genealogy, whereas red blood (*sang rouge*) figures the link between mother and daughter.[48] In this maternal order, there would be no need for the daughter to repudiate her mother (as lacking the phallus); it would now be possible for the mother and daughter to coexist, just as it would now be feasible for women to relate without the rivalry necessitated by patriarchy. The notion of contiguity and metonymy are crucial, because they allow for multiplicity rather than a system of (metaphoric) replacement and substitution. This means not that women are fused with one another in a relationship that obliterates the individual subject, but that subject-to-subject relations among women could now exist. The difference made possible by this realm of multiplicity, which is signaled by the two lips, provides the basis "*both* for sexual difference (and thus of the sexual relation) *and* of a female homosexual economy."[49] Diana Fuss glosses Irigaray's emphasis on multiplicity in Irigaray's own words: "Both at once." A woman is both singular and double, or, as Irigaray puts it, "*She is neither one nor two.*"[50]

The problem of enumeration is precisely Irigaray's point, for the impossibility of fixing woman to a specific number that is mutually exclusive is what also prevents setting up a hierarchy of original and copy. Whereas my interpretation of the mirror scene in Donne's "Sappho to Philaenis" stressed Sappho's desire for a fusion that is continually undercut by the poem's rhetoric ("Likeness" begets "*self flattery*," "touching myself, all *seems* done to thee," "Me, in my glass, I *call* thee"; emphasis mine), a rhetoric that emphasizes the impossibility of the endeavor, Irigaray subverts the logic of this relation:

47. Whitford, *Luce Irigaray* 180.
48. Ibid., 118–19.
49. Ibid., 182.
50. Irigaray, *This Sex* 26; Fuss, *Essentially Speaking* 58.

The fact that you live lets me know I am alive, so long as you are neither my counterpart not my copy. How can I say it differently? We exist only as two? We live by twos beyond all mirages, images, and mirrors. Between us, one is not the "real" and the other her imitation; one is not the original and the other her copy. Although we can dissimulate perfectly within their economy, we relate to one another without simulacrum. Our resemblance does without semblances: for in our bodies, we are already the same. Touch yourself, touch me, you'll "see." (*This Sex* 216)

Where the mirror becomes the vehicle for union in Donne's epistle, a necessary supplement to the proclaimed doubleness and self-sufficiency of the female body, for Irigaray the mirror is a sign of patriarchal mimesis. According to her, there is no need for an external representation of doubleness because the two lips already disturb and displace the economy of similitude. The specular image is thus a sign of a deathly sameness: "the strange way they divide up their couples, with the other as the image of the one. Only an image. So any move toward the other means turning back to the attraction of one's own mirage. A (scarcely) living mirror, she/it is frozen, mute" (207). Although Donne's poem incorporates the tactile,[51] Sappho's summoning of the absent Philaenis still depends upon vision, and it is the tears which dim her eyes that eventually destroy the illusion of her lover's presence. Irigaray, by contrast, condemns this "age-old oculocentrism" (48) that is the basis of Freudian distinctions of sexual difference, and she substitutes touch instead as the sense that will reshape perception in general. Again, the two lips provide the paradigm, since theirs is a perfectly mutual touching in which there is no distinguishable subject and object, no division into what is touched and what is touching. As she says in a phrase that registers a grammatical multiplicity of senses, "You will always have the touching beauty of a first time, if you aren't congealed in reproductions" (214).

Irigaray's most radical reshaping of the Order of the Same in "When Our Lips Speak Together" is directed to language itself. She reflexively returns to the question of how to reclaim the phrase "I love you," how to put it differently. Ultimately, it entails inventing a language, finding a language of the body, a language accompanied by enough gesture and movement to resist the immobilizations of patriarchal definition, of petrification as statues (214). Diana Fuss has suggested that the use of "statue" in this context refers to Irigaray's critique of Lacan's Seminar XX on women, most notably his infamous remark on St. Theresa's *jouissance*: "you only have to go and look at Bernini's statue in Rome to understand immediately that

---

51. Scarry, "Donne" 88, has drawn attention to Donne's extraordinary emphasis on touch, which she argues is his model for the senses. While this is true, his sense of touch is often mediated or supplemented by vision.

she's coming, there's no doubt about it."[52]   That Lacan should presume to understand women's pleasure from art and from an art created by a male artist ("In Rome? So far away? To look? At a statue? Of a saint? Sculpted by a man? What pleasure are we talking about? Whose pleasure?"; *This Sex* 91) graphically displays the dangers of ventriloquism. By contrast to Lacan's interpretation of Bernini's statue, Irigaray offers the fluency of female language, a flux and current of words that continually resist solidification. Rather than defining what this language would sound like, she argues that the female voice is defined precisely by this fluidity, this lack of fixed boundaries, this definition that always resists definition.[53]

52. Qtd. in Mitchell and Rose, *Feminine Sexuality* 147.

53. Irigaray's idea of female language has been condemned by feminists like Moi (*Sexual/Textual Politics*) because it was seen to be essentialist (since it emanated from a supposedly essential female body). Both Fuss, *Essentially Speaking*, and Whitford, *Luce Irigaray*, have challenged this reading in ways that have far-reaching implications for future Anglo-American readings of French feminists' texts. My own reading emphasizes the dimension of mimicry at work in Irigaray's texts; by providing a historical context for her metaphor (the two lips, the double mouths), I argue that she is subversively employing a traditionally patriarchal definition of women.

FIVE

Sappho in Early Modern England:
A Study in Sexual Reputation

Harriette Andreadis

In this study, I seek to recover some aspects of public discourse about female sexuality in sixteenth- and seventeenth-century England—before a language of lesbian sexuality as we know it became available. To explore public discourse about female same-sex sexuality, I examine contemporary references to the mythologized reputation of the Greek poet Sappho, who was for the English, as she was for the French and other Europeans, "the original poet of female desire."[1] Though Joan DeJean, in her influential book on Sappho, has indicated that English texts on Sappho merely mimic French views of Sappho of a half century earlier,[2] a closer examination of sixteenth- and seventeenth-century texts available in England reveals that the English rediscovery of Sappho did not wait for the French translations of Anne Le Fèvre Dacier and the turn of the eighteenth century; the complexities of Sappho's sexuality as they were represented in the ancient world were indeed disseminated and elaborated in England well before the Sapphic fictions of Addison and Pope in the eighteenth

I want to thank Shawn Maurer, Doreleis Kraakman, and Howard Marchitello for their attentive commentaries on various drafts; Nancy Tubbs for her enthusiastic assistance with research; Steve Oberhelman for help with translations from the Latin; and, for their encouragement and suggestions, the audiences at the National Women's Studies Association, the University of Amsterdam, the Folger Shakespeare Library's Women in the Renaissance colloquium, the Women's Studies seminar at Texas A & M University, the Berkshire Conference on the History of Women, and the University of Maryland's "Attending to Women in Early Modern Europe" conference. The English Department at Texas A & M University provided release time and an Undergraduate Research Opportunity Award as well as a collegial environment in which to think and write.
    1. DeJean, *Fictions of Sappho*, 6.
    2. Ibid., 5, 121.

century.[3] Sappho's passionate involvements with other women were, in fact, well known to those able to read Latin, if not always to those who could not.

My investigations thus far indicate that there were three primary modes of representing Sappho in early modern England: she was portrayed as a mythologized figure who acts the suicidal abandoned woman in the Ovidian tale of Sappho and Phaon; she was used as the first example of female poetic excellence, most often with a disclaimer of any sexuality (or what Abraham Cowley called "ill manners" [sig. c1]); and she was presented as an early exemplar of "unnatural" or monstrous sexuality. In this essay, I will describe in detail each of these modes of figuring Sappho in a variety of sixteenth- and seventeenth-century texts before going on to examine their implications for the discourse(s) about female same-sex eroticism (or sapphism) in early modern England. Although I have used these three modes as a means of organizing this discussion, it is important to keep in mind that these representations were not always discrete but rather functioned in ways that were interconnected and overlapping.

THE MYTH OF SAPPHO AND PHAON

The myth of Sappho and Phaon was given currency by Ovid's rewriting, in the *Heroïdes*, of Sappho's sexual reputation, following the reputedly scurrilous example of a number of Attic comedians, including Menander. The myth as shaped by Ovid seems to have provided a nexus for the destruction of Sappho's power as a poet/artist and for her reduction, through his appropriation of her voice and his ventriloquizing of her grief, to the status of a tribade debilitated by unrequited heterosexual passion. For reasons that are not clear, in part because their plays are no longer extant, the Athenian comedians had conflated the real person of Sappho with a myth about the ferryman Phaon (also Phaethon, as noted by Nagy)[4] and the goddess Aphrodite; they gave impetus to the myth perpetuated and elaborated by Ovid, who used the language of her poetry to accentuate her pathos in the shaping of his tale: Ovid's Sappho has rejected her female companions and, overwhelmed by grief, laments her unrequited passion for the much younger Phaon; in despair at his rejection, she ends her life by leaping from the Leucadian Rock to her death at sea. Ovid's fictionalized representation of Sappho gained currency throughout early modern Europe in edition after edition of the *Heroïdes*.

3. Donoghue, *Passions between Women* 243, has also remarked DeJean's lack of familiarity with the rich variety of texts available to English readers before the Enlightenment.

4. See Nagy, "Phaethon."

The complexities of Ovid's stance toward Sappho in the fifteenth epistle have already been examined in depth by Howard Jacobson, Florence Verducci, and Joan DeJean.[5] For the purposes of this study, it is sufficient to recognize in the text Ovid's deep ambivalence: a resentful, grudging admiration toward his influential female precursor and his misogynist eagerness to obliterate her preeminence as a rival poet. Consequently, in his reconfiguration of the myth, Sappho is seduced away both from her art and from her female companions by a self-destructive heterosexual obsession and finally commits suicide. As has already been observed by Gregory Nagy, the original myth was suffused by overtones of death and rebirth/regeneration and of the relation of the sun/light god to the sea;[6] the absence of these elements from the Ovidian version serves to diminish the profundity of the myth and, by extension, the significance of this representation of Sappho's suffering.

Commentators in the many editions of the *Heroïdes* were not shy in glossing Sappho's farewell to her women friends, nor were they overscrupulous in describing her presumed erotic activities in their brief biographies, comments that perpetuate the view of the eleventh-century lexicon known as the *Suda* that Sappho's relations with her friends were transgressive: "Sodales ejus amicæ fuerunt tres, Atthis, Telefippa, Megara: cum quibus etiam turpem confuetudinem habuiffe dicebatur (with whom she is said even to have had shameful habits, or intimacies)." As early as the *Suda*, then, classical representations of Sappho had become integrated into the Western literary tradition. In keeping with this tradition, the Venetian editions of the *Heroïdes* of 1538 and 1543 reproduce the commentary of one "Domitius," which includes the following remarks: "Erynna was the concubine (*concubina*) of Sappho ... [he gives the names of three of her friends (*amicas*)] who it is said she used libidinously (*ad libidinem*).... Ovid indicates that her poems were lascivious (*lasciva*).... [S]he did not fail to love [them] in the manner of a man, but was with other women a tribade, this is abusing (*insultando*) them by rubbing, for tribein is to rub, which we say according to Juvenal and Martial, and she was named by Horace *mascula Sappho* ..." (sig. N1 in both editions). There is no question here that Sappho's tribadism was an integral part of her representation in Europe at this early date. Similarly, the first Latin edition of the *Heroïdes* published in England, in 1583, somewhat abbreviates the fullness of detail in the Venetian editions, but retains enough of it to convey the crucial point of her tribadism, maintaining the definition of *tribas* and interpreting the Horatian epithet as referring

5. Jacobson, *Ovid's Heroides* 277–99; Verducci, *Ovid's Toyshop of the Heart* 123–79; DeJean, *Fictions of Sappho* 60–78.

6. See Nagy, "Phaethon."

to Sappho's same-sex erotic stance ("In XXI. Epistolam Argumentum" sigs. H14–H14v).

Sappho's presumed erotic connections with women were thus implicated in Ovid's representation of her as driven and destroyed by an unrequited heterosexual passion. She was punished for her aberrant erotic tastes as well as for the threatening and dangerous (to men) power of her art. This construction of her "life" was available to educated sixteenth-century English readers of Latin. This construction was also available, though less explicitly, to a wider English audience in the translation of Ovid's text, published in 1567 by George Turberville, without gloss and without an additionally appended "life" of Sappho:

> Pyrino is forgot,
> ne Dryads doe delite
> My fancie: Lesbian Lasses eke
> are now forgotten quite.
> Not Amython I force,
> nor Cyndo passing fine:
> Nor Atthis, as she did of yore,
> allures these eyes of mine.
> Ne yet a hundreth mo
> whom (shame ylayd aside)
> I fancide erste: thou all that love
> from them to thee hast wride.
>
> (sig. O5v)

> My lowring Lute laments for wo,
> my Harpe with doole is dombe.
> Ye Lesbian Lasses all
> that border on the Lake:
> And ye that of the Aeolian towne
> your names are thought to take,
> Ye Lesbian Lasses (that
> for cause I looved you sore
> Breede my defame) unto my Harpe
> I charge you come no more.
>
> (sig. P4)

Early in the next century, Wye Saltonstall's 1636 translation for "the Vertuous Ladies and Gentlewomen of England" modified both these passages in such a way as to undercut their explicit references to Sappho's erotic activities with her own sex. Compare his bowdlerized translation with Turberville's earlier one:

> I hate Amythone, and Cyndus white,
> And Atthis is not pleasant in my sight.

And many others that were lov'd of me,
But now I have plac'd all my love on thee.

(sig. L6)

Yea, Lesbian Nymphs that mariage do desire,
Yea, Nymphs so called from the Lesbian Lyre.
Ye Lesbyan Nymphs whose love advanc'd my fame:
Come not to heare my Harpe, or Lyrick straine.
For that sweet vaine I had in former time,
My Phaon took away, who is not mine.

(sig. L8)

In Saltonstall's later version, Sappho's rejection of the "Lesbian Nymphs" is emphatic, even a bit contemptuous, while the nature of her love for women might not be apparent to those not already familiar with her reputation; further, the nymphs not only fail to reciprocate her love but desire (heterosexual) marriage. Underlined here as well is the connection between Sappho's excessive and futile passion for Phaon and the acute diminishing of her artistic powers. This is a pathetic Sappho indeed, having lost the "sweet vaine" of her "Lyrick straine" for a Phaon who abandoned her. Saltonstall seems to have been sufficiently aware of the implications of Ovid's representation that he chose to reconfigure his own Sapphic voice so as to reinforce those sentiments in a manner appropriate to the "Vertuous Ladies" for whom he wrote.

Three years later, in 1639, John Sherburne's translation gives us a lasciviously heterosexual Sappho. References to her same-sex erotic partners are in some ways less explicit than those of Turberville, but also rather less evasive than in Saltonstall's "Ladies' " version:

Vile's *Amython*, vile *Cydno*. [sic] too the white,
Vile *Althis*, once most gratefull in my sight,
And hundreds more with whom my sins are knowne.

(sig. G9v)

In addition to disgust with her former friends and erotic partners as the consequence of her newfound self-destructive heterosexual passion, this Sappho is burdened by what we might term tribadic promiscuity, a male fantasy of hedonistic and exotic pleasures with "hundreds more," "sins" (rather than "crimes") she must regret and expiate through heterosexual suffering. Sherburne's Sappho has been, perhaps, suspiciously Christianized by a discourse that echoes the orientalizing and "othering" of tribadism to Middle Eastern locales during this period.[7]

---

7. Valerie Traub, in "Psychomorphology of the Clitoris," explores the theoretical implications of this orientalizing. The connection between tribadism and exotic locales seems to have

These examples suggest that as Ovid's epistle of Sappho to Phaon began to reach a larger reading audience in English translation, the clearly delineated tribadism familiar to those who could read Latin was reconfigured in favor of a representation of the preeminent female poet creatively and emotionally debilitated, sacrificing herself on the altar of heterosexual passion. Apart from what this might suggest about patriarchalism in early modern England, it does seem to indicate that there was sufficient consciousness about female same-sex eroticism and a reasonably clear understanding of the meaning of tribadism, at least among educated males, that discourse in the vernacular was being inhibited, particularly when it was addressed or made available to respectable women. Where Ovid's epistle is concerned, the representation of Sappho as a model of behavior was clearly in need of reconfiguration. In contrast to the relatively straightforward presentation of Sappho's putative tribadism by sixteenth-century Latin commentators, seventeenth-century translators are more self-consciously ambiguous in their handling of the complexities of her erotic behaviors.

Other contemporary versions of the Sappho and Phaon story substantiate this view. They do not with any consistency adhere to the conventional scenario presumably established by Ovid; even less do they hint at any earlier irregularities in Sappho's sexuality. In his late-sixteenth-century play *Sapho and Phao* (1584), John Lyly, a writer of elaborately rhetorical prose fictions and of courtly, mythological plays for the boys' theatrical companies, uses the figure of Sappho to compliment Elizabeth: in his version, Sappho turns the tables on Phao (who serves, presumably, as a suitor to Elizabeth), by rejecting *his* love and taking control of Cupid and Venus. Far from succumbing to love for Phao, Lyly's Sappho emerges triumphant over the potentially disruptive powers of Venus and Cupid. There is perhaps an oblique suggestion— though not in a manner inappropriate in a compliment to Elizabeth— that she might have preferred the company of members of her own sex. Here, as Janel Mueller has suggested,[8] Lyly is in all probability drawing plot complications from Sappho's prayer-poem, the ode to Aphrodite, to

---

been current during a considerable period of time. We find it, for example, in 1671, in Jane Sharp's *Midwives Book*: "[the clitoris] hangs forth at the flit like a Yard, and will fwell and ftand ftiff if it be provoked, and fome lewd women have endeavoured to ufe it as men do theirs. In the *Indies*, and *Egypt* they are frequent, but I never heard but of one in this Country, if there be any they will do what they can for fhame to keep it clofe" (45); and again in 1749, in the anonymous *Satan's Harvest Home*: "[tribadism] is practis'd frequently in Turkey, as well as at Twickenham at this Day" (18).

8. Mueller, "A Letter from Lesbos" 18–19, 48 n. 41. But see also the richly textured reading of this play provided by Berry, *Of Chastity and Power* 120–24: "emphasis on the queen's withdrawal into an exclusive feminine world as another Diana is invested with a certain innuendo by its conjunction with the name of Sappho" (123).

structure his dramatic situation until its "reversing dénouement." Lyly uses a version of the familiarly mythical name of Phaon, but for all practical purposes ignores the substance of Ovid's epistle.

A second and later English version of the myth appears as a digression in the obscure William Bosworth's justifiably forgotten 1651 romance, "The Historie of Arcadius and Sepha."[9] This mid-seventeenth-century version bears very little resemblance to any Latin sources, to Lyly's play, or to any of Sappho's then-known works. It is sheer fantasy in an outmoded Elizabethan vein, except that Bosworth—unlike Lyly—retains Sappho's status as an artist. In Bosworth's version, Phaon is a knight, complete with shield and sword, come to Lesbos to renew his patrimony. A young Sappho (in Ovid she is well past her prime) falls in love with him; he does not return her love but, for reasons not clearly explained in the text, kills himself. Sappho then drowns herself in a stream and is mourned by yet another knight. Thus has the drama of the Leucadian Rock degenerated: Lesbos has been domesticated, complete with a romantic grotto and stream. Gone are Sappho's Ovidian monologue of lovelorn despair and any hint of sexual transformation or loss of artistic capacities. Bosworth's digression is a genteel exemplum of thwarted lovers.

This Sappho, like Lyly's very different one, has little connection with the tortured lover portrayed by Ovid. It is fair to say that, although English readers were no doubt familiar with the myth perpetuated by Ovid, the story of Sappho and Phaon as it made its way into the vernacular—the drama and popular romance of the seventeenth century—failed to maintain the complexly misogynistic elements of the Ovidian epistle or the Renaissance humanists' " 'defamation of Sappho,' "[10] or even to hint at Sappho's love for women and the erotically transgressive nature of her poetry. What remained were the mythologized names and some semblance of a narrative of love.

The 1601 English translation by Philemon Holland of the Roman naturalist Pliny's (ca. 23–79 C.E.) encyclopedic compendium of natural lore, *Historie of the World or The Natural History*, was a widely distributed and popularly known standard reference work in early modern England. Pliny's description of the herb white eryngion, "the reason (men say) that ladie *Sappho* was so enamoured upon the yong knight *Phao* of Lesbos" (sig. L6), consequently would have had wide currency. Interestingly, in this attribution of the motive for Sappho's infatuation to the magic properties of an herb, Pliny neatly dispensed with the entire mythic superstructure of goddesses and rocks and seas and relieved Sappho of responsibility for her lovesickness. Holland's

9. I have been unable to discover any other writings by Bosworth.
10. Mueller, "Troping Utopia" 187.

translation thus made available to seventeenth-century English readers yet another bowdlerized version of Ovid's myth.

The historical trajectory of Ovid's attempted defamation of Sappho is demonstrated as well by the fate of his well-known reference to her in the *Tristia*, written in exile, lamenting that he has been punished for his sexual escapades while others, among whom is Sappho, have not: "Lesbia quid docuit Sappho, nisi amare puellas?" (What did Lesbian Sappho teach the girls if not love?; Cambridge 1638 sig. B8). Early modern English translations of this Ovidian passage, whose erotic implications are clear enough in Latin and in any literal translation, while initially faithful in their rendering of the original, move toward an obscuring of Sappho's progressively more problematic relations with her own sex. In 1572 Thomas Churchyard translated this line as "What hath dame *Sapho Lesbia* learnde, but maydens fayre to love" (sig. B6); in 1633 Wye Saltonstall translated it as "And *Sappho* doth instruct mayds how to love" (sig. D3); and in 1639 Zachary Catlin rendered the English as "What taught the *Lesbian Sappho* but to love?" (sig. C8). By mid-seventeenth century, then, "puellas" is finally eliminated and Sappho's tribadism is obliterated from the English Ovid. Again we see that by mid-seventeenth century in England the treatment of Sappho's tribadism has become increasingly self-conscious and ambiguous when not altogether obliterated.

SAPPHO AS THE FIRST EXAMPLE OF
FEMALE POETIC EXCELLENCE

That Sappho's preeminence in the world of letters was generally acknowledged in the ancient world is also evidenced by the numerous surviving encomia to her. In his *Rhetoric*, Aristotle pointed out that "everybody honors the wise ... and the Mytilineans honored Sappho although she was a woman."[11] Though her works were lost during the depredations of the early Christians, and it was left to the late nineteenth and twentieth centuries to recover fragments of her poems in papyri abandoned in ancient refuse heaps, two of her poems and a number of fragments were preserved in Renaissance Europe. The French led in the recovery of her work when in 1566 the great printer Henri Estienne [Henricus Stephanus] published the two odes preserved in their entirety by Dionysius of Halicarnassus and by "Longinus," as well as all known fragments, in his second edition of the Greek lyric poets (C1 ff.).[12] The English were much later in publishing her

11. Arist. *Rhet.* 1389b; qtd. in Barnstone, *Sappho* 167.
12. See DeJean, *Fictions of Sappho* 313 ff., for a listing of sixteenth- and seventeenth-century French editions of Sappho, and Mueller, "Lesbian Erotics" 109, 127 nn. 15, 16, for other

work, only in 1695 including both odes in a Latin/Greek edition of the odes of Anacreon published in London. No doubt, before the end of the seventeenth century, those English speakers who wanted to read her in Greek could obtain a French edition, or they could read the French translations of the odes that had become available. Those who had not read her extant work had probably heard of her.

A portion of Sappho's work became well known, as did the fact that both odes—the ode to Aphrodite and *Phainetai moi*, in which the speaker's passion for her beloved is triangulated by a man—addressed love between women. Despite the ambiguities of her sexual reputation, Sappho's became the one name associated with female poetic excellence; she was the sole ancient model to which contemporary women writers might compare themselves and to whom they might be compared. Plato had called her "the tenth Muse" and that epithet became more or less inevitably, and conventionally, attached to her name in literary circles.

In the latter half of the seventeenth century in England, Sappho's name was used to apostrophize female poets, most often with a disclaimer about their sexuality or erotic proclivities. This was, at least at first, almost certainly a fashionable echo of Mme de Scudèry's having styled herself the second Sappho and having rewritten her own fiction of Sappho in book 10 of *Artamène où le Grand Cyrus* (1649–53), which included an acknowledgment— albeit subtle—of Sappho's erotic interest in women. In the seventeenth century, male contemporaries referred to Katherine Philips, who was also an admirer of Mme de Scudèry, as "the new Sappho," making certain always to emphasize Philips's exemplary virtue. Philips's friend, the poet Abraham Cowley, writes:

> They talk of *Sappho*, but, alas the shame
> Ill Manners soil the lustre of her fame.
> Orinda's [Philips's *nom de plume*] inward Vertue is so bright,
> That, like a Lantern's fair enclosed light,
> It through the Paper shines where she doth write.[13]

The compliment was later taken over, without the sexual disclaimer, by women writers who used it among themselves. Delarivier Manley and Catharine Trotter, as well as others, describe each other as and compare each other to Sappho in the commendatory poems that preface their plays. For example, Mary Pix addressed Delarivier Manley on her play *The Royal*

---

editions. Mueller, "Troping Utopia" 184 ff., also furnishes a good account of the Sappho doxography and citation in humanist scholarship, especially by Politian and Giraldi. Bonnet, *Un choix*, provides an account of Continental commentary.

13. In K. Philips, *Poems* sigs. cl–cl'. See Andreadis, "The Sapphic-Platonics" 51–55, for a fuller account of comparisons between Philips and Sappho.

Mischief (1696) as "Like Sappho Charming...."[14] Sappho's literary reputation was, in this way, well established in seventeenth-century England,
though often—especially when referred to by men—with an evident unease
about her sexuality, with what nineteenth-century England was to name
"Sapphism."

SAPPHO AS AN EARLY EXAMPLE OF
FEMALE HOMOSEXUALITY

Sappho was, then, already being used in England as an Ovidian example
of tribadism in literary discourse and she was, in fact, probably the most
prominent exemplar of erotic behaviors between women. In the discourse
of medical literature, in the Latin anatomies available in England in the
sixteenth century, it is usual to find some brief mention of tribadism in the
description of the clitoris, so that it is clear that among educated males female same-sex eroticism was acknowledged and was already a topic of some
interest. The 1562 edition of Fallopius and the 1595 edition of Laurentius
are good examples of these descriptions and convey a sense of their characteristic tone. Fallopius remarks the role of the clitoris in female same-sex
relations:

> Auicen[na] ... meminit cuiufdam partis in pudendo muliebri fitam, quam virgam
> vel albathara vocat. Hanc Albucafis ... tentiginem appellat, quae folet aliquando
> ad tantum incrementum peruenire, vt mulieres hanc habentes coeant cum aliis,
> veluti fi viri effent. Partem hanc graeci κλητορίδα vocârunt, vnde verbum κλη-
> τορίζειν obfcœnum diductum est. Anatomici verò nostri penitus neglexerunt,
> neque verbum quidem de ipfe faciunt. (sig. p4v)

> Avicenna makes mention of a certain member situated in the female genitalia
> which he calls *virga* or *albathara*. Albucasis calls this *tentigo*, which sometimes will
> increase to such a great size that women, while in this condition, have sex with each
> other just as if they were men. The Greeks call this member *clitoris*, from which
> the obscene word *clitorize* is derived. Our anatomical writers have completely
> neglected this and do not even have a word for it.

While Fallopius emphasizes the way in which these behaviors imitate
male-female sexuality ("veluti fi viri effent"; "as if they were men") and
makes a verb (attributed to Greek authority) of the noun *clitoris*, Laurentius
quotes Fallopius and then, next to the marginal gloss "vfus clitoridis," goes
on to provide the language most commonly used to describe female same-sex
behaviors:

---

14. Manley, *The Royal Mischief* sig. A3v. See as well Trotter's *Agnes de Castro* (1696) and *Fatal
Friendship* (1698).

Huius vfum agnofcimus, vt perfricata torpentem excitet facultatem. Crefcit in quibufdam tam importuné, vt extra rimam pendeat mentulæ inftar, eafefe mutuò fricent mulieres, quas propterea tribades feu fricatrices dicunt. (sigs. Ll4v–Mm1)

I have become aware of the use of this [clitoris], whereby after being rubbed all over it excites the sluggish faculty. It increases in some people to such an inappropriate extent that it hangs outside the fissure the same as a penis; women then often engage in mutual rubbing, such women accordingly called *tribades* or *fricatrices*.

Laurentius makes clear that the Greek *tribades* and the Latin *fricatrices* were used interchangeably to describe women who enacted these behaviors, described—and understood—primarily as mutual "rubbing" ("eafefe mutuò fricent mulieres"; "women mutually rub each other") of an enlarged member (elaborating on Fallopius's "ad tantum incrementum peruenire" (to increase to such a great size) with "Crefcit in quibufdam tam importuné, vt extra rimam pendeat mentulæ inftar" (it increases in some people to such an inappropriate extent that it hangs outside the fissure the same as a penis). Later, seventeenth-century anatomies in English tend to devote more space to their descriptions of the clitoris in order to add additional commentary of a judgmental nature. In 1615, Helkiah Crooke in his English anatomy repeats the commentaries of his Greek and Latin predecessors; next to the marginal gloss "*Tribades odiofæ feminæ*," he remarks:

although for the moft part it [the clitoris] hath but a fmall production hidden vnder the *Nymphes* and hard to be felt but with curiofity, yet fometimes it groweth to fuch a length that it hangeth without the cleft like a mans member, efpecially when it is fretted with the touch of the cloathes, and fo ftrutteth and groweth to a rigiditie as doth the yarde of a man. And this part it is which thofe wicked women doe abufe called *Tribades* (often mentioned by many authours, and in fome ftates worthily punifhed) to their mutuall and vnnaturall luftes. (sig. Y5v)

Quite apparent in Crooke's description are both the contemporary obsession, surely bred by anxiety, with the homologies between the clitoris and the "yarde," and a growing contempt for female same-sex eroticism, the two no doubt interconnected. The 1634 translation of the anatomy of Ambroise Paré by Thomas Johnson makes the usual references to earlier authorities, especially to Realdo Columbo and to Fallopius, and then coyly adds the following:

Columbus cals it *Tentigo, Fallopius Cleitoris*, whence proceeds that in*f*amous word *Cleitorizein*, (which fignifies impudently to handle that part.) But becaufe it is an obfcene part, let thofe which defire to know more of it, read the Authors which I cited. (sig. M5v)

That the terms of description used for the clitoris remain remarkably consistent, with authors echoing their predecessors, over a quite long period

of time is evidenced repeatedly. Alexander Read's comments in his 1642
Manvall of the Anatomy are characteristic:

> [the] Clytoris . . . is a nervous and hard body: within, full of a black and fpongious
> matter, as the laterall ligaments of the yard. . . . And as it doth reprefent the prick
> of a man, fo it fuffereth erection, and falling; It may be called a woman's prick.
> In some women it hath been as big as a mans. (sig. F5v–F6)

The anatomical connection with Sappho seems to have been made rather
later, toward the middle of the seventeenth century, as prurient interest in
the clitoris was evidently continuing to increase. In 1653, Thomas Bartholin,
the Swedish anatomist, revised, expanded, and translated into English his
father's 1633 Latin anatomy of the human body. The Latin of Caspar
Bartholin clearly describes contemporary understanding of female same-
sex sexual activity, but it does not include the anecdotal embellishments and
example of Sappho added by the younger Bartholin twenty years later in the
English translation. The entry "Of the Clitoris" includes engravings of that
part, with explicit comparisons to the penis, or "yard," and the following
description:

> The Greeks call it *clitoris*, others name it *Tentigo*, others the womans Yard or Prick:
> both because it resembles a Mans Yard, in Situation, Substance, Composition,
> Repletion, with Spirits and Erection. And Also because it hath somewhat like the
> Nut and Fore-skin of a Mans Yard, and in some Women it grows as big as the Yard
> of a man: so that some women abuse the same, and make use thereof in place of a
> mans Yard, exercising carnal Copulation one with another, and they are termed
> *Confricatrices* Rubsters. Which lascivious Practice is said to have been invented
> by Philaenis and Sappho, the Greek Poetress, is reported to have practised the
> same. And of these I conceive the Apostle Paul speaks in the I. of *Romans* 26.
> And therefore this part is called *Contemptus virorum* the Contempt of Mankind.
> (sigs. Z2–Z2v)

He goes on to say that an unusually large clitoris is "praeternatural and
monstrous" and comments further that "the more this part encreases, the
more does it hinder a man in his business" (sig. Aa1). The androcentrism
of Bartholin's commentary and his thinly disguised prurience may be too
obvious to need commentary, yet it is important to underline the particular
form they take here: male anxiety is expressed not only in the presence of the
female assumption of male sexual prerogative (i.e., "make use thereof in place
of a mans Yard") but also in the prospective thwarting of his own perceived
prerogatives and just deserts (i.e., being "hinder[ed] in his business"). Indeed,
as we have seen, these anxieties and the androcentrism and prurience to
which they give rise typify contemporary accounts.[15] Bartholin's description

---

15. Park, "Hermaphrodites and Lesbians," provides an important analysis of this material.

of the clitoris consequently furnished a model for the semipornographic medical treatises that were to follow in the eighteenth century.[16]

It also furnishes us with evidence that lesbianism as we know it, with Sappho as its chief exemplar, had entered vernacular discourse in England by the middle of the seventeenth century. Though *tribade* was the term most often used by educated males, *confricatrices* —a pseudo-Latinate nonce word—becomes, literally, the English "rubsters," an epithet that eventually, in the eighteenth century, yields to "tommies," perhaps as an analogue for the male homosexual "mollies."[17] Bartholin's account of the clitoris thus most importantly suggests to us the language through which what since the early twentieth century has been called lesbianism originally entered verbal consciousness in the vernacular.

After the middle of the seventeenth century, we also remark the appearance of literary documents by English women that portray explicitly female same-sex erotic behaviors: the duchess of Newcastle's play, *The Convent of Pleasure* (1668); Anne Killigrew's poem of erotic flagellation, "Upon a Little Lady Under the Discipline of an Excellent Person" (1686); Aphra Behn's poem "To the Fair Clarinda, Who Made Love to Me, Imagined More than Woman" (1688); and Delarivier Manley's "new *Cabal*" in her roman à clef *The New Atalantis* (1709) are perhaps the best known of these works. Except for Anne Killigrew, whose poem is accompanied by her father's disclaimer of her authorship, these writers were all in some way considered infamous or associated with scandal.

Margaret Cavendish, the duchess of Newcastle, was generally regarded as a Tory eccentric whose discourse was described, dismissively, by at least one contemporary as "airy, empty, whimsical and rambling" and who "in her rhetoric of dress and behaviour aimed at a blurring of the boundaries between genders similar to that produced by *The Convent of Pleasure*."[18] Aphra Behn's notoriety as a spy in Antwerp for Charles II, her incarceration in

16. These materials are very usefully surveyed by Wagner, "The Discourse on Sex."

17. See Norton, *Mother Clap's Molly House*, esp. 232 ff. Norton cites the "history of lesbianism" provided by the anonymous author of *Satan's Harvest Home*; it is striking that, in 1749, as a new vocabulary is becoming current, Sappho continues to be the chief exponent of female same-sex transgressiveness: "*Sappho*, as she was one of the wittiest Women that ever the World bred, so she thought with Reason, it would be expected she should make some Additions to a *Science* in which Womankind had been so successful: What does she do then? Not content with our Sex, begins *Amours* with her own, and teaches the Female World a new Sort of Sin, call'd the *Flats*" (*Satan's Harvest Home* 18). Norton glosses "the Game of Flatts" as "a reference to games with playing cards, called 'flats,' and an allusion to the rubbing together of two 'flat' female pudenda" (233).

18. Tomlinson, "My Brain the Stage" 158; the contemporary comment is from Mary Evelyn, qtd. in Tomlinson 159.

debtor's prison, her advocacy of education for women, her contributions to the rise of the novel, and her theatrical writings were all rather well known to her contemporaries and helped shape her reputation and, one is tempted to add, her self-fashioning as a woman who consciously transgressed social norms and challenged social values. Like Cavendish, Delarivier Manley was a strong royalist in her political sympathies; she was, however, more than merely eccentric. Manley was involved in a bigamous marriage that she exploited for literary materials on polygamy; moreover, *The New Atalantis*, her "Tory-motivated exposé of the supposed 'secret' lives of rich and powerful Whig peers and politicians of the reigns of the Stuart kings and queens from Charles II to Anne I,"[19] was suppressed on publication and she was taken into custody. Creating scandal in her fictions and theatrical productions, she also lived it.

These works were not, then, generally considered "respectable." But they do demonstrate the willingness of unconventional women to contribute to a public discourse about the erotic activities of women with each other. Similar observations might be made about John Donne's explicitly erotic heroical epistle *Sapho to Philaenis* in which Donne (like Ovid before him) assumes the voice of Sappho, but (unlike Ovid) explores in detail the utopian dynamics of female desire.[20]

Read in the context of other contemporary materials, this survey of literary texts in which the figure of Sappho appears indicates that in the sixteenth century female homoerotic behavior was treated often misogynistically, but also with relative matter-of-factness and as a curiosity. In the seventeenth century, however, this eroticism is presented with increasing ambiguity and self-consciousness on the part of authors and translators until, by mid-century, public discourse about lesbians is increasingly relegated to medical treatises, erotica, and literary works by unconventional women and at least one male poet, where it also becomes much more detailed and explicit in describing the sexual activities of women with each other. This change in the treatment of lesbianism in written texts suggests both the growing opprobrium directed by society at what had been known as tribadism and the growing interest in, even prurience toward, this behavior on the part of at least some segments of English society.

I would like to conclude, tentatively, that my reading of these materials confirms that there was a change in discourse about female same-sex eroticism in England in or around the mid-seventeenth century. The language of literature and respectable society seems to have become more evasive as the

19. Ballaster, introduction to *New Atalantis* v.
20. See Mueller, "Lesbian Erotics" and "Troping Utopia." Holstun, " 'Will You Rent,' " and Harvey, "Ventriloquizing Sappho," develop differing perspectives.

existence of lesbianism was increasingly acknowledged by other dimensions of public discourse.

Although there has been some contention about the shifts, both discursive and behavioral, in the understanding of male same-sex eroticism, my analysis seems to confirm with regard to women the hypothesis initially proposed by Mary McIntosh in 1968. Using a structuralist functionalist approach, McIntosh argues that a specific male homosexual *role* —as distinguished from merely homosexual *behavior*—of the effeminate sodomite emerged under the particular historical circumstances of the late seventeenth century, a role that "keeps the bulk of society pure in rather the same way that the similar treatment of some kinds of criminal helps keep the rest of society law abiding."[21] In concurring with McIntosh's chronology, Alan Bray uses the evidence of legal theory and of court cases to demonstrate that an identifiable male homosexual *subculture* —at least in London, if not in other provincial English cities—crystallized and took recognizable shape some time after the mid-1600s and by the close of the seventeenth century. Bray's evidence suggests that before the mid-1600s, "So long as homosexuality was expressed through established social institutions, in normal times the courts were not concerned with it; and generally this meant patriarchal institutions— the household, the educational system, homosexual prostitution and the like.... Despite the contrary impression given by legal theorists, so long as homosexual activity did not disturb the peace or the social order, and in particular so long as it was consistent with patriarchal mores, it was largely in practice ignored."[22] That is to say, from the close of the Middle Ages to the mid-1600s, homosexual behavior was "not socialized to any significant degree at all" and did not coalesce into "a specifically homosexual world, a society within a society" made up of molly houses and other casual meeting places, until some time later, between the mid-1600s and the turn of the eighteenth century.[23] Before about the mid-seventeenth century, then, before the apparent emergence of a social role within an identifiable subculture, the Elizabethans had "the unwelcome difficulty ... in drawing a dividing line between those gestures of closeness among men that they desired so much [in 'the orderly relationship of friendship'] and those they feared" [in "the

21. McIntosh, "The Homosexual Role" 184.

22. Bray, *Homosexuality in Renaissance England* 74.

23. Ibid., 80, 85. Trumbach, "Sodomitical Subcultures," takes issue with McIntosh and Bray, though he finally comes to agree with McIntosh, but with reservations. See also Weeks, *Sex, Politics, and Society* 96 ff.; Sedgwick, *Epistemology of the Closet* 182 ff.; and Bray, "Homosexuality and the Signs of Male Friendship," for a fuller discussion of the issues at stake in this scholarship. Whatever the outcome of the contested historicizing of a homosexual role and subculture, it is crucial to keep in mind that the construction of sexuality in London certainly differed from that in other northern European capitals, as it did also from that in the rest of England.

profoundly disturbing image of the sodomite, that enemy not only of nature but of the order of society and the proper kinds and divisions within it"].[24]

We may speculate that an analogous female homosexual subculture might also have emerged in or around the same period in London. Its visibility, or rumors of its existence, could certainly have precipitated the evasiveness and eventual silence of the discourse of "respectable" society, as well as the transgressiveness and prurience we have observed in other quarters with respect to erotic relations between women. As several recent scholars have observed, attempts to define *lesbian* seem inevitably to founder on the Scylla of essentialist, transhistorical meanings and the Charybdis of feminist controversies between a "lesbian continuum" of romantic friendship and the necessary sexualizing of female erotic relations; definitional impasses are no longer surprising, are almost to be expected, in current lesbian theoretical writing.[25] It does seem clear, however, that the discourse of transgressive female same-sex relations in early modern England was increasingly relegated to medical and other texts that could provoke and satisfy pruriently misogynist interests, as well as to the writings of women willing or able to be unconventional.

With the approach of the eighteenth century, the definition of female same-sex relations seems to have become even more narrowly focused on a specific set of forbidden sexual behaviors. On the one hand, discursive representations of transgressive female sexuality continued in the eighteenth century to employ Sappho as their vehicle, as witnessed by Alexander Pope's 1712 translation of Ovid's epistle "Sapho to Phaon" or Nicholas Venette's 1750 manual *Conjugal Love; or, The Pleasures of the Marriage Bed*; yet, on the other hand, this forbidden sexuality seems to have been increasingly circumscribed and split off from representations and understandings of the relations between "respectable" women.[26] This splitting off, or bifurcation, of

---

24. Bray, "Homosexuality and the Signs of Male Friendship" 51–54.

25. The phrase "lesbian continuum" was first introduced into feminist discourse in 1980. See Vicinus, "Lesbian History," and Jagose, *Lesbian Utopics* 1–24, for lucid commentaries on these issues.

26. Pope's translation reads as follows:

> No more the *Lesbian* Dames my Passion move,
> Once the dear Objects of my guilty Love;
> All other Loves are lost in only thine,
> Ah youth ungrateful to a Flame like mine!
> (ll. 17–20)

Venette describes the clitoris and Sappho thus:

> According to the opinion of some authors, there is a part above the nymphae longer more or less than half a finger, called by anatomists clitoris; the which I may justly term the fury and rage of love; there Nature has placed the seat of pleasure and

discourses creates a space for the development, in the mid-to-later eighteenth century, of the language of female romantic friendship as the dominant discourse defining "virtuous" female friends.[27] That the relations between "respectable" women might be highly eroticized, might even partake of behaviors not defined as sexual because not modeled on valorized male penetrative action, would have been of little import. For those who were defined as transgressing were ever more conclusively ostracized and relegated to a liminal existence in a subculture that would also ensure the acceptability of those women not so relegated.

---

lust, as it has on the other hand in the glands of man; there it has placed those excessive ticklings, and there is lechery and lasciviousness established; for, in the action of love, the clitoris fills with spirits, and afterwards stiffens as a man's virge, which part it resembles. One may see its pipes, its nerves, and muscles: neither is there a gland or prepuce wanting; and if it was hollow through, one would say it was altogether like a man's member.

This part lascivious women often abuse. The lesbian Sappho would never have acquired such indifferent reputation, if this part of hers had been less. (18–19; sigs. B7v–B8)

27. The examples of Eleanor Butler and Sarah Ponsonby (see the account of Mavor, *The Ladies of Llangollen*) and of Sarah Scott's autobiographical *Description of Millenium Hall* (1762) are perhaps the best known. Faderman's *Surpassing the Love of Men* is the *locus classicus* for a (de-eroticizing) discussion of romantic friendship.

SIX

Sex and Philology: Sappho and the Rise of German Nationalism

Joan DeJean

At the beginning of his scholarly autobiography, J.J. Bachofen, the theoretician of "mother right," proclaims, "I was drawn to the study of law by philology."[1] Bachofen's placement of philology at the origin of his work parallels that of virtually all the influential intellectual systems to come out of nineteenth-century Germany: in the beginning, there was philology. The study of language and of literature became the keystone of law and ethics, as well as of history and the history of art. Never has wider reaching importance been attributed to literary texts, especially to founding literary texts like Sappho's. And never has literary commentary appropriated for itself with such confidence the right to apply its conclusions to other domains, even to assume that textuality was at the center of all knowledge. The philological science, as it was defined by its founders in the late eighteenth and early nineteenth centuries, was an intellectual totality, a world unto itself that at the same time gave access to the essence of nations. In particular, philology was the tool German scholars would use to rehabilitate antiquity and reveal the Greeks as the standard for beauty, grandeur, and national genius. In the process, these scholars would guarantee for themselves a role as privileged interpreters of the essence of that genius. The dimensions of the mission philology assigned itself are evident in nineteenth-century German Sappho commentary, where the reader can expect arguments that lead well beyond Sappho's corpus, beginning with her sexuality

---

This essay was originally published in slightly different form as "Sex and Philology: Sappho and the Rise of German Nationalism," *Representations*, no. 27 (1989) 148–71.

1. Bachofen, *Myth, Religion, and Mother Right* 3.

and concluding with the foundations of Greek nationalism and the source of Greek artistic power.[2]

The founders of philology (notably the Schlegel brothers, August Wilhelm and Friedrich von Schlegel) were brought into contact with Sappho at the turn of the nineteenth century in the place Stendahl termed the "Estates-General of European opinion," Germaine de Staël's salon in exile in Switzerland. There, intellectuals from all over Europe debated the political implications of the transition from revolutionary values to Napoleonic ideology, undoubtedly using the newly coined French vocabulary of nationalism.[3] There also, because of Staël's lifelong obsession with the original woman writer, the intellectual community was introduced to two fictions of Sappho that reflected contemporary political values.[4] In the decade prior to the Revolution, French commentators had concocted a politically subversive Sappho, forced into exile after an unsuccessful revolt against a dictator, and the most tireless promoter of this vision was none other than Staël herself. During Napoleon's rise to power, an antidote to the French vision of a seditious Sappho began to be circulated, most notably in a future outpost of his empire, Italy. In the tradition initiated by Alessandro Verri's 1782 novel *Le Avventure di Saffo*, Phaon, the mythical lover presented by Ovid as the poet's downfall, replaces her at the heroic center of the Sapphic plot.[5] In this new fiction, there is no mention of Sappho's political activities; narrative energy is concentrated instead on a hypermasculinized Phaon. Authors from Verri to the fanatical Napoleon loyalist J.-B. Chaussard, whose *Fêtes et courtisanes de la Grèce* appeared in 1801, linger over the powerful beauty of Phaon's young flesh in a protofascist hymn to the male body as well-oiled machine for the domination of anyone, for example female revolutionaries, who threatens the patriarchal order.

---

2. Perhaps the most convincing testimony to the pivotal role philology intended for literature in the historico-politico-religious system it presented as the foundation of the modern nation-state, as well as its presentation of the Germans as the modern direct heirs of the Greeks, is found in Friedrich von Schlegel's study of ancient and modern literature, an origin of the discipline today called comparative literature, *Geschichte der alten und neuen Litteratur*; first English translation, *Lectures on the History of Literature, Ancient and Modern*.

3. According to Robert's *Dictionnaire de la langue française*, *nationalisme* entered French in 1798, *nationalité* in 1808.

4. One of the teenage Germaine Necker's first literary efforts in the early 1780s, "Romance to the Tune: We Loved Each Other from Childhood," is an adaptation of Ovid *Her.* 15. Her last work is the tragedy *Sapho* (published 1816).

5. Since in many, if not most, periods what was believed to be Sappho's story did not include female homosexuality, I maintain a distinction between *Sapphic* and *sapphic* and between *Sapphism* and *sapphism*. In lowercase, adjective and noun correspond to standard usage and refer to female same-sex eroticism, without necessarily implying a vision of Sappho's sexuality. In uppercase, adjective and noun convey the plot decreed for Sappho in a given period.

The group that formed around Staël at Coppet was eventually associated with the dissemination throughout Europe both of the concept of nationality as national identity and of philology as the science that defines national identities (and that would help inspire German nationalism). From about 1815 until World War II, knowledge of Sappho was diffused simultaneously, and often jointly, with philology and nationalism. Throughout this period, the issue at the heart of pan-European Sapphic speculation was Sappho's relation to the nation-state, especially the role she could be assigned in the development of (modern) national identity.

At the origin of modern Sappho scholarship can be found the invention by early philologists of the most influential theory in the history of her inter-pretation, the theory of Sappho's "chastity." Despite its evident absurdities, that conception clearly responded to a deep-seated desire on the part of nu-merous commentators, who promoted it with enthusiasm for over a century and in many cases refuse to abandon it today. In their theory of Sapphic chastity, early philologists made two surprising connections. First, yielding to an ideological attraction so powerful that it crossed the lines normally drawn both between national scholarly traditions and between high and low culture, they made the revitalized masculinity of Napoleonic nation-alist fictions a necessary correlative of the German doctrine of Sappho's chastity.[6] Second, they consistently linked discussion of Sappho's chastity to the phenomenon now most frequently referred to in German as *Knaben-liebe* (boy love) and in English as "ideal love" or "Greek love." By thus recurrently defining the parameters of their discussion, nineteenth-century German Sappho commentators (involuntarily) established a nexus of issues in which the construction of gender, the foundations of the philological science, the origins of German nationalism, and the idealization of homoeroticism were linked.

The idealized masculinity essential to Napoleonic Sapphic fictions was a product of the period that witnessed the dissemination throughout Europe of J.J. Winckelmann's aesthetic system. Surely Winckelmann's most influential contribution was his definition of Greek ideal beauty and his equation between the cult of that ideal beauty and the essence of Greek national identity. The most recent German philologist to situate Sappho in the

---

6. This affinity is all the more startling in view of the climate of military hostility that sepa-rated French and Germans in Napoleonic Europe: the first theoretician of Sapphic chastity, F. W. Welcker, enlisted twice in the campaigns against Napoleon in the years just prior to the publication of the treatise that initiated this theory, *Sappho von einem herrschenden Vorurteil befreyt*. Welcker's student and heir, perhaps the most celebrated Hellenist of the early twen-tieth century, Ulrich von Wilamowitz-Moellendorff, still comments on these sensationalistic Napoleonic fictions *as though he were dealing with serious scholarly commentaries* in his *Sappho und Simonides* (Berlin, 1913).

context of Greek ideal beauty and love, Hans Licht (Paul Brandt), proclaims Schiller's 1795 slogan from *On Naive and Sentimental Poetry*, "At that time nothing was sacred but the beautiful," as "the key to the understanding of Greek life in general."[7] Certainly these words are crucial to the understanding of what Greek life represented to the nineteenth-century German intellectual and, after the success of philology, to European intellectuals in general. And certainly in their contemporaneous volumes Schiller and Winckelmann laid the foundation for the powerful influence of philology by guaranteeing that Greek culture would play a privileged role in the creation of German national identity and values.[8]

Key terms of Winckelmann's definition of the Greek aesthetic ideal, accepted and passed down by the philologists who set the standard for Sappho commentary, can help us understand the tenaciousness of the most influential presentation of Sappho to date. Most notable is Winckelmann's privileging of the athletic young male body as the measure of the Greek aesthetic ideal. He states repeatedly that "beautiful virile youth" provides the almost exclusive model for the masterpieces of Greek art. He treats in great detail the types of male beauty glorified by the ancients, while dismissing the value of the female body as an artistic model in summary fashion: "Few observations can be made about the beauty of women."[9] Winckelmann repeatedly lingers over descriptions of the nude as the summit of Greek art, and especially over the evocation of naked youths in what he terms "schools of beauty," the gymnasium where they exercised and the stadium where they competed. He even contends that the extraordinary sensitivity to beauty that is at the origin of the greatness of Greek art resulted from Greek men having been exposed so often to the sight of the naked young male body.[10]

---

7. The Hellenist Paul Brandt wrote his 1909 study of Sappho under his own name but used the pseudonym Hans Licht to sign his 1925–28 *Sexual Life in Ancient Greece*. I cite the expanded 1932 English edition of this work (183).

8. This article is part of a study of Sappho's place in the French tradition. Because of this larger context, in citing Winckelmann I limit myself to the works available in translation to the contemporary French public.

9. Winckelmann, *Histoire de l'art chez les anciens* 374, 395.

10. See Jenkyns, *The Victorians and Ancient Greece*, esp. 132–34, on Winckelmann's belief that the Greek aesthetic sense originated with the omnipresence of male nakedness. Jenkyns suggests that Winckelmann's views, as well as those of some of the Victorians whose fascination with Greece he documents, were influenced by their homosexuality. The same argument has been put forward about almost all of the German philologists I will discuss in this article. See, for example, Ernest Borneman's judgment that Hans Licht's views of Greek culture are all colored by his homosexuality, cited by Tubach, "Female Homoeroticism in German Literature" 80. See also Stein, "The Iconography of Sappho" 197 n. 61, 319 n. 125, on Welcker's homosexuality. Whereas knowledge of the sexual orientation of these scholars does not seem irrelevant to my reasoning here, I would prefer to keep such information marginal.

The fact that Winckelmann's theory is prescriptive as well as descriptive helps account for its importance in an age of rising nationalism. He resurrects the glories of ancient art and society as a model for a new nation-state: "The only way to become great and, if possible, inimitable, is to imitate the ancients." Those who would become the new Greeks must begin by cultivating an awareness of "ideal beauty," that is, beauty that is "more" than "the most beautiful nature," beauty "in a Platonic sense." The new Greeks will be led to this ideal by "the true connoisseur," who is "capable of judging the works of the Greeks" and who, as guide to aesthetic and civic greatness, cannot simply be "knowledgeable about beauty in general." Winckelmann stops just short of saying that the beauty of female forms must be ignored; he does say that one must pay no attention to "beauty to which woman is sensitive." The true aesthetic leader can only be "touched by the beauties of our sex," that is, by the male body, "the statues of men."[11] National greatness will only be achieved if the young male body is the exclusive aesthetic ideal—and if the gaze admiring and objectifying that body is exclusively male.

The philologists who followed in Winckelmann's wake had mastered this lesson in aesthetics; certainly the bizarre circumlocutions of the work that inaugurates the modern tradition of Sappho interpretation are incomprehensible apart from it.[12] Friedrich Gottlieb Welcker's *Sappho von einem herrschenden Vorurteil befreyt* (1816) reveals a pattern that is repeated by all his followers: Welcker presents his philological argument only through a complex but seemingly inevitable excursion no longer into Winckelmann's primary subject, Greek art, but into the subjects Winckelmann had annexed to it—the origin of Greek nationalism, the primacy of the male aesthetic model—as well as into a subject only hinted at in Winckelmann's privileging of the erotic gaze of male upon male, *pederastia*.

Of the generation that inaugurated philology, Welcker is hardly the most celebrated today, but he was a true founding father with a career that covered the first half of the century and a long tenure as editor of the influential

---

In general, I agree with the position expressed by K. J. Dover in his influential study, *Greek Homosexuality*, that "the cogency of a philosophical argument, its power over the imagination, its moral and social value, and its influence over subsequent thought do not depend on the sexual orientation of its proponent" (153). In addition, for the period that concerns me here (1815–1920), the simple knowledge of an individual's own homosexual orientation does not seem sufficient to me: the degree of official persecution of homosexuality as well as the degree of personal repression of it seem to me both more relevant to the argument I will be advancing here, and in general more difficult to evaluate.

11. Winckelmann, *Recueil des différentes pièces sur les arts* 95, 99, 244.

12. On nineteenth-century German interpretations of Sappho, see Frenzel, *Stoffe der Weltliteratur*; Rüdiger, *Sappho*; and Tubach, "Female Homoeroticism in German Literature."

Rheinisches Museum für Philologie. He was also the dominant influence on Ulrich von Wilamowitz-Moellendorff, whose work spans the nineteenth and twentieth centuries and still commands respect today.[13] In the annals of Sappho scholarship, Welcker was known for more than a century as Sappho's "defender," as one who, as his work's title indicates, "freed Sappho from a reigning prejudice" in arguing for her chastity. Welcker himself never explains where or when the prejudice from which Sappho required salvation was dominant, an unfortunate omission since at no point in classical commentary or in modern interpretations before his day had a homosexual Sappho "reigned." Welcker also generally avoids naming the "prejudice" in question, although he on occasion speaks of "female homosexuality" (*Hetärisstrien*). This avoidance points to the crucial omission in his text, that of any discussion of either Sappho's homosexuality or of female sexuality in general.

Indeed, the logic behind Welcker's chastity argument is so convoluted as almost to defy reconstruction. Welcker admits that Sappho's poetry shows love for women, but he disclaims the existence of any "basely sensual," "punishable," or "reprehensible" element in that love. This claim, on which his entire theory rests, is based on no evidence more concrete than a personal conviction that "no educated Greek would have thought these were beautiful love poems if something monstrous and disgusting had been going on in them."[14] Welcker then promotes the fiction really "reigning" at the dawn of the nineteenth century, a fiction that had become accepted as much because of the influence of popular novelists such as Verri as because of Ovid's account, where, after an early marriage, Sappho becomes a young widow with a daughter and is virtuous until she meets the unfaithful Phaon. Yet Welcker never suggests—and this is the only point on which he was subsequently attacked—that Sappho wrote a poetry of heterosexual love. It is as if Sappho's real passion had engaged him as little as the forms of female beauty had interested Winckelmann—which suggests that the acceptance of male homoerotic relations in the scholarship inaugurated by Winckelmann somehow *required* the female to be asexual in the subsequent discussions of Sappho.

The subject that really does engage Welcker, the issue for which the study of Sappho serves as a pretext—whether consciously or unconsciously—is male homosexuality. Ironically, Welcker offers no new fiction or knowledge about Sappho at the same time that he formulates what seems to be the first modern defense, even eulogy, of male homosexuality, or at least of the

---

13. Welcker himself is still cited, e.g., by Page in *Sappho and Alcaeus.*
14. Welcker, *Sappho* 69; further citations will be given in parentheses in the text.

Greek practice of *pederastia*.[15] Sappho is used by Welcker to reformulate a Platonic concept important to philologists throughout the century, the distinction between a completely sensual eros and an eros that is, "if not completely devoid of sensuality, at least blameless" (15). Woman, Welcker claims, can only know the baser, sensual eros and never its higher form. The Greeks understood this and hence suppressed the possibility of Sappho's homosexuality. Welcker implies that modern readers are so feminized that they no longer know the purer, masculine eros and hence have difficulty understanding the concept of an erotics without sensuality, "not just a difference of degree but a complete break" (15). Here Welcker resurrects Winckelmann's uncontested primacy of male aesthetic values in which the philologist, as seer, is alone able to decode the language of the lost utopia and therefore to lead his contemporaries to greatness. "Only a few men," Welcker admits, will understand what he is saying, but that select few, like Winckelmann's connoisseur, keep alive the knowledge of an ethos that ennobled mankind.

Welcker shares this almost forgotten knowledge by composing a detailed rehabilitation of Greek love. Two points of his argument—that this love was so widespread that it should be understood as "an inclination particular to the Greeks," and that this bond was ennobling because it "assumed part of the character of fatherly love and took over the pedagogical role" (52)—are often simply repeated by Welcker's followers. But on at least two points Welcker was bolder than any scholar was willing to be for well over a century. First, he speaks not solely of "love of boys" (*Knabenliebe*) but interchangeably of "love of boys" and "love of men" (*Männerliebe*). He thereby implies that his argument is applicable not only to a phenomenon particular to Greek society—the bond between a mature man and a youth—but to the larger context of homoerotic relations in general. Second, Welcker refuses, unlike many of his followers, to deny completely the sensual content of "love of men" by claiming that the phenomenon existed solely for pedagogical purposes.

The boldness of his formulation is especially important in view of his conclusion. Welcker repeatedly stresses the status of male homosexuality as an essential part of what he terms the Greek "national character" (e.g., 52). He makes this claim only some twenty years after Winckelmann and Schiller had sounded the rallying cry that would echo throughout the philological tradition: the Germans will be the new Greeks and will become thereby inimitably great. Implicit in Welcker's polemic, therefore, is the argument that the Germans, in order to become the new Greeks, should adopt not

---

15. I will initially adopt the often controversial position, implicitly Welcker's, that *pederastia* can be defined as what is today known as homosexuality.

only their male-centered aesthetic model but also the sexual orientation that could explain such an aesthetic ideal.

And where is Sappho in all this? Remarkably, the scholar known as her "champion" and credited with founding modern Sappho scholarship is consistently unconcerned with the tenth Muse. His implicit reasoning is that women could never have participated in a national project as great and ennobling as "love of men." Welcker wants to demonstrate that Sappho does not offer a female variant of *Männerliebe*. This said, he never bothers to grant her a sexual orientation; she is left simply a blank, one that Welcker's disciples soon began to fill in with their attempts at characterizing Sappho.

I want to stress that no German scholar ever pointed out any deficiency in Welcker's argument; the master had spoken, and his disciples, undoubtedly in awe of his authority, simply set about continuing to "free Sappho from prejudice." In the process, they developed the initial set of arguments for Sapphic purity. In less than a decade, Johann Christian Neue published the first edition of the fragments designed to illustrate what he imagined to be Welcker's position. In his discussion of the variants to the "Ode to Aphrodite," Neue dismisses the homosexual reading of the poem that some German scholars were beginning to propose: "We would embrace this [reading of l. 24] if the accent were moved back"—as though his objection is purely technical and the question simply one of metrics uncolored by sexuality.[16] In his introduction, Neue enshrines the myth of Welcker, before whom, he claims, all had believed the "calumny" that Sappho was a "tribade," but who had demonstrated that "this monstrous desire was ... detestable to the ancients." Neue concludes his eulogy by adding a new "proof" in the Welckerian tradition of demonstration through absence of evidence: if the ancients had believed such "slander," they would never have held up Sappho, along with Diotima and Theano, as part of the "complete image of the perfect woman" (7–8). This notion of Sappho as example for womankind was soon Christianized by other disciples of Welcker, among them Johann Richter, who speaks of Sappho's "virgin purity" (*jungfräulicher Reinheit*).[17] The interpretative tradition, thus launched, had defined its central goal: the establishment of Sappho's chastity, her purity, her virginity. There is another agenda, however, in the logic of Welcker's linkage between Sappho and Greek love.

Welcker's central scholarly project (not only in his work on Sappho, but in his entire corpus) is the resurrection of *pederastia* in Greek literature. He is

---

16. Neue, *Sapphonis Mytilenaeae Fragmenta* 27; further citations will be given in parentheses in the text. Neue's position is blind but not absurd, since any convincing reconstruction of the line must be metrically accurate.

17. J. Richter, *Sappho und Erinna* 22.

afraid that Sappho will be labeled a homosexual—not, however, because he fears this stain on her reputation but because he fears that *pederastia* will be contaminated and weakened by association with a female figure. He cannot go so far as to add a new "calumny" by strengthening Sappho's association to the basely sensual heterosexual eros, but he does not intend to proclaim her chaste. Welcker's followers are guilty of a double misreading, however, when they attempt to demonstrate Sappho's "virgin purity" and at the same time proclaim the complete spirituality of *pederastia*. In other words, the association between Sappho and Greek love in Welcker leads, with them, to a double overreaction that eventually cuts off both Sapphism and *pederastia* from sensuality.

Indeed, after Welcker only one influential German theorist dares proclaim the physicality of Greek love. In his 1837 *Paederastia*, M. H. E. Meier attacks both those who condemn homosexuality *and* "those singular minds" who have invented "apologetic theories in order to idealize and glorify" this love.[18] Meier does not deny either the central role played by *pederastia* in Greek society or the particular character of Greek love. On the contrary, he contends that "the strange mixture of materiality and spirituality" has never existed elsewhere (7). However, Meier refuses to see idealization as the price of glorification, sublimation as the cost of sublimity. He alone offers a pragmatic reading of the Platonic version of *pederastia*. Homosexuality existed, so Socrates gave it a central role to play in his project of "perfecting human nature." This meant neither that, as post-Welckerian philologists habitually contended, Socrates saw eros only as "a method of moral instruction" nor that he felt that pederastic relations could be sexually chaste (123–25). "It is wrong to believe that, even in its noblest forms, the love that the Greeks had for boys was something exclusively spiritual, a purely aesthetic satisfaction in the presence of beauty." Meier alone develops the hint of sensuality present in Welcker; he alone refuses the connoisseur theory that those who do not have special knowledge of the Greeks are unable to understand it; and he alone refuses to divorce *pederastia* from modern practice: "The spiritual elements of this affection were always mixed with a highly sensual element, the pleasure inspired by the physical beauty of the beloved; lovers then did not evaluate this beauty any differently than they would judge female beauty today" (18).

---

18. Meier, *Histoire de l'amour grec*. The most influential German commentaries on *pederastia* were always translated. Probably because Meier openly asserts the sensuality of homosexuality, his study only appeared in French a century later. Further citations will be given in parentheses in the text.

In this debate over the nature of male erotic experience in antiquity, some readers will recognize the opposing positions in the current controversy about the existence of a pre-nineteenth-century tradition that can be characterized by the nineteenth-century word *homosexual*. The issue, in David Halperin's formulation, is "first of all, how to recover the terms in which the experiences of individuals belonging to past societies were actually constituted and, second, how to measure and assess the differences between those terms and the ones we currently employ."[19] Contemporary opposing views of this issue are represented most notably, on the one hand, by K. J. Dover and John Boswell, who believe that pederasty should be considered part of a homosexual tradition.[20] On the other hand, Jeffrey Weeks and others such as Halperin contend that, in Weeks's words, "clear lesbian and gay identities" have recently been developed for the first time, a development that has its roots in late-nineteenth-century capitalism, at the time when the sexologists' commentaries on sexual practices gave homosexuality "potentially the embryo of an identity."[21]

However, if we take a long-range view of the current controversy and situate it in the context of the speculation that led to the development of the sexologists' position on homosexuality, it may be possible to mediate somewhat between the two positions. At the very least, an examination of key texts of nineteenth-century German commentary on ideal love illuminates the origin of the widespread fin de siècle medical curiosity, verging on the obsessional, about homosexuality. The German philologists' conception of ideal love, which set both Sappho scholarship and the discussion of Greek homoerotic relations on a resolutely binary course, moreover, has continued to be the subject of debate. Michel Foucault has argued that the relations between sexuality, sexual abstinence, and access to truth were formulated by the Greeks with reference to "boy love," whereas Christianity reformulated these questions with reference to heterosexuality, and the nineteenth century—he gives the example of Goethe's "eternal feminine"— finally linked them to "love of woman, her virginity, her purity, her fall, and her redemptive power."[22]

Goethe's contemporaries, however, formulate "boy love" as the male counterpart of the eternal feminine, purified of the fall. They thereby decree, as it were, the existence of the countertradition that will define homosexuality as a sin, a perversion. The medical tradition that originated in Germany in the mid-nineteenth century, and that culminated in such syntheses as Richard

19. Halperin, "One Hundred Years of Homosexuality" 34–45, 38.

20. Dover, *Greek Homosexuality*; Boswell, *Christianity, Social Tolerance, and Homosexuality*.

21. Weeks, *Sexuality and Its Discontents* 92.

22. Foucault, *L'Usage des plaisirs* 27, 251–52.

Krafft Ebing's *Psychopathia Sexualis* (1888) and Havelock Ellis's *Studies in the Psychology of Sex* (1897), defines homosexuality, male and female, as a "rare and possibly diseased form of access to pleasure,"[23] an illness it rebaptizes "sexual inversion." The abundant recent literature on homosexuality generally considers this the original tradition of scholarly treatment of homosexuality. Those who grant the greatest power to the literature of perversion—I think most notably of Lillian Faderman and Weeks—trace the modern notion of homosexuality to the late nineteenth century and attribute a formative role to the commentary on sexual inversion. The dictionary conspires to lend credence to this view: the *Oxford English Dictionary* credits C. G. Chaddock with having introduced *homosexual* into English in 1892 in his translation of Krafft-Ebing.[24]

But the dictionary is wrong. *Homosexual* appears to have first been used in English by John Addington Symonds, who speaks of "homosexual relations" in *A Problem in Greek Ethics*, a text available at least as early as 1883.[25] This detail is of significance only because Symonds, even though his study is subsequently included as an appendix to Ellis, really writes as a representative of the ideal love tradition. It is surely no accident that this tradition has almost been effaced from the history of homosexuality by many recent historians, to such an extent that Boswell feels obliged to develop at some length an argument that concludes, "If the term *homosexual* has any significance at all, it clearly includes relations between men and boys no less than between men and men or boys and boys"—and to such an extent that Halperin contends that it is still to be decided whether "Athenian pederasty is primarily a matter for philological investigation."[26] But let us return to the nineteenth-century

23. Lanteri-Laura, *Lecture des perversions* 32.

24. The word is only granted admission in the 1933 supplement to the *OED*. For more information on the medical tradition, see Lanteri-Laura, *Lecture des perversions*. See Chauncey, "Female Deviance," and Faderman, *Surpassing the Love of Men*, on the literature of sexual inversion.

25. In the introduction to the edition I consulted, Symonds says that he wrote *A Problem in Greek Ethics, Being an Inquiry into the Phenomenon of Sexual Inversion* in 1873 and that the text was first published in 1883. I have found no trace of the 1883 edition in national library catalogues. Boswell, *Christianity, Social Tolerance, and Homosexuality* 17 n. 25, states that the work was originally "privately printed" in 1873, but I have found no trace of an 1873 edition. The work must have been available before it was included, without the consent of Symonds's executor, in Ellis's 1897 *Studies in the Psychology of Sex*. Symonds also uses *homosexual* in *A Problem in Modern Ethics* (1891); see Boswell 42 n. 4. According to the *Dictionnaire de la langue du dix-neuvième et du vingtième siècle*, the word was first used in German in 1869 by K. Kertbeny (pseudonym K. M. Benkert). Alain Corbin claims that the word first appeared in French in 1809, but he gives no information about this otherwise undocumented occurrence; Corbin et al., *Histoire de la vie privée* 4:587.

26. Boswell, *Christianity, Social Tolerance, and Homosexuality* 28; Halperin, "One Hundred Years of Homosexuality" 44.

philological tradition to see how it succeeded in decreeing the virginity of both *pederastia* and Sappho and in making them "primarily matter[s] for philological investigation," and how in the process it pushed those who refused to deny the sensuality of homoeroticism to view it as diseased.

With the generation of 1820, philology came into its own and was able to consolidate some fifty years of work, to make good on its claim of being an intellectual totality, that is, of using the study of language to reach the essence of nations. At the forefront of this generation stood <u>Karl Otfried Müller, Welcker</u>'s successor at Göttingen, whose syntheses of Greek culture were quickly translated. Müller establishes all the patterns that dominate the nineteenth-century scholarly vision of Sappho: he devotes separate studies to her and to *pederastia* and he uses parallel arguments when asserting their chastity. Yet when read together, Müller's history of the Dorians (1820–24), a foundation of the ideal love tradition, and his history of Greek literature (1841) make it plain that, when both become "matters for philological investigation," Sapphic passion will be purified but never glorified like *pederastia*.[27]

In Müller's history of the Dorians, which established his scholarly reputation, he proposes that civilization as the model for the Greek genius and *pederastia* as the origin of that genius. Müller contends that he will not examine Greek love from a "moral point of view" (2:306), but he then attempts to prove that it is a phenomenon without moral content: *pederastia* must not be confused with "the vice to which in its name and outward form it is so nearly allied" (2:310). The custom he is characterizing belongs to the domain of nationalism and pedagogy: precisely, therefore, the domain of philology. Müller provides the kind of detailed description of the pedagogical function of *pederastia* as a tool for civic and military values that is missing from Welcker's polemic. He traces the origin, the spread, and the official "encouragement" of Greek love "in the race of all the Greeks the most distinguished for its healthy, temperate, and even ascetic habits" (2:311), and he does so with a moderation absent from Welcker's more propagandistic text.

But when Müller subsequently turns to literature, the eulogy begins. In addition, he strengthens the bond between Sapphic purity and *pederastia* in his presentation of Sappho, in what is probably the most influential history of Greek literature in the nineteenth century. In his discussion of lyric poetry Müller, as we will see, flagrantly privileges Alceus, especially Alceus's erotic (homosexual) poetry. He has hardly begun his presentation of Sappho before he launches into a discussion of a poem then still unknown

---

27. Müller, *The History and Antiquities of the Doric Race* and *Histoire de la littérature grecque*. I cite the English translation of the former because the work was revised and expanded for this edition; further citations will be given in parentheses in the text.

except for a reference in Herodotus (it subsequently turned up in the early-twentieth-century papyri discoveries), in which she scolds her brother for his relation with the courtesan Rhodopis. It quickly becomes evident why Müller elects this aberrant introduction: Sappho's alleged moral "severity" in the conjectured poem "allows us to determine the principles that she followed in her own life.... The conscience of a young girl of *immaculate* honor raised with modesty is ... plainly evident in the lines" (1:356, my emphasis). Having thus established Sappho's immaculateness on the basis of an unknown poem, Müller proceeds to unveil her "innocent artlessness" in poems of more certain provenance. The "Ode to Aphrodite" is a youthful effort, and even then she wrote to the goddess rather than the man; when she was older, she sent men away. The fragments addressed to women were composed for the "association" she directed whose object was to promote music and poetry.

Just how uninspired Müller's reading of Sappho really is becomes evident as soon as it is compared with his treatment of Alceus. There he expresses at length his regret that we do not have more of Alceus's erotic poetry: "What charming thoughts ... natural and true, the poetry Alceus addressed to beautiful adolescents must have contained.... These erotic poems revealed no trace of an effeminate sybarite, a libertine only thinking of sensual pleasures. One saw throughout them the vigorous man ... and the tumult of war and political struggle formed their background" (1:349–50). The passage ends with Müller's strongest explicit formulation of his admiration for *pederastia* as "noble love." Indeed, much of his consideration of Alceus is really a Welckerian eulogy, with more emphasis on the bond between Greek love and military capabilities. The pretext of describing the content of poems now lost to us allows Müller to define *pederastia* as a virile relation cleansed of eroticism by the instruction of manly virtue.

For Müller, because Sappho's poetry provides no instruction in the acquisition of virility it is unworthy of the official sanction of either the Greek state or the German philologists who are its modern interpreters. This means finally that Sappho's poems will essentially not be read or discussed, beyond perfunctory remarks about her candor and ingenuous frankness, by the philologists who claim to understand her essence. A brief look at two of the most respected philologists of the early twentieth century is sufficient to demonstrate how Müller's conjectural reading was preserved intact for the next century.[28]

---

28. Perhaps the clearest lesson I learned from the study of four centuries of Sappho scholarship is never to underestimate the power of tradition. Once a theory had gained authority, commentators were immensely reluctant to reject it.

Paul Brandt, like Müller, devotes separate studies to the tenth Muse and to *pederastia*. His 1905 *Sappho* is remarkably close to Müller's 1841 presentation. Sapphic friendship is initially justified with a description of "the noble bonds of friendship" between men and boys that "are bound up with essence of the Greek being," yet Brandt's only justifications of how Sappho's poetry plays a role in the ennobling enterprise he is describing are his vague claims that it is full of "delight in nature" and that her "songs" to Atthis are "higher hymns full of majesty."[29] Brandt never confronts the difficulty of reconciling a poetry that praises the female body with the type of sublimating aesthetic his own work glorifies, that is, one that considers the male body the aesthetic norm: "The Greeks knew nothing of the tyrannical law that saw beauty only in women," Brandt proclaims at the outset.[30]

Brandt's project, more than others, raises the possibility that Sappho may have functioned as a smoke screen against censorship for the apologists of ideal love. When Brandt published his full-blown eulogy of *pederastia* some twenty years later, he did so only under the pseudonym "Hans Licht," even though his position in *Sexual Life in Ancient Greece* is no bolder than that earlier expressed under his own name, if more likely to attract attention because of his work's announced subject matter. Licht's study is initially puzzling because of his refusal to recognize his precursors. He contends that to date the Greek pederast had been less studied than the hetaera, so that the reader unfamiliar with Greek sources would have the idea "that Greek homosexuality was a subsidiary phenomenon," whereas Licht—the initiate, the connoisseur—knows it to be, on the contrary, "*the* key to the understanding of the whole Greek culture."[31]

Indeed, Licht's monumental study is geared less to the presentation of the history of sexuality than to the demonstration of this sweeping axiom. His concluding sentence, for example, offers the most common defense of *pederastia* used throughout the ideal love tradition: "But anyone who is able to set himself free in the spirit from modern views, and to penetrate with unprejudiced mind into the thoughts of these ancient peoples, will comprehend the lofty ethics of the Hellenes, whose highest ideal expresses

29. Brandt, *Sappho* 9, 47, 35.

30. Ibid., 9. Directly related to this question of the gender of the aesthetic norm is the status of Sappho's person. Philologists often stressed the description, widely accepted in antiquity, of the tenth Muse as small, dark, and ugly—the opposite, in other words, of the Aryan physical type. Poliakov, *The Aryan Myth* 190 ff., traces the beginning of the Aryan myth to the period during which philology and the cult of *pederastia* also are initiated. Indeed, no less important an originator of philology than Friedrich von Schlegel is identified by Poliakov as the origin of the Aryan myth.

31. Licht [Brandt], *Sexual Life in Ancient Greece* 412–13. Further citations will be given in parentheses in the text.

itself in 'the beautiful both in body and soul' " (525). It is only in the chapter devoted to "Perversions of Greek Sexual Life," however, that the explanation for Licht's attempt to divorce himself from the philological tradition becomes clear: here he contests the view that Greek homosexuality "at least" should be considered part of the domain of *psychopathia sexualis* (499). Licht provides the only contemporary evidence that philologists were aware of the usurpation of their authority over the history of homosexuality by the new school of medical morbidity.

Licht responds to the German medical tradition with perhaps the strongest formulation ever made of ideal love as virile nationalism, an argument of seemingly guaranteed appeal in Germany between the wars. Licht's rhetoric seems directed at those who sought to renew Germany's prestige by restoring its military capabilities: "Everything that created for the Greeks a civilization that will be admired as long as the world exists has its roots in the unexampled ethical valuation of the masculine character in public and private life" (440); "The love of boys was not persecuted, but fostered, to become the power that maintained the State and upheld the foundation of Greek ethics" (441); "We are indebted to their heroic lovers ... for Europe's freedom" (434). But in an atmosphere in which homosexuality had been officially recast as "sexual psychopathy," the philologist no longer attached his name to this program for renewed national grandeur through the promotion of virile pederasty. And once "the unexampled ethical valuation of the masculine character" had become the clearly formulated goal of the ideal love tradition, Sappho's usefulness was over.

The culmination of the philological representation of Sappho, the study destined to carry the nineteenth-century vision over into her depiction in twentieth-century erudition, exposes Sappho's fate once it is divorced from that of ideal love. Ulrich von Wilamowitz-Moellendorff's 1913 *Sappho und Simonides*, dedicated "to the memory of Friedrich Gottlieb Welcker," shows how far the heir of the nineteenth-century tradition is prepared to go in order to reduce the story of the tenth Muse to her chastity. Even though by the early twentieth century Phaon had been dismissed by most scholars as a legendary figure whose fate had, by mistake or by design, been entwined with Sappho's, Wilamowitz nearly resurrects Aphrodite's boatman as what he clearly considers the ultimate proof of Sappho's chastity, that is, her freedom from the sin of lesbianism. The love she felt for the beloved girls who were pupils in her school did have a sexual component, but it was never realized since it was understood that the girls were to be married. Sappho herself led the way for them by falling for Phaon. As soon as Wilamowitz evokes Phaon, however, as though sensing the outlandishness of this scholarly backsliding, he retreats into a position already proposed by Müller: "Whoever first spoke of Sappho's love for Phaon conveyed her nature so truly and so beautifully as though in a picture."[32] The philologist is free to act as though Phaon had existed because he is fulfillment of the philological science's privileged understanding of Sappho's nature, the "true" and "beautiful" image of her heterosexuality.

In fact, Wilamowitz is not content simply to promote Sapphic heterosexuality. He sees marriage, the ceremony that would seal the respectability of her pedagogical establishment, where it had never been suspected before. Thus fragment 31 becomes a poem about the preparations for the wedding of one of Sappho's beloved students, and the man in the ode is presented as the girl's husband (54 ff.). And with the accumulated authority of a century of philology behind them, Wilamowitz's views came to dominate the twentieth-century official vision of Sappho, to such an extent that in 1955 Denys Page still feels obliged to devote the most extensive section of his commentary on fragment 31 to a scornful dismissal of the scenario imagined by Welcker's heir.[33]

Thus Wilamowitz finally manages to confine Sappho to the status philology had wanted for her for a century. The purpose of her pedagogy was to prepare girls for marriage, to fuel the official institution whose existence interests the philologists only insofar as it is needed to produce new citizens. Witness the conclusion of Licht's *Sexual Life*, in which he presents *pederastia* and marriage as unions whose complementarity was recognized by a state that sanctioned "love of boys" as a "necessary supplement" to marriage, a supplement undoubtedly made necessary by the inability of any union with a woman to ennoble her partner and make him thereby the heroic warrior citizen. Philology's passion for Sappho could be laid to rest once a place had been found for her in the nationalistic program for civic virtue. Wilamowitz finally manages to take account of the similarity first formulated by Maximus of Tyre—"The love of Sappho . . . was surely the same as the art of love practiced by Socrates"—without according her any share in the unique and essential Greek pedagogical enterprise. Sappho is granted status as "an immortal woman," if it is accepted that she won immortality by defending the modern patriarchal view of the importance of virginity. by watching over in her role as "teacher of the Lesbian virgins" (71) the chastity of future mothers of beloved boys.

Among nineteenth-century German thinkers, only J. J. Bachofen, in his 1861 *Myth, Religion, and Mother Right*, attempts to resensualize the virginal Sapphic body. Bachofen alone seeks to establish a parallel behind the recurrent pairing of Sappho and ideal love by making Sapphism the result, and in some sense the fulfillment, of *pederastia*. The goal of the sexual political

---

32. Wilamowitz, *Sappho und Simonides* 60. Further citations will be given in parentheses in the text.

33. Page, *Sappho and Alcaeus* 30 ff.

history Bachofen traces often seems a familiar tale of the ennobling powers of a politicoaesthetic institution: the "ultimate form" in the development of classical history is the "Apollonian purity" of "the paternal system of Athens."[34] Even his "Lesbos" section initially appears to be only the ideal love theory enriched with exotic elements. He recounts the legend that traces the poetic genius of Lesbian women to the friendly welcome they gave Orpheus's head when it arrived singing on Lesbos. Orpheus, prophet of Apollo, had proclaimed the importance of "masculine loves"[35] as "an ethical transcending of the lower Eros" that "raises man ... to a higher stage of existence" (203). When the women of Lesbos begin to follow "the Orphic life," they initiate "a higher spiritual development which culminated in Sappho and her circle." Bachofen pronounces this "love of women for their own sex" "equivalent" to the Orphic masculine love by which it was inspired (204). Since Bachofen alone grants Sapphism equal status, it is in his description of its function that we can measure his independence from the ideal love tradition.

After a familiar beginning—"Here again the sole purpose was to transcend the lower sensuality, to make physical beauty into a purified psychic beauty"—we find a new pedagogical justification for same-sex love when Sappho is portrayed as a protofeminist: "Her task was to elevate and educate her sex" (205). We also find a new vocabulary of religious "enthusiasm," almost of spiritual frenzy: Sappho's "enthusiasm" "*seized* upon the sensuous"; "Eros *drove* her to all [the Lesbian maidens]"; "Wherever she found physical beauty, Eros *impelled* her to create spiritual beauty as well" (204–5, my emphases). The cool sublimation of Müller's heroic lovers has been replaced by Bachofen's vision of Sappho as a wildly driven, mad priestess of Aphrodite—and of doctrines more mysterious still. Because of the place he accords Sappho and female powers, Bachofen's reading goes against the grain of the philological tradition. The Lesbos section of *Myth, Religion, and Mother Right* culminates in a eulogy, not of the powers of sublimation, but of the force of "woman's sublimity," "a consequence of her relation to the hidden doctrine" and "the source of her enthusiasm" (206). Sappho becomes a repository of Pythagorean mysteries and attains immortality not for her chastity but for her access to doctrines hidden from men.

34. Bachofen, *Myth, Religion, and Mother Right* 76. Further citations will be given in parentheses in the text.

35. Bachofen and his editors perform a similar dance around the term to be used here. He switches from German to Greek and uses *arrenes erōtes*; the German editors add in brackets "die Männerlieben." In the English edition, the term is initially given in Greek, a literal version of "male loves," and translated in parentheses (incorrectly) as "male homosexuality." This multilingual rite of onomastic avoidance may originate with Bachofen's implicit desire to position himself at a slight angle from commentary on *Knabenliebe*.

The fulfillment of Bachofen's vision of a resensualized Sappho may well be found in the texts of the one individual whose work truly spans both nineteenth-century traditions of commentary on homoeroticism, the ideal love school and the school of medical morbidity. John Addington Symonds follows the philological model in a number of ways, the most obvious being his composition of parallel studies of Sappho (in *Studies of the Greek Poets*) and *pederastia*. *A Problem in Greek Ethics*, written in 1873 and gradually made public over the next twenty-five years, parallels Bachofen's attempt to add mysticism to the philologist's concept of ideal love as sublimation. For the most part, Symonds merely replicates the arguments proposed by the philologists to portray *pederastia* as a program for noble virility, in his formulation "closely associated with liberty, manly sports, severe studies, self-sacrifice, self-control and deeds of daring."[36] However, Symonds refuses to follow them in their denial of the sensuality of what his near-contemporary sensualizer Bachofen calls "male loves": he distinguishes at some length between what he terms "heroic love" on the model of Achilles and Patroclus—which, he contends, "existed as an ideal rather than as an actual reality" (4)—and what he terms "Greek love," defined as a mixture of "heroic and vulgar" love (7–8). Furthermore, in his conclusion Symonds forces his reader to question the degree to which an acceptance of male sexuality would affect the comprehension of female sexuality.

Like other commentaries on ideal love, Symonds's has a strange structure, as though it bore conscious marks of its author's fear of censorship, or unconscious marks of his self-censorship. This perhaps most exhaustive eulogy of Greek love ends with three brief sections: on "The Relation of Paiderastia to Greek Art," on female homosexuality in Greece, and a final section in which Symonds reviews the development of history, and not just the history of homosexuality, from Greece to "modern times" in three short paragraphs. Symonds's discussion of the centrality of Greek love to the Greek "esthetic morality" (69) is still straight out of the philological tradition and in no way hints at the surprises he holds in reserve for his last four pages. The next section has become such a commonplace in subsequent histories of Greek homosexuality that it would be easy to skip over it, too: Symonds explains that it is difficult to assess its importance, not because "homosexual love between females" did not exist, but because "feminine homosexual passions were never worked into the social system, never became educational and military agents" (71). Symonds does not state, as more recent authors do, that the absence of institutional status would explain the absence of documents; he seems only interested in separating, in the best philological

---

36. Symonds, *A Problem in Greek Ethics* 44. Further citations will be given in parentheses in the text.

manner, female sexuality from male and in classifying it as less important, "unhonored" (72). Rather than explain this section away on the basis of its similarities with subsequent commentary, however, I would like to explore the strangeness of Symonds's brief innovation—which may well contain the first usage in English of the female form of *homosexual*.[37]

On several occasions Symonds points out what he considers the "parallelism" between "the two Platonic conceptions of love," that is, *pederastia* and the "chivalrous enthusiasm for women" (see, e.g., 54–55). The notion that chivalry marked the continuation of ideal love becomes more than an implication only in the enigmatically elliptical final section: "Greek love did not exist at Rome—Christianity—Chivalry—The *modus vivendi* of the modern world." Throughout his study, Symonds develops his arguments with great care, more carefully than any member of the ideal love school. At the end, however, he adopts the jump-cut progression of his precursors for this review of the history of sexuality after Greece: the Romans of the Decadence corrupted Greek love to mere "lust" and thereby provoked the early Christians to cut man off from tainted "nature" by pronouncing a mind-body dualism and to confine woman to "the convent." But escape to the convent was not the answer, for redemption was to come now from woman, a "truth" "for the first time truly apprehended" by "the Teutonic converts to the Christian faith." This idea was a nineteenth-century commonplace, but Symonds's final sentences reveal the innovation of his *pederastia* / chivalry comparison: "The mythology of Mary gave religious sanction to the chivalrous enthusiasm; and a cult of woman sprang into being to which, although it was romantic and visionary, we owe the spiritual basis of our domestic and civil life. The *modus vivendi* of the modern world was found" (73).

With this flourish comes to an abrupt halt the work that has been referred to as "the first thorough account of [homosexuality in ancient Greece] in English,"[38] the work that seems to have made *homosexual* an English word. Symonds's study marks at the same time the ne plus ultra of the ideal love tradition and the revitalizing of the Sappho tradition. The price eventually paid for the recuperation of Greek homosexuality as ennobling love was

37. The section's title, "Sexual Inversion Among Greek Women," repeats the hesitation with regard to onomastic innovation evident at the study's outset. In his title, Symonds calls male homosexuality "sexual inversion," a term borrowed from the sexologists rarely found in his text. The linguistic dichotomy may signal either a simple reluctance to coin a noun based on an adjective only just created in Germany, or a decision to use the at least slightly more familiar term in the title and the (preferred) neologism in the text. In any event, Symonds simply shifts immediately from *sexual inversion* to *homosexual* in his first page (as he does in the opening paragraph of his section on female homosexuality) without calling attention to his innovative use of neologisms.

38. Boswell, *Christianity, Social Tolerance, and Homosexuality* 17.

to deny homosexuality any life after classical Greece. Outside the Greek ethical aesthetics, Symonds implies, homosexuality can only be corrupted to "lust." Unlike the philologists, Symonds has no message about the implicit revival of male same-sex love necessary to create a race of "new Greeks"; he proposes only the relatively innocuous recuperation of Greek homosexuality as a "noble synthesis" that can never be made to function as it once did. Yet Symonds does implicitly suggest a modern continuation of the idealizing sublimation necessary for *pederastia*. In an act of homage more reminiscent of Bachofen than of any other nineteenth-century German thinker, Symonds implies that the modern pederast-homosexual worships at the shrine of the ultimate in female mysticism or chivalric womanhood, the Virgin Mary.

Moreover, the strange unfolding of Symonds's argument suggests a second way in which the potential of the ideal love tradition may be realized. When he glides from the aesthetic value of *pederastia* to sapphism to the Virgin Mary, Symonds establishes a rhythm whereby Sappho—chaste in a Bachofenian rather than a Welckerian manner—finally assumes the role that the philologists had implicitly assigned her all along, as precursor of the Virgin Mary. By the same progression, "homosexual passions among females," in a move the attentive reader of the philological speculation on ideal love may have anticipated for some time, become central to the "*modus vivendi* of the modern world." I believe that the possibility of this conflation of the ancient and the modern formulations of the relation between sexuality and access to truth had been all along at the root of philologists' attempts to dissociate Sappho from homosexuality: in the age of the "eternal feminine," Sappho, and no longer those Symonds calls "the heroic lovers," was the logical center of a cult of sublimated homosexuality. The enormously elliptical presentation of Symonds's final sections makes it impossible to determine just how far he intended to carry this line of reasoning. But we must not forget that, unlike more recent commentators on male homosexuality in ancient Greece who must feel that at least a nod in the direction of women is mandatory, Symonds was not obliged to recreate the philological bond between Sappho and *pederastia*. Furthermore, the juxtaposition of the only two female figures in his study invites the reader to compare Sappho and the Virgin Mary.

With *A Problem in Greek Ethics*, Symonds becomes part of an unexpected movement by which the philologists' theories, so marked by the German nationalism that crested during World War II, were co-opted—and feminized—by an interconnected group of fin de siècle decadents in England and France who tried to realize Symonds's conclusion that Sapphism is the "*modus vivendi* of the modern world." Thus for his defense at his 1895 trial, Oscar Wilde evokes the classic topoi of ideal love theorists—David and Jonathan (the "modern" Achilles and Patroclus) and Plato. Pierre Louÿs, who corrected the French for Wilde's *Salomé*, dedicated the *Chansons de Bilitis*, the fiction that drove Wilamowitz to a frenzied attack, "to the young women of the future society," a dedication that soon became a battle cry for the first female commentators on Sappho, the members of the movement known as "Sapho 1900," in proclaiming both their feminism and their homosexuality.

This milieu also generated what Bram Dijkstra terms a "relatively rare explicit early treatment of lesbianism," that 1864 *Sappho and Erinna in the Garden of Mytilene* by Simeon Solomon, who moved in the same circles as Swinburne and Symonds.[39] This lush garden scene is among the few unequivocally homoerotic depictions of Sappho at any time, the only visual representation, to my knowledge, of the poet actively initiating an embrace with another woman. Judith Stein cites William Gaunt's testimony that Solomon's drawings of Antinous and of Sappho decorated the Oxford rooms of the initiates in the 1860s.[40] This suggests that, perhaps under Symonds's influence, Sappho had already assumed the role of patron saint of modern (homo)sexuality that is forecast for her at the end of *A Problem in Greek Ethics*, and that the peaceful cohabitation that Symonds predicts between the ideal beloved boy and the poet who immortalized her beloved girls had already become at least an iconographic reality. The juxtaposition of Sappho and Antinous in Symonds's circle may also imply an invocation of her patronage for a modern renewal of *pederastia*. Sapphism, as K. J. Dover correctly stresses, differs from the pederastic model in a major way: it replaces "the usual distinction [in *pederastia*] between a dominant and a subordinate partner" with "a marked degree of mutual eros."[41] This mutual eros could explain Sapphism's attraction for Symonds, who, in his finale to *A Problem in Greek Ethics*, may have wanted to suggest its attraction for a homoerotic "future society" rather than attempt still another evocation of the redemptive value of sublimation typical of ideal love commentary.

The proof that this position is implicit in the philological presentation of Sappho was supplied some seventeen years before Symonds wrote by no less than the man who forged the link between Sappho and ideal love, Welcker. For decades, Welcker had received only praise for the "salvation" of Sappho, and his simple rejection of female homosexuality had been amplified into a theory of Sappho's "virgin purity." Suddenly he came under attack from an outsider, an Englishman always identified as "the Colonel," William Mure.[42] In his history of Greek literature, Mure devotes a major part of the entry

---

39. Dijkstra, *Idols of Perversity* 153. When Swinburne proclaimed Sappho "the greatest poet who ever was at all" (*Letters* 4:124), he echoed the exceptional status that Symonds, unlike German ideal love theorists, accorded her poetry in *Studies of the Greek Poets*.

40. Stein, "Iconography of Sappho" 296–97.

41. Dover, *Greek Homosexuality* 177.

42. Mure, *A Critical History of the Language and Literature of Ancient Greece*; "Sappho" in vol. 3.

on Sappho to a refutation of the ideal love/chastity theory on the grounds
that its proponents were naively trying to cover up the existence of female
homosexuality in general and Sappho's double homo- and heterosexual
promiscuity in particular. In his response, Welcker disdains Mure for having
tried to attribute to German scholars opinions that "even in England no
one could ever believe they had expressed."[43] Welcker is prepared to deny
that any German had ever even implied, much less openly argued, that
Sappho was chaste. He feels obliged to jettison this byproduct of his 1816
study in an effort to win an absolute victory for what is now shown to be
the essential proposition for him, the chastity of *pederastia*. He is prepared
therefore to condemn Sappho to heterosexual lust—anything to keep her
off the territory of heroic male sexuality and to guarantee the sublimity
and the sublimation of that sexuality: "Surely a task far more difficult than
the theologian's of converting someone who cannot believe in God and
immortality is the task of the philologist of bringing over to his own views
someone who is determined not to believe in that state of falling-in-love
which does not dream of unchastity."[44]

The theologian-philologist resorts to a triple negation to retain his power
over the mysteries of ideal love, a syntactic weakness that exposes the extent
to which philology had allowed its authority to become bound up with the
definition of this conception. Behind Welcker's determined resistance to
Sappho lay from the beginning the realization that she had the power to
become the mystical, redemptive Virgin who would preside over much of fin
de siècle decadence. Once Sappho had been empowered by a connection
to chastity, the relation between sexuality and access to truth formulated
by the Greeks and the philologists with reference to "boy love" could be
transferred to her. Chastity was a powerful attribute for the century that
finalized the cult of Mary as pure virgin when the Immaculate Conception
became dogma in 1854.

The most original and compelling late-nineteenth- and early-twentieth-
century visions of Sappho are all related to this rebellion against philology
that created the chaste priestess of sensuality. This does not mean, however,
that philology's authority was broken. On the contrary, until virtually the
mid-twentieth century, the most respected Hellenists everywhere preached
the pure doctrine of German philology, despite the decreasing frequency
of powerful philological arguments for ideal love after the mid-nineteenth
century.[45] Both the French and the English, after Colonel Mure's skirmish

43. Welcker, "Über die beiden Oden der Sappho" 236.

44. Ibid. Though Welcker had previously waffled about the status of Phaon, he now
resurrects Aphrodite's boatman to guarantee Sappho's heterosexuality.

45. What I term the pure doctrine of philology with respect to *Knabenliebe* continues to
be preached today, virtually without alteration. See the two most recent studies, Patzer's

with the formidable Welcker, fell into the German line, so that by the time the turn-of-the-century papyri discoveries made Sappho the object of renewed attention, her purity had been universally decreed.

The English philological tradition, following the German, supplied proofs for the chastity theory with a zeal that went far beyond that of its originator. J. M. Edmonds's commentary is a perfect example of the English tradition of reading Sappho's poetry to show why it could not be the product of a "bad" woman.[46] But my favorite examples of this interpretative style are from the work of an American, David Robinson, in his 1924 study of Sappho, which is still widely cited today. Robinson—and I hasten to stress that his reasoning is only slightly more ludicrous than that common in all national scholarly traditions for decades under the influence of the chastity theory—devotes page after page to a demonstration of why homosexuality and Sappho's poetry are irreconcilable. Exercising utmost restraint, I will permit myself only one pared-down example from a vast stock:

> It is against the nature of things that a woman who has given herself up to unnatural practices which . . . throw the soul into disorder . . . should be able to write in perfect obedience to the laws of vocal harmony. . . . Sappho's love of flowers, moreover, affords another luminous testimony. A bad woman might love roses, but a bad woman does not love the small and hidden wild flowers of the field as Sappho did.[47]

Robinson finally makes explicit the often implicit philological position that sexuality is an affair of metrics: moral corruption (homosexuality) is incompatible with metrical perfection.

Not the least of Welcker's dubious accomplishments is the way in which he set the terms according to which the history of Sappho scholarship was written. In his wake and at least until the 1930s, all those who followed his point of view and proclaimed either Sappho's chastity or her lukewarm heterosexuality are known as Sappho's "defenders," while those who believed in her homosexuality are known, if not as her attackers, as those who "calumniate" her. Under the influence of the myth of philology—that the study of Greek, made scientific, would permit the perfect recovery of Greek genius—Sappho's modern history was limited to the theory of her chastity, and "*the* tradition" of Sappho scholarship allowed into its ranks only those

---

Die griechische Knabenliebe and Sergent's *L'homosexualité initiatique dans l'Europe ancienne.* Sergent still repeats what is essentially Wilamowitz's view of Sappho's school preparing virgins for marriage.

46. Edmonds, *Sappho in the Added Light of the New Fragments.*

47. Robinson, *Sappho and Her Influence* 44–45. See also Edmonds, *Sappho in the Added Light* 25–26, on Sappho's love of flowers. The enthusiastic persistence with which this argument is evoked by Anglo-American scholars has made me wonder if scholarly traditions inevitably repeat clichés of national characteristics.

who proclaimed this doctrine. From the late nineteenth century to the eve of World War II, the debate on Sapphism must have seemed to the reigning philologists to have been concluded.

The chastity theory's success story corresponds perfectly to the paradigm for sexual politics articulated so famously by Luce Irigaray in *Speculum of the Other Woman*: men found a cultural order through the creation of a shared discourse of female sexuality.[48] Such a discourse conveys no information about the actual reality of women's lives, in this case that of a female intellectual in antiquity; rather its fiction of the feminine was convincing to men at the time of its articulation in that it corresponded to their fantasy of woman's place in the sociocultural order. The chastity theory survived because it served as a rite of scholarly coming of age, the initiation of the individual philologist into the cultural order.

The tradition inaugurated by Welcker demonstrates that the overwhelming modern scholarly preference in fictions of Sappho is for the vision of chaste handmaiden serving the interests of the state. The inability on the part of its proponents to deal with the issue of female homosexuality and their concomitant desire to speak only of (sublimated) male homoerotic bonds provides further confirmation of Irigaray's paradigm. This is consistent with the inspiration for Irigaray's theory in Freud's treatment of female homosexuality: in Freud's "Psychogenesis of a Case of Homosexuality in a Woman," for example, Irigaray identifies a detour of desire in which the woman serves only as a pretext for the creation of a male homoerotic scene.[49] When read in the context of the nineteenth-century German philological position on Sappho, the original psychoanalytic treatment of female homosexuality seems perfectly compatible with the then authoritative view of the original female homosexual. In this area as in others, Freud can be seen as a product of a specific historical moment. His theories, as well as those of the sexologists and of the medical morbidity school, bear the mark of the philological discourse that reigned over the German nineteenth century. Such theories, therefore, now thought to have played a formative role in the creation of a modern homosexual identity, cannot be read in isolation from the ideal love commentary privileged by philologists. No more than the contemporary dual Sapphic image of virgin and whore, the opposing nineteenth-century visions of male homoerotic relations as *pederastia* or perversion cannot be dissociated from each other.

48. Irigaray, *Speculum*. In "Why Is Diotima a Woman," Halperin proposes a parallel reading of Plato's *Symposium*.

49. Irigaray, *Speculum* 98–104.

SEVEN

146 / 63

Sappho Schoolmistress

Holt N. Parker

If we show that poetry . . . is not one thing for men and another for women but the same, by comparing the poems of Sappho with those of Anacreon . . . will anyone have any reason to find fault with the demonstration?

PLUTARCH, *ON THE VIRTUES OF WOMEN* 243B

INTRODUCTION

"Monique Wittig and Sande Zeig in their *Lesbian Peoples: Material for a Dictionary* devote a full page to Sappho. The page is blank." So John Winkler began one of the most perceptive articles of recent years on Sappho.[1] Wittig and Zeig's blank page is a salutary warning that we know nothing about Sappho. Or worse: Everything we know is wrong. Even the most basic "facts" are simply not so or in need of a stringent critical reexamination. A single example. We are told over and over again that Sappho "was married to Kerkylas of Andros, who is never mentioned in any of the extant fragments of her poetry."[2] Not surprising, since it's a joke name:

A version of this paper was originally presented at the 1991 APA meeting in Chicago in a panel session, "Looking Inward and Looking Outward: New Directions in the Study of Sexuality in the Ancient World," sponsored by the Lesbian/Gay Caucus. I would like to thank the organizer of the session, Philip Kovitz, and the members of the Women's Classical Caucus. References to Sappho and Alcaeus follow the numbering of Lobel and Page, *Poetarum Lesbiorum Fragmenta* (L.-P.) and Page, *Supplementum Lyricis Graecis* (P.), supplemented by Voigt, *Sappho et Alcaeus* (V.); lyric poets according to Page, *Poetae Melici Graeci* (*PMG*) supplemented by Davies, *Poetarum Melicorum Graecorum Fragmenta* (*PMGF*); elegists and iambists according to West, *Iambi et Elegi Graeci*; many of the testimonia on Sappho and Alcaeus are gathered in Campbell, *Greek Lyric* vol. 1, those of Alcman in Calame, *Alcman*, and Campbell, *Greek Lyric* vol. 2. This essay was originally published in slightly different form as "Sappho Schoolmistress," *Transactions of the American Philological Association* 123 (1993) 309–51.

1. Winkler, "Double Consciousness" 162.
2. Snyder, *The Woman and the Lyre* 3.

he's Dick Allcock from the Isle of MAN.[3] It's been over 139 years since
William Mure pointed this out, and it is there in Wilamowitz and easily
accessible in the *Real-Encyclopädie*.[4] The only source for this factoid is the
Suda, and it is clearly taken from one of the numerous comedies on Sappho.[5]
Yet one finds this piece of information repeated without question from book
to book, usually omitting the dubious source, usually omitting any reference
at all.[6]

3. From χέρχος, "penis"; cf. Henderson, *The Maculate Muse* 128. I might be willing to
accept Kerkylas as a real person if the name were ever attested anywhere else and if he
came from any other place on the planet except Andros (an island, not a city, *pace* Lardinois,
"Lesbian Sappho" 22). The etymology is quite sound. For other such names built to χέρχ-,
e.g., Κερχίδας (PW 21:292–93, s.v., for the etymology), see Bechtel, *Die historische Personennamen*
482.
4. Mure, *A Critical History* 3:278, and Calder, "Welcker's *Sapphobild*" 147, 150; Wilamowitz,
Sappho und Simonides 24; Aly, "Sappho," in PW, 2nd ser., 1:2361.
5. *Sappho* by Ameipsias (Kock 1.674), Amphis (Kassel-Austin [K.-A.] 2.228), Antiphanes
(K.-A. 2.424–26), and Diphilos (who has Archilochus and Hipponax as her lovers; K.-A. 5.94),
Ephippus (K.-A. 5.148), Timocles (K.-A. 7.777). Other comedies possibly about Sappho:
Phaon by Plato Comicus (K.-A. 7.508–17) and Antiphanes (K.-A. 2.437–38, if not identical
with *Sappho*); *Leucadia* by Menander (Körte 2.96–98) and Diphilus (K.-A. 2.387); *Antilais*
by Epikrates (K.-A. 5.156). Also a *Leucadia* by Turpilius telling the story of Phaon, based
presumably on Menander (Ribbeck 2.113–18; Rychlewska, *Turpilius* 29–37). See Aly, "Sappho"
2366; Campbell, *Greek Lyric* 1:27.
6. So for standard works subsequent to Aly, see Schadewaldt, *Sappho* 9; Hadas, *A History of
Greek Literature* 51; Bowra, *Greek Lyric* 176; R. Cantarella, *Storia della letteratura greca* 203; Flacelière,
Histoire littéraire de la Grèce 126; Lesky, *A History of Greek Literature* 139; Campbell, *Greek Lyric Poetry*
261 (who notes Aly's doubt later in *Greek Lyric* 1:5 n. 4); West, "Burning" 328; Tarditi, *Storia della
letteratura greca* 73; Fränkel, *Early Greek Poetry* 171; Kirkwood, *Early Greek Monody* 101; Pomeroy,
Goddesses 54; Levi, *A History of Greek Literature* 82 (in a passage still gallantly defending her against
charges of homosexuality); E. Cantarella, *Pandora's Daughters* 71, and *Bisexuality* 78. None of
these cites the source of the information. Rose, *A Handbook of Greek Literature* 94–95, is unique in
citing Aly and explicitly arguing against him. Wilamowitz, *Sappho und Simonides* 73, defends
her as a "noble woman, wife, and mother," and though he recognizes that the husband's
name is a joke (24), the husband himself must still have existed to account for the daughter
Kleis (so too Schadewaldt, *Sappho* 9, and Lardinois, "Lesbian Sappho" 22). Mure, "Sappho"
591, had already pointed out the basis of this argument: "My opponent [Welcker] and his
fellow apologists every where assume that Sappho was married; on the ground chiefly that
she had a daughter, and the daughter of so exemplary a woman must necessarily have been
a legitimate child" (see Calder, "Welcker's *Sapphobild*" 153). Others working to rehabilitate her
as a nineteenth-century schoolmistress flatly assert that she was unmarried and consequently a
virgin; so Schmid and Stählin, *Geschichte der griechischen Literatur* 417 and n. 9, baldly state: "She
can hardly have been married. . . . The rich husband Kerkylas of Andros (Suid. s. Σαπφώ)
belongs to legend. . . . Once the husband disappears so does the daughter" (failing to cite Aly,
missing the point that Kerkylas comes from comedy, criticizing Wilamowitz for tastelessness in
doing so, and evidencing the same curious assumptions about the birth of children); so too
Jaeger, *Paideia* 133.

Thus the note I am sounding is cautionary and my purpose in this paper is primarily negative. I hope to foster an atmosphere of skepticism. Whenever anyone presents a statement about Sappho, I want us to ask, "How do you know? Says who and where?" I wish to remind us to distrust.[7]

My purpose in this brief animadversion is not to attack the straw men of previous centuries, nor to rehearse the fascinating history of the critical fortunes of Sappho.[8] Rather, I wish to reconsider a single interpretive paradigm that continues to have remarkable influence: Sappho as schoolmistress. I want first to examine this picture of Sappho and what, if any, evidence has been used to construct it, then to look at the models that (explicitly or implicitly) have formed the basis for this picture. Next, I turn my attention to two particular attempts to rescue this image— Sappho as music teacher and Sappho as sex educator. To support these models there has arisen a curious double movement of assimilation and isolation. Her sexuality (the expression of which she shares with no one else)[9] has been absorbed into a male model of pederastic power and aggression, while her poetry (the expression of which she shares with many) has been cut off from all other poets. Finally, I consider a different paradigm for understanding Sappho, which I believe is truer to the few facts we do possess.

II. PALIMPSEST

Perhaps an even better image for Sappho than the blank page is the palimpsest. There does exist a text of Sappho, but it is so thickly written over with critical accumulation that it is almost impossible to make out the words beneath. This repetition of statements and assumptions from book to book is indicative of what seems to me to be a widespread tendency in the study of Sappho, where statements are taken from previous works without any critical evaluation, frequently without citation, as if they were facts so basic that "everyone" knows them. Further, this lack of critical evaluation toward Sappho stands in sharp contrast to the generally skeptical approach to the other lyric poets, for example Alcaeus.[10] Specifically, there

7. Welcker, *Sappho* 80, in his defense of Sappho on the charge of being a homosexual quotes Epicharmus (250 Kaibel) as his epigraph: νᾶφε καὶ μέμνασ' ἀπιστεῖν ἄρθρα ταῦτα τᾶν φρενῶν (Be sober and remember to distrust that organ of the mind). Though Welcker had a different ax to grind, his attempt at an attitude of skepticism is commendable. See Calder, "Welcker's *Sapphobild*."

8. See Lefkowitz, "Critical Stereotypes"; for France, see DeJean, *Fictions of Sappho*.

9. That is, the first-person expression of desire by a woman for a woman.

10. For this widespread attitude Lesky, *A History*, can be taken as an exemplar. While he warns against the romanticized "legend founded mainly on the writings of Alcaeus himself"

is a failure to try as far as possible to look at the text without first reading the commentary.

The reasons are in part understandable and even creditable. The text of Sappho is in fragments, which we must shore against their ruin. The language is difficult, the society obscure. We turn to the handbooks and commentaries for aid. But this means that we come to Sappho already blinded by the largely unexamined assumptions of the previous generations of scholars;[11] and in the case of Sappho the accumulation of assumptions is millennia deep and includes Greek comedies, Italian novels, and French pornography. The case is worse for Sappho than for any other author, including Homer. For here we are dealing not only with archaic literature but with sexuality; the commentaries are heavily endued with emotion and our own preconceptions. More importantly, we are dealing with homosexuality (or rather what we construct as homosexuality)[12] and women's sexuality. Sappho creates idiocies and raises questions that simply are never asked of any male poets.

It is not that these various constructions and reconstructions of Sappho are necessarily wrong. Rather, they are largely unprovable and completely unexamined. My note throughout will be that there is simply no evidence for many of the statements so decisively made. Rather than argue *ex silentio*, I hope to point out that much of what we read in the handbooks is an *argumentum ex nihilo*, based solely on unexamined tradition, presupposition, and prejudice. Classicists experience a *horror vacui* (especially of biographical data) perhaps more strongly than others and few have been able to resist the temptation to fill in the blanks.[13] Every age creates its own Sappho. Her

---

and advises "emphasiz[ing] the few ascertainable facts rather than make up a continuous narrative" (130–31), he directs the reader's attention uncritically to the "many biographical details about [Sappho], mostly derived from her own writings" (138). For two examples of the ongoing novelization of Sappho, see Lesky 146 on fr. 150, "When her daughter is mortally ill she forbids loud wailing." The citation is taken from Max. Tyr. (18.9) and actually says, "He [Socrates] was angry with Xanthippe when he was dying, and she [Sappho] with her daughter." See also Fränkel, *Early Greek Poetry* 171: "She herself, *by her own account* [my italics], was small and dark and not very pretty." Her "own account," of course, is Ovid (well, perhaps), *Her.* 15.31–40, backed by Max. Tyr. 18.7 (259 V.) and *POxy.* 1800 (T 1 Loeb = 252 V.); they may indeed have drawn on her poetry, but that is an inference, not a fact. For the novelistic and romantic treatments of Alcaeus, see DeJean, *Fictions of Sappho* 158–60, 190–91, 258–59.

11. Cf. the remarks of Lefkowitz, "Critical Stereotypes" 65, and Jenkyns, *Three Classical Poets* 6–7.

12. Cf. Dover, *Greek Homosexuality* vii: "I know of no topic in classical studies on which a scholar's normal ability to perceive differences and draw inferences is so easily impaired."

13. Cf. ibid., 173.

position as *the* woman poet (as Homer is the male poet),[14] the first female voice heard in the West, elevates her to a status where she is forced to be a metonym for all women. Sappho ceases to be an author and becomes a symbol. She is recreated in each age to serve the interests of all who appropriate her, whether friend or enemy. We, of course, are doing the same. All we can hope to do is be as little blind as we can be to what evidence there is and explicitly to acknowledge the limitations of our knowledge and the bases for our assumptions.

III. SAPPHO SCHOOLMISTRESS

In its strongest form, Sappho Schoolmistress is the well-known creation of Wilamowitz, who was concerned with defending Sappho from charges of homosexuality, in particular Pierre Louÿs's recently published *Chansons de Bilitis* (1895). To do so, Wilamowitz took over the theories of Karl Otfried Müller and Friedrich Gottlieb Welcker and recast Sappho as a virgin schoolmistress.[15] This whole construction was created to explain away Sappho's passion for her "girls," allowing her the emotion of love but denying it any physical component, by recasting it in the form of an explicitly "Platonic" and propaedeutic love.[16] Calder and DeJean have dealt with this at length.[17] I will merely point out that it arises from a historically conditioned construct of feminine psychosexual development, unique to England and Germany, springing in part from an attempt to justify the role of and allay anxieties about the current regime of single-sex schools. Thus, Sappho is cast as a friendly spinster teacher at a boarding school—this is not an exaggeration—educating girls before turning them over to a normal life of marriage and motherhood.[18] The girls in turn pass through a phase of a

14. Antipater *AP* 7.15, Galen 4.771.18 Kühn [K] (Marquandt 2.35.14, not *Protr.* 2 as stated by Aly, "Sappho" 2368, the source of fr. 50). Cf. Antipater of Thessalonica *AP* 9.26, where Anyte is the female Homer.

15. Wilamowitz, *Sappho und Simonides*; Müller, *Geschichte* 1:172–78, *History* 228–36; Welcker, *Sappho* 98. Welcker and Müller had a precedent in the novels of Billardon de Sauvigny, *La Parnasse de dames* 1:64 (who speaks of her female disciples), and Barthélemy, *Voyage du jeune Anacharsis* 2:69 (= Beaumont, *Travels of the Young Anacharsis* 2:63, where Sappho is in charge of a literary school); see DeJean, *Fictions of Sappho* 139, 341 n. 20.

16. Müller, *Geschichte* 1:319–22, and *History* 1:234–36. Cf. Wilamowitz, *Sappho und Simonides* 77; Schmid and Stählin, *Geschichte* 418; Jaeger, *Paideia* 1:143–44; Flacelière, *Histoire* 128. The comparison between Sappho and Socrates is originally made by Max. Tyr. 18.9 (T 20 Loeb); see below.

17. Calder, "Welcker's *Sapphobild*"; DeJean, *Fictions of Sappho* 198–220. See also Jenkyns, *Three Classical Poets* 1–4, and Rüdiger, *Sappho*.

18. Welcker, *Sappho* 97, and following him Wilamowitz, *Sappho und Simonides* 73, and Schmid and Stählin, *Geschichte* 418, let us know that the school was in Sappho's house (on the basis

crush on an older teacher which somehow or other "prepares" them for normal heterosexuality (see section VIII below). With the authority of Wilamowitz, Sappho the Schoolmistress came to be enshrined in the canonical pages of the *Real-Encyclopädie* by Aly, in Schmid and Stählin's *Geschichte der griechischen Literatur* (1929)—and once embalmed there, it seems as if it can never be buried. It passed to Jaeger, Flacelière, Campbell, Gerber, Arthur, and beyond.[19] It reaches its ultimate point of absurdity in Devereux's now infamous picture of Sappho waking up one morning, realizing she has no penis, and dashing off fragment 31 in a (literally) hysterical seizure. He comments:

> These findings [of Sappho's "authentic lesbianism"] can neither prove nor disprove that she was *also* a schoolmistress or a cult-leader. If she was either (or both), this would prove no more than that in Lesbos, quite as much as in some modern societies, female inverts tended to gravitate into professions which brought them in contact with young girls, whose partial segregation and considerable psycho-sexual immaturity—and therefore incomplete diffentiatedness—made them willing participants in lesbian experimentation.[20]

Perhaps the most astonishing thing in this quote is the word "professions." Devereux shows no hesitation in recreating archaic Mytilene on the basis of *Mädchen in Uniform*.[21] Sappho Schoolmistress has become Sappho Gym Teacher.

In the midst of all this reconstruction (or rather romancing), one most important (and most frequently ignored) fact must be pointed out: nowhere in any poem does Sappho teach, or speak about teaching, anything to anyone. Page demolished the silly notion of Sappho in some sort of formal teaching position in 1955, and since then we have had to be reminded by Lefkowitz, Kirkwood, Pomeroy, Snyder, and others that there is simply no evidence

---

of fr. 150); so too Kranz, *Geschichte der griechischen Literatur* 88 (complete with curriculum); West, "Other Early Poetry" 38 ("a group of unmarried women or girls who gathered at Sappho's house to practice music and song"); Burnett, *Three Archaic Poets* 211 n. 8.

19. Jaeger, *Paideia* 1:111; Flacelière, *Histoire* 125; Campbell, *Greek Lyric Poetry* 261; Gerber, *Euterpe* 161; Arthur, "Early Greece" 42. Wilamowitz, *Griechische* 41, proposed an analogy: "If one does not mind the modern tone, it might be termed a girls' boarding school [*Mädchenpensionat*]." His analogy has passed to others as part of the baggage of Sappho Schoolmistress; two examples, Flacelière 125: "Sappho, then, directed a sort of boarding school [*pensionnat*] for young girls which reminds one of Mme de Maintenon's Saint Cyr"; Arthur 42: "It is difficult to define the exact nature of this circle, but since it was frequented by girls only during a brief interval between childhood and marriage, it is perhaps most analogous to a finishing school." See E. Cantarella's remarks quoted in the text below.

20. Devereux, "The Nature of Sappho's Seizure" 31.

21. See the criticisms of Marcovich, "Sappho Fr. 31."

for Mistress Sappho's School for Young Ladies.[22] Yet despite these efforts, this image of Sappho continues to be taken as gospel.[23] So we encounter Eva Cantarella flatly asserting: "But Sappho was not only mistress of the intellect—her girls learned about the weapons of beauty, seduction, and charm: they learned the grace (*charis*) that made them desirable women. Here the description finishing school is not incorrect, but it is certainly insufficient."[24] Though Cantarella does not tell us how she came by a copy of the syllabus at Sappho's school, we can see that she took the details from Schmid and Stählin, and if we ask where *they* got them from, we find out they just made them up. Since Sappho had a school—something we all know—it must have had a curriculum, and they grub through the poems in search of details. Anything mentioned in the poems becomes a course offering. Thus the wedding of Hector and Andromache (fr. 44) is part of a series of "Stories from Greek Myth" for her pupils, nor they do fail to list the lessons in cosmetics.[25] On this basis, Sappho 16 would be proof that she trained her girls in cavalry maneuvers. In "Sappho und ihr Kreis," Merkelbach accepted Wilamowitz's *Mädchenpensionat* "cum grano salis," but still provides a syllabus including "weibliche Arbeiten" (women's work), for which his evidence is fragment 102 (in which a girl tells her mother she can no longer spin; no mention that she learned to do so at Sappho's Boarding School), Inc. Auct. 17 (which he assigns to Sappho, apparently *because* it speaks about spinning), and the existence of sewing circles in Germany and other cultures. Burnett writes: "Cult, deportment and dress were all apparently matters for study among Sappho's girls, but music was at the core of their curriculum."[26] The college catalogue is derived from the various descriptions of clothes; the deportment from 57 (a rustic girl) and

22. Page, *Sappho and Alcaeus* 111–12; Lefkowitz, "Critical Stereotypes" 63; Kirkwood, *Early Greek Monody* 101; Pomeroy, *Goddesses* 53; Snyder, "Public Occasion and Private Passion" 12.

23. The unquestioning attitude of classicists bears a share of responsibility for the distortions of Sappho in works written by nonclassicists. Here, for example, are quotations from two popular reference works: "In time she returned to her homeland and there became mistress of a school for the daughters of the aristocracy" (Gettone, "Sappho" 1153). And "Sappho: Director of a girls' school on the island of Lesbos; widely known poet of her time" (Kramarae and Treichler, *A Feminist Dictionary* 400, citing Boulding, *The Underside of History* 262); it is all the more upsetting to note the order of presentation of these last two sentences in a work with its title.

24. E. Cantarella, *Pandora's Daughters* 86–87, and *Bisexuality* 79 (cf. 3–4). Supplying a Greek word is essential to make it appear as if there were any ancient support for these statements. Cf. the comments on the use of *thiasos* below. Cantarella is led into making direct misstatements. So she claims (*Pandora's Daughters* 86; *Bisexuality* 79) that the *Suda* calls Sappho a *didaskalos*.

25. Schmid and Stählin, *Geschichte* 419–20, 422 n. 9; see Page's strictures (*Sappho and Alcaeus* 111 and n. 1). For the cosmetics, cf. Saake, *Zur Kunst Sapphos* 200 (quoted below).

26. Burnett, *Three Archaic Poets* 215.

16 (Anactoria's walk): a love poem is reduced to a report card. Most recently Lardinois: "Sappho's teaching need not have been restricted to music and dance, however. An impression of all the activities Sappho performed with her girls is to be found in fragment 94."[27] Flowers, garlands, perfumes, soft beds on which to expel desire, shrines, groves, and dance become parts of a course description.

IV. THE NEW PARADIGM: "GIRLS" AND RITUAL

Thus Sappho's School for Girls still seems to be a going concern. Yet despite these periodic attempts to close it, one thing remains untouched and unquestioned, which shows the lingering influence of Sappho Schoolmistress even among those who ignore it or explicitly reject it. Sappho is still assumed in nearly every book, monograph, and paper to be an older woman with some kind of power over a group of young unmarried girls. This is the unquestioned assumption we have inherited from the handbooks that still forms the basis for discussion of Sappho. Oddly enough then, it is the most Victorian, anachronistic, sexist, and perverse part of Müller and Wilamowitz's picture of Sappho that continues to exert the strongest influence.

A new paradigm has grown up. In this view, which is the dominant interpretive model (apart from making Sappho a headmistress outright), she is still seen as an older woman presiding over an organization devoted to educating young girls before they leave for marriage, but now she does so in a *ritual* context. The all-pervasiveness of this assumption left over from Sappho Schoolmistress is shown by the pandemic use of the words "girls," "Mädchen," "jeunes filles," "fanciulle," and the like.

The new model is informed primarily by the growing realization of the importance of the oral performance of lyric poetry and by anthropological studies.[28] This important stressing of the primarily oral nature of Sappho's poetry provides the basis for the important new interpretations of, among others, Merkelbach, Hallett, Burnett, and Gentili.[29] Sappho sang, and she must have sung to an audience. However, all of these scholars unquestioningly assume, still on the basis of the old all-pervasive paradigm, that her

---

27. Lardinois, "Lesbian Sappho" 26.

28. On oral performance, see Merkelbach, "Sappho und ihr Kreis"; Russo, "Reading the Greek Lyric Poets"; Segal, "Eros and Incantation"; Gentili, *Poetry and Its Public* 3–23, with 235 n. 2 for a full bibliography. For anthropological studies, see Brelich, *Paides*; Calame, *Les chœurs*.

29. Merkelbach, "Sappho und ihr Kreis"; Hallett, "Sappho and Her Social Context"; Burnett, *Three Archaic Poets*; Gentili, *Poetry and Its Public*.

audience consisted entirely of unmarried girls. For this, to put the matter briefly, there is no credible evidence at all.[30]

V. THE EVIDENCE

Three factors have contributed to this dominant belief: the lingering influence of Wilamowitz and others in the handbooks, certain late testimonia, and an anachronistic model of female homoerotics derived from Sparta. I will deal with the last two in turn. Since so much has been built on the ancient citations, it seems necessary to quote them in full and treat them at some length. Five late testimonia speak of Sappho as a "teacher" in some sense. None of them is evidence that Sappho ran an institution of any sort. The earliest is Ovid *Tristia* 2.363–65:

> quid, nisi cum multo Venerem confundere vino,
> praecepit lyrici Teia Musa senis?
> Lesbia quid docuit Sappho, nisi amare, puellas?

> What, except how to mingle Venus with much wine, did the Teian Muse of the old lyric poet teach? What did Sappho of Lesbos teach the girls, except how to love?

Here, of course, Ovid is no more imagining Sappho running a school for love than he is imagining Anacreon running an drinking academy. Maximus of Tyre (ca. 125–85 C.E.) in his oration τίς ἡ Σωκράτους ἐρωτική compares Sappho to Socrates:

> ὁ δὲ τῆς Λεσβίας [ἔρως] ... τί ἂν εἴη ἄλλο ἢ αὐτό, ἡ Σωκράτους τέχνη ἐρωτική; δοκοῦσι γάρ μοι τὴν καθ' αὐτὸν ἑκάτερος φιλίαν, ἡ μὲν γυναικῶν, ὁ δὲ ἀρρένων, ἐπιτηδεῦσαι. καὶ γὰρ πολλῶν ἐρᾶν ἔλεγον καὶ ὑπὸ πάντων ἁλίσκεσθαι τῶν καλῶν. ὅ τι γὰρ ἐκείνῳ Ἀλκιβιάδης καὶ Χαρμίδης καὶ Φαῖδρος, τοῦτο τῇ Λεσβίᾳ Γυρίννα καὶ Ἀτθὶς καὶ Ἀνακτορία· καὶ ὅ τί περ Σωκράτει οἱ ἀντίτεχνοι Πρόδικος καὶ Γοργίας καὶ Θρασύμαχος καὶ Πρωταγόρας, τοῦτο τῇ Σαπφοῖ Γοργὼ καὶ Ἀνδρομέδα· νῦν μὲν ἐπιτιμᾷ ταύταις, νῦν δὲ ἐλέγχει καὶ εἰρωνεύεται αὐτὰ ἐκεῖνα τὰ Σωκράτους. (Max. Tyr. 18.9a–d = T 20 Loeb)

> What else was the love of the Lesbian woman except Socrates' art of love? For they seem to me to have practiced love each in their own way, she that of women, he

---

30. Page, *Sappho and Alcaeus* 111, refers rightly to "the copious but inane biographical tradition." Lardinois, "Lesbian Sappho," might be taken as emblematic. In what purports to be a critical and skeptical reexamination of whether Sappho was a lesbian, he provides fairly copious documentation. He then states (17): "It is, however, certain that these poems concern young girls. Sometimes Sappho herself refers to them as such and the testimonia confirm this repeatedly." He has just referred to the testimonia as "a collection of fiction, truths, and half-truths" (15) but here provides not a single reference for a statement central to his reconstruction.

that of men. For they said that they loved many and were captivated by all things beautiful. What Alcibiades and Charmides and Phaedrus were to him, Gyrinna and Atthis and Anactoria were to the Lesbian. And what the rival craftsmen Prodicus and Gorgias and Thrasymachus and Protagoras were to Socrates, Gorgo and Andromeda were to Sappho. Sometimes she upbraids them, sometimes she refutes them and uses irony, like Socrates.

Maximus's concern here is to show the nobility of love. He no more states that Sappho ran a school than he sets up one for Hesiod, whom he cites for comparison with Socrates immediately before this passage or for Archilochus or Anacreon, whom he quotes immediately afterward (18.9l–m). Further, the important point is missed that not even *Socrates* ran a "school." As Page points out: "There is no suggestion of any formal association."[31] The comparison is made on the basis of their love of beauty and a certain ironic and sarcastic tone that Maximus finds in his quotations.[32] And, we should note, even Maximus does not speak of "girls" and "boys," but of "men" and "women." It is as wrong to deduce that Sappho was surrounded only by prepubescent girls as it would be to deduce that Socrates never spoke to anyone except males under the age of eighteen.

Maximus is our only source for such "rivals." Yet by taking his comparison in a naively literal fashion, there has sprung up the widespread vision not just of Sappho's Academy but of a Lesbos littered with warring boarding schools.[33] This in turn has had profound effect on the interpretation of the poems. Thus when Atthis leaves to do to Andromeda (131), some scholars speak of her "defecting" from Sappho to Andromeda's possibly "larger group,"[34] despite the fact that apart from this one, late, broad, humorous, and superficial analogy there is no indication that Andromeda is anything other than a rival *lover*, nor is there even a mention that any of the women whom Sappho dislikes had a "circle" of young girls. This idea of "defection"

31. Page, *Sappho and Alcaeus* 111 n. 2.

32. Max. Tyr. is a source for frs. 47, 49b, 57, 130, 150, 155, 159, 172, 188. A reading of the entire passage will how superficial his comparison is and is meant to be. Cf. the citation in n. 10 above.

33. E.g., Schadewaldt, *Sappho* 11; Page, *Sappho and Alcaeus* 133; Merkelbach, "Sappho und ihr Kreis" 5; Fränkel, *Early Greek Poetry* 183; Lesky, *A History* 145; Gentili, "La veneranda Saffo" 49; Rivier, "Observations" 89 (who conjures up a vision of each "new girl" being sworn into Sappho's school in a religious ceremony which constitutes a "contract"); Calame, *Les chœurs* 1:370; Burnett, *Three Archaic Poets* 212 (who misquotes Max. Tyr.); Podlecki, *The Early Greek Poets* 88 (who plays down the formal aspects of "schools"); E. Cantarella, *Pandora's Daughters* 87, and *Bisexuality* 79; Gentili, *Poetry and Its Public* 80–83. Scholars have plunged headlong into creating rival girls' schools, taking Maximus's comparison as literally true for Sappho, without stopping to realize that it is not even literally true for Socrates. To what extent were Gorgias & Co. "rival craftsmen" of Socrates?

34. E.g., Kirkwood, *Early Greek Monody* 125.

is applied even to poem 1, where the woman Sappho loves is said to be "deserting the Sapphic *thíasos* for the community of a rival."[35] But Sappho says nothing of a *thiasos*, or a community, or desertion, or even a rival; there is only Aphrodite and Sappho, and a woman who does not love Sappho back. This is absurdly out of hand. Compare the situation of Anacreon 357: there is only Dionysus, Anacreon, and a boy who does not love him back; or compare Theognis 250–54 or 1299–304. Yet does anyone say that Kleoboulos or Kymos had "defected" from the "*thiasos*" of Anacreon or Theognis and joined that of a "rival"?

Philostratus (ca. 200 C.E.) in the *Life of Apollonius of Tyana* writes about a Pamphilian woman:

ἡ δὲ Σαπφοῖ θ' ὁμιλῆσαι λέγεται ... καλεῖται τοίνυν ἡ σοφὴ αὕτη Δαμοφύλη καὶ λέγεται τὸν Σαπφοῦς τρόπον παρθένους θ' ὁμιλητρίας κτήσασθαι ποιή-ματά τε ξυνθεῖναι τὰ μὲν ἐρωτικά, τὰ δ' ὕμνους. (Philostr. *VA* 1.30 = T 21 Loeb)

Who is said to have associated with Sappho.... This wise woman was called Damophile and is said also to have gathered maidens as disciples in the manner of Sappho and to have written love poetry as well as hymns.

Again the model envisaged for Damophile, and by implication for Sappho, is that of Socrates and his "pupils" (ὁμιλητρίας), and again this does not show the existence of a formal school. Dover cites this passage "for what it is worth—and this is very little, except as an indication of the form of the Sappho-legend in much later times" and comments: "If in the generation after Sappho there were other women poets in the Eastern Aegean, Lesbian tradition will have regarded them as pupils of Sappho."[36]

Two sources, however, speak more directly of Sappho as teaching, but neither is remotely solid evidence for Sappho "running a school." The oldest is a fragment of an anonymous commentary on Sappho dating to the second century C.E.: ἡ δ' ἐφ' ἡσυχία[σ] παιδεύουσα τὰς ἀρίστας οὐ μόνον τῶν ἐγχωρίων ἀλλὰ καὶ τῶν ἀπ' Ἰωνίας (But she in peace educating the best women not only from the natives [of Lesbos] but also of Ionia; 214b V. = S 261a P.). The contrast in the ἡ δὲ (the papyrus begins ὁ μὲν ...) is apparently between Sappho's quiet life in teaching and Alcaeus's stormy life in politics.[37] We have no idea of the commentator's sources or accuracy and Treu rightly

35. Gentili, *Poetry and Its Public* 80.

36. Dover, *Greek Homosexuality* 175.

37. So Gronewald, "Fragmente" 114. Burnett, *Three Archaic Poets* 210 n. 4, translates ἐφ' ἡσυχίας as "at her leisure," commenting "surely ἐφ' ἡσυχίας must mean that Sappho acted as a private citizen, not as a priestess or the appointed leader of an initiation group." While I agree with her conclusion, the contrast of ἡσυχία here following a reference to κρατοῦσι is with war (cf. Thuc. 3.12), not with public status. Burnett cites Strabo 13.2.4 for "the foreign membership" of Sappho's circle, but he says nothing of the sort, merely mentioning

comments, "We are not required to believe him."[38] Likewise the *Suda* seems to make a distinction between comrades and pupils:

ἑταῖραι δὲ αὐτῆς καὶ φίλαι γεγόνασι τρεῖς, Ἀτθίς, Τελεσίππα, Μεγάρα· πρὸς ἃς καὶ διαβολὴν ἔσχεν αἰσχρᾶς φιλίας. μαθήτριαι δὲ αὐτῆς Ἀναγόρα Μιλησία, Γογγύλα Κολοφωνία, Εὐνείκα Σαλαμινία. (*Suda* Σ107 = T 2 Loeb)

She had three companions and friends, Atthis, Telesippa, and Megara, for whom she was slandered as having a shameful love. Her pupils were Anagora of Miletus, Gongyla of Colophon, and Eunica of Salamis.

Megara, Telesippa, and Eunica of Salamis are mentioned only here in the surviving evidence as is Anagora of Miletus, unless she is the same as (or a mistake for) Anactoria,[39] while Gongyla is mentioned but in poems too fragmentary to tell if Colophon was mentioned (22, 95, 213, 213a, 214a). The *Suda* is merely continuing the standard process of turning poetry into biography.[40] The prosopography of Sappho contains more than six entries, and the distinction the *Suda* makes between three friends and three pupils is illusory. It is also clear on what basis the *Suda* makes that distinction: the "companions and friends" all appear without a geographical designation, the "pupils" are foreign. That is, wherever the *Suda* or its sources found some reason for thinking a character was not from Lesbos, they explained her presence by assuming she was a "pupil."[41] The idea of Sappho with

---

that Hellanicus, the historian, and Kallias (ca. 200 B.C.E.), the commentator on Sappho and Alcaeus, were from Lesbos.

38. Treu, "Sappho," in PW suppl. 11:1235. Note that the first part of the fragment (on Sappho's teaching) is not attributed to any source. Burnett, *Three Archaic Poets* 210 n. 4, mistakenly says that the authority is Kallias (see n. 37). Rather, he is cited only for Sappho's subsequent reputation. Further, as Dover notes, *Greek Homosexuality* 175, "Kallias will probably have based his statement about 'high favour' on tradition as he knew it, not on evidence giving direct access to the sentiment of the Lesbians in Sappho's lifetime." Calder, "Welcker's *Sapphobild*" 140 n. 49, accurately says, "Kallias of Mytilene is invoked."

39. So Page, *Sappho and Alcaeus* 135 n. 1.

40. See Fairweather, "Fiction in the Biographies"; Lefkowitz, "Critical Stereotypes."

41. These foreign women have played an important role in the history of Sappho Schoolmistress. Three points need to be made. (1) The presence of foreign women on Lesbos is attested only by this bit of the *Suda* and by the Cologne commentary quoted above, which may share a common source and that source, like so much else, might be comedy (see n. 5 above). There may be some truth hidden here (Ionia matching up with Colophon and Miletus). However, if we are to use Ovid as evidence, he ought to be used consistently: the *Heroides* mentions no lover of Sappho's coming from further afield than Lesbos (15.15–16, 201) and implies that Anactoria (the *Suda*'s Anagora of Miletus?) is a native (15.17). Lardinois, "Lesbian Sappho" 17 and 29, attempted to explain why these two sources say that foreign women were on Lesbos: "The regions to which some of the girls, *according to the poems* [my emphasis], went *after* their stay in Sappho's circle, may have been held to be their places of origin. In most cases the girls were married there." The last statement has no evidence at all to

pupils, common to these two sources, rests on this basis alone. There is still no mention of any sort of "school" and, let us note, even the wretched evidence of the *Suda* has been misinterpreted: it limits her "shameful love" to her "companions and friends," not to her students. On the value that can be assigned to such Byzantine speculation we need only recall that both Erinna (*Suda* H521, Eust. *Il.* 326.46) and Nossis (*AP* 7.718 in the lemma) are turned into pupils of Sappho.[42]

Seven testimonia present some sort of picture of Sappho consorting with "girls." Ovid (*Tr.* 2.365, quoted above; *Her.* 15.15) and Horace (*Carm.* 2.13.24–35) speak of her as in love with *puellae*. They may be imagining prepubescents here, but *puella*, of course, is used equally of girls, mature women, and goddesses, especially as objects of love, and Horace calls Sappho herself a *puella* at *Odes* 4.9.12. There is an implication in the passages of Philostratus, Maximus of Tyre (Alcibiades, Charmides, and Phaedrus were young men), and the Cologne Commentary (παιδεύουσα) that Sappho had young women as students. Even then there is no indication that these women were girls on their way to the marriage market. Himerius (*Or.* 28.2 = T 50 Loeb) speaks of her singing of the beauty of a young girl (παρθένος).

Chronologically, the earliest witness (Horace) is six hundred years after Sappho. As evidence the testimonia are valueless, again turning poetry into biography. They do not prove that Sappho ran a school. They do not prove that Sappho loved only nubile girls. What they do show is something quite familiar to feminists: the wholesale restructuring of female sexuality and society on the model of male sexuality and

---

back it up. In 16 Anactoria is gone, but we don't know where; in 96 someone has left for Sardis, but we don't know who (but see n. 110). Lardinois has accepted others' speculations as facts and then convinced himself that he has read them in the poems. (2) Unlike Lardinois, I do not find the idea of foreign women on Lesbos inherently improbable. However, even if they did come to Lesbos, it does not follow, as he and many others think, that they therefore came because of Sappho. (3) Even if they were on Lesbos, and there because of Sappho, it does not follow that they were little girls there to *study* with Sappho, much less to live with her in her house. We find nowhere in the Greek world an equivalent for unmarried girls being shipped around the Mediterranean by their fathers. This picture would be odd even for adult males: Gorgias comes to Athens, not the other way around. The idea that the women were on Lesbos to "study" with Sappho arises from the preconception that they were prepubescents. In turn, the idea that they were "pupils" is used as proof that they were "girls." If the presence of these nonnative women is indeed a fact, why could they not have been there with their (native or not) husbands and families?

42. Further on the dubious chronology of the sources, Hermesianax makes her the contemporary of Anacreon (Ath. 13.598b–c) perhaps as a deliberate joke (so Ath. 13.599c–d), while Pausanias (9.29.8) makes her a borrower from Pamphos, whom he apparently believed to be pre-Homeric, but who seems to be Hellenistic (see Maas, PW 18.3:352).

society.[43]   This is precisely the type of construction we find in Lucian's portrayal of the women of Lesbos in *Dialogue of the Courtesans* 5. The analogy, whether stated or assumed, for the relation of Sappho to her lovers is that of *paiderastia*, a power relation of older to younger, teacher to pupil, initiator to initiated. Sappho wrote of love; she therefore must be the (necessarily older) *erastēs*, those about whom she sang the (necessarily younger) *erōmenoi/ai*. Lardinois is at least explicit: "She appears to have been a kind of female pederast."[44]   Surely, this ought to make us suspicious. This reinscription of Sappho along the lines of male power relations is implicit in Maximus of Tyre and explicit in several other texts. So the Oxyrhynchus commentary (252 V. = T 1 Loeb) says that she was accused of being a γυναικ-ε[ράσ]τρια, a nonce-formation meaning "(female) *erastēs* of women."[45]   Porphyrion, on Horace's use of *mascula* to describe Sappho, comments (ad *Ep.* 1.19.28 = T 17 Loeb): "vel quia in poetico studio est ⟨incluta⟩, in quo saepius viri, vel quia tribas diffamatur fuisse" (either because she was famous for her talent in poetry in which men figure more often or because she is slandered as having been a tribade). Themistius (*Or.* 13.170d = T 52 Loeb) writes: Σαπφοῖ μὲν γὰρ καὶ Ἀνακρέοντι συγχωροῦμεν ἀμέτρους εἶναι καὶ ὑπερμέτρους ἐν τοῖς ἐπαίνοις τῶν παιδικῶν (We allow Sappho and Anacreon to be unrestrained and excessive in the praises of their beloveds). Themistius uses παιδικά, a technical term for the *erōmenos*, the younger boy partner in a male pederastic relationship.[46]

To a large extent, I believe it is precisely this reinscription that accounts for the extraordinary power of Sappho Schoolmistress over the imaginations of so many, despite the total lack of evidence for it. I can illustrate this best, perhaps, by bringing up an incidental criticism of Sappho Schoolmistress. Why is Sappho always called the "leader" of her "*thiasos*"? Poets were important figures in the life of the polis to be sure, but there is no evidence to show that they "led" anything other than songs. Alcaeus is never called the "leader" of his *hetairia*. Sappho comes to interpretation already presumed to be the older woman in control of younger girls. Again, the model is of controlling male to controlled Other, and reveals a disturbing obsession with power and hierarchy. Sappho, the female poet, is being assimilated as much as possible to the male, in order to neutralize her. There is absolutely nothing in her poetry to show that Sappho was an older woman.[47]

43. For the Roman world, see Hallett, "Female Homoeroticism," for the construction of the *tribas* on the model of masculine sexuality.

44. Lardinois, "Lesbian Sappho" 17–18.

45. See Dover, *Greek Homosexuality* 174.

46. Ibid., 16.

47. Old age is referred to in 58.13–14, but we do not know whose.

There is nothing in the texts to show that her addressees were young children, or that they left her care for marriage. This latter widespread assumption seem to be built entirely on the fact that she wrote epithalamia— as if that were all she wrote. Outside of the obvious wedding songs (27, 30, 105, 107, 113, 114, 194), where the youth and virginity of the bride are mentioned, there are exactly six references in the surviving fragments, some of which might also be epithalamia, to the age of the women for whom or about whom she is singing. On this slender basis has been erected the whole tower of Sappho Schoolmistress. In 140a, she refers to the celebrants as κόραι. But the Adonia was everywhere that we know of a private festival including adult women, and κόραι is ritual language, not age description.[48] At the mutilated end of 17, a prayer to Hera, in what seems to be part of a ritual, she probably refers to maiden(s): π]αρθ[εν . . . , though the reference is not necessarily to the celebrants. In 56, in an unknown context, she says that no girl will have such skill. In 153, again in an unknown context, she refers to a "sweet-voiced girl," using πάρθενος both times. In 122 a tender child (παῖδ' †ἄγαν† ἀπάλαν) is plucking flowers; the context is unknown and may well be mythological. Finally, in the most famous example (49), she says, ἠράμαν μὲν ἔγω σέθεν Ἄτθι πάλαι ποτά (I loved you once, Atthis), and elsewhere, σμίκρα μοι πάις ἔμμεν ἐφαίνεο κἄχαρις (You seemed to me to be a small child and graceless). Even if we accept that these two lines are consecutive or even necessarily belong to the same poem or referred to the same person, which I do not,[49] there is nothing here that shows that Sappho was an older woman. Indeed, the imperlfect ἐφαίνεο could equally argue quite the opposite, that Sappho speaks here to an age-mate about the time when both Sappho and the woman were children. That is certainly what is implied by Terentianus Maurus's recasting of 49a (2154–5 6.390.4–5 Keil): "cordi quando fuisse sibi canit Atthida / parvam, florea virginitas sua cum foret" (when she sings that she loves little Atthis, when her own virginity was in flower); the *virginitas sua* in question is Sappho's. This notion of Sappho surrounded by agemates is further strengthened by a fragment, which, since it does not gibe with the *communis opinio*, has been ignored; this is fragment 24a.2–5:

]. [μ]εμνάσεσθ' ἀ[
κ]αὶ γὰρ ἄμμες ἐν νεό[τατι
ταῦτ'! [ἐ]πόημμεν·
πόλλα [μ]ὲν γὰρ καὶ κά[λα

---

48. Winkler, "Double Consciousness" 189 with n. 2. Cf. the same use in Telesilla (717). It would, in any case, presumably apply to the poet as well.

49. The only reason for connecting these two fragments, which are nowhere quoted by the same source, is the fact that Terentianus Maurus (see text) uses the adjective *parvam*.

... you will remember ... for we also did these things in our youth. For many beautiful things ...

Here, despite the damage to the papyrus, we have clear picture of age-mates, who shared common experiences while growing up together. In the same papyrus, we find fragment 23:

ὡς γὰρ ἄν]τιον εἰσίδω σ[ε,
φαίνεταί μ' οὐδ'] 'Ερμιόνα τεαύ[τα
ἔμμεναι,] ξάνθαι δ' 'Ελέναι σ' εἰσ[x]ην
οὐδ' ἔν ἄει]χες

> [for when] I look directly at you [not even] Hermione [seems to me to be] equal to you, and to compare you to blonde Helen [is not] unsuitable.

Now although Hermione, Helen's daughter, might be a proper comparison for a young girl, Helen is the *comparanda* for a mature woman.[50] No male lyric poet compares his *pais* with the adult male gods or heroes.[51] The same comparison to goddesses is made in 96.3 and 21–23, and the statement that Λάτω καὶ Νιόβα μάλα μὲν φίλαι ἦσαν ἔταιραι (Leto and Niobe were dear companions; 142) may also have introduced a comparison to Sappho and a friend (see n. 118). The fragments, therefore, point not to Sappho the predatory gym teacher of Devereux's fancy, but to a woman in love with women of her own generation. The only thing odd about this picture is that is not generally held.[52]

Most importantly, in none of the epithalamia is the girl getting married addressed by name; in none is she spoken of as loved by Sappho. Nor in any of the poems in which Sappho speaks to or about her companions is there a mention of their marriages, their having "studied" with Sappho in preparation for their marriages, or anything else to indicate that they were

50. The speaker may not be Sappho, though I am assuming that she probably is, and it is not impossible that these two, like 27 and 30, are epithalamia; see Page, *Sappho and Alcaeus* 125. Helen in fr. 16 is the image not for the beloved but the lover (contra Lardinois, "Lesbian Sappho" 19).

51. Instead, for an example, cf. Pind. *Ol.* 10.104–5, where the boy victor Hagesidamos is compared to Ganymede.

52. Cf. Stigers [Stehle], "Sappho's Private World" 52 (though she seems to be imagining an older Sappho, cf. 45). If, however, Sappho and Atthis are age-mates, we have something very similar to Erinna's *Distaff*; to show that this is not a matter of feminine poetics, see Theog. 1063–68 for an explicit statement that there is nothing sweeter for men and women than to sleep together all night after a party with one of their own age group (ὁμῆλιξ). Further, whatever we make of Anacreon 358, if the "girl" (νῆνι) from Lesbos does refer to a woman in love with another woman (about which I am uncertain), we have again an image of the young girl herself as lover. For the most recent work on this puzzle, see Marcovich, "Anacreon"; Renehan, "Anacreon Fragment 13"; Gentili, *Poetry and Its Public* 94–96; Pelliccia, "Anacreon 13."

other than what Sappho calls them (160): her "companions," ἑταίραις.[53] In short, the "girls" of the epithalamia and the "companions" of the lyric poems are simply not at all the same people, a point rightly made by Winkler.[54] Only the presuppositions of Sappho Schoolmistress has caused them to be so mistaken.

VI. SPARTA

The search for formal occasions involving young girls has led many into invoking Alcman's partheneia.[55] Yet as Treu succinctly says, "However, the nearest parallels, Alcman and the band of girls of his girl choruses, provide no support." Alcman is not the same as Sappho nor doing the same things as Sappho.[56] Alcman is a man, hired by the community, to provide choral songs, on civic occasions, for choruses composed of young women and of young men, to whom he evidences no individual erotic emotions.[57] Sappho is a woman, independent of any demonstrable civic role, a lyric poet performing

53. At 96.6–7, a companion now stands out among the women (γυναίκεσσιν) of Sardis. McEvilley, "Sapphic Imagery" 262, presupposes that the woman has left Sappho a virgin to go to Sardis to be married and so translates γυνή as "wife," arguing: "In the other occurrences of γυνή, for example, the γυναῖκες or matrons, are specifically distinguished from the πάρθενοι, or unmarried girls." This is not so: γυνή occurs only two other times in Sappho, both in 44; at l. 15, they are indeed contrasted with the virgins, but 44.31 refers only to γύναικες … προγενέστερα[ι, "the older women," a contrast with the young matrons, if with anyone. Further, in Alcaeus, our only close dialectal *comparandum*, γυνή simply means "woman" (130b.19, 347.4, 390; 41.21 is fragmentary; cf. also Inc. Auc. 35.6 V.). If the use of γυνή in 96 is evidence of anything, it is evidence that the unnamed woman of 96 was indeed a *woman*.

54. Winckler, "Double Consciousness" 165.

55. The first uses of this comparison that I know are Diels, "Alkmans Partheneion" 352, and Wilamowitz, "Der Chor" 259–60.

56. Treu, "Sappho" 1235. Even Gentili, *Poetry and Its Public* 77, writes: "It hardly needs saying, of course, that Alcman composed his partheneia on commission for the Spartan *thiasoi* of his time, whereas Sappho, being a poet, composed songs for performance in her own *thiasos*."

57. In the surviving frs. Alcman talks about his relation to the chorus only at 26 (his lament that he is too old to dance with them) and 34: Ἀλκμὰν τὰς ἐπεράστους κόρας λέγει ἀίτιας (Alcman calls beloved girls "*aitis*"); some, like the Thessalians (no mention of Dorians) use ἀίτιας for ἐρώμενος, according to the scholiast on Theocritus 12 (cf. 12.14, *Anecd. Bekk.* 348.2 = Ar. fr. 738). Lardinois, "Lesbian Sappho" 27, implies that the masc. ἀίτας is known to have been in official use at Sparta (for the facts, see Gow, *Theocritus* 2:224, and Dover, *Greek Homosexuality* 193 n. 16; contra Cartledge, "Spartan Pederasty" 391 n. 18; for a possible Laconic attestation, see Gallavotti, "Alcmane") and writes that the fem. was the term "for a young girl in a sexual relationship." Even if this were so, with whom? Not necessarily each other or older women as he seems to assume; the word, of dubious etymology, seems to mean no more than "comrade, beloved." E. Cantarella, *Bisexuality* 84, implies that *aitis* was a term in general use. Contrast this with Sappho's expressions of love for women, and compare her lack of expressions of love for the brides in the epithalamia.

solo songs, who also writes choral works for private marriage ceremonies, singing often to individual women, with whom she is in love.

Not only is Sappho lumped in with Alcman, but their societies are held to be identical. However, archaic Lesbos and archaic Sparta share only a single factor: expressions of desire by women for women.[58] The assumption underlying their facile equation, therefore, is a form of sexual essentialism: all female homosexuality is the same, and therefore the societies are the same. This is logically fallacious as well as theoretically and anthropologically naive. We know little about archaic Lesbos apart from Sappho and Alcaeus; we know little about archaic Sparta apart from Alcman; but it seems unlikely that the two had much in common, whatever picture one may form of Alcman's Sparta by contrast with Tyrtaeus or the austere *mirage spartiate* of later times.[59] To compare the two on the basis of this shared ignorance does not profit us much.

In a famous sentence in the *Life of Lycurgus*, Plutarch says of the Spartan type of paedeutic male homoeroticism:

οὕτω δὲ τοῦ ἐρᾶν ἐγκεκριμένου παρ' αὐτοῖς, ὥστε καὶ τῶν παρθένων ἐρᾶν τὰς καλὰς καὶ ἀγαθὰς γυναῖκας, τὸ ἀντερᾶν οὐκ ἦν, ἀλλὰ μᾶλλον ἀρχὴν ἐποιοῦντο φιλίας πρὸς ἀλλήλους οἱ τῶν αὐτῶν ἐρασθέντες, καὶ διετέλουν κοινῇ σπουδάζοντες ὅπως ἄριστον ἀπεργάσαιντο τὸν ἐρώμενον. (Plut. *Lyc.* 18.9)

This love was so approved among them, that even the beautiful and good [i.e., noble] women loved virgins. But rivalry in love did not exist. Rather those men [specifically masculine] who were in love with the same boys made it a starting place for friendship between themselves, and continued to strive in common to make the beloved boy [masc.] the best.

Note here that Plutarch mentions *female* homoeroticism only in order to show the high regard the Spartans had for *male* homoeroticism. He does not allot women a part of the *agōgē*.[60] Scholars have shown remarkably little

58. Page, *Alcman* 66–67, and Lardinois, "Lesbian Sappho" 28, deny that the language of the girls of Alcman's chorus is erotic, but Diels, "Alkmans Partheneion" 86–97, had already rightly noted its character; and see Calame, *Les chœurs* 2:86–97. So Lardinois 28–29 in a circular argument says that Lesbos resembled Sparta because "in both cases we are dealing with highborn women. . . . Also the age of the Spartan girls and those of Sappho's circle appear to be similar."

59. For the difficulty of the sources see Forrest, *A History of Sparta* 16. For what little we know or surmise about Alcman's Sparta, see Huxley, *Early Sparta* 61–62; Michell, *Sparta* 11–28; Fitzhardinge, *The Spartans* 129–35. For the social role of women at Sparta, see Redfield, "The Women of Sparta"; Cartledge, "Spartan Wives."

60. So rightly Hallett, "Sappho and Her Social Context" 452; and cf. the cautious assessment of Cartledge, "Spartan Pederasty" 405. E. Cantarella, *Pandora's Daughters* 87, in her paraphrase mistakes the Greek: "At Sparta, says Plutarch, the best women loved girls, and

restraint in taking this single remark and recasting Alcman's Sparta, some seven hundred years earlier, on its basis, and then using that reconstruction of Sparta as a model for Lesbos.[61] Gentili, for example, swings back and forth from Sappho's Lesbos to Alcman's Sparta to Plutarch's Sparta, with a breathtaking disregard of both space and time. Thus when he reaches his "single, unambiguous conclusion" that Alcman's "partheneion is an epithalamium composed for ritual performance within the community to which the girls belonged"—that is, a homosexual ritual quasi-marriage between Agido and Hagesichora—he is able to cut immediately away and state, "Himerius, writing in the fourth century A.D., and interweaving his orations and paraphrases and citations from archaic lyric, particularly that of Sappho and Anacreon, bears witness in one passage [*Or.* 9.4 194 Loeb] to the presence of an internal ceremony of exactly this sort [i.e., two women in a formal marriage]."[62] In passing, beside the dubious methodology of employing

when it happened that more than one adult fell in love with the same girl, they were rivals with one another but joined forces to educate the beloved," an error repeated in *Bisexuality* 84. She therefore believes that the women and their lovers also were viewed as having a separate but equal form of education and writes: "It is perhaps no accident that it is a man (Plutarch) who stresses the pedagogical function of the relationship between women, whereas Sappho—though she insists on the educational and ennobling aspect of life in the *thiasos* —stresses instead the affective and erotic aspect of the relationship" (*Pandora's Daughters* 89; cf. *Bisexuality* 84). This is typical of the problems created by the presuppositions involved in Sappho Schoolmistress. Note: (1) the facile equation of Plutarch's remarks on Sparta with Sappho's situation; (2) the statement that Sappho insists on ennobling education, in the complete absence of anything of the sort in the poems; (3) the uncritical use of "*thiasos*" to validate the reconstruction; and (4) the isolation of Sappho: how does Sappho's emphasis on the "affective and erotic" differ from that of any other poet?

61. An additional piece of remarkably misunderstood evidence is cited by Calame, *Les chœurs* 1:434, followed by Bremmer, "An Enigmatic Rite" 292; E. Cantarella, *Bisexuality* 84 n. 25; and Lardinois, "Lesbian Sappho" 27. Calame states that a certain Academic philosopher, Hagnon, tells us that Spartan women had sexual relations with young girls before their marriage. The source is Ath. 13.602e, which clearly says that among the Spartans πρὸ τῶν γάμων ταῖς παρθένοις ὡς παιδικοῖς νόμος ἐστὶν ὁμιλεῖν (it is the custom to have intercourse with virgins before marriage as with *paidika*), i.e., anal intercourse (so rightly Devereux, "Greek Pseudo-Homosexuality" 83; Dover, *Greek Homosexuality* 188; Cartledge, "Spartan Pederasty" 407 n. 69). The Greek is unmistakable, but Calame asserts, with the aid of a misleading French translation, that because the context of the passage is "homosexuality," we can be certain that the custom is that of adult females, thus anachronistically ascribing to the Greeks our lumping together of male and female homoeroticism as forms of the same "deviancy." He protests against Devereux by saying, "la Sparte antique n'est pas un pays latin et catholique," apparently ignorant of the fact that the custom was not unknown to Greece (Hdt. 1.61) and was a standing joke about the Spartans (Ar. *Lys.* 1173–74); see Dover, "Eros and Nomos" 37. The entire discussion is not about "homosexuality" but *Knabenliebe*; no women have been mentioned for pages.

62. Gentili. *Poetry and Its Public* 72–89; quotations from 75, 76.

a fourth century C.E. paraphrase of Sappho as if it were evidence about seventh-century B.C.E. Sparta, Gentili mistakes a metaphorical treatment of Sappho's poetry as a description of a real event, turns the textual mess †γράφειτ† παρθένους ⟨εἰς⟩ νυμφεῖον (writes[?] maidens ⟨into⟩ the bridal chamber) into evidence for lesbian marriage in Sparta/Lesbos, and ignores Alcman 81 and S 5b (*PMGF*), where the poet has the chorus of maidens ask for a husband.

Gentili states: "We know from Plutarch (*Lyc.* 18, 9) that homoerotic female relationships were also allowed in archaic Sparta, in communities of more or less the same type as the Lesbian ones. And it has been demonstrated ... that the partheneia of Alcman are full of stylemes, metaphors and typical expressions that derive from the language of love and are extensively paralleled in Sappho."[63]   But we "know" nothing of the sort. We don't know what, if any, source Plutarch had for this statement; we don't know that female erotic relationships in archaic Sparta were in the form Plutarch imagines for them; we don't know anything about Spartan women's "communities" (in the plural) nor of Lesbian "communities," nor that they were "more or less the same type."   What we do have is ample evidence for Plutarch's back-projection of his assumptions about contemporary Sparta onto the time of Lycurgus.[64]   Plutarch may well be right about the existence of female homoeroticism in contemporary Sparta or even the Sparta of Alcman's day.   However, we must be suspicious of his construction of it.   Even Cantarella notes: "In some way, then, one senses that female homosexuality was culturally 'constructed' on the model of the male and presented—by the few male sources that allude to it—as a copy of this."[65]

I do not know exactly what is going on in Alcman's partheneia, but there is no trace of this male type of *erastēs* to *erōmenos*, older to younger love, in them.   Instead, we find something quite different: expressions of love between age-mates, each for the other.[66]   In the Louvre Partheneion, the

63. Ibid., 73.

64. See Ollier, *Le mirage* 2:187–215; Redfield, "The Women of Sparta" 146; and Plutarch's own opening statement in *Lyc.* 1.1.

65. E. Cantarella, *Pandora's Daughters* 89. By 1988 she was, rightly, even more suspicious of the male construction of female (homo)sexuality: "My feeling, in short, is that female homosexuality ... was constructed from the outside—which is to say, by men—on the model of pederasty" (*Bisexuality* 83–84). She shows, however, a curiously split vision on this point. While arguing against any sort of initiatory function (e.g., for marriage) for ancient Greek female homosexuality in general and Sappho in particular, she is yet unable to rid herself of the notion of Sappho as teacher and sex instructor before marriage.

66. The erotic language is directed only at each other; see above, n. 58. Yet the effect of Sappho Schoolmistress is so powerful that it can blind scholars even to this.   So

singers, including Hegesichora and Agido, are ten girls together (99), who call Agido their cousin (52).[67] Outside the circle of the chorus stands the shadowy figure of Aenesimbrota but she is not a candidate for a role of elder female *erastēs*. In 73–77 the chorus sings:

οὐδ' ἐς Αἰνησιμβρ[ό]τας ἐνθοῖσα φασεῖς·
Ἀσταφίς [τ]έ μοι γένοιτο
καὶ ποτιγλέποι Φίλυλλα
Δαμαρ[έ]τα τ' ἐρατά τε ϝιανθεμίς·
ἀλλ' Ἁγησιχόρα με τείρει.

Nor going to Aenesimbrota's house will you say:
"Let Astaphis be mine"
and "Let Philylla look at me
and Damareta and lovely Vianthemis."
But Hagesichora wears me out.[68]

First, let us admit that we have no idea who Aenesimbrota is. All we know is that she has some connection with the four girls named here. Page suggests that she is "one to whose house you would go if you were looking for Astaphis, Philylla, and the rest." This seems reasonable, though in fact all the text says is that her house is a place to go to say things about the four girls.[69] However, Page's next sentence quite oversteps the evidence: "In short, the text indicates, without the least obscurity, that she is the keeper of

---

Lardinois, "Lesbian Sappho" 28, in order to save his model of a pederastic female homosexuality, is prepared to deny that the girls' language is at all erotic: "There is, however, no reason to suppose that relationships also existed among the girls themselves. The *other sources* [emphasis mine] also refer only to relationships between adult women and girls."

67. Page, *Alcman* 46. For the choruses consisting of age-mates, see Calame, *Les chœurs* 1:63–70.

68. On the reading τείρει and its meaning, see Page, *Alcman* 91; Merkelbach, "Sappho und ihr Kreis" 3.

69. West, "Alcmanica" 199–200, has the bizarre suggestion that she might be a dispenser of love potions, followed by Griffiths, "Alcman's Partheneion" 22; Puelma, "Die Selbstbeschreibung des Chores" 40. The suggestion is tentatively raised by Campbell, *Greek Lyric* 2:367; Lefkowitz, *First-Person Fictions* 19; and Lardinois, "Lesbian Sappho," who adds, "Otherwise she might have been a woman who allocated the girls among the women of Sparta" (28). Aenesimbrota has become the offical civic lesbian procuress (so explicitly Hooker, *The Ancient Spartans* 79). Again, it is possible to see the strange slant that the discussion of female sexuality can occasion. The point in all these authors is a supposed parallelism between male and female versions of the *agōgē*. Yet despite all that we do know about the formal male *agōgē* and all the commentary that has been written on it (for which see Brelich, *Paides* 113–207; Cartledge, "Spartan Pederasty"), no one has ever suggested that the boys had recourse to love potions or that there was an official civic boy bursar.

a training school for choir-maidens."[70] While Hagesichora's leading of the chorus is explicit in the text (44, 84, beside her name), there is no mention of any "training" by Aenesimbrota. There would seem to me to be a superfluity of trainers: the chorus leader Hagesichora, her second-in-command Agido, now Aenesimbrota, all of whom leave very little for Alcman to do.[71] Page's suggestion may very well be so, but there is more obscurity here than he was willing to admit. An equally possible (and equally unprovable) scenario is that Aenesimbrota is the mother of the four girls, especially if the chorus consisted of actual cousins,[72] and this notion receives some support from Pindar's fragmentary *Partheneion II*.[73]

Yet whatever Aenesimbrota was to the girls, there is one thing that she most definitely was not, and that is their lover. Even Calame believes that Aenesimbrota was a teacher to the chorus, "but one who remained outside their love affairs."[74] In short, there is no evidence for the sort of masculine *erastēs* to *erōmenos* relationship that Plutarch envisions for Spartan women to be found in Alcman at all.

Aenesimbrota cannot be turned into Sappho. I doubt she was a professional chorus trainer. Even if she was, Sappho wasn't. Page explicitly denied any comparison to Sappho's "school,"[75] but others were and continue to be less circumspect. Thus we have a vicious circle: the image of Sappho Schoolmistress is invoked to explain (and misinterpret) Alcman's Sparta, which in turn is used to justify Sappho Schoolmistress. We simply cannot turn Plutarch into Alcman and Alcman into Sappho.

70. Page, *Alcman* 65. He heads the section, "The Academy of Aenesimbrota." For Aenesimbrota as teacher, cf. also Bowra, *Greek Lyric Poetry* 57.

71. On Agido, see rightly Page, *Alcman* 44–46. If Aenesimbrota is a trainer, she seems to be responsible for only half the chorus—less one leader—and Page himself (48, 57–62) has fairly well demolished the idea that there were semichoruses, in the singing at any rate. Further, why would the trainer of one half of the chorus be mentioned and not the other?

72. See Page, *Alcman* 67–68. The arguments of West, "Alcmanica" 196, and Griffiths, "Alcman's Partheneion" 29, for some vague use of "cousin" (explicitly influenced by English usage) are extremely weak. Gentili, *Poetry and Its Public* 259 n. 16, flatly proclaims it an "institutional designation." The sensible suggestion of Aenesimbrota as mother is made by Campbell, *The Golden Lyre* 189.

73. 94b Snell-Maehler (83 Bowra, *Greek Lyric Poetry*), a civic ritual of the *daphnēphorikon* at Thebes. The relationships between the named persons in the partheneion are uncertain, but they seem all to be members of the family of Aeoladas, his son Pagondas, and his grandson Agasicles. Andaesistrota, who instructed the chorus leader with her arts (Ἀνδαισιστρότα ἂν ἐπάσκησε μήδεσ[ι]; 94b.71–72 Snell) is most likely the maiden's mother. For a new text, discussion, and review of the previous literature, see Lehnus, "Pindaro" (esp. 83), who is followed by Lefkowitz, *First-Person Fictions* 17–19 (cf. Lefkowitz, "The First Person in Pindar" 188–90).

74. Calame, *Les chœurs* 2:97.

75. Page, *Alcman* 65–66.

VII. SAPPHO MUSIC TEACHER

The lingering influence of Wilamowitz, the search for a ritual setting to "explain" her poetry, and the invocation of Alcman as a parallel have led to a very popular by-form of Sappho Schoolmistress, that of casting Sappho as music teacher. Thus Dover writes:

> In what, if anything, did Sappho "educate" Lesbian and Ionian girls? Most obviously, in that in which she herself excelled, poetry and music, establishing a female counterpart to a predominately male domain; there would be a certain improbability in supposing that Lesbian girls of good family were sent by their parents to a school of sexual technique, but none in supposing a school which enhanced their skill and charm (charm is within the province of Aphrodite) as performers in girls' choruses at festivals.[76]

Dover is right to reject the notion of a "school of sexual technique," but a "charm" school (confined to the natives) fares no better.[77] Again, it is necessary to point out that in no extant poem does Sappho "teach" anything to anyone. But Dover points out a way that Sappho Schoolmistress might yet be saved. Since she wrote choral poetry, she would have, presumably, *taught* the chorus her songs.[78] However, as Page notes: "There is no evidence or indication that any of Sappho's poetry apart from the Epithalamians [and 140, a fragment of a song for an *Adonia*] was designed for presentation by herself or others (whether individuals or choirs) on a formal or ceremonial occasion, public or private."[79] Along with Page and others, I am presuming here that Sappho's epithalamia are actual songs for actual ceremonies on Lesbos,[80] but they cannot be pressed into service to turn Sappho into a

76. Dover, *Greek Homosexuality* 175. He refers to fr. 214b = S 261a P., quoted above.

77. For music as part of the curriculum at Sappho's school, cf. the citations in section III above; Wilamowitz, *Sappho und Simonides* 73; Aly, "Sappho" 2371, 2377–78; Schmid and Stählin, *Geschichte* 421 (who include poetry lectures and verse composition); Kranz, *Geschichte* 88; R. Cantarella, *Storia* 203: "Sappho was head of a 'thiasos' of young ladies ... a type of college or school for girls where, in an atmosphere of refined elegance, they took what was a 'good education' at that time, in particular music, singing, and dancing"; Fränkel, *Early Greek Poetry* 175; West, "Other Early Poetry" 83; Burnett, *Three Archaic Poets* 215; E. Cantarella, *Pandora's Daughters* 72: "It was 'female' education emphasizing music, singing and dance," and *Bisexuality* 79; Lardinois, "Lesbian Sappho" 26 (quoted above).

78. For a summary of the evidence for the poet as *didaskalos*, see Herington, *Poetry into Drama* 183–84.

79. Page, *Sappho and Alcaeus* 119; cf. 72, 126. On fr. 140, see Page 119 n. 1.

80. Ibid., 120, 122. The epithalamia are frs. 27, 30 (in Sapphics), perhaps 104–6(?) (dactylic hexameter), 107–9 (prob. dactylic hexameter), 110–17 (a variety of meters, some uncertain). Only these last are in what might be choral meters. Demetr. *Eloc.* 167 says that her epithalamia are not suitable for the lyre or the chorus, but this is criticism of her choice of prosaic words rather than an indication of the modes of performance.

professional music teacher. Dover and others are correct to state that Sappho presumably "taught" these songs to her chorus. The mistake comes not in calling her therefore a "chorus teacher" but rather trying to use the ambiguity of that word to imply some sort of modern idea of "teacher," as if "chorus teacher" were the name of a profession, a specific social role distinct from that of poet.

There are two extremely important differences between Sappho's epithalamia and the type of choral songs that Dover is imagining, and between Sappho and Alcman (the poet to whom she is explicitly or implicitly compared), Pindar, Bacchylides, or later tragic and comic poets. First, epithalamia are part of the private, familial ritual of the marriage.[81] They are not a public, civic, or political rite. Alcman is said to be the διδάσκαλος for the traditional choruses of girls and of boys at Sparta,[82] maintained then, one presumes, at public expense to provide the chorus for public ceremonies, such as the partheneia. This is a completely different situation than Sappho's, whose epithalamia were created for the specific private occasion of individual marriage ceremonies, consisting of the relatives and friends of the bride and groom. Unlike Alcman, Sappho was not hired by the city for the occasion nor was the entire polis expected to attend. Partheneia and epithalamia are distinct genres and the mere fact that choruses of young girls feature in both does not mean that they are the same thing, have the same poetics, or serve the same societal function, a fact that Calame rightly points out. Thus the civic *chœurs de jeunes filles* that he studied have, by his own admission, simply nothing to do with Sappho.[83]

Second, there did not exist, as far as we know, anywhere in the Greek world, an institution of standing choruses. Even for the greatest of civic celebrations, the tragic festivals at Athens for example, each chorus was put together for a single specific occasion. Nowhere did there exist choral "schools" in which the citizens of even a single polis enrolled to learn a job skill, much less a Panhellenic choral academy. Alcman was the "teacher" of his choral verses to the sons and daughters of Sparta, yet no one has ever suggested that he ran a "school" there. Pindar was in demand throughout

---

81. Maas, "Hymenaios" in PW 17.1:130–34; Muth, "Hymenaios"; Keydell, "Epithalamium" 927–31.

82. *POxy* 2506, called by Page the "Commentarius in Melicos" = *PMG* 10.32–43 (T 5 Calame): διδάσκαλον τῶν θυγατέρων καὶ ἐφή[βω]ν πατρίο[ις] χοροῖς. Cf. also test. A 11b *PMGF* (T 29 Loeb), which mentions his παιδείας, "training."

83. Calame, *Les chœurs* 1:167. For Calame's remarks on partheneia, see 1:18–20, 167; on epithalamia, 1:159–62. Cf. also [Plut.] *De mus.* 17.1136f = Alcman test. B 2 *PMGF* (T 15 Loeb), where Plato knows partheneia by Alcman, Pindar, Simonides, and Bacchylides (also *prosodia* and paeans), with no mention of Sappho. Sappho is doing something quite different in the epithalamia from the partheneia of the other poets.

the Hellenic world, but no one speaks of his "school." He did not travel with a band, nor were children or citizens sent to any kind of central music academy run by him in order to learn how to sing and dance in his choruses.[84] Alcman and Pindar have a precise social role: it is not "teacher," not even "chorus teacher," it is "poet." These kind of suggestions are never made about any male poet, only about Sappho. There is indeed improbability—and, more importantly, no evidence—in supposing a school to train "performers in girls' choruses at festivals." And the epithalamia were not in fact sung at public festivals, but private weddings. The picture of girls being sent from all over Asia Minor to enter an academy in order to form a permanent chorus of bridesmaids belongs to Gilbert and Sullivan, not archaic Greece.[85]

VIII. SAPPHO SEX EDUCATOR

Earlier authors looking for details of Sappho's educational program in her poems forced the epithalamia into this role. And there has been a return, again in ritual guise, of the idea of Sappho as sex educator.[86] Schmid and

84. Instead, Pindar on occasion sent his poem with a *chorodidaskalos* to teach it (*Ol.* 6.87–91; with scholia on 87–88 = 148a, 149a Drachmann). We do, however, hear of choruses traveling to other festivals, as in Pind. *Ol.* 6.98–100. *POxy* 2389 fr. 35, col. i, 16–18 (Alcman 11 *PMGF*) may speak of "the women of Dyme" going to Pitane (Spartan villages) to do something with the women of Pitane, but the text is severely damaged (Podlecki, *The Early Greek Poets* 111, is overly confident). According to Paus. 5.25.2–4, the Messinians regularly sent a boys' chorus, with *didaskalos*, to Rhegium. What we do not find is the Messinians sending their sons to Rhegium to be trained. For other evidence, see Herington, *Poetry into Drama* 189–91.

85. Further, the fact that the epithalamia fit so neatly into the image of Sappho School-mistress has led to a strange forgetfulness of Sappho's lyrics. So Tarditi, *Storia* 73: "Sappho was a χοροδιδάσκαλος [chorus trainer] with the job of preparing choruses for public and private festivals, and headed a *thiasos*," with no mention that she was a lyric poet as well. Again, note the use of Greek words to authenticate the unauthentic.

86. Cf. Dover, *Greek Homosexuality* 175, quoted above; Lardinois, "Lesbian Sappho," evidences his own two minds about Sappho. While recognizing that calling Sappho a homosexual "is necessarily anachronistic" (25), he operates with a purely mechanical definition of lesbianism: if she touched the girls, she's gay. He too seems more concerned to deny the "charge" of lesbianism than to question what would constitute proof. The question of "sincerity" raises its pointless head. He admits that "probably she engaged in sexual relations with the girls," but describes her poetry as "conventional" and warns that "it is impossible to gather from her poem her personal feelings. . . . [O]ne cannot infer that Sappho was a lesbian at heart" (20). Later, he says that "we are dealing with an institutionalized type of sexuality, in which the preferences of those involved may have been of little consequence" (30). It might then not have been Sappho's fault; society is to blame. Again, a contrast with male poets is instructive; no one has ever claimed that Alcaeus or Theognis was forced into writing homosexual poetry by convention. This necessitates his belittling the very poetry he seeks to defend (24–25): "Could it be that her frivolous songs praising the beauty of young girls gave rise to the assumption that she would also have been more than willing to sleep with numerous men, preferably

Stählin, as well as Merkelbach, speak vaguely of "instruction and preparation for marriage."[87] For other examples of "sex education" courses at Sappho's school, compare Cantarella's remarks about "beauty, seduction, and charm" quoted above.[88] Hallett, in a perceptive article, is one of the few to have thought seriously about what *ritual* purpose Sappho's erotic monodies might have served.[89] However, I cannot agree with her view of Sappho as a "sensual consciousness-raiser," since it begins from the assumption that Sappho's circle consisted of girls being educated before marriage and that her love poetry was written only to these girls.[90] Further, I find no evidence that Greek fathers or husbands wanted their daughters' or wives' sensual consciousness raised. The emphasis throughout the society is on the repression of female sexuality rather than its encouragement.[91] A wife who enjoys sex too much is a potential adulteress, not a valuable commodity.[92]

Burnett presents the most explicit picture of Sappho's Sex Academy:

> Soon the girls of these youthful groups would marry, and it was to this end that their elegant accomplishments were acquired. Their value was being increased, so that their fathers could boast more fulsomely [sic] to their prospective grooms, but they were not just polished for the market—they were being prepared for marriage itself.

> Ideally they were to have enough understanding of Eros to bring their husbands pleasure. . . . Their lessons were in part practical, for . . . they, as her age-mates, accompanied the bride almost to her bed. Sappho taught them just what to do.

> Ritual songs of this sort were a form of instruction in the corporal side of marriage.[93]

Burnett's insistence on an educative/ritual function for every song leads ultimately to a distorted picture. There is simply no evidence for any of this.[94] There is no sex education in the epithalamia. The purpose of an

---

in a shameless manner?" Sappho's poetry has been called many things before, but never "frivolous."

87. Schmid and Stählin, *Geschichte* 421; Merkelbach, "Sappho und ihr Kreis" 4, cf. 12–16.

88. E. Cantarella, *Pandora's Daughters* 86–87.

89. Hallett, "Sappho and Her Social Context."

90. Ibid., 460. See also Stigers' [Stehle's] response, "Romantic Sensuality, Poetic Sense," and Winkler, "Double Consciousness" 187.

91. See Arthur, "Early Greece," for a excellent overview.

92. E.g., Hes. *Op.* 373–75, 695–705; Sem. 48–54, 90–91, or Homer's and Aeschylus's portraits of Klytemnestra; Ar. *Lys.* 163–66 is the remarkable exception.

93. Burnett, *Three Archaic Poets* 216, 218, 219.

94. Himerius *Or.* 9.4 (T 154 Loeb) and *AP* 7.406.6 (T 58 Loeb) are sometimes pressed into service, but they simply mean that Sappho wrote epithalamia; see above.

epithalamion is to praise the bride (103b V., 108, 112, 113, 117a) not to give her advice on the finer points of intercourse on her way to the wedding chamber. What we find instead is regret for the loss of virginity (105c, 107, 114). There is nothing said about "attendant joys."[95] And how exactly all this was supposed to work is left misty. Are we to imagine Sappho falling in love with just one girl at a time, or all of them indiscriminately, or as each one comes to market? Lardinois alone has tackled this ticklish problem head on: "Sappho had a circle of young girls around her, and it is unlikely that she had a sexual relation with all of them."[96] His solution is that Sappho slept only with the head girl at her boarding school, who was then appointed the "*choragos*" of the school choir.

What I find curious about this reconstruction is that its origins so clearly lie in the products of masculine fantasy. This does not mean that it is *therefore* incorrect. But when dealing with a reconstruction—and it must be emphasized that it is only a reconstruction—that has its origins in Victorian sexism and sexology, we should be at least suspicious.[97] This idea of a homoerotic "phase," either of "crushes" or of sexual experimentation, leading (being tamed or transformed) to "normal" heterosexual, reproductive sex is a commonplace of both the literature of pornography and developmental psychology. It has a venerable history in both. For the first, see Nicolas Chorier's *Satyra Sotadica de Arcanis Amoris et Veneris*, which has claims to be the first pornographic best-seller.[98] Better known is Cleland's *Fanny Hill*. Compare the way in which Sappho is imagined to Cleland's description of Phoebe Ayres, Fanny's first lover, "whose business it was to prepare and break such fillies as I was to the mounting block; and she was accordingly, in that view, allotted me for a bedfellow; and to give her the more authority, she had the title of cousin conferred on her by the venerable president of this college."[99] Elaine Marks emphasizes the importance of the school setting to much of this literature. For psychology, Helen Deutsch popularized the notion of the "pashes" of Anglo-German school girls as a stage in a universal feminine psychosexual development.[100]

The result is that Sappho's very lesbianism and poetry are forced into the service of normative male heterosexuality. Sappho falls *in love* and writes

95. Hallett, "Sappho and Her Social Context" 456.

96. Lardinois, "Lesbian Sappho" 29.

97. Cf. E. Cantarella's remarks above and n. 65.

98. Chorier, *Satyra* 31–39. Chorier published this dialogue novel under the name of the Spanish humanist and poet Luisa Sigea, in another of the ongoing series of sexual attacks on learned women.

99. Cleland, *Fanny Hill* 47.

100. Marks, "Lesbian Intertextuality"; Deutsch, *The Psychology of Women* 1:30–32, 85–87, 119–20.

poetry on commission, it would seem, in order to benefit men. Sappho, whether she touches the girls (Burnett) or not (Wilamowitz), still warms them up and hands them over to men for the real thing. She is left behind, blindly jealous or tenderly regretful, as you wish, in any case not threatening. This picture borders on the literally porno-graphic.[101]

IX. FORMAL ISOLATION

We find ourselves trapped in a particularly vicious hermeneutic circle. Aware to a greater extent perhaps than the New Critics of old that a poem can only be understood in terms of the society in which it was created, modern critics frequently wind up reconstructing a society on the basis of its poetry and then interpreting the poetry on the basis of that reconstruction. This can turn out to be only a slightly more sophisticated version of the biographical fallacy. It has, however, been the dominant form of interpretation of Sappho since antiquity. Compare Lefkowitz's warning: "Thus biography, itself derived from interpretation of her poems, is in turn reapplied to the poems and affects our interpretation of them."[102] The problem is that we are almost completely ignorant of what that social background was. This is particularly true in the cases of archaic Lesbos and Sparta. The objection is made that one must have *some* lens through which to view the poetry in order to be able interpret it. The problem arises when the glass darkens what we see. A distorting construct is a danger, not an aid—a point already made by Kirkwood in a lengthy and perceptive footnote.[103] Here again I want to urge a greater skepticism in distinguishing what we know (and where we know it from) from what we were told, from what we assume is likely, and from what we see as parallels in other societies.[104]

This ignorance about the circumstances of performance accounts for the large element of arbitrariness applied to assigning formal, ritual social settings for poems. This arbitrariness applies to three categories: the degree of formality envisioned, the types of poems, and the poets themselves.

First, the degree of formality can be easily overstated. An audience does not, as Merkelbach, Schadewaldt, and Lasserre think, necessarily

---

101. See Kappeler, *The Pornography of Representation* 44; Bunch, "Lesbianism" 90–94. See section VI above for a similar view of Alcman's Aenesimbrota.

102. Lefkowitz, "Critical Stereotypes" 62.

103. Kirkwood, *Early Greek Monody* 267–68 n. 76.

104. Thus Gentili ("La veneranda Saffo" 48, *Poetry and Its Public* 77) offers the fact that a friend once told Simone de Beauvoir that there were lesbian marriages in Singapore and Canton as evidence that second-century C.E. Sparta was just like sixth-century B.C.E. Lesbos. Snyder, *The Woman and the Lyre* 2–3, makes the point well.

imply a ritual.[105]   Winkler's remarks are to the point: "The view of lyric as a subordinate element in celebrations and formal occasions is no more compelling than the view, which I prefer, of song as honored and celebrated at least sometimes in itself. Therefore I doubt that Sappho always needed a sacrifice or dance or wedding *for which* to compose a song."[106]

Second, it is selectively applied to particular types of poems.[107] It is easy to visualize the social settings for choral poetry, for *skolia* and epithalamia. But we are almost completely ignorant of the circumstances under which solo lyric poetry might have been performed in fifth-century Athens, much less seventh-century Lesbos. The problem of "occasion" is particularly acute for erotic poetry. We can say little beyond that—for men at least—a sympotic setting seems likely.[108]

A fuller realization of the element of performance in a still predominately oral culture has, however, led to a certain monolithic approach in some scholars. Since the epithalamion is an easily imagined social occasion, Sappho's poems are forced to be epithalamia whether they wish it or not. Thus Merkelbach and others have taken fragment 17 as a "propemptikon for the passage of a bride over to her new home and country." The same is true for 94 and 96: they became a new genre of "Trostgedichte" (consolation songs) for when the girls leave Sappho's school to get married.[109] The absence of any mention of bride, husband, or wedding does not seem to bother him.[110] This is hardly less absurd than Wilamowitz's reading of fragment 31 as a epithalamion, which Merkelbach also endorses with the change of heterosexual jealousy (*Eifersucht*) into homosexual regret for the loss of a

105. Merkelbach, "Sappho und ihr Kreis"; Schadewaldt, "Zu Sappho"; Lasserre, "Ornements érotiques." See the strictures of Jenkyns, *Three Classical Poets* 6–7; Burnett, *Three Archaic Poets* 209 n. 2; Herington, *Poetry into Drama* 36. Cf. the discussion at Russo, "Reading the Greek Lyric Poets" 720–21.

106. Winkler, "Double Consciousness" 165.

107. Merkelbach, "Sappho und ihr Kreis" 7 and n. 1 admits the difficulty of finding an occasion for some poems: "Sappho 1 remains a difficult problem."

108. See West, *Studies* 10–13; Crotty, *Song and Action* 76–103; Herington, *Poetry into Drama* 36, 60, 195; Gentili, *Poetry and Its Public* 89–104; Bremmer, "Adolescents, Symposion, and Pederasty." The chief ancient source for the sympotic setting and for repeat performances of solo song (here elegiacs) is Theog. 237–54.

109. Merkelbach, "Sappho und ihr Kreis" 5; cf. 23–35; 12–13.

110. Kirkwood, *Early Greek Monody* 269, is mistaken in saying that Merkelbach calls it an epithalamion but correct when he writes: "Even Fr. 17 ... is called an epithalamion by Merkelbach, apparently because it cannot be proved not to be." So for fr. 96, Wilamowitz, *Sappho und Simonides* 54; Rose, *Handbook* 98; Gentili, *Poetry and Its Public* 82; Lardinois, "Lesbian Sappho" 17 and 29.

pure beloved to "normal" life.[111] Thus in an recent article entitled "Public Occasion and Private Passion in the Lyrics of Sappho of Lesbos," Snyder shows how difficult it is to determine which poems fell into what category, and West appeals to an equally subjective sense of decorum at symposia.[112]

Most importantly, a degree of ritual formality is invoked for Sappho that is not invoked for any male poet. Sympotic themes make it easy to discuss Alcaeus or Theognis as operating within a formalized social setting, and it has been suggested that "ritual" occasions are sought for Sappho more often than for male poets because she lacks such a clear sympotic setting. However, there are many poems by male poets that are difficult to imagine as sung at a symposium or in any other formal setting; they are not therefore labeled "ritual." Kirkwood's observations still apply:

> I am not conscious of any concern to determine the specific occasion of Alcaeus 130, the remarkable description of the poet in exile . . . or the occasion of Archilochus's famous song of hatred . . . (79a), or the specific occasion of any poem of Archilochus, Alcaeus, or Anacreon, except where the subject of the poem readily suggests its occasion, as in some of Alcaeus' drinking songs. Only for Sappho are the efforts of scholarship bent on providing occasions.[113]

So for Sappho, Kraus calls the existence of her school, "only an assumption, but a necessary one."[114] I think it a most unnecessary assumption, certainly an assumption no one finds necessary for any other poet. Could Sappho not have written poetry except at a ladies' seminary? Male poets are simply left to be poets but Sappho, it seems, needs to be explained away, isolated in a cult or shut away in a school. Like many a woman of genius, Sappho has been institutionalized.

X. THE NONEXISTENT "THIASOS"

The sign of this attitude is the constant use of the word *thiasos* in connection with Sappho. This word is never used anywhere in any of the poems of Sappho (or Alcaeus), nor is it ever used anywhere in any ancient source about her. Yet it is approaching its hundredth anniversary, copied from Wilamowitz to Aly, Rose, Hadas, Schadewaldt, Latte, Fränkel, Flacelière, Raffaele Cantarella, Tarditi, Russo, Stigers, Tsagarakis, Eva Cantarella,

---

111. Merkelbach, "Sappho und ihr Kreis" 7. Again one would imagine the stake had been fairly well driven into this one by Page, *Sappho and Alcaeus* 30–33, but it rises still in Fränkel, *Early Greek Poetry* 176, and as recently as E. Cantarella, *Pandora's Daughters* 73, and *Bisexuality* 80.

112. West, "Burning Sappho" 309, 318.

113. Kirkwood, *Early Greek Monody* 267–68.

114. Kraus, "Sappho" 1546.

Crotty, Burnett, and Commoti.[115] Its only purpose, whether conscious or not, is to lend a spurious air of antiquity to a modern creation, and to make it sound as if we actually knew what Sappho's *"thiasos"* was.[116] I am officially announcing its death. It should never be used again in connection with Sappho. Merkelbach writes, "Whether one calls this group a 'thiasos' or a 'hetairia' is naturally a matter of indifference."[117] But it does make a difference: the word *thiasos* is not used in connection with anyone but Sappho. And its primary purpose is to isolate Sappho from all other lyric poets. Alcaeus calls his comrades ἕταιροι (129.16; 150.4); he has a *hetairia*. Sappho calls her comrades ἕταιραι (160.1); she has a *thiasos*.[118] Alcaeus has friends; Sappho has a cult.

XI. POETIC ISOLATION

This isolation extends not only to the circumstances in which we visualize Sappho singing but also to her songs themselves. She is segregated as a poet from consideration with other poets. Thus Gentili describes the topics and

115. I have not chased the application of the term to Sappho back further than Wilamowitz's article on Alcman, "Der Chor" 259–60. See Aly, "Sappho" 2357, 2371, 2377–78; Rose, *Handbook* 97; Hadas, *History* 51; Schadewaldt, *Sappho* 11; Latte, review of Fränkel 35; Fränkel, *Early Greek Poetry* 175; Flacelière, *Histoire* 128; R. Cantarella, *Storia* 196; Tarditi, *Storia* 73; Russo, "Reading the Greek Lyric Poets" 721; Stigers [Stehle], "Retreat from the Male" 92–93, 98; Tsagarakis, *Self-Expression in Early Greek Lyric* 70 n. 5; E. Cantarella, *Pandora's Daughters* 71, 86, and *Bisexuality* 107 f.; Crotty, *Song and Action* 80; Burnett, *Three Archaic Poets* 211; Commoti, *Music* 21.

116. See also Calame's warning (*Les chœurs* 1:367) about its use ("granted, the indications of the existence of a genuine Sapphic thiasos are extremely thin and the word is never used in connection with the poetess of Lesbos"), which does not prevent him from tossing the term about elsewhere (27, 362, 429, 438). Likewise Fernandez-Galinano, *Safo* 56: "This circle ... is not a thiasos, nor a brotherhood, nor a boarding school, nor an academy, nor a school for poetry"; and West, "Burning Sappho" 324: "θίασος, for example, which some modern writers readily apply, does not occur either in Sappho or in Alcaeus."

117. Merkelbach, "Sappho und ihr Kreis" 4 n. 1. The word "natürlich" is a warning. Lanata, "Sul linguaggio amoroso" 66, says the same thing.

118. Further, Ath. 11.463e continues his quotation of fr. 2 with τούτοισι τοῖς ἑταίροις ἐμοῖς γε καὶ σοῖς (for my companions and yours), so some such words may have been in Sappho (Page, *Sappho and Alcaeus* 39; for a summary of positions, Burnett, *Three Archaic Poets* 275 n. 128). In fr. 126 she writes δαύοις ἀπάλας ἐτα⟨ί⟩ρας ἐν στήθεσιν (May you sleep on the breast of your tender companion). Athenaeus quotes 142 to show that Sappho called her friends ἕταιραι: Leto and Niobe were dear companions (φίλαι ἕταιραι); and the commentary at 90 (fr. 10a) seems to say, if it is about this passage, that Sappho compared her friendship to Atthis to these two, i.e., once friends, now enemies. Even the *Suda* (Σ 107, 4.322 Adler = T 2 Loeb) speaks of ἕταιραι δὲ αὐτῆς καὶ φίλαι, as well as her μαθήτριαι (see above). So throughout Gentili, *Poetry and Its Public* 72–104, "The Ways of Love in the Poetry of *Thiasos* and Symposium": cf. 3, 56, 81 ("male clubs ... female communities"), 259 n. 16. So Snell, *Poetry and Society* 30–33 on Alcaeus's "hetairia" vs. Sappho's "circle" (44).

formats of the lyric poetry of praise and blame as "political and social polemic, the occasional anecdote based on some commonplace episode of ordinary life, personal abuse, moralizing invective, cynical criticism of traditional ideas and the poets who are their spokesmen."[119] Such is the poetry, he says, of Archilochus, Hipponax, Semonides, Xenophanes, Solon, Theognis, Alcaeus, and especially Anacreon; in short of everyone, except Sappho. Yet all these themes (except perhaps a "cynical" criticism) are found in her poetry. Burnett describes the circle of Alcaeus: "Met together for pleasure, they celebrated common cults and entertained one another with songs of every sort—hymns and exhortations, but also riddles, jokes, abuse, and salutes to the victories and defeats, departures and reunions, as well as to the sexual adventures, that made up their mutual lives."[120] Again, this differs not at all from what we find in Sappho, save in perhaps substituting "love" for "sexual adventures" in both poets.

Modern scholars have ancient precedent for segregating Sappho by sex from her fellow lyric poets. Strabo (13.3.3 = T 7 Loeb), Antipater of Thessalonica (*AP* 7.15 = T 57 Loeb; 9.26: a list of nine women poets), Galen (4.771.18 K), and an anonymous author (*AP* 9.190.7–8 = T 35 Loeb) compare her only with other women, while Antipater of Sidon (*AP* 7.14 = T 27 Loeb, 9.66), Plato (*AP* 9.506 = T 60 Loeb), and Plutarch (*Amat.* 18) make her a Muse, not a poet.[121]

But there exists another ancient tradition that counted her simply as one of the nine lyric poets (Anon. *AP* 9.184, Gell. 19.3 = T 53 Loeb, Ath. 14.639e). Sappho sang of love. A wide variety of authors recognized that her subject matter was more important to her poetry than her gender and compared her with other poets who sang about love. Above all they compared her with Anacreon.[122] So Clearchus (ca. 300 B.C.E., Ath. 14.639a = T 39 Loeb) treats their love songs together, as do Horace (*Carm.* 4.9.9–12), Ovid (*Tr.* 2.363–65, quoted above), Pausanias (1.25.1), Aulus Gellius (19.9.3 = T 53 Loeb), Maximus of Tyre (18.9l–m, see above), Themistius (fourth century C.E., *Or.* 13.170d–71a = T 52 Loeb), and Plutarch (*De mul. virt.* 243b = T 54 Loeb), who provides my epigraph. Apuleius (*Apol.* 9 = T 48 Loeb) says the only difference between the love songs of Sappho and Anacreon, Alcman, or Simonides is dialect. Menander Rhetor (9.132, 134 = T 47 Loeb) sees no difference in the kletic hymns of Sappho and Anacreon or Alcman. Dionysius of Halicarnassus (*Dem.* 40 = T 42 Loeb) chooses Sappho, Anacreon, and Hesiod

119. Gentili, *Poetry and Its Public* 109.

120. Burnett, *Three Archaic Poets* 121. Note here that Alcaeus is not the *leader* of his *hetairia*.

121. Anon. *AP* 9.571 cuts her from the nine lyric poets to add her to the nine Muses. Cf. also Dioscorides *AP* 7.407; Anon. *AP* 9.189, 521.

122. Winkler, "Double Consciousness" 163.

as representing the polished (γλαφυρά) style. Demetrius (*Eloc.* 132 = T 45 Loeb) in a famous passage summed up "the whole of Sappho's poetry" as νυμφαῖοι κῆποι, ὑμέναιοι, ἔρωτες (gardens of nymphs, wedding songs, love affairs). These are not unique to Sappho. What is unique to Sappho is the desire to lock her up in the garden.

Sappho sang hymns, wedding songs, love songs, songs of blame, and songs of praise. Russo on what he terms "the great Question of Sapphic studies" writes: "I find it easier to assume that some special *purpose* lay behind the existence of Sappho's circle of women, and that some degree of formal organization existed to carry out that purpose."[123] My question is, why is that purpose made more formal than that which bound together Alcaeus's circle? Why is she alone made the *leader* of a *thiasos*, a schoolteacher, a priestess of Aphrodite and the Muses? For all his hymns, Alcaeus is never called the leader of a *thiasos*.[124] For all his choral poetry, no one says that Alcman set up a school for young boys. For all his erotic verse, no one calls Theognis a "sensual consciousness-raiser."

XII. A DIFFERENT READING/READING OTHERWISE

The interpretive model of Sappho as Schoolmistress, Sappho as Ritual leader does not work. It has no evidence to support it and it leads to some grotesque misinterpretations of the poetry. But if Sappho was not a Schoolmistress, what was she?

Let us turn from Victorian fantasy and modern reconstructions to the one indisputable fact about Sappho: *she was a poet.* Let us look then at what *poets* did. It is time we ceased this double standard. I wish to propose an alternative reconstruction of Sappho's social world. She calls her comrades φίλαι (43) and ἕταιραι (142, 160.1). She calls herself "a firm friend" (φίλα φαῖμ' ἐχύρα γέ[νεσθαι; 88.17). She should therefore be seen, not in a *thiasos* (whatever that might be) but, like Alcaeus, in a *hetairia*, an association of friends. I am not raising this point for the first time, but it seems to have been powerless against so entrenched a series of preconceptions. So Burnett has written: "Sappho sang for an audience in some ways very much like the fraternity that Alcaeus fought with during the day and drank with at night. Her circle, like the *hetairai*, had a customary role to play in Lesbian society, and it too was aristocratic, musical, and constrained only by bonds of love and loyalty." So too Winkler: "It is by no means certain that her own poems are either for a cult-performance or that her circle of women friends (*hetairai*) is identical in extension with the celebrants in a festival she

---

123. Russo, "Reading the Greek Lyric Poets" 721.
124. For his hymns see Page, *Sappho and Alcaeus* 244–72; Campbell, *The Golden Lyre* 169–72.

mentions."[125] Trumpf compared the *hetairia* of Alcaeus to Sappho's circle and writes, "The poet's sphere of activity is the half cult, half political-social form of organization of the clubs and *hetairiai* with their attendant institutions."[126] Any overly stringent attempt to separate the cultic from the sociopolitical is fundamentally mistaken—I doubt if any Greek would have understood the distinction we were trying to make—though civic celebrations (involving the whole polis) can be differentiated from private ceremonies.[127] The point I wish to make is that there is no justification for imposing on Sappho a greater degree of ritual, formality, or institutionalization than on any other (male) poet. Sappho has a social role—it is that of poet. Since she does the same things as other poets and writes the same things as other poets, why is she not treated like all other poets? This rhetorical question has an answer: scholars for the most part are still refusing to treat Sappho as a poet and instead are turning her into a "wonderful thing" (θαυμαστόν τι χρῆμα; Strabo 13.2.3 = T 7 Loeb), that is, a freak of nature.[128] A single example: Gentili says: "The closeness to the Muses can only be explained by the hypothesis of an actual cult in their honor within the community."[129] May I offer another hypothesis? Sappho invokes the Muses because she is a poet. Alcaeus invokes the Muses. Why do these remarks not apply to him, or to Archilochus, or Pindar, or anyone else who ever wrote poetry in the entire history of Greek literature?

Men got together with other men in a variety of formal and informal settings at which poetry might be sung. These included civic festivals and competitions, banquets (θαλία, ἑορτή, θυσία), and above all the symposium.[130]

---

125. Burnett, *Three Archaic Poets* 209; Winkler, "Double Consciousness" 165.

126. Trumpf, "Über das Trinken" 160.

127. Cf., for example, McEvilley, "Sapphic Imagery" 268: "Fragment 94 does not present exactly a rite nor exactly a party, but a private occasion which involved the symbolic objects common to both." This draws a line that did not exist in Greece and asks on which side particular occasions fell. Every party began with a sacrifice; every sacrifice was followed by a party.

128. For this attitude as basic to more interpretations of the work of women poets, see Lefkowitz, "Critical Stereotypes," and Gubar, "Sapphistries."

129. Gentili, *Poetry and Its Public* 84.

130. On banquets as a place for poetry, and the synonymy of these words, see Schmitt-Pantel, "Sacrificial Meal." I follow her usage of the term "banquet" to indicate the falsity of applying modern distinctions of "secular" activity from "sacred." E. Cantarella in a curious section (*Bisexuality* 86–88) invokes symposia as sites for lesbian love. She, however, is imagining the *hetairai* at men's symposia falling for each other. How much this is influenced by modern notions of the lesbian hooker, I don't know, though her remarks certainly point in that direction (87). She can, however, offer no evidence apart from Anacreon 358 (see above n. 52), which may not be about female homosexuality and fails to mention symposia, and Alciphron *Ep.* 4.14.4, a buttock beauty contest between two *hetairai*, which she reads as a "homosexual turn-on"

What might these occasions have been for Sappho? Bearing in mind that we know little about archaic Lesbos, we must go primarily on the basis of her own and Alcaeus's poetry. If, however, we strip away the blinkers of Sappho Schoolmistress, we find her celebrating the same or similar occasions in settings neither more or less formal or cultic than those celebrated in the circles of friends that included Alcaeus, or Mimnermus, or Ibycus, or Theognis, or Anacreon.

There is no theme, no occasion, in Sappho that we do not find in other poets. For identifiable occasions, those that seem to us to be more "formal" are Sappho writing choral song for an Adonia,[131] singing about some sort of all night celebrations,[132] singing about choruses (70.10, 94.27), and (according to an anonymous epigram) leading a chorus of women to the precinct of Hera.[133] The Adonia was a women's festival and Praxilla wrote an famous (and derided) hymn to Adonis (747).[134] Pindar describes an all-night festival (*Ism.* 4.65–68).[135] Alcman, of course, speaks of χορός, "dancing" (besides the partheneia, see 10(b)11, 15; 27.3), as do Alcaeus (249), Anacreon (386), Ion (26.1, 11), Pratinas (708, 709), [Socrates] 3.1 (Ath. 14.628e), Theognis 779 (of a paean), and an anonymous drinking song (900). Alcaeus (129) invokes

---

(88). The lavishly illustrated world of the symposium offers no such images. The Apollodorus vase (*Para.* 333,9bis; illustrated in Dover, *Greek Homosexuality* 173 [R207]; Keuls, *The Reign of the Phallus* 85 [fig. 515]; Boardman, *Eros in Greece* 110–11), sometimes offered as evidence of lesbian masturbation (as Dover), rather shows one *hetaira* perfuming the pubic hair of another (note the perfume jar) and is comparable to the bathing scenes (see Boardman, Keuls). Such a scene would not be impossible: vase painting does show women drinking by themselves (e.g., psykter by Euphormios, *ARV* 16,15 = Boardman, *Athenian Red Figure Vases* no. 27; hydria by Phintias, *ARV* 23,7 = Boardman, *Athenian Red Figure Vases* no. 38) and is not shy about showing women masturbating with dildos (ubiquitous; e.g., Keuls, *Reign* 82–86) or by hand (Thalia painter, *ARV* 113,7 = Boardman, *Athenian Red Figure Vases* no. 112).

131. 140a; cf. 168, 221 b iii, *AP* 7.407 (Dioscorides 18 Gow-Page = T 58 Loeb). For the Adonia, see Détienne, *The Gardens of Adonis*, and Winkler's criticisms, "Laughter of the Oppressed."

132. Frs. 30.3, 43, 149, perhaps 126, 151, 157; cf. 154. Since 30 is certainly an epithalamion, there is a possibility that some of the others are also. For 43, the direct address to friends and the end of the poem seem to indicate a nonnarrative context; we cannot know the character of the occasion. For 154, the presence of the altar seems more "cultic," but cf. Xenoph. 1.11 (below). Further, the past tenses might indicate either simply an antecedent setting, or the narration perhaps of a myth. Frs. 23.12 and 126 may simply be about spending the night with a companion.

133. *AP* 9.189 = T 59 Loeb; Hera is also mentioned at 9 and 17. Perhaps the mysterious "beauty contests" of Lesbos fit in somewhere, though Sappho in what survives makes no mention of them. The testimonia are conveniently assembled by Treu, *Sappho* 120–21 (with German trans.).

134. For other poets apparently writing choral works for the Adonia, cf. Cratinus, *Boukoloi* (3.16 Kock = K.-A. 4.131). A certain "Glykon" told his story (Adespota [Ad.] 1029).

135. For which see Parke, *Festivals of the Athenians* 49–50.

Hera; Alcman (3) writes a partheneion in her honor.[136] Numerous poets have invoked numerous gods. Only Sappho is turned into a priestess.

A principal occasion for women (and men) gathering together in a less "cultic" setting for Sappho's songs is the wedding.[137] Alcman wrote wedding songs (*hymenaia*);[138] Homer, Hesiod, and Aristophanes know of them;[139] Licymnius (768) and Telestes (808) wrote dithyrambs about Hymenaios. Only Sappho sets up a school for bridesmaids.

But most of all, we find Sappho singing about (and I presume at) banquets. She speaks of the θαλία at a temple grove to which she summons Aphrodite (2.15). So do Archilochus (11, 13), Theognis (778, 983), Pindar (*Ol.* 7.94, 10.76; *Pyth.* 1.37, 10.34; *Pae.* 6.14), Ion of Chios (23.3), and Xenophanes.[140] She speaks of a ἑορτή for Hera (9.3); so do Anacreon (410.2) and Pindar (*Ol.* 3.34, 5.5, 6.69, 6.95, 10.58; *Pyth.* 8.66; *Nem.* 9.11, 11.27; frs. 59.4, 128b.15, 193.1).[141] She refers to sacrificial meals (θυσία, θύω);[142] the same words are used by Alcaeus (306A(b)24), Hipponax (104.48), Simonides (519 fr. 73(c)2), Theognis (1146), Timotheus (783), Philoxenus of Cythera (823), Pindar (*Ol.* 6.78, 7.42, 10.57, 13.69; *Pyth.* 5.86; *Isth.* 5.30, *Pae.* 3.96, 6.62, 12.6; frs. 59.23, 78.2, 86a), and the anonymous drinking song the "Harmodius" (895.3). And everywhere she speaks of garlands.[143] So do Alcaeus, Alcman, Anacreon, Hipponax, Simonides, Stesichorus, Theognis, and Xenophanes.[144] To say that Sappho's θαλία is a cult but Archilochus's is a party, that Sappho's

---

136. Also in praise of Hera: the author of the *Homeric Hymn* and the shadowy Olen of Lycia (Paus. 2.13.3); cf. Bacch. 11 on the just wrath of Hera. For Alcman 3 as a choral work for Hera, see Campbell, *The Golden Lyre* 155, and Calame's cautious assessment, *Les chœurs* 2:107–8.

137. For the festival setting of the wedding, see Gernet, *The Anthropology of Ancient Greece* 23–25.

138. According to Leonidas *AP* 7.19 = 159 *PMG* (= T 3 Loeb), of which 4c, 81, and 107 *PMG* might be examples; they are not partheneia. Griffiths, "Alcman's Partheneion" 11, quotes Gow and Page, *Hellenistic Epigrams* 2:366, with approval for the existence of Alcman's epithalamia: "We can hardly suppose Leonidas to have been mistaken or to have confused *partheneia* with *epithalamia*"; he then does just that by interpreting Alcman's *Partheneion* 1 as an epithalamion for Agido and an unnamed man, in which he is followed by Gentili, *Poetry and Its Public* 73–77, who turns it into a wedding song for Agido and Hagesichora (see above).

139. *Il.* 18.491–96; Hes. *Scut.* 273–80; Ar. *Pax* 1316–57, *Av.* 1722–65.

140. Cf. Stesich. 210 (the opening of the *Oresteia*).

141. Cf. Alcman 56.2 on the feasting of the gods.

142. Frs. 19, 40. For the sacrificial meal, see Détienne and Vernant, *The Cuisine of Sacrifice*, esp. 87–92, and, for the bibliography of 1979–89, Schmitt-Pantel, "Sacrificial Meal."

143. Frs. 81.7, 92.10, 94.12–17, 98a.8, 125, 191; 168c V. if by Sappho (fr. Adesp. 964) refers merely to the earth producing garlands. See also West, "Burning Sappho" 321.

144. Alc. 48.17, 296b.8, 306 A(b)14, 362.1, 436; Alcman 58; Anac. 352.2, 396.2, 410.1, 434.1, 496; Hippon. 60; Simon. 506.2, 519, fr. 77.3, fr. 80.5; Stesich. 187.3; Theog. 828; Critias 4.1; Xenoph. 1.2. Also Critias, Philoxenos of Leucas in the dithyramb "The Banquet" 836(a)3, (b)4, 43; the drinking songs Skol. 885.2, 956, Ad. 1018(b)7; Ad. eleg. 30.9(?). Corinna 654(a) col. i.26 is mythological.

garlands belong to ritual but Anacreon's belong to banqueting, is a false distinction and special pleading.[145] Pollux (6.107 = Sappho 191 = Alc. 436) and Athenaeus (15.674c–d = Alc. 362 = Sappho 96.15) make no distinction in quoting Anacreon, Sappho, and Alcaeus together for the use of garlands at banquets.[146] She speaks of myrrh (94.18, 20) not as a matter of cosmetics,[147] but as part of a celebration, exactly as do Alcaeus (45.7, 50.1, 362.3; cf. 36), Anacreon (363.3, 444), Archilochus (205), Theognis (730), and Xenophanes (1.3). Finally, it is clear that wine was present at some of the celebrations at which Sappho sang. She certainly thinks it suitable for the weddings of gods (141b.1) and heroes (44.10).[148] And in fragment 2, she refers to the nectar given by Aphrodite who pours the wine (οἰνοχόαισον; 2.15–16: cf. 96.27, also of Aphrodite and nectar) into their *kylixes*, the cup for drinking wine (cf. 44.29, on the wedding of Hector and Andromache; 192, a description of cups from an unknown context). Athenaeus (11.463e) quotes the poem as part of a series of descriptions of the features of a perfect symposium[149] and Page explicates the role of Aphrodite: "The wine which Sappho and her companions drink is conceived of as being, or including, nectar poured by the hand of their invisible but unquestionably present patroness."[150]

For Bowra, Sappho 2 "has certainly the air of cult about it, and though Sappho's position may not be official, she certainly officiates." Saake sees her as a priestess. Gentili calls it a "ritual invocation."[151] But Sappho does not rule a cult; she sings a song. Burnett rightly criticizes West's flippant

---

145. For the significance of garlands, see Von der Muhll, *Ausgewählte kleine Schriften* 486.

146. Both show that the setting is sympotic.

147. Saake, *Zur Kunst Sapphos* 200, is typical of this belittling approach, in speaking of "cosmetics" and "'medicamina faciei femineae,' the essences, oils, and ointments of the cultivated toilette." Apparently the girls were at a makeup party. Sappho merely refers to myrrh. Cf. the attack of Semon. 7.65.

148. At 173, Sappho mentions the vine, but this might be some piece of incidental description.

149. Ath. 11.463a–63c is the source of Xenophanes' famous description (1), as well as Anac. *Eleg.* 2 West (96 Diehl), Ion 27, Theophr. fr. 120 (Wimmer), Alexis *Tarentines* (2.377 Kock), and Sappho 2.13–16.

150. Page, *Sappho and Alcaeus* 43. So also Bowra, *Greek Lyric Poetry* 198, and West, "Burning Sappho" 317. For nectar as a metonymy for wine, cf. Arch. 290, Ion 26.9, Philoxenos of Leucas 836(d)1. Yet, this has not prevented certain interpretations in which the actual wine of the celebration has been ignored in the search for the poetic meanings of the nectar of Aphrodite. So Burnett, *Three Archaic Poets* 275: "Aphrodite is to mix nectar, the matter of the gods, into the immaterial festivity of her followers." Yet she acknowledges the materiality of the images of that festivity. That the nectar "bestows the sweet intoxication of love" (Theiler and Von der Muhll, "Das Sapphogedicht" 25) may be true but ignores that these images begin in the concrete fact of actual feasting.

151. Bowra, *Greek Lyric Poetry* 196; Saake, *Sapphostudien* 63; Gentili, *Poetry and Its Public* 79.

tone, but he is correct to call the setting of fragment 2 a "picnic,"[152] an outdoor banquet of a well-known type.[153] We may not wish to call any of these banquets symposia as such,[154] those exclusively male drinking parties, but if we compare Xenophanes 1, his description of the perfect symposium, with Sappho 2, 94, and others, we find all the same elements; cups, wine, wreaths, perfume.[155] Even the incense, altars, and hymns are as much a feature of the symposium as of the sacrifice.[156] Sappho is not serving as a priestess to girls; she is attending a banquet with friends.

XIII. CONCLUSION

Just as Sappho's poetry shares concerns and subject matter with Alcaeus and the other lyric poets, so Sappho's society should also be regarded as a *hetairia*. Analogous to Alcaeus's circle, Sappho's society was a group of women tied by family, class, politics, and erotic love. Like any other association, it cooperated in ritual activities, cult practice, and informal social events. Her subjects, like those of the other lyric poets, were praising her group's friends, attacking its enemies, celebrating its loves, and offering songs for its banquets. This picture has I believe a greater fidelity to the facts. It removes a distorting series of assumptions and reveals an exciting world, where women as well as men are concerned with love and politics and where Sappho is no longer a schoolmistress but a poet.

152. West, "Burning Sappho" 317. He refers later dismissively to "jolly outings" (322). See Burnett, *Three Archaic Poets* 265.

153. Gernet, *The Anthropology of Ancient Greece* 14–15.

154. So West, "Other Early Poetry" 38: "a women's society which was the mirror image of the men's, with their own symposia and love affairs."

155. Fränkel, *Early Greek Poetry* 180, rightly invokes men's banquets and compares Xenoph. 1 and Sappho 2.

156. For incense: Sappho 2.3–4, cf. Xenoph. 1.7 (both specifically frankincense); altar: Sappho 2.3, cf. Xenoph. 1.11. Xenophanes tells of the men hymning the gods, and I would have no difficulty in seeing Sappho's kletic hymns 1 and 2 in exactly this sort of festive setting.

EIGHT

184~90

H.D. and Sappho:
"A Precious Inch of Palimpsest"

Erika Rohrbach

Like all deeply famous figures, Sappho keeps her anonymity. I do not mean this in the sense that Sappho is no one; rather, she could be anyone. Having borne witness to the 1890s' boom of interest in her, modernists were well aware of the interpretative leeway that Sappho's ambiguous biography and minced verse grant readers. They saw in her a woman whose life had been erased, her poetry fragmented and written over, and yet whose style had been canonized. We think of modernist writers like H.D. and Richard Aldington, for whom the classical era represented the keystone of their own aesthetic, as attempting to rescue Sappho from centuries of scholarly misinterpretation and bad translation. But even though they set themselves up to be the archaeological Red Cross, these modernists knew that the "real" Sappho was an unrecoverable ideal. Hence, they explored the one aspect of study open to them: Sappho's transmission through the ages.

I want to argue that H.D.'s identification with Sappho is primarily a poetic one, and furthermore, that the layers of interpretation insulating Sappho's fragments provided H.D. with as much of a stylistic model as did the fragments themselves. For a number of modernists, much was at stake in the reading of Sappho, but particularly fascinating about H.D. is the way in which she turned this palimpsestic reading relationship into a writing style. In her own fragment poems H.D. used Sappho to expand her poetic relation to imagism, while encoding her personal relationship with Aldington. Aldington too had masked feelings for H.D. in his "Letters to Unknown Women," and capitalized on Sappho and other classical figures to promote his own aesthetic of antiacademism. His presence, then, is an important inclusion in any consideration of H.D.'s relation with Sappho, for it enlarges and complicates the accepted belief that H.D. mostly sought refuge in Sappho's lesbianism as a poetic escape from real heterosexual trauma.[1] Like Aldington, whose classicism was enmeshed in his reaction to classicism, and Virginia Woolf, whose intellectual pursuit of Sappho was aggravated by the sexism of her male peers, H.D. used Sappho as a projection of her life, not as she wished it to be, but as it was.

The *Egoist* provided Aldington the forum to engage the same kind of life projection through classical writers that H.D. would accomplish with Sappho. By late 1915, he had been married to H.D. for two years, and, with her help, was editing *The Egoist* 's Poets' Translation Series. The Translation Series was Aldington's brainchild and amounted to six pamphlets published between 1915 and 1916. At Aldington's provocation, the second pamphlet in the series, published in 1915, consisted of Edward Storer's *Poems and Fragments of Sappho*.[2] Storer's introduction to his translation had a strong impact on Aldington and H.D., and was most likely read by Ezra Pound, Marianne Moore, James Joyce, Amy Lowell, F. S. Flint, Harriet Shaw Weaver, Dora Marsden, and T. S. Eliot, who were also frequent *Egoist* contributors.

> Sappho was born in the island of Lesbos about 612 B.C. Her name in her own language is "Psappha." She was a contemporary of Alkaios and Stesichoros. At some period of her life she was exiled from Lesbos. An inscription in the Parian Chronicle says: "When Aristokles reigned over the Athenians Sappho fled from Mitylene and sailed to Sicily." But it is through her own poems that we see most clearly into the beauty and tragedy of her life. She is there revealed to us as a woman of ardent nature, noble, delicate-minded, and fond of pleasure. That her poems were chiefly love-poems, and love-poems written to women, is clear even from the mutilated fragments which remain. Any other explanation destroys at once their art and their reality. Yet sedulous hypocrites are to be found to-day who will wilfully mistranslate and misconstrue in order to envelope the manners of antiquity in a retrospective and most absurd respectability.[3]

Storer's portrait of Sappho is significant on a number of counts. First, he presents us with the poet in exile, which must have struck a familiar chord

---

1. Susan Gubar popularized this view in "Sapphistries." She argues that H.D. and Renée Vivien wished to form a "fantastic collaboration" (203) with Sappho as a poet, and importantly as a fellow lesbian poet. Gubar's reading is plausible, but her basis for this claim—that H.D.'s fragment poems are a tribute to Bryher (Winifred Ellerman)—is, as I will show, unfounded.

2. See also his article in *The Egoist*, "Poems and Fragments of Sappho." Storer (1880–1944) produced two volumes of poetry, *Inclinations* (1907) and *Mirrors of Illusion* (1908), which contain rather ineffective experiments with free verse. According to Zilboorg, he dropped out of the modernist poetry scene after 1908, and Pound writes to Flint in 1915 that imagism was "most emphatically NOT the poetry of friend Storer" (qtd. in Harmer, *Victory in Limbo* 45). For more on his relationship with Aldington, see Zilboorg, *Richard Aldington and H.D.*

3. Storer, "Poems and Fragments" 153.

in the modernist vein. Then he asks us to join him in reading Sappho's life "most clearly" through her poems. If we then follow him and read her life through her poems, we discover it not only in fragments but *"mutilated fragments."* Having thus collapsed Sappho's body into her work, Storer finally rebukes those contemporary, "sedulous hypocrites" for attempting to envelope her lesbian "manners of antiquity" in the "most absurd" cloak of modern heterosexual "respectability."

Under the guise of rescuing Sappho from Victorian misconstruction, Storer turns her "mutilated fragments" into the muted body of Philomela. His portrayal of Sappho as a woman whose artistic work ultimately saves her from isolation and violation focuses our attention on the poetry and the process by which it becomes fragmented. It also places Storer (or any translator) in Procne's position as the lone reader capable of restoring to Sappho "the beauty and tragedy" of her life. For modernist poets who identified with Sappho's queerness, fragmentation, ambiguity, and alienation—as well as her artistry—this was the most important aspect of the Sapphic reading relationship. Whatever form of textual harassment they chose to address, for modernists, rescuing Sappho meant reading modernly: that is, with one eye on the text in hand and the other on whose hand the text is in. On the one hand, Sappho as Philomela mandates attention to the history of the fragments' transmission; on the other, it warrants the modernists' preoccupation with their unique position as readers.

For these reasons, Aldington (and H.D.) embraced Storer's reading. In the first of his "Letters to Unknown Women," which appeared in *The Dial*, 14 March 1918, Aldington describes the lengths one must go to in addressing these "unknown," Philomela-like figures:

> Helen the queen and Sappho the poet are "unknown" to us because their legends have been altered and overlaid by so many men of different personalities that we have difficulty in deciphering the true character from the additions. Like all very great people they have become what we wished them to be, and those who seek the truth about them must search for it among a thousand lies. (226)

Aldington's point here of course is not that these women are "unknown" to us like strangers we pass on the street, but that they have been made unknowable by centuries of "men's," read here scholarly, mishandling. If we wish to learn the "truth" about them, *we* must seek it out; Sappho and Helen alone can tell us nothing. This is an important point driven home in Aldington's second "letter," published 9 May 1918 in *The Dial*:

> To Sappho of Mitylene:
>   Like so many notorious characters in history you have become an enigma, as ambiguous as an oracle. (430)

Here, as in Storer's portrait, is the second half of the Philomela story. If Sappho has been "mutilated" to the extent that only her work can reveal her suffering, this forces on subsequent readers Procne's burden of privileged reading; if Sappho is "as ambiguous as an oracle," she is that much in need of interpretation and a qualified interpreter.

Enter Aldington with the Poets' Translation Series, assembled by his handpicked coterie of poet-translators. The statement of objectives for the series embodies familiar imagist tenets, as Caroline Zilboorg observes; more importantly, it stresses the backgrounds of the translators:

> The object of the editors of this series is to present a number of translations of Greek and Latin poetry and prose, especially of those authors who are less frequently given in English. This literature has too long been the property of pedagogues, philologists, and professors. Its human qualities have been obscured by the wranglings of grammarians, who love it principally because to them it is so safe and so dead.
>
> But to many of us it is not dead. It is more alive, more essential, more human than anything we can find in contemporary English literature. The publication of such classics, in the way that we propose, may help to create a higher standard of appreciation of the writers of antiquity, who have suffered too long at the hands of clumsy metrists. . . .
>
> These translations will be done by poets whose interest in their authors will be neither conventional nor frigid. The translators will take no concern with glosses, or notes or any of the apparatus with which learning smothers beauty.[4]

Note the emphasis on these translators being warm-blooded, bohemian poets set apart from the cold, convention-bound set of "pedagogues, philologists, and professors." Zilboorg argues that Aldington's objectives stem from his belief in there being "an audience to whom one was linguistically and morally responsible,"[5] but if anything, his views merely reflect a wish to salvage the integrity of the classical source. Crucially, the audience is left out of this aesthetic imperative. Remember, Procne and Philomela were sisters. Aldington clearly believes that only footnote-free contemporary poets and authors can resuscitate their muted classical counterparts.

This strike against academia should not, however, be read as any sort of attempt to take the classics to the people. Largely because he was never afforded easy access to the classics, Aldington concerned himself mainly with the modern translator or reader of Greek, as opposed to the translator's audience. In a letter dated 22 December 1918, he listed his motives for

---

4. Aldington, trans., *The Poems of Anyte of Tegea* 7–8, cited in Zilboorg, "Joint Venture" 90. Zilboorg's thorough studies of Aldington and H.D. have proven instrumental to my understanding of their roles as modernists and of Sappho's meaning to them.

5. Zilboorg, "Joint Venture" 90.

wanting to rejuvenate the translation series: "I want it first to establish a canon of taste, *our* taste, against a mob of clergymen and schoolmasters and professional critics; that will give us a point d'appui for defense of our own work. Then I want it also for the pleasure of doing that work and getting a number of people to work on it. If my plan is properly carried out the series will be an important contribution to modern English culture."[6] Thus the series offers Aldington, whose family's slim means deprived him of an Oxbridge education, and his renegade band of poets both the authorization and the means to plunder the stores of what Jane Marcus has called the "intellectual aristocracy."[7]

The sexism to which Marcus notes Virginia Woolf and the women of her circle were subjected by their male Oxbridge peers for wanting to know Greek carries with it the overriding academic classism that so galled Aldington and his troupe. Much as Woolf and company make Sappho the object of study for the formation of their own insular female "society,"[8] Aldington and his modernist translators choose Sappho and other maligned classical figures to subvert the influence of the intellectual aristocracy and ratify their own outlaw status as poets. Perhaps more than any other classical figure, Sappho authorized these modernist arbiters of taste to be what they were.

In this light we are now ready to deal with H.D., who, like Aldington, Storer, and others, adopted Sappho as a persona and not as an alternative to her life. She wrote five poems that take their epigraphs from Sappho: "Fragment 113," published in *Hymen* (1921), and "Fragment Thirty-six," "Fragment Forty," "Fragment Forty-one," and "Fragment Sixty-eight," published in *Heliodora* (1924); she also wrote an essay entitled "The Wise Sappho" between 1918 and 1920. Like Aldington, she was an accomplished translator of Greek and was familiar with other contemporary Sappho translations.[9] Susan Gubar has suggested that H.D. sought in Sappho a motherly precursor, and

6. Cited ibid., 82. The letter is addressed to Bryher, H.D.'s companion after Aldington; she was also a young writer with strong classical leanings.

7. Marcus, *Virginia Woolf and the Languages of Patriarchy* 92.

8. Woolf, "A Society" (1921).

9. Two translations H.D. consulted were H. T. Wharton's *Sappho* (1885) and Renée Vivien's *Sapho* (1903). Storer's introduction recommends Wharton's as the best English translation ("Poems and Fragments" 153), and in a letter from Aldington, dated 13 December 1918, in which he outlines his plans for the second Poets' Translation Series—among them, making H.D. Greek editor—Aldington tells H.D.: "Any foreign books you may need, whether Greek or French—any of Renée Vivien for example—you may need; order from David Nutt . . ." (qtd. in Zilboorg, *Richard Aldington and H.D.* 167). H.D.'s own numbering of the fragments follows Wharton's, which is based on that of the standard Greek edition at the time, Bergk's *Poetae Lyrici Graeci*.

that the incorporation of Sappho into her verse is an homage to the lesbian relationship she began in 1918:

> While Sappho's lyrical evocation of Aphrodite triumphs over the pain and confusion of mortal love, H.D.'s lyrical invocation of Sappho testifies to her own artistic survival, which was in large measure due to the companion who took her to the Hellas she associated with Helen, her mother. Indeed, just as H.D. is empowered to find the strength and integrity to create poetry out of the pain of abandonment by turning to the intensity she associates with Sappho, in her life she survived male rejection by returning to Bryher, a woman who quite literally shared her visions.[10]

But H.D. wrote three of the fragment poems two years before she had even met Bryher. The poems in question, "Fragment Forty," "Fragment Forty-one," and "Fragment Sixty-eight," were originally composed under the titles "Amaranth," "Eros," and "Envy" at Corfe Castle in 1916. They did not appear with the epigraphs until 1924, shuffled, retitled, and purged of direct male references.[11] Given that some of H.D.'s Sapphic allusions precede both Bryher's arrival by two years and the later addition of the epigraphs, it would seem that something other than the neat recuperation of Sappho in Bryher's image is at stake here.

While 1916 reveals nothing relating to Bryher, it marks a significant moment in H.D.'s relationship with Aldington. In late May, Aldington and his friend Carl Fallas enlisted as infantry privates in the Eleventh Battalion of the Devonshire Regiment, and by June, Aldington wrote to F. S. Flint that he had twice consummated the erotic attraction (which had sprung up in March) between him and Flo Fallas, Carl's wife. H.D. knew of the affair, and initially did not find it particularly threatening, as both she and Aldington believed in and, at various times, practiced "free love." By the fall, however, H.D. was "fearful that perhaps it was a more serious relationship, although there was little evidence for this conclusion."[12] So if we are to interpret H.D.'s fragment poems via her life, we should read with the Aldington rift and not the Bryher refuge in mind.

---

10. Gubar, "Sapphistries" 212.

11. I am indebted to Louis L. Martz, whose introduction and notes to the *Collected Poems* lucidly detail the composition and revisionary history of the fragment poems. See H.D., *Collected Poems*, esp. xiv–xix, 613, 616, 617–18. All citations of H.D.'s poetry are to this edition. Martz relates that the original triad of poems was "preserved in a carefully bound typescript containing only these poems and bearing on the flyleaf the inscription in H.D.'s hand, 'Corfe Castle – Dorset – summer 1917 – from poems of *The Islands* series – ' The date should probably be 1916, for that was the summer she spent at Corfe Castle, while Richard Aldington was beginning his military training nearby" (xiv).

12. Zilboorg, *Richard Aldington and H.D.* 23. Zilboorg derived this information from H.D.'s letters to John Cournos during this period.

Remembering that H.D. sat on those three soon-to-be fragment poems for eight years, during which time she composed "The Wise Sappho" and the remaining two "fragments," and during which she also rather permanently broke with Aldington and took up with Bryher, one might argue that Bryher's devotion prompts her to overtly summon Sappho and omit the obviously male-directed sections in the revised works. When compared with only one identification H.D. offers in "The Wise Sappho," this reading becomes nearly irresistible. She states:

> True, Sappho has become for us a name, an abstraction as well as a pseudonym for poignant human feeling, she is indeed rocks set in a blue sea, she is the sea itself, breaking and tortured and torturing, but never broken. She is the island of artistic perfection where the lover of ancient beauty (shipwrecked in the modern world) may yet find foothold and take breath and gain courage for new adventures and dream of yet unexplored continents and realms of future artistic achievement. She is the wise Sappho.[13]

Could it be one pseudonym (H.D.) molding Sappho as such to represent another—Bryher? Possibly. Given that this Sappho embodies both a feeling and a place where H.D. "may yet find foothold," one must note that in "The Islands" (published in 1920, and to which the "Amaranth-Eros-Envy" triad is linked), "beauty" cannot connect with it.

> But beauty is set apart,
> beauty is cast by the sea,
> a barren rock,
> beauty is set about
> with wrecks of ships,
> upon our coast, death keeps
> the shallows—death waits
> clutching toward us
> from the deeps.
>
> Beauty is set apart;
> the winds that slash its beach,
> swirl the coarse sand
> upward toward the rocks.
>
> Beauty is set apart
> from the islands
> and from Greece.
>   (section V, 126–27)

Obviously if Sappho or Bryher is the island, that could not be who is setting "beauty" or H.D. apart from it, and here I divorce my interpretation of H.D.'s poetic Sappho of any references to Bryher, for they produce an

---

13. H.D., "The Wise Sappho" 67. Further citations will be given in parentheses in the text.

unreasonably inconsistent Sappho. Turning instead to "Amaranth" 's final two sections, which H.D. did not include in her revision of the poem as "Fragment Forty-one," we witness the speaker's rage at her lover's leaving her for another.

> But I,
> how I hate you for this,
> how I despise and hate,
> was my beauty so slight a gift,
> so soon forgot?
>
> I hate you for this,
> and now your fault be less,
> I would cry, turn back,
> lest she the shameless and radiant
> slay you for neglect.
>
> Neglect of finest beauty upon earth
> my limbs, my body and feet,
> beauty that men gasp
> wondering that life
> could rest in so burnt a face,
> so scarred with her touch,
> so fire-eaten, so intense.
>
> (from section V, 314)

While these lines sizzle in bursts of Sapphic imagery and condensation, they address a man as Sappho's do not. H.D.'s lover, "Atthis," who leaves her for Andromeda, is not Sappho's female Atthis mentioned in section II of the poem, but a play on the male fertility god "Attis," who was driven mad by the goddess Cybele to castrate himself, and whose story was immortalized by Catullus.[14] Just the hint of Catullus here makes me think that quite possibly H.D. was using "Atthis," a name by which Aldington actually referred to himself,[15] in the same fashion in which Catullus employed the pseudonym "Lesbia" in his poems to mask the identity of his great love.

14. H.D. also transforms another Sapphic fragment in "Amaranth" 's first section, by setting "Andromeda, shameless and radiant" in place of Sappho's "Aphrodite, shameless and radiant." By deifying Andromeda, H.D. makes Atthis's attraction toward her somehow more comprehensible to speaker and reader, while at the same time commenting on the unreality of such a tryst and the dangerous frivolity of the caprice.

15. In a letter to H.D. dated 12 June 1918 Aldington wrote: "Pardons à ton vieux amant tous ses torts et tous ses petitesses et ne te souviens que de cette partie de lui que tu as aimé autrefois—Atthis" [trans. by Zilboorg] "Let's pardon your old lover all his faults and all his pettiness and remember only that part of him that you used to love—Atthis" (qtd. in Zilboorg, *Richard Aldington and H.D.* 65–67).

In "Fragment Forty-one" H.D. removes all readily identifiable evidence of the poem's original male address and direct mention of Atthis, going so far as to further fragment the Sappho epigraph by printing only "...*thou flittest to Andromeda*," and not "But to thee, Atthis, the thought of me is hateful; thou flittest to Andromeda."[16] In this version, H.D. restores Aphrodite as the goddess addressed throughout, and hints that her flitting lover is a man only in the last stanza.

> I offer more than the lad
> singing at your steps,
> praise of himself,
> his mirror his friend's face,
> more than any girl,
> I offer you this:
> (grant only strength
> that I withdraw not my gift,)
> I give you my praise and this:
> the love of my lover
> for his mistress.
>   ("Fragment Forty-one" 184)

In "Amaranth," the third last line of this stanza reads, "I give you my praise for this"—a distanced, passive release of the speaker's lover; whereas in the revised "I give you my praise *and* this," the speaker actively offers two gifts, her praise and her lover's love, ostensibly to the goddess Aphrodite. Here, applying to the line a sound bit of advice from Adalaide Morris, who says that in reading H.D., "to listen well is to listen loosely,"[17] we not only hear "and this," but "Atthis." I read this as an echo of Attis that anticipates the surprising "his" in the poem's last line, and reinforces the placement of a heterosexual fissure at the core of the work.

After witnessing a similar scattering and spackling of personal trauma involving Aldington from "Eros" to "Fragment Forty" and "Envy" to "Fragment Sixty-eight," we cannot help but wonder: why Sappho? Had H.D. somewhat randomly slapped on the epigraphs and revised the poems to fit them, one could claim that she applies the Sapphic Band-Aid to protect a deep heterosexual wound, while simultaneously airing her revised, lesbian lifestyle. But while these epigraphs do not introduce the texts of "Amaranth," "Eros," and "Envy," we can readily identify their presence, and that of other

16. Three translations have been indispensable to this study, only one of which could have been consulted by H.D.: Wharton's *Sappho*, which houses the exact translations of the epigraphs she chose. The second is Campbell's new Loeb edition, *Greek Lyric* vol. 1, and the third is Rayor, *Sappho's Lyre*. I have used Wharton's translation of the fragment both he and H.D. number 41.

17. Remark made during "An H.D. Retrospective" at Poet's House, New York, 14 November 1991.

Sapphic fragments, within these poems. And then what do we do with "Fragment 113" and "Fragment Thirty-six"? I suggest we return to "The Wise Sappho."

"Little, but all roses," is how H.D. begins this lyric essay (57). Not her words, nor even Sappho's, but the tribute of Meleager—"late Alexandrian, half Jew, half Grecian poet" (67). Starting with the color of those roses, she then reads down through rock, island, country, and planet, to arrive at a world of emotion imaginable only "by the greatest of her own countrymen in the greatest period of that country's glamour, who themselves confessed her beyond their reach, beyond their song, not a woman, not a goddess even, but a song or the spirit of a song. A song, a white star that moves across the heaven to mark the end of a world epoch or to presage some coming glory" (58–59).

The song without a throat to sing it, the shooting star that must be seen and interpreted—these images set up the same kind of oracular reading relationship as Storer's and Aldington's view of Sappho. H.D. devotes a few pages to romanticizing Sappho but finally extols her, like Plato, for her wisdom.

> Wisdom—this is all we know of the girl, that though she stood in the heavy Graeco-Asiatic sunlight, the wind from Asia, heavy with ardent myrrh and Persian spices, was yet tempered with a Western gale, bearing in its strength and its salt sting, the image of another, tall, with eyes shadowed by the helmet rim, the goddess, indomitable.
>
> This is her strength—Sappho of Mitylene was a Greek. And in all her ecstasies, her burnings, her Asiatic riot of colour, her cry to that Phoenician deity, "Adonis, Adonis—" her phrases, so simple yet in any but her hands in danger of overpowering sensuousness, her touches of Oriental realism, "purple napkins" and "soft cushions" are yet tempered, moderated by a craft never surpassed in literature. The beauty of Aphrodite it is true is the constant, reiterated subject of her singing. But she is called by a late scholiast who knew more of her than we can hope to learn from these brief fragments, "The Wise Sappho." (63)

H.D.'s Sappho is blessed by not only the radiantly tressed Aphrodite but also the helmeted, crafty Athena, goddess of wisdom. Like Aldington and other modernists, H.D. is fascinated by her unsurpassed craft, as well as its transmission through the ages. She writes: "Legend upon legend has grown up, adding curious documents to each previous fragment; the history of the preservation of each line is in itself a most fascinating and bewildering romance" (68).

I believe that there are two roots to H.D.'s "bewildering romance" with Sappho; one is to be found in the archival history surrounding each fragment. H.D. reaches back to her chosen epigraphs as much for emotional content and superior craft as for historical context. Each of H.D.'s epigraphs survives in a classical source, all of which are books on writing. "Fragment 113" appears in Tryphon's *Figures of Speech*; "Fragment Thirty-six" in Chrysippus's *Negatives*; "Fragment Forty" and "Fragment Forty-one" may have been consecutive in Hephaestion's *Handbook on Meters*; and "Fragment Sixty-eight" is found in Stobaeus's *Anthology* (on folly).[18] Viewing the fragment poems from this perspective grants us and H.D., a poet obsessed with palimpsest, access to Sappho only through another writer's personal history. And here we must not overlook the titles of the fragment poems, taken from random numbers assigned by a modern scholar, as opposed to directly from Sappho or as one of H.D.'s interpretative gestures.

The other root to H.D's Sapphic "romance" is buried in her bewildering relationship with Aldington. The palimpsestic layering of personalities inherent in any reading of Sappho sets the stage for the rhetorical encoding of H.D. and Aldington's own relationship. As we saw hints of Catullus's castrated Attis running around in "Amaranth," in "Fragment Sixty-eight," with its epigraph "*. . . even in the house of Hades*," H.D. subtly uses Sappho to cut down Aldington. Read in conjunction with the abandoned section from "Envy," one could view this poem as H.D.'s somewhat hyperbolic jealousy of Aldington's increased chances of dying a soldier's noble death, while she molders away at home, abandoned by him as lover and friend. The omitted section reads:

> Could I have known
> you were more male than the sun-god,
> more hot, more intense,
> could I have known?
> for your glance all-enfolding,
> sympathetic, was selfless
> as a girl's glance.
>
> Could I have known?
> I whose heart,
> being rent, cared nothing,
> was unspeakably indifferent.
>   ("Envy," section III, 321)

H.D. concludes both versions of the poem, "Do not pity me, spare that, / but how I envy you / your chance of death," leading us to think that the speaker too wishes to die, as well as conjuring up the Swinburnean image of a cliff-diving Sappho. But if we examine the remainder of the fragment from which H.D. excerpts "Fragment Sixty-eight" 's epigraph, we find that its ending foretells a much less dismal conclusion: "*But thou shalt lie dead, nor shall*

18. See Campbell, *Greek Lyric* 1:159, 97, 147, 149, 99.

there ever be any remembrance of thee then or thereafter, for thou hast not of the roses of Pieria; but thou shalt wander obscure even in the house of Hades, flitting among the shadowy dead."[19] In this fragment Sappho not only envisions a salon rival's death but directs her to Hades. Rayor interprets it as "an invective against someone who does not share the Muses' gift of poetry. She was a nonentity in life and once she has died, she will remain unknown among the obscure dead."[20] This epigraph suggests that H.D. is really telling Aldington to go to hell, that he will die an obscure poet, and that the woman he is involved with is as talentless and "selfless" as he. Here H.D. uses Sappho's classical pen to open a modern vein.

On a less personal stylistic level, she does the same in "Fragment 113." H.D. chooses for an epigraph perhaps Sappho's most famous line, *"Neither honey nor bee for me,"* which Campbell tells us comes down from Tryphon's *Figures of Speech* and is referred to in Diogenian's *Proverbs* as "used of those who are not willing to take the bad with the good."[21] I read "Fragment 113," the lone fragment poem published in *Hymen* in 1921, as basically H.D.'s attempt to work out the Sapphic style. Here H.D. adopts the Greek priamel, imitating the repetition of negation and recurrent images to recapture its melodic line. Particularly Sapphic is the final stanza.

> not iris—old desire—old passion—
> old forgetfulness—old pain—
> not this, nor any flower,
> but if you turn again,
> seek strength of arm and throat,
> touch as the god;
> neglect the lyre-note;
> knowing that you shall feel,
> about the frame,
> no trembling of the string
> but heat, more passionate
> of bone and the white shell
> and fiery tempered steel.
>
> (131–32)

The speaker moves away from past desire in what seems to me an echo of the *Homeric Hymn to Demeter*, with the withdrawal from the lushness of both honey and fruit tree, the fertility of the bee, and association with the iris. Here too I think we find H.D. turning away from imagism, and it is important to keep in mind how her stylistic proximity to Sappho enabled H.D. to make this move.

19. Wharton, trans., *Sappho* 90.
20. Rayor, *Sappho's Lyre* 165.
21. Campbell, *Greek Lyric* 1:159.

Many of the imagist tenets we find so exquisitely enacted in H.D.'s verse are equally applicable to Sappho's: for example, direct treatment of subject, as few adjectives as possible, individuality of rhythm, and the exact word.[22]

Of all the fragment poems, "Fragment Thirty-six" best reflects imagism, Sappho, and H.D.'s wrestling to expand her relation to both. This intricately woven poem begins with the most generative of the epigraphs: "*I know not what to do. / my mind is divided.*" Rayor translates the fragment, "I don't know what I should do— / I'm of two minds," noting that "what I should do" could mean " 'what I should set down,' in regard to composing poetry."[23] John Winkler further suggests that the speaker's dilemma might hinge upon the revelation of some women-only secrets, offering "I am not sure which things to set down and which to keep among ourselves, my mind is divided," as a possible meaning.[24] Undoubtedly H.D. plays upon this double entendre in the poem's first stanza:

> I know not what to do,
> my mind is reft:
> is song's gift best?
> is love's gift loveliest?
> I know not what to do,
> now sleep has pressed
> weight on your eyelids.
>   (165–66)

This is the only poem in which H.D. actively debates her recuperation of Sappho—will it be through song or love? Is it a poetic gift that enables her to craft the Lesbian song, or lesbian perspective that empowers H.D. to read Sappho? Does H.D. dare break her meter to translate Sappho into her own imagist language?

> Shall I break your rest,
> devouring, eager?
> is love's gift best?
> nay, song's the loveliest:
> yet were you lost,
> what rapture
> could I take from song?
> what song were left?
>   (stanza 2, 166)

22. I take these characteristics from Aldington's review of *Des Imagistes*, which appeared in *The Egoist*, 1 June 1914, and included a list of the imagists' "fundamental doctrines" (202).

23. Rayor, *Sappho's Lyre* 80, 169.

24. Winkler makes the compelling argument that it is the "many-mindedness" of the varying perspectives offered in Sappho's poetry itself that encourages a diversity of readings. See "Double Consciousness," esp. 166–67.

Notice the crossing here—"love's gift" becomes "best" and "song's the loveliest." The two blend, "each strives with each," and she fears privileging one over the other. Should the poet transmit her passion through Sappho and risk disturbing her icy perfection?

> I know not what to do:
> to turn and slake
> the rage that burns,
> with my breath burn
> and trouble your cool breath?
> so shall I turn and take
> snow in my arms?
> (is love's gift best?)
> yet flake on flake
> of snow were comfortless,
> did you lie wondering,
> wakened yet unawake.
>   (stanza 3, 166)

Were H.D. to adopt Sappho's cool control, taking "snow" in her arms, would it stir her; is the remedy to "slake / all the wild longing [. . .] as two white wrestlers / standing for a match" (stanzas 4–5, 166–67)? Throughout the poem, waves of sound and phrase surge over one another, forcing the speaker's doubled mind to hesitate above passion and song, waiting for one to "fall" into the other.

> I know not what to do:
> will the sound break,
> rending the night
> with rift on rift of rose
> and scattered light?
>
> will the sound break at last
> as the wave hesitant,
> or will the whole night pass
> and I lie listening awake?
>   (final stanzas [8–9], 167–68)

The poem ends as it began with the poet's reft mind now waiting to see if sound will split the night "with rift on rift of rose / and scattered light." And suddenly we are back to roses and "The Wise Sappho," yet no nearer either poet than before. H.D. leaves us in these poems to find her wise Sappho, "a great power, roses, but many, many roses, each fragment witness to the love of some scholar or hectic antiquary searching to find a precious inch of palimpsest among the funereal glories of the sand-strewn Pharaohs" (69).

The intimate rose, with its lesbian and Sapphic resonances, and the dusty palimpsest, the measure of centuries of scholastic interest, represent the twofold reading relationship that H.D. sees in Sappho and then reproduces in her own work. Part of the reason the fragment poems are such successful artistic ventures is because they move away from the impersonal object-dependence of imagism without ever moving back toward the poet. H.D.'s fragments, like Sappho's, are extremely potent and invite the direct atten-tion of the reader—saying, "I hate," or rendering her speaker's touch "so fire-eaten, so intense"—yet like Sappho's, they too have been alternately fragmented and written over. Like Aldington, H.D. notes the presence of complex relationships surrounding the fragments and writes her own Atthis into the poems; then she takes that knowledge one step further by writing him out. It is important to see that the fragment poems' later revisions were prompted not by the love of Bryher, nor even by a need to kill Aldington, but by H.D.'s desire to emulate Sappho: queerness, craft, fragmentation, and all. The fragment poems then testify not only to H.D.'s skill as a modern poet, but to the depth and nature of her understanding as a modernist reader.

NINE

Sapphistries

Susan Gubar

>] called you
>] filled your mouth with plenty
>] girls, fine gifts
>] lovesong, the keen-toned harp
>] an old woman's flesh
>] hair that used to be black
>] knees will not hold
>] stand like dappled fawns
>   ] but what could I do?
>] no longer able to begin again
>   ] rosy armed Dawn
>   ] bearing to the ends of the earth
>   ] nevertheless seized
>   ] the cherished wife
>   ] withering is common to all
>   ] may that girl come and be my lover
> I have loved all graceful things [   ] and this
> Eros has given me, beauty and the light of the sun.

"SAPPHO 146" IN GUY DAVENPORT, *ARCHILOCHUS, SAPPHO, ALCMAN*

From the poems by Katherine Philips, "The English Sappho," celebrating female friendship to the provocative blank page under the entry for Sappho in Monique Wittig and Sande Zeig's *Lesbian Peoples: Material for a Dictionary* (1979), from Elizabeth Barrett Browning's translations and Christina

I am indebted throughout this paper to Sandra M. Gilbert. My title comes from Pat Califia's book on lesbian sexuality, *Sapphistry*, and from Jane Marcus's paper on Virginia Woolf, delivered at the 1981 English Institute and reprinted as "Liberty, Sorority, Misogyny," esp. 81, 87. Finally, I have profited from the generous advice of Elyse Blankely, Don Gray, Donna Hollenberg, Dori Katz, Lawrence Lipking, Susan Friedman, and Dolores Rosenblum. This essay was originally published in slightly different form as "Sapphistries," *Signs* 10 (1984) 43–62.

Rossetti's variations to recent publications like Sidney Abbott and Barbara Love's *Sappho Was a Right-On Woman* (1972) and Pat Califia's *Sapphistry* (1980), the person and poetics of Sappho have haunted the female imagination.[1] Since the late nineteenth century, of course, the words we use to describe female homosexuality derive from the poet of Lesbos, although the 1971 edition of the *Oxford English Dictionary* actually defines "Sapphism" as "unnatural sexual relations between women," and "Lesbian rule" as "a mason's rule made of lead. . . ." In a manner that might have surprised the lexicographers, however, doubtless because of a flood of male-authored classic scholarship and decadent poetry at the turn of the century, Sappho influenced women writing in the early decades of the twentieth century. Just when translators of Sappho were beginning to honor her choice of a female pronoun for her beloved and classicists were disputing the legends and facts about her life,[2] Sappho's status as a female precursor empowered a number of female modernists to collaborate in exuberant linguistic experiments.

Like "Michael Fields" (pen name of Katherine Bradley and Edith Cooper), whose volume of Sapphics were entitled *Long Ago*, Isadora Duncan viewed Sappho as a legendary survivor from a paradise lost long ago; while Edna St. Vincent Millay identified her as a lovelost suicide, Sara Teasdale idealized Sappho as a mother-poet crooning to her daughter Cleis, Elizabeth Robbins meditated on a Sappho who is "the nursing mother of intellectually free women," and Isak Dinesen associated her with prostitution.[3] Despite their differences, however, all evince the same desire to recover Sappho that impels Virginia Woolf's women's studies collective in her 1921 short story, "A Society." When the members of this Society of Outsiders evaluate the world of culture created by men, they discover one Professor Hobkin's edition of Sappho, which is primarily devoted to a defense of Sappho's chastity. As Jane Marcus has shown, Hobkin's gynecological obsession with

1. The indispensable background for the lesbian tradition in literature is Faderman, *Surpassing the Love of Men;* see esp. 69–71 on Katherine Philips (see Philips, "To My Most, Excellent Lucasia: On Our Friendship"). Significantly, Barrett Browning's only mention of a female precursor in "A Vision of Poets" is Sappho (see ll. 11. 318–21), and Rossetti's "Sappho" (1846) and "What Sappho Would Have Said Had Her Leap Cured Instead of Killing Her" (1848) were excised from her collected work by William Michael Rossetti (see Hatton, "Unpublished Poems of Christina Rossetti").

2. The poet Anne Winters, of Berkeley, Calif., describes the shift from T. W. Higginson's male pronouns (1871) to J. A. Symonds's female pronouns (1873) in an unpublished paper.

3. [Bradley and Cooper], *Long Ago;* Duncan, *My Life* 58, 116–22; Millay, "Sappho Crosses the Dark River into Hades"; Teasdale, "To Cleis (The Daughter of Sappho)"; Elizabeth Robbins, *Ancilla's Share* 125; Dinesen, *Out of Africa* 316. Robinson discusses Teasdale's "Phaon and the Leucadian Leap" in *Sappho and Her Influence* 227–28. Watts, *The Poetry of American Women* 75–82, analyzes the use of Sappho in nineteenth-century American poetry by women.

"some implement which looks remarkably like a hairpin" dramatizes Woolf's recognition that exceptional women like Sappho have been used not for but against the nurturing of a female literary tradition.[4] One year before writing "A Society," moreover, Woolf discerned in Desmond MacCarthy's newspaper article on the paucity of women's poetry precisely the sentence her society would read in the newspaper: "Since Sappho there has been no female of first rate." In a letter of rebuttal, Woolf claimed that "external restraints" have inhibited the growth of women's literary history after Sappho, for Sappho lived in a time that accorded "social and domestic freedom" to women who were "highly educated and accustomed to express their sentiments." The conditions that make possible the birth of Sappho are first, artistic predecessors; second, membership in a group where art is freely discussed and practices; and third, freedom of action and experience: "Perhaps in Lesbos," Woolf speculates, "but never since have these conditions been the lot of women."[5]

Significantly, however, some of Woolf's contemporaries were in the process of recovering the artistic freedom they, too, associated with this classical literary foremother who evaded masculine definitions and therefore freed them from the anxiety of authorship suffered by so many women writers.[6] As if to illustrate the problem creativity continued to pose for twentieth-century women artists, as late as 1944 Edith Sitwell complained that "women's poetry, with the exception of Sappho" and a few poems of Christina Rossetti and Emily Dickinson, "is *simply awful*—incompetent, floppy, whining, arch, trivial, self-pitying."[7] Whether the woman poet confronted no poetic tradition of her own or a tradition only of what Sitwell termed "ghastly wallowing," she suffered isolation and feelings of inferiority. Like so many women writers, both Woolf and Sitwell mulled over the inadequacy of their classical education, specifically the inadequacy of their knowledge of Greek, which made it difficult for them to be what Woolf called Sappho, "an inheritor as well as an originator."[8] Yet, in order to become originators inheriting Sappho's poetic genius, both Woolf and Sitwell would have certainly agreed with Willa Cather that, "If all of the lost riches we could have one master restored to us, . . . the choice of the world would be for the lost nine books

4. Marcus, "Liberty, Sorority, Misogyny" 87.

5. See "Affable Hawk's" review of Arnold Bennett's *Our Women* and Otto Weininger's *Sex and Character* in *The New Statesman* (2 October 1920) 704, and Woolf's exchange with him (9 October 1920) 15–16; (16 October 1920) 45–46. The quotations are taken from the second letter.

6. Sandra M. Gilbert and I analyze the anxiety of authorship in *The Madwoman in the Attic* 45–92.

7. Sitwell, *Selected Letters* 116.

8. Woolf, *A Room of One's Own* 113.

of Sappho," for "those broken fragments have burned themselves into the
consciousness of the world like fire."[9] To be sure, male writers from Catullus
to Lawrence Durrell also turned to Sappho, thereby providing women artists
with a prism through which to view their only classical precursor.[10] But, as
Louise Bogan has explained, women readers search for the lost fragments
of Sappho "less with the care and eagerness of the scholar looking for bits
of shattered human art, than with the hungry eyes of the treasure hunter,
looking for some last grain of a destroyed jewel."[11]

Sappho represents, then, all the lost women of genius in literary history,
especially all the lesbian artists whose work has been destroyed, sanitized,
or heterosexualized in an attempt to evade what Elaine Marks identifies
as "lesbian intertextuality."[12] Antithetically, the effort to recover Sappho
illustrates how twentieth-century women poets try to solve the problem of
poetic isolation and imputed inferiority. For the woman poet who experiences herself as inadequate or inadequately nurtured by a nonexistent or
degraded literary matrilineage, for the lesbian poet who looks in vain for a
native lesbian poetic tradition, Sappho is a very special precursor. Precisely
because so many of her original Greek texts were destroyed, the modern
woman poet could write "for" or "as" Sappho and thereby invent a classical inheritance of her own. In other words, such a writer is not infected
by Sappho's stature with a Bloomian "anxiety of influence," because her
ancient precursor is paradoxically in need of a contemporary collaborator,[13]
or so the poetry of Renée Vivien and H.D. seems to suggest. What Sandra
Gilbert would call a "fantasy precursor" or what I would term a "fantastic
collaboration" simultaneously heals the anxiety of authorship and links these
two women poets to an empowering literary history they could create in their
own image.

Sappho's preeminence provides Vivien and H.D. with evidence that the
woman who is a poet need not experience herself as a contradiction in
terms, that the woman who achieves the confessional lyricism of Sappho will
take her place apart from but also beside a poet like Homer. Through the
dynamics of their collaboration with Sappho, feminist modernists like Renée
Vivien and H.D. present themselves as breaking not only with patriarchal
literary tradition, but also with nineteenth-century female literary history.
Replacing the schizophrenic doubling Sandra Gilbert and I have traced

9. Cather, "Three Women Poets," in *The World and the Parish.*
10. Lipking in "Sappho Descending" examines how male and female poets interpret
Sappho's "Second Ode."
11. Bogan, *A Poet's Alphabet* 429.
12. Marks, "Lesbian Intertextuality" 353–77.
13. Bloom, *The Anxiety of Influence.*

throughout Victorian women's literature with euphoric coupling in which the other is bound to the self as a lover, such poets also offer divergent interpretations of what lesbianism means as an imaginative force. The fantastic collaborations Vivien and H.D. enact through their reinventions of Sappho's verse are not unrelated to the eroticized female relationships that quite literally empowered them to write. By recovering a female precursor of classical stature, moreover, Vivien and H.D. could mythologize the primacy of women's literary language. Whether the recovery of Sappho results in a decadent aesthetic, as it does for Vivien, or in a chiseled classicism, as for H.D., it holds out the promise of excavating a long-lost ecstatic lyricism that inscribes female desire as the ancient source of song. Only in the later work of writers like Amy Lowell and Marguerite Yourcenar would the liabilities of such a collaboration be uncovered.

Like Cather, who especially admired Sappho's creation of "the most wonderfully emotional meter in literature," Renée Vivien was fascinated with Sappho's resonant lines that, in Cather's words, "come in like a gasp when feeling flows too swift for speech."[14]   But, unlike Cather, Vivien self-consciously dramatized her efforts to regain Sappho's erotic language specifically for lesbians. Curiously, in 1900, Vivien met the woman she would desire and resist all her life: at a theater, Natalie Barney was reading a letter from Liane de Pougy that would be published the next year in her *Idylle saphique*. And, as Elyse Blankely has shown, Sappho's legend continued to provide the scenic background for the stormy relationship Vivien and Barney pursued, as well as being the central symbol of their respective arts.[15]   Motivated at least in part by her friendship with Pierre Louÿs, the famous author of *Chansons de Bilitis* (1894) and *Aphrodite* (1896), Natalie Barney published *Cinq petits dialogues grecs* in 1902. In 1906 she produced her *Acts d'entr'actes*, with Marguerite Moreno playing the leading role of a Sappho who dies not from love of the boatman Phaon, as the followers of Ovid claimed, but because of her desire for a girl promised in marriage.[16] During this same period, after teaching herself Greek, Vivien published *Sapho* (1903), a collection of translations and imitations of Greek fragments that the Anglo-American Vivien composed in French. In 1904, she and Natalie Barney traveled to Mytilene where Vivien eventually purchased a house of her own. In that same year, she published *Une femme m'apparut* (*A Woman Appeared to Me*), a roman à clef that focused on an androgynous avatar

14. Cather, "Three Women Poets" 147.

15. Blankely, "Returning to Mytilene"; Wickes, *The Amazon of Letters;* Chalon, *Portrait of a Seductress;* and Rogers, *Ladies Bountiful.*

16. Foster, *Sex Variant Women in Literature* 154–73. Also see Harris, "The More Profound Nationality of Their Lesbianism."

and disciple of the poet of Mytilene who argues not only that Phaon is the vulgar invention of low humorists but also that Sappho is the only woman poet of distinction because she did not deign to notice masculine existence, which is "the Unaesthetic par excellence." [17]

In both her poetry and her novel, Vivien appropriates the sadistic Sappho so prevalent in the late-nineteenth-century work of Baudelaire and Swinburne.[18] In a setting of voluptuous, "evil" flowers and narcissistic mirrors like those associated with Swinburne's vampire and suicidal heroine Lesbia Brandon, Vivien's Sappho morbidly sings, "I believe I take from you a bit of your fleeting life when I embrace you"; like Baudelaire, who portrays the sinful delights of Lesbos, Vivien identifies Sappho with Satan, the incarnation of cunning and the antagonist of both God and his poet, Homer.[19] This satanic Sappho is, of course, the same haunted figure Colette perceived in Vivien herself, living shrouded in the scented darkness of fin de siècle decadence, wasting away in a twilight of anorexic self-incarceration.[20] But while in her life Vivien clearly did suffer the consequences of such internalization, in her art she tapped the energy of the decadents' alienated lesbian. The unholy excess and implacable cruelty of lesbian desire in Vivien's fiction and poetry—the tormented hair, unappeased breasts, insatiable thighs, and ardent hands of the lovers described by Vivien—uncover the demonic power that drew Baudelaire and Swinburne to the lesbian femme fatale. Indeed, Vivien suggests that the "unnatural" longing of the decadents' Sappho turns the lesbian into a prototypical artist, for her obsession with a beauty that does not exist in nature is part of a satanically ambitious effort against nature to attain the aesthetic par excellence.

Vivien therefore implicitly reveals the centrality of the lesbian in decadent poetry to claim this image for herself. Like Proust, who had declared "Femmes damnées" the "most beautiful [long poem] that Baudelaire had written," Vivien must have been struck by what Proust called the "strange privilege" Baudelaire assigned himself in "Lesbos": "For Lesbos of all men on this earth elected me / To sing the secret of its flowering virgins / And as a child I was admitted to the dark mystery."[21] Swinburne, with less presumption, responded to a friend's critique of his Sapphopersona by explaining, "It is as near as I can come; and no man can come close to

17. Vivien, *A Woman Appeared to Me* 34.

18. Praz discusses the lesbian female fatale in *The Romantic Agony* 236–40, 260–61, as does Faderman, *Surpassing the Love of Men* 269–75. See also Foster, *Sex Variant Women* 76–80, 104, 114.

19. A recitation of San Giovanni, Sappho's avatar in *A Woman Appeared to Me* 17; see Rubin's introduction, viii.

20. Colette, *The Pure and the Impure* 71.

21. Baudelaire, *Flowers of Evil* 106–7. I have departed somewhat from this translation. Also see Proust, "A propos of Baudelaire" 125–26.

her."[22] As if diagnosing his and Baudelaire's efforts to "come close," the Sapphic androgyne of Vivien's novel explains the limits of such voyeuristic masculine fantasies of lesbianism: "Men see in the love of woman for woman only a spice that sharpens the flatness of their regular performance. But when they realize that this cult of grace and delicacy will permit no sharing, no ambiguity, they revolt against the purity of a passion which excludes and scorns them."[23] Vivien implies that Baudelaire, who originally gave the title *Les Lesbiennes* to *Les Fleurs du mal*, and Swinburne, who spoke to "Anactoria" in the accents of a passionately depraved Sappho, were themselves excluded from what she is elected to sing: the secrets, the dark mysteries of Mytilene. She subversively implies, moreover, that the lesbian is the epitome of the decadent and that decadence is fundamentally a lesbian literary tradition.

No wonder, then, that this Anglo-American girl christened Pauline Tarn seems to have renamed herself after the insinuating seductress Vivien of Arthurian legend: in Tennyson's *Idylls of the King* and Burne-Jones's *Beguiling of Merlin*, the enchantress Vivien literally steals Merlin's magical book, which contains a powerful charm to enthrall women to men.[24] Like the Arthurian Vivien, Renée Vivien appropriates the male-authored book of power to usurp male authority and to break what Gayle Rubin calls the male monopoly over women.[25] Of course, as critics like Sandia Belgrade and Pamela Annas have noted, when Pauline Tarn renamed herself Renée Vivien she was also effecting a transformation in which she was reborn (re-*née*), even as she was insisting on retaining her maiden name (*née*) and her maidenhood.[26] Like the sinister but sensuous figure in her poem "Viviane," who has "changed her name, her voice, her visage," Vivien is "born anew" ("elle renaît").[27] Just as the Arthurian Vivien casts Merlin in a lifeless spell, just as Vivien's

---

22. Swinburne, *Selected Poetry and Prose* 328–29. Klaich, *Woman Plus Woman* 143, sees Vivien as victimized by Swinburnean decadence.

23. Vivien, *A Woman Appeared to Me* 36.

24. Both of these popular Victorian works of art would have been familiar to Vivien. I am indebted to Elliot Gilbert for my understanding of Tennyson's *Idylls of the King*. Sandra M. Gilbert and I place Vivien's pseudonym in the context of other feminist modernist names of power in "Ceremonies of the Alphabet."

25. Gayle Rubin's brilliant introduction to *A Woman Appeared to Me* provides an indispensable introduction to Vivien (iii–xx). Auerbach, *Woman and the Demon* 74–81, 104–6, discusses the relationship between the female and the demonic in Pre-Raphaelite painting and in Swinburne's poetry.

26. Belgrade, introduction to *At the Sweet Hour of Hand in Hand* xv; Annas, "Drunk with Chastity."

27. "Viviane" is translated in *At the Sweet Hour* 47–49. Unless otherwise indicated, I am using the Naiad Press translations of Vivien's poetry because they are a pioneering achievement that makes possible the teaching and study of Vivien in this country. For those who wish to see the original, a collected *Poèmes de Renée Vivien* has been reprinted in facsimile by Arno Press.

"Viviane" weaves so that "you fall asleep in her eternal arms," Vivien is reborn a lesbian poet; thus she evades heterosexual consummation with *its* vampiric consumption of women, for in her view the penetration of women ensures the perpetuation of patriarchy.

In a number of poems, therefore, Vivien flouts heterosexual homophobia: "You will never know how to tarnish the devotion / Of my passion for the beauty of women"; in others, she praises female virginity as virility:

> I shall flee imprint
> And soiling stain.
> The grasp that strangles, the kiss that infects
> And wounds shall I shun.[28]

For Vivien, Sapphism, precisely because it is what the decadents called "barren," provides access not to the future of the human species but to the present of the female of the species. "Our love is greater than all loves," Vivien declares in "Sappho Lives Again," for "we can, when the belt comes undone, / Be at once lovers and sisters."[29] Similarly, in "Union," Vivien begins, "Our heart is the same in our woman's breast," and she explains, "Our body is made the same"; "we are of the same race"; "I know exactly what pleases you"; "I am you."[30] Because the beloved feels so much like oneself, however, the realization of her separateness is tormenting. Vivien's feelings about Barney's promiscuity, to which Sappho's poems on the loss of Atthis could serve as utterance, underscore this sense of aloneness, allowing Vivien to privilege lesbianism as the preferred eroticism because it raises crucial issues of fusion and identity.[31]

By opening up the relationship of women to eroticism, Vivien admits an influx of jealousy and self-abasement as well as of consolation and pleasure. Sapphic desire implicates the lover in the beloved's abandonment and the rival's competition, both of which complicate the monolithic ideal of sisterhood that informed so much feminist rhetoric in her time: "For Andromeda," Vivien laments in one Sapphic meditation, "the lightning of your kiss," while she herself is left with only "the grave cadences" of Atthis's voice.[32] Even when the beloved is present to the lover, their lovemaking offers

28. Vivien, "The Disdain of Sappho" and "I shall be always a virgin" in *The Muse of the Violets* 46, 44.

29. Vivien, "Sappho Lives Again," in *At the Sweet Hour* 2–4.

30. Vivien, "Union," in *Muse of the Violets* 73.

31. The best analysis of Sappho's poetry in terms of the "illusion of perfect union, the inevitability of parting," is Stehle [Stigers], "Romantic Sensuality, Poetic Sense" (quotation on 467). Adrienne Rich addresses the issue of privileging lesbianism as the preferred eroticism in "Compulsory Heterosexuality and Lesbian Existence."

32. Vivien, "For Andromeda, she has a beautiful recompense," in *Muse of the Violets* 36.

paradoxical intimations of their separateness: in "Chanson," for example, Vivien sees in her beloved a "form . . . that leaves me clutching emptiness" and a "smile . . . that one can never clasp."[33] The need to "evoke the fear, the pain and the torment" of such love repeatedly turns Vivien toward Sappho:

O perfume of Paphos! O Poet! O Priestess!
Teach us the secret of divine sorrow,
Teach us longing, the relentless embrace
Where pleasure weeps, faded among the flowers
O languors of Lesbos Charm of Mytilene
Teach us the golden verse stifled only by death,
    Of your harmonious breath,
    Inspire us, Sappho[34]

Vivien's dramatic poems—"La Mort de Psappha" ("The Death of Sappho"), "Atthis délaissée" ("Atthis Abandoned"), and "Dans un verger" ("In an Orchard")—are elegies mourning not only the death of the poet of fugitive desires but also the death of desire itself.[35] Paradoxically, however, "Sappho Lives Again" in these elegies, reborn as Vivien: "Some of us have preserved the rites / Of burning Lesbos gilded like an altar."[36] Prefaced with fragments of Sappho's, Vivien's French becomes an aspect of the other muted languages of languor in the poetry: the lexicon of scents, the syntax of flowers, the sign language of fingers on flesh, the intonation of swooning voices sighing in broken phrases. While Vivien's French aligns her poetry with the flagrant fragrance of Continental eroticism in the *belle époque* and thereby frees her to speak the unspoken, prefaced with Sapphic phrase, set off with ellipses, her most fragmentary translations seem to attest to a form of aphasia, symptomatic of an ontological or sexual expatriation, for Vivien's French is as foreign to her native English as her homosexuality is to the hegemonic heterosexual idiom. At a loss for words, Vivien signals her exile from Lesbos, her expatriation from a native language of desire.

Two of the finest of Vivien's original poems that equate the recovery of Sappho with the rediscovery of a distant but distinct female country and the translation of the poet carried across the seas and the centuries to this country are "En débarquant à Mytilène" ("While Landing at Mytilene")

33. Vivien, "Chanson," in *Muse of the Violets* 24; thanks to a gift from Elin Diamond, I have taken the original, "Sonnet," from *Études et preludes* 24.

34. Vivien, "Invocation," in *Muse of the Violets* 59. The original appears in *Cendres et poussiers* 2–4.

35. Although Vivien's verse dramas have not yet been translated into English, they are available in French in *Poèmes de Renée Vivien.*

36. Vivien, "Sappho Lives Again," in *At the Sweet Hour* 2; but I have departed from this translation here with the help of Star Howlett.

and "Vers Lesbos" ("Toward Lesbos").[37] In the first, the poet begins with an effort at return: "From the depths of my past, I turn back to you / Mytilene, across the disparate centuries." Similarly, in "Toward Lesbos," she speaks to a beloved on board a ship headed for Mytilene: "You will come," she tells her lover, "your eyes filled with evening and with yesterday." In both poems, fine fragrances fill the air: in the first, the poet brings her love "like a present of aromatics," and in the second, "our boat will be full of amber and spices." In both poems the trip to Greece involves dying into a new life; the poet discovers waves, trees, and vines, a place in which to "melt and dissolve." Or again the boat is "frail like a cradle," as the lovers, sleeping through the risks and rites of passage, wonder if they will be able to move to where "we will live tomorrow." Most important, in both poems the Greek island is a place of the female erotic imagination: in the first, Mytilene is quite simply a woman's body rising out of the sea, "golden-flanked Lesbos"; in the second, the lovers on board hear "mysterious songs," the intimation of "supreme music," as they approach "the illusionary island."

This utopian yearning for a visionary land and language of female primacy also impelled the American-born poet H.D. The Englishwoman Bryher saved H.D.'s life in 1919 by caring for her through influenza and a difficult childbirth when she had been abandoned both by her husband and by the father of her child; and in 1920 Bryher took H.D. to the Greek islands to recuperate.[38] H.D. describes the events that led to her recovery in the first section of her novel *Palimpsest*: her heroine, Hipparchia, is a translator of Moero, an ancient woman poet whose imagery resembles Sappho's, although Hipparchia has renounced the struggle to recapture Sappho "as savouring of sacrilege."[39] After she is visited by a girl who has memorized all her translations, Hipparchia embarks on the regenerative voyage which taught H.D. that "Greece is not lost" because "Greece is a spirit."[40] Two or three years after her trip with Bryher, H.D. may have visited Lesbos with her mother, an experience she apparently found overwhelming.[41] Yet, while Vivien and H.D. took imaginative and actual passage to Greece in a similar spirit, they excavate two quite different Sapphos: Vivien's Sappho is languorous and tormented, H.D.'s stark and fierce in her commitment to artistic perfection—a shift in attitude that doubtless reflects the translation history of Sappho's

---

37. Vivien, "While Landing at Mytilene" and "Toward Lesbos," in *At the Sweet Hour* 25–26, 64–65.

38. The most recent biography of H.D. is Barbara Guest's *Herself Defined;* see 118–20, 123–26. Also see H.D., *Tribute to Freud* 49.

39. H.D., *Palimpsest* 129.

40. Ibid., 131.

41. Wolle's account of H.D.'s life records such a visit (*A Moravian Heritage* 58). However, Guest argues that there is no other evidence of such a trip (*Herself Defined* 167).

texts in this period. Also, unlike Vivien, who exclusively defines Sappho as a satanic lesbian, H.D. is strikingly reticent about the homosexual content of Sappho's verse. Instead, placing Sappho in a Greek context that extends from Homer to Euripides, H.D. explicitly adopts Sappho's texts as anachronistic literary models to remove herself from the contamination of contemporary sentimentality, even as she implicitly demonstrates that lesbianism furnishes her with a refuge from the pain of heterosexuality and with the courage necessary to articulate that pain.

H.D.'s first use of Sappho, "Fragment 113," is an original poem that presents itself as an exploration of Sappho's fragment "Neither honey nor bee for me."[42] Organized around a series of negatives, this poem refrains from assenting to an old desire. "Not honey," the poet reiterates three times in the first stanza, refusing thereby "the sweet / stain on the lips and teeth" as well as "the deep plunge of soft belly." The voluptuous plight of the plundering bee is associated with sweetness and softness. "Not so" would the poet desire, "though rapture blind my eyes, / and hunger crisp, dark and inert, my mouth." Refusing "old desire—old passion—/old forgetfulness—old pain—," H.D. speculates on a different desire:

> but if you turn again,
> seek strength of arm and throat
> touch as the god;
> neglect the lyre-note:
> knowing that you shall feel,
> about the frame,
> no trembling of the string,
> but heat, more passionate
> of bone and the white shell
> and fiery tempered steel.

Bone, not belly, shell, not lyre; fiery tempered steel instead of the stealings of the plundering bee: as in her essay on Sappho, H.D. finds in Sappho's poems "not heat in the ordinary sense, diffused, and comforting," but intensity "as if the brittle crescent-moon gave heat to us, or some splendid scintillating star turned warm suddenly in our hand like a jewel."[43]

Sappho's imagery—the storm-tossed rose, lily, and poppy; the wind-swept sea garden; the golden Aphrodite—dominates H.D.'s early poetry. The lyricism of both poets is characterized by a yearning intensity expressed through direct address and situated in a liminal landscape.[44] In her notes

---

42. H.D., "Fragment 113," in *Collected Poems* 131–32.

43. See H.D.'s "The Wise Sappho" 57–58.

44. See the excellent discussion of Sappho's poetry in Friedrich, *The Meaning of Aphrodite* 107–28.

on Sappho, entitled "The Island," H.D. imagines Sappho as "the island of artistic perfection where the lover of ancient beauty (shipwrecked in the modern world) may yet find foothold and take breath and gain courage for new ventures and dream of yet unexplored continents and realms of future artistic achievement."[45] Certainly, from H.D.'s earliest imagist verse to her later, longer epics, the Greek island is a place of female artistry. Specifically, from her dramatization in "Callypso" of Odysseus fleeing Calypso's island, to her paradisal vision in *Trilogy* of "the circles and circles of islands / about the lost center-island, Atlantis," to the central section of *Helen in Egypt*, which is situated on Leuke, *l'île blanche*, H.D. affirms what she proclaims in her last volume, *Hermetic Definition*, that "the island is herself, is her."[46]

Susan Friedman has explained that "Sappho's influence on imagists no doubt helped to validate H.D.'s leadership role in the development of the modern lyric."[47] Just as important, Sappho's Greek fragments furnished H.D. a linguistic model for the poems that would define the imagist aesthetic. "Fragment 113" presents itself as a numbered remnant, a belated version of a mutilated vision, a translation of a lost original. As H.D. knew, Sappho's texts, excavated in 1898 from Egyptian debris, survived as narrow strips torn from mummy wrappings. Her own poems, narrow columns of print with not a few phrases broken off with dashes, meditate on a loss they mediate as the speaker's series of negatives, presumably a response to a prior sentence omitted from the poem, seems to imply that the text has been torn out of an unrecoverable narrative context. H.D.'s lifelong effort to recreate what has been "scattered in the shards / men tread upon"[48] is reflected in her early fascination with Sappho's poetry, as in her recurrent presentation of herself as a translator of unearthed texts that can never be fully restored or understood. Certainly, H.D. uses the runes of Sappho as the fragments she shores up against her own ruin.

"Fragment 113" was published in the volume *Hymen* in 1921. Significantly, in the title piece of this volume, H.D. begins to extend her short lyrics in the direction of narrative. A cluster of poems describes the bride's impending fate, the loss of her virginity, in terms of the plundering bee who

45. H.D., "The Wise Sappho" 67. The heading, a section title, is found in the manuscript "Notes on Euripides, Pausanias, and Greek Lyric Poets" (1920), Beinecke Library, Yale University.

46. H.D., "Callypso," in *Collected Poems* 388–96; *Trilogy* 15; *Helen in Egypt* 109; *Hermetic Definition* 29.

47. Friedman, *Psyche Reborn* 10. Adalaide Morris has noted that the existence of women poets like Sappho, Nossis, and Telesilla illuminates H.D.'s attraction to classical literature ("Prospectus for Gender and Genre Session on H.D"). Kenner describes Pound's use of Sappho in "The Muse in Tatters."

48. H.D., *Trilogy* 36.

"slips / Between the purple flower-lips."[49] In the context of Sappho's "Neither honey nor bee for me," H.D.'s image of the bee's penetration brings to the foreground the silence and isolation of the veiled, white figure of the bride. In addition, as Alicia Ostriker has pointed out, the very title, "Hymen," with its evocation both of female anatomy and of a male god, turns this celebratory sequence into a somber meditation on the predatory pattern of homosexuality,[50] a pattern explicitly associated with the simultaneity of the bride's marriage and her divorce from the female community. H.D. transforms Sappho's epithalamia into the choruses of girls, maidens, matrons, and priestesses accompanying the silent bride. The stage directions between the lyrics consist of descriptions of musical interludes (flute, harp), of costumes (tunics, baskets), and of the spatial arrangement of figures in their processionals before the temple of Hera. Linking the lyrics together into a liturgy, these italicized prose passages solve the poetic problem H.D. faced as she struggled to extend a minimalist form without losing the intensity she associated with the image. "Hymen" therefore epitomizes the way in which Sappho empowered H.D. to turn eventually toward a reinvention of Homeric epic in *Helen in Egypt*, where she perfected the interrelationships between individual lyrics and a prose gloss that contextualizes them.

Unlike her husband, Richard Aldington, who published a book of voluptuous Sapphic lyrics, *The Love of Myrrhine and Konales* (1926), and unlike Ezra Pound, whose elegiac point in *Lustra* (1917) was that Sappho's fragments could not be reconstituted, H.D. uses the other five meditations on Sapphic fragments that she wrote early in her career to address the contradiction for the woman poet between artistic vocation and female socialization.[51] Heightening this contradictory need for autonomy as a lyricist and dependence as a desiring woman is the sense she has of her own fragility and frigidity; two poems directly confront these complex emotions. In "Fragment Forty-one" (". . . thou flittest to Andromeda"), H.D. describes her beloved's betrayal while defending herself against his charges: "I was not asleep," she declares; or "I was not dull and dead." In "Fragment Forty" ("Love . . . bitter-sweet"), Sappho's bittersweet love becomes H.D.'s honey and salt, an unnerving blend of tastes that epitomize the grief of love's abandonment.[52] In these two poems, H.D. is "deserted," "outcast," "shattered," "sacrificed," "scorched," "rent," "cut apart," and "slashed open" by her love for a man who is absent or unfaithful. Paradoxically, however, it is precisely the torment of rupture

49. H.D., "Fragment 113," in *Collected Poems* 109.

50. Ostriker, "The Poet as Heroine."

51. This point is made by both Swann, *The Classical World of H.D.* 109–21, and Quinn, *Hilda Doolittle* 43–46.

52. H.D., "Fragment Forty-one" and "Fragment Forty," in *Collected Poems* 181–84, 173–75.

that sparks the poetry of rapture associated by H.D. with Sappho's ecstasy, her ex stasis, her breaking out of the self into lyric song.[53] In "Fragment Forty-one," the poet discovers her strength in a supremely generous gift, namely, "the love of my lover / for his mistress." Similarly, at the close of "Fragment Forty," she admits that "to sing love, / love must first shatter us."

That Eros is "he" in "Fragment Forty" and that the poet's lover is in love with "his mistress" in "Fragment Forty-one" unmistakably and—in the Sapphic context—surprisingly mark desire as heterosexual. Why would H.D. invoke the celebrated poet of lesbianism to articulate what Rachel Blau DuPlessis has called her "romantic thralldom" to a series of male mentors?[54] While it is certainly true that H.D. writes obsessively about her desire for the mastery of such men as Pound, Aldington, and Lawrence, her poetry is motivated less by their presence than by their absence. Like her autobiographical prose, which frequently dramatizes her frigidity when she is with these men,[55] H.D.'s revisions of Sapphic fragments articulate her effort to accept the intensity of desire that, transcending the beloved and his inevitable desertion, compels the poet to translate erotic abandonment into poetic abandon. The very number of Sappho's beloveds—Atthis, Anactoria, Gyrinno, Eranna, Gorgo—implies that her confessional poetry is an occasion for experiencing and expressing "an island, a country, a continent, a planet, a world of emotion" that H.D. considers the "spirit of a song."[56] For H.D., then, inspiration and abandonment (by men) are inextricably intertwined. Both Sappho and lesbianism function as a refuge for her, a protective respite from heterosexual deprivation, not unlike the maternal deities she celebrates in her later epics.

While Sappho's lyrical evocation of Aphrodite triumphs over the pain and confusion of mortal love, H.D.'s lyrical invocation of Sappho testifies to her own artistic survival, which was in large measure due to the companion who took her to the Hellas she associated with Helen, her mother. Indeed, just as H.D. is empowered to find the strength and integrity to create poetry out of the pain of abandonment by turning to the intensity she associates with Sappho, in her life she survived male rejection by returning to Bryher, a woman who quite literally shared her visions: repeatedly, in the autobiographical prose, H.D. describes not only how Bryher encouraged her to maintain the heretical concentration necessary to sustain the mystical

53. Barnstone, *The Poetics of Ecstasy* 29–41, discusses Sappho's poetry.

54. DuPlessis, "Romantic Thralldom in H.D."

55. H.D., *HERmione* 73; *Bid Me to Live* 51, 55, 160; *Tribute to Freud* 16. D. H. Lawrence captures this "frozen" quality in two of his fictionalized portraits of H.D., the priestess of Isis in *The Man Who Died* and Julia in *Aaron's Rod*.

56. H.D., "The Wise Sappho" 58–59.

experiences that would inform H.D.'s poetic development but also how Bryher occasionally saw such visions "for" H.D.[57] While Bryher herself is perceived as a brother in a poem like "I Said,"[58] their joy—which cannot be spoken "in a dark land"—puts H.D. in touch with the prophetic wisdom she associates with Hellas (Helen). If, as Susan Friedman has argued, Adrienne Rich was drawn to H.D. because of Rich's "desire to recreate a strong mother-daughter bond through her reading,"[59] H.D. herself accomplished such a task through both Bryher and Sappho.

While the dynamic of collaboration impels the linguistic experimentation of both Renée Vivien and H.D., it is analyzed most consciously by Amy Lowell, a poet who used Sappho's images to celebrate her passionate response to her lifelong companion, Ada Russell.[60] In "The Sisters" (1926), a poem explicitly about literary matrilineage, Lowell explores not only the significance of Sappho as the first female lyricist, but also the problematic limitations of precisely the collaboration with Sappho that Vivien and H.D. attempted to sustain. Sappho is first "remembered" by the author of "The Sisters," as she is by Vivien and H.D., at the moment when she is wondering why there are so few women poets: "There's Sappho, now I wonder what was Sappho."[61] Imagining a conversation with Sappho, Lowell supposes that she could surprise Sappho's reticence by flinging her own to the wind in order to learn how this irrepressibly sensuous "sister" came at the "loveliness of [her] words." For Lowell, as for Vivien and H.D., Sappho (who is neither a "Miss" nor a "Mrs.") embodies the elemental grandeur of "a leaping fire" and of "sea cliffs," in direct opposition to a poet like Mrs. Browning who writes "closeshuttered" and "squeezed in stiff conventions." Unlike the Victorian poetess, who is shut up in the parlor of propriety, once again Sappho represents the physical release of wind, sea, and sun as well as the mental relief from reticence associated with the "tossing off of garments" and with female conversation. Yet, for all her attraction to Sappho, Lowell also implies that the gulf between the ancient tenth Muse and the modern woman poet may not be negotiable: Lowell does not actually talk with Sappho; she wishes that she could. Imagining what "One might accomplish" in a conversation with Sappho, speculating on Mrs. Browning speculating on Sappho, Lowell

57. Rich has written about the collaborative vision H.D. shared with Bryher on Corfu in her introduction to *Working It Out*. See also H.D., *The Gift* 142, and *Tribute to Freud* 56, 130; and the discussion of female friendship in Bernikow, *Among Women* 163–92.

58. H.D., "I Said," in *Collected Poems* 22–25.

59. Friedman, " 'I go where I love,' " esp. 229.

60. In *Tendencies in Modern American Poetry*, Lowell defended H.D.'s poetry, which she also published in three imagist anthologies. See poems like "A Decade" and "Opal" in Lowell's *Complete Poetical Works* 217, 214.

61. Lowell, *Complete Poetical Works* 459.

describes the first sister of her "strange, isolated little family" as "a burning birch-tree" who wrote like "a frozen blaze before it broke and fell."

Although both Vivien and H.D. reject Ovid's influential version of Sappho leaping suicidally from the Leucadian cliff because of her unrequited love for Phaon, both seem to agree with Lowell that the intensity of Sappho's passion presages a fall: Vivien literally starves and poisons herself, and H.D. writes a number of poems—most notably "Oread"[62]—asking to be obliterated on the shore by the oncoming waves. Both therefore illustrate what Lawrence Lipking has called the "poetics of abandonment."[63] Just as potentially destructive, Lowell implies, is the strangely isolated situation of a classical poet defined not as a powerful foremother but as a vulnerable sister. From this point of view, the hegemonic position of Sappho in female poetic history privileges personal sincerity and passionate ecstasy as the lyricism perceived to be appropriately "feminine." In the context of lesbian literature, moreover, Sappho's preeminence as a model paradoxically sets up a single standard for writers defining themselves by their sexual difference, a standard that personalizes experiences already painfully privatized. Writing colloquially and conversationally, Lowell concludes "The Sisters" by admitting to Sappho and her descendants, "I cannot write like you. . . ." Indeed, all of her older "sisters" leave her feeling "sad and selfdistrustful."

A number of contemporary women writers express this same distrust of Sappho. For every Rita Mae Brown, writing "Sappho's reply" to protect those "who have wept in direct sunlight" with Sappho's voice, which "rings down through thousands of years," there is a Muriel Rukeyser who, rejecting Sappho "with her drowned hair trailing along Greek waters," calls out, "Not Sappho, Sacco"; or an Ann Shockley who uncovers the implicit racism of elitist Sapphic cults in "A Meeting of the Sapphic Daughters."[64] Equally suspicious, for various reasons, are poets from Sylvia Plath to Robin Morgan: Plath begins her poem "Lesbos" with the satiric line, "Viciousness in the kitchen" while Carolyn Kizer begins "Pro Femina" by considering the poetic line, "From Sappho to myself," only to remind herself that it is still "unwomanly" to discuss this subject; Susan Griffin writes marginalia to her poems that condemn them as "too much an imitation of Sappho"; and Robin Morgan exclaims defiantly, "get off my back, Sappho. / I never liked that position, / anyway."[65] Perhaps May Sarton explains Lowell's resistance

---

62. H.D., "Oread," in *Collected Poems* 55.

63. Lipking, "Aristotle's Sister," esp. 75.

64. R. M. Brown, "Sappho's Reply"; Rukeyser, "Poem out of Childhood"; Shockley, "A Meeting of the Sapphic Daughters."

65. Plath, "Lesbos," in *Collected Poems* 227; Kizer, "Pro Femina"; Griffin, "Thoughts on Writing" 115; Morgan, *Monster* 73.

to Sappho best when, placing Sappho in the company of Emily Dickinson and Christina Rossetti, she claims, "Only in the extremity of spirit and the flesh / And in the renouncing passion did Sappho come to bless." She thus demonstrates that "something is lost, strained, unforgiven" in the woman poet.[66]

These writers may help to explain why Djuna Barnes, the historian of Natalie Barney's salon in Paris, and Gertrude Stein, the center of her own coterie, only refer to Sappho tangentially, even sardonically, although they were themselves in the process of creating what Lillian Faderman calls "Lesbos in Paris."[67] Like Lowell's, their swerve from Sappho seems less a fear of being obliterated by her power as literary foremother, as it would be if Bloom's "anxiety of influence" were in effect, than a fear that Sappho was herself enmeshed in contradictions that threatened to stunt their own creative development. But it is Marguerite Yourcenar's treatment of Sappho that directly engages Lowell's reservations in order to question the dynamic of collaboration with Sappho. Although Yourcenar does not situate herself in the lesbian literary tradition, she, like most of the writers discussed here, was to become an expatriate. Her prose poem, "Sappho, or Suicide," concludes *Fires*, a work she wrote in French in 1935, four years before her departure for America with Grace Frick, and some four decades before she became the first woman to be elected to the French Academy. Reversing the immigration pattern of her predecessors, Yourcenar dramatizes the tragic demise of the dream of a separate sphere for women and thereby engages the tradition we have been tracing here—as she would, too, in her first translation work, of Virginia Woolf's *The Waves*.

"Just as in ancient times she was a poetess," Yourcenar's Sappho is an impoverished, graying acrobat, a "star" in the circus, a "magnetic creature, too winged for the ground, too corporal for the sky."[68] Because she cannot hold her lovers' bodies very long in "this abstract, space bordered on all sides by trapeze bars" (117) and because she is fated to worship in her female lovers "what she has not been" (118), she loses Attys, only to fall in love with a Phaon who seems like a "bronze and golden god" (125). Just at this point of thralldom, she begins to neglect "the discipline of her demanding profession" (125) and, after seeing Phaon dressed up to impersonate Attys, she discovers that he "is nothing more than a stand-in for the beautiful nymph" (126). Sappho's final act can only be to search above the spotlight in the highest

66. Sarton, "My Sisters, O My Sisters."

67. Faderman, *Surpassing the Love of Men* 70–72. Barnes, in her *Ladies Almanack* 71–72, invokes "a peep of No-Doubting Sappho, blinked from the Stews of Secret Greek Broth, and some Rennet of Lesbos" in one of its potent potions.

68. Yourcenar, *Fires* 116. Further citations will be given in parentheses in the text.

reaches of the arena's canopy for "a place to fall." Climbing the rope of her "celestial scaffold" (127) high above what Sylvia Plath would call in "Lady Lazarus" the "peanut-crunching crowd,"[69] Yourcenar's Sappho must make her art itself a form of suicide: unable to lose her balance, "no matter how she tries" (128), she dives, "arms spread as if to grasp half of infinity" (129). Yet "those failing at life run the risk of missing their suicide," and she is ultimately pulled from the mesh nets "streaming with sweat like a drowning woman pulled from the sea" (129).

While such a summary hardly catches the subtle brilliance of Yourcenar's lyrical meditation, it does illustrate how she insists on the lonely isolation of the woman artist who can neither break nor keep "the pact that binds us to the earth" (116). For Yourcenar, clearly, this aerial artist, this light princess with a heavy heart, is a divided creature. Finally, then, Sappho falls not only from lesbianism into heterosexuality, but from the fluid and supple women who were her "sky companion[s]" (117) to the unfortunate girl to whom she can only offer a maternal and tender "form of despair" (121) and ultimately to the "weight of her own sex" (126) when she knows herself to be captivated by a man who infiltrates the image of Attys. As it does so often, the revision of Sappho's story here provides a vision of lesbianism. Like Djuna Barnes in *Nightwood* (1936), Yourcenar sets her fable in the "international world of pleasure-seekers between the wars" (xii) to explore the disintegration of the lesbian community, implying that lesbianism can degenerate when it replicates the hierarchy implicit in heterosexual relationships. Her title, "Sappho, or Suicide"—with its ambiguous "or"—seems to assume on the one hand that the woman writer must choose either suicide or a lifeline to Sappho, her personal "sky companion," who is destined to be revived and retrieved over and over again; on the other hand, Sappho's second name may be suicide, for the writer who invokes Sappho's fame may be collaborating with the enemy; she may be destined to associate the grace and daring of her art with the anguish of a fated, if not fatal, eroticism. In either case, by the 1930s, the dream of recovering Mytilene had degenerated for Yourcenar into a circus act. She sees lesbianism as an artful and courageous but doomed effort to defy the laws of gravity.

Yet in *Fires*, Yourcenar describes that effort in a mode that preserves the utopian grandeur of the lesbian aesthetic project in the modernist period. For, like her soaring acrobatic Sappho, the writers in this tradition were clearly attempting a radical redefinition of the barren grounds of heterosexual culture in general and of a male-dominated literary history in particular. Their two forms of collaboration—writing "for" the admired

69. Plath, "Lady Lazarus," in *Collected Poems* 245.

precursor and/or writing "for" the beloved other—challenge assumptions about the autonomy/authority of the author and the singularity of the subject: to use the language of Gertrude Stein, the writer who analyzed most fully the mechanisms of her own collaboration with Alice B. Toklas, to be "one" is to know oneself as "two."[70] The act of writing cannot be said to originate from a single source, these writers seem to suggest—as Amy Lowell does, too, when she entitles her sequence of Sapphic poems "Two Speak Together."[71]

Early-twentieth-century lesbian poets had to reach back into antiquity to find a literary foremother, whose texts had been falsified by classical legends and partially obliterated by patristic injunctions. Clearly, they were empowered to do so by the formation of autonomous female communities that the friendships of nineteenth-century women poets could only adumbrate. It is a striking biographical contrast, the shift from the seclusion of Emily Dickinson or the familial sisterhood of Christina Rossetti or the married life of Elizabeth Barrett Browning to the bonding between women that we find in the erotic unions and female friendships of Vivien, H.D., Lowell, and Yourcenar, and also of Cather, Sitwell, Woolf, and Barnes. In other words, even as it situates itself on the margins, at the edge, of patriarchal culture, the lesbian tradition may serve as a paradigmatic solution to the problem creativity posed to nineteenth-century women artists.

Finally, then, the sapphistries of Vivien, H.D., Lowell, and Yourcenar demonstrate how feminist modernists found—if only fleetingly—what Woolf had thought lost in Lesbos: artistic predecessors, membership in a group where art is freely discussed and practiced, and freedom of action and experience. Living, all but one of them, *ex patria*, outside of their fathers' country, they represent their exile as a privileged marginalization that paradoxically exposes the homogeneity of heterosexual culture, the heterogeneity of homosexual coupling. Together, they draw on the strength of collaboration in much the way Sappho had prayed for an empowering union with Aphrodite:

> Come, then, loose me from cruelties.
> Give my tethered heart its full desire.
> Fulfill, and come, lock your shield with mine.
> Throughout the siege.[72]

70. The anxiety of becoming the other is dramatized in Stein's depression after the popularity of *The Autobiography of Alice B. Toklas* (1933), her fear that the public was more interested in her personality than in her work; on the other hand, in works like "Ada" and "Lifting Belly," she articulates the pleasure and merriment of speaking for and with the one who is the lover.

71. Lowell, *Complete Poetical Works* 209–18.

72. Sappho's "Ode to Aphrodite," in Davenport, *Archilochos, Sappho, Alkman* 121.

BIBLIOGRAPHY

Aldington, Richard, trans. *The Poems of Anyte of Tegea*. London: Egoist Press, 1915.

Alfonsi, L. *Otium e vita d'amore negli elegiaci Augustei*. Vol. 1 of *Studi in onore di Aristide Calderini e Roberto Paribeni*. Milan: Ceschina, 1956.

Allen, Don Cameron. "Donne's Sappho to Philaenis." *English Language Notes* 1 (1964) 188–91.

Allen, M. J. B. "Marsilio Ficino, Hermes Trismegistus and the US?? *Corpus Hermeticum*." In *New Perspectives on Renaissance Thought: Essays in the History of Science, Education and Philosophy in Memory of Charles B. Schmitt*, edited by John Henry and Sarah Hutton, 38–47. London: Duckworth, 1990.

André, Jean Marie. *L'Otium dans la vie morale et intellectuelle romaine, des origines a l'époque augustéenne*. Paris: Presses universitaires de France, 1966.

Andreadis, Harriette. "The Sapphic-Platonics of Katherine Philips, 1632–1664." *Signs* 15 (1989) 34–60.

Annas, Pamela. "Drunk with Chastity: The Poetry of Renée Vivien." *Women's Studies* 13 (1986) 11–22.

Armstrong, Alan. "The Apprenticeship of John Donne: Ovid and the *Elegies*." *ELH* 44 (1977) 419–42.

Arthur, Marilyn B. "Early Greece: The Origins of the Western Attitude toward Women." *Arethusa* 6 (1973) 7–58. [Reprinted in *Women in the Ancient World: The Arethusa Papers*, edited by John Peradotto and J. P. Sullivan, 7–58 (Buffalo: SUNY Press, 1984).]

Auerbach, Nina. *Woman and the Demon*. Cambridge: Harvard University Press, 1982.

Baca, Albert R. "Ovid's Epistle from Sappho to Phaon (*Heroides* 15)." *Transactions of the American Philological Association* 102 (1971) 29–38.

Bachofen, J. J. *Myth, Religion, and Mother Right*, translated by Ralph Manheim. Princeton: Princeton University Press, 1967.

Ballaster, Rosalind. Introduction to *New Atalantis*, by Delarivier Manley, v–xxi. New York: Penguin Books, 1992.

Barnard, Mary. *Assault on Mount Helicon: A Literary Memoir*. Berkeley: University of California Press, 1984.

———. *Collected Poems*. Berkeley: Far Corner Books, 1979.

————, trans. *Sappho: A New Translation*. Berkeley: University of California Press, 1958.

Barnes, Djuna. *Ladies Almanack*. 1928. Reprint, New York: Harper and Row, 1972.

Barnstone, Willis. *The Poetics of Ecstasy: From Sappho to Borges*. New York: Holmes and Meier, 1983.

————. *The Poetics of Translation: History, Theory, Practice*. New Haven: Yale University Press, 1993.

————, trans. *Sappho: Lyrics in the Original Greek with Translations*. New York: New York University Press, 1965.

Barthélemy, Jean-Jacques. *Voyage du jeune Anacharsis en Grèce*. 7 vols. Paris, 1790.

Bartholin, Caspar. *C. Bartholini Anatomicae institutiones corporis humani*. Oxford, 1633.

Bartholin, Thomas. *The Anatomical History of Thomas Bartholin*. London, 1653.

Battersby, Christine. "Unblocking the Oedipal: Karoline von Guenderode and the Female Sublime." In *Political Gender: Texts and Contexts*, edited by Sally Ledger, Josephine McDonagh, and Jane Spencer. New York: Harvester Wheatsheaf, 1994.

Baudelaire, Charles. *The Flowers of Evil/Les Fleurs du mal*, edited by Wallace Fowlie. New York: Bantam, 1964.

Bayle, Pierre. "Sappho." In *Dictionnaire historique et critique*, edited by M. des Maizeaux. 4th ed. Amsterdam: P. Brunel, R. and J. Wetstein, etc., 1730.

Beattie, A. J. "Sappho Fr. 31." *Mnemosyne*, ser 4, 9 (1956) 103–11.

Beaumont, W., trans. *Travels of the Young Anacharsis in Greece*. 4. London, 1806.

Bechtel, Friedrich. *Die historische Personennamen des Griechischen*. Halle a. d. S., 1917.

Behn, Aphra. "To the Fair Clarinda, Who Made Love to Me, Imagined More Than Woman" (1688). In *The Norton Anthology of Literature by Women: The Traditions in English*, edited by Sandra M. Gilbert and Susan Gubar, 116. 2nd ed. New York: Norton, 1996.

Belgrade, Sandia. Introduction to *At the Sweet Hour of Hand in Hand*, by Renée Vivien. Tallahassee, Fla.: Naiad Press, 1979.

Benjamin, Walter. *Illuminations*, translated by Harry Zohn. Glasgow: Fontana/Collins, 1982.

————. *Reflections: Essays, Aphorisms, Autobiographical Writings*, translated by Edmund Jephcott, edited by Peter Demetz. New York: Schocken Books, 1978.

Bergk, Theodor, ed. *Poetae Lyrici Graeci*. 3 vols. Leipzig: Reichenbach, 1843.

Bernikow, Louise. *Among Women*. New York: Crown, 1980.

Berry, Philipa. *Of Chastity and Power: Elizabethan Literature and the Unmarried Queen*. London: Routledge, 1989.

Billardon de Sauvigny, Louis-Edme. *Le Parnasse de dames*. 7 vols. Paris, 1773.

Blankely, Elyse. "Returning to Mytilene: Renée Vivien and the City of Women." In *Women Writers and the City: Essays in Feminist Literary Criticism*, edited by Susan Squier, 45–67. Knoxville: University of Tennessee Press, 1984.

Bloom, Harold. *The Anxiety of Influence*. New York: Oxford University Press, 1973.

Boardman, John. *Athenian Red Figure Vases: The Archaic Period*. London: Thames and Hudson, 1975.

————. *Eros in Greece*. Milan: A. Mondadori, 1975.

Bogan, Louise. *A Poet's Alphabet: Reflections on the Literary Art and Vocation*, edited by Robert Phelps and Ruth Limmer. New York: McGraw-Hill, 1970.

Bolling, George Melville. "Textual Notes on the Lesbian Poets." *American Journal of Philology* 81 (1961) 151–63.

Bonnet, Marie-Jo. *Un choix sans équivoque: Recherches historiques sur les relations amoureuses entre les femmes XVIe–XXe siècle.* Paris: Denoël, 1981.

Boswell, John. *Christianity, Social Tolerance, and Homosexuality.* Chicago: University of Chicago Press, 1980.

Bosworth, William. "The Historie of Arcadius and Sepha." In *The chast and lost lovers* (1651). [London], 1653.

Boulding, Elise. *The Underside of History: A View of Women through Time.* Boulder: University of Colorado Press, 1976.

Bowra, C. M. *Greek Lyric Poetry.* Oxford: Oxford University Press, 1961.

Bradley, Katherine, and Edith Cooper. *Long Ago.* London: G. Bell and Sons, 1889.

Brandt, Paul. *Sappho.* Leipzig: Friedrich Rothbarth, 1905.

———. [Hans Licht]. *Sexual Life in Ancient Greece*, translated by J. H. Freese. London: Routledge, 1932.

Bray, Alan. "Homosexuality and the Signs of Male Friendship in Elizabethan England." In *Queering the Renaissance*, edited by Jonathan Goldberg, 40–61. Durham: Duke University Press, 1994. [Reprinted from *History Workshop Journal* 29 (1990) 1–19.]

———. *Homosexuality in Renaissance England.* London: Gay Men's Press, 1982.

Brelich, Angelo. *Paides e Parthenoi.* Rome: Edizione dell'Ateneo, 1969.

Bremer, Jan M. "A Reaction to Tsagarakis' Discussion of Sappho Fr. 31." *Rheinisches Museum* 125 (1982) 113–16.

Bremmer, Jan N. "Adolescents, Symposion, and Pederasty." In *Sympotica: A Symposium on the Symposion*, edited by Oswyn M. Murray, 135–48. Oxford: Oxford University Press, 1990.

———. "An Enigmatic Indo-European Rite: Pederasty." *Arethusa* 13 (1980) 279–83.

Bronfen, Elisabeth. *Over Her Dead Body: Death, Femininity, and the Aesthetic.* New York: Routledge, 1992.

Brown, Judith. *Immodest Acts: The Life of a Lesbian Nun in Renaissance Italy.* New York: Oxford University Press, 1986.

Brown, Rita Mae. "Sappho's Reply." In *Lesbian Poetry*, edited by Elly Bulkin and Joan Larkin, 163. Watertown, Mass.: Persephone Press, 1981.

Brown, Susan. "A Victorian Sappho: Agency, Identity, and the Politics of Poetics." *English Studies in Canada* 20 (1994) 205–25.

Bunch, Charlotte. "Lesbianism and Erotica in Pornographic America." In *Take Back the Night: Women on Pornography*, edited by Laura Lederer, 91–94. New York: Bantam, 1980.

Burnett, Anne Pippin. *Three Archaic Poets. Archilochus, Alcaeus, Sappho.* Cambridge: Harvard University Press, 1983.

Bury, J. B., S. A. Cook, and F. E. Adcock, eds. *Greek Literature from the Eighth Century to the Persian Wars.* Vol. 4 of *Cambridge Ancient History.* Cambridge: Cambridge University Press, 1926.

Butler, Judith. "Imitation and Gender Insubordination." In *Inside/Out: Lesbian Theories, Gay Theories*, edited by Diana Fuss, 13–31. New York: Routledge, 1991.

Byron, Lord George Gordon. *Don Juan*, ed. T. G. Steffan, E. Steffan, and W. W. Pratt. New Haven: Yale University Press, 1973.

Calame, Claude. *Les chœurs de jeunes filles en Grèce archaïque.* 2 vols. Rome: Edizioni dell'Ateneo e Bizzarri, 1977.

———, ed. *Alcman fragmenta.* Rome: edizioni dell'ateneo, 1983.

Calder, William M., III. "F. G. Welcker's *Sapphobild* and Its Reception in Wilamowitz." In *Friedrich Gottlieb Welcker*, edited by Calder, 131–56. Hermes Einzelschriften 49. Stuttgart: Franz Steiner Verlag, 1988.

Califia, Pat. *Sapphistry.* Tallahassee, Fla.: Naiad Press, 1980.

Campbell, D. A. *The Golden Lyre: The Themes of the Greek Lyric Poets.* London: Duckworth, 1983.

———. *Greek Lyric.* 5 vols. Loeb Classical Library. Cambridge: Harvard University Press, 1982–93.

———. *Greek Lyric Poetry.* London: Macmillan, 1967.

Cantarella, Eva. *Bisexuality in the Ancient World*, translated by Cormac O'Cuilleanain. New Haven: Yale University Press, 1992.

———. *Pandora's Daughters: The Role and Status of Women in Greek and Roman Antiquity*, translated by Maureen B. Fant. Baltimore: Johns Hopkins University Press, 1987.

Cantarella, Raffaele. *Storia della letteratura greca.* Milan: Nuova Accademia, 1962.

Carey, John. *John Donne: Life, Mind, and Art.* London: Faber and Faber, 1981.

Carson, Anne. *Eros the Bittersweet.* Princeton: Princeton University Press, 1986.

———. "'Just for the Thrill': Sycophantizing Aristotle's *Poetics.*" *Arion* 1.1 (1990) 142–54.

Cartledge, Paul. "The Politics of Spartan Pederasty." In *Sexualität und Erotik in der Antike*, edited by Andreas Karsten Siems, 385–415. Darmstadt: Wissenschaftliche Buchgesellschaft, 1988. [Reprinted from *Proceedings of the Cambridge Philological Society* 27 (1981) 17–26.]

———. "Spartan Wives: Liberation or Licence?" *Classical Quarterly* 31 (1981) 84–105.

Cather, Willa. *The World and the Parish: Willa Cather's Articles and Reviews, 1883–1902*, edited by William M. Curtin. Lincoln: University of Nebraska Press, 1970.

Catlin, Zackary, trans. *Ovid, De Tristibus: or mournefull elegies.* London, 1639.

Cavendish, Margaret, Duchess of Newcastle. "The Convent of Pleasure: A Comedy." In *Plays, never before printed*. London, 1668.

Chalon, Jean. *Portrait of a Seductress: The World of Natalie Barney*, translated by Carol Barko. New York: Crown, 1979.

Chase, Cynthia. *Decomposing Figures: Rhetorical Readings in the Romantic Tradition.* Baltimore: Johns Hopkins University Press, 1986.

Chauncey, George. "Female Deviance." *Salmagundi*, nos. 58–59 (1982–83) 114–46.

Chorier, Nicolas. *Aloisiae Sigeae Toletanae Satyra Sotadica de Arcanis Amoris et Veneris sive Joannis Meurii Elegantiae Latini Sermonis* (1660), edited by Bruno Lavagnini. Catania: R. Prampolini, 1935.

Churchyard, Thomas, trans. *The thre first bookes of Ovids de tristibus.* London, 1572.

Cixous, Hélène. "The Laugh of the Medusa." In *New French Feminisms*, edited by Elaine Marks and Isabelle de Courtivron, 245–64. New York: Schocken Books, 1981.

Cleland, John. *Fanny Hill, or, Memoirs or a Woman of Pleasure* (1748–49), edited by Peter Wagner. Harmondsworth: Penguin, 1985.

Colette. *The Pure and the Impure*, translated by Herma Briffault. 1932. Reprint, New York: Penguin, 1971.

Commoti, Giovanni. *Music in Greek and Roman Culture*, translated by Rosaria V. Munson. Baltimore: Johns Hopkins University Press, 1989.

Corbin, Alain. *Histoire de la vie privée.* Vol. 4. Paris: Editions du Seuil, 1987.

Cowley, Abraham. "Upon Mrs. 'K. Philips' her Poems." In *Katherine Philips, Poems.* London, 1667.

Crooke, Helkiah. *Microcosmographia: A Description of the Body of Man*. London, 1615.

Crotty, Kevin. *Song and Action: The Victory Odes of Pindar*. Baltimore: Johns Hopkins University Press, 1982.

Culler, Jonathan. "Changes in the Study of Lyric." In *Lyric Poetry: Beyond New Criticism*, edited by Chaviva Hosek and Patricia Parker, 38–54. Ithaca: Cornell University Press, 1985.

———. *The Pursuit of Signs: Semiotic, Literature, Deconstruction*. Ithaca: Cornell University Press, 1981.

———. "Reading Lyric." In *The Lesson of Paul de Man*; special issue of *Yale French Studies* 69 (1985) 98–106.

Dacier, Anne Le Fèvre, trans. *Les Poésies d'Anacréon et de Sapho*. Paris, 1681.

———, trans. *Les Poesies d'Anacreon et de Sapho, Traduites en François, avec des remarques*. Amsterdam, 1716.

Davenport, Guy, trans. *Archilochos, Sappho, Alkman: Three Lyric Poets of the Late Greek Bronze Age*. Berkeley: University of Califorinia Press, 1980.

Davies, Malcolm, ed. *Poetarum Melicorum Graecorum Fragmenta*. Oxford: Oxford University Press, 1991.

Degani, Enzo, and Gabriele Burzacchini. *Lirici greci*. Florence: La Nuova Italia, 1977.

DeJean, Joan. "Female Voyeurism: Sappho and Lafayette." *Rivista di letterature moderne e comparate* 40 (1987) 201–15.

———. "Fictions of Sappho." *Critical Inquiry* 13 (1987) 787–805.

———. *Fictions of Sappho, 1546–1937*. Chicago: University of Chicago Press, 1989.

———. "Sappho's Leap: Domesticating the Woman Writer." *L'Esprit Créateur* 15 (1985) 14–21.

———. "Sex and Philology: Sappho and the Rise of German Nationalism." *Representations*, no. 27 (1989) 148–71.

de Man, Paul. *Allegories of Reading: Figural Language in Rousseau, Nietzsche, Rilke, and Proust*. New Haven: Yale University Press, 1979.

———. "Autobiography as De-Facement." In *The Rhetoric of Romanticism*, 67–81. New York: Columbia University Press, 1984.

Derrida, Jacques. "Des Tours de Babel," translated by Joseph Graham. In *Difference in Translation*, edited by Joseph Graham, 165–207. Ithaca: Cornell University Press, 1985.

Détienne, Marcel. *The Gardens of Adonis: Spices in Greek Mythology*, translated by Janet Lloyd. Princeton: Princeton University Press, 1977.

Détienne, Marcel, and Jean-Paul Vernant. *The Cuisine of Sacrifice among the Greeks*, translated by Paula Wissig. Chicago: University of Chicago Press, 1989.

Deutsch, Helene. *The Psychology of Women: A Psychoanalytic Interpretation*. 2 vols. New York: Greene and Stratton, 1944.

Devereux, George. "Greek Pseudo-Homosexuality and the 'Greek Miracle.'" *Symbolae Osloenses* 42 (1967) 69–92. [Reprinted in *Sexualität und Erotik in der Antike*, edited by Andreas Karsten Siems, 206–31 (Darmstadt: Wissenschaftliche Buchgesellschaft, 1988).]

———. "The Nature of Sappho's Seizure in Fr. 31 LP as Evidence of her Inversion." *Classical Quarterly*, n.s. 20 (1970) 17–31.

Diels, H. "Alkmans Partheneion." *Hermes* 31 (1896) 339–74.

Dijkstra, Bram. *Idols of Perversity*. New York: Oxford University Press, 1986.

Dinesen, Isak. *Out of Africa*. 1936. Reprint, New York: Random House, 1965.

Docherty, Thomas. *John Donne, Undone*. London: Methuen, 1986.

Domitius. "Domitius in Sappho Ovidii." In *Ovid, Heroides*. Venice, 1538; 2nd ed., 1543.

Donne, John. *The Poems of John Donne*, edited by Herbert Grierson. 2 vols. 1912. Reprint, London: Oxford University Press, 1960.

Donoghue, Emma. *Passions between Women: British Lesbian Culture, 1668–1801*. London: Scarlet Press, 1993.

Doolittle, Hilda. *See* H.D.

Dörrie, Heinrich. *P. Ovidius Naso: Der Brief der Sappho an Phaon mit literarischen und kritischen Kommentar im Rahmen einer motivgeschichtlichen Studie*. Zetemata 58. Munich: C. H. Beck, 1975.

Dover, K. J. "Eros and Nomos (Plato *Symposium* 182a–185c)." *Bulletin of the Institute of Classical Studies* 11 (1964) 31–42.

———. *Greek Homosexuality*. Cambridge: Harvard University Press, 1978.

Dryden, John. *An Essay of Dramatic Poesy, Selected Works of John Dryden*, edited by William Frost. New York: Holt, Rinehart, and Winston, 1964.

Duban, J. M. *Ancient and Modern Images of Sappho: Translations and Studies in Archaic Greek Love Lyric*. Classical World Special Series 2. Lanham, Md.: University Press of America, 1984.

duBois, Page. Introduction to *The Love Songs of Sappho*, translated by Paul Roche. New York: Penguin, 1991.

———. *Sappho Is Burning*. Chicago: University of Chicago Press, 1995

Duncan, Isadora. *My Life*. New York: Liveright, 1955.

Dunston, J. "Studies in Domizio Calderini." *Italia Medioevale e Umanistica* 11 (1968) 71–150.

DuPlessis, Rachel Blau. "Romantic Thralldom in H.D." *Contemporary Literature* 20 (1979) 178–203.

Edmonds, J. M. *Lyra Graeca, being the Remains of all the Greek Poets from Eumelus to Timotheus excepting Pindar*. Vol. 1, *Including Terpander Alcman Sappho and Alcaeus*. Loeb Classical Library. London: William Heinemann, 1922.

———. *Sappho in the Added Light of the New Fragments*. Cambridge: Cambridge University Press, 1912.

Ellis, Havelock. *Studies in the Psychology of Sex*. London: University Press, 1897.

Estienne, Henri [Henricus Stephanus]. *Carminum poetarum novem, lyricae poesews [sic] principum fragmenta*. Paris, 1566.

Evans, R. O. "Remarks on Sappho's 'Phainetai moi.' " *Studium Generale* 22 (1969) 1016–25.

Faderman, Lillian. *Surpassing the Love of Men: Romantic Friendship and Love Between Women from the Renaissance to the Present*. New York: William Morrow, 1981.

Fairweather, Janet A. "Fictions in the Biographies of Ancient Writers." *Ancient Society* 5 (1974) 231–75.

Fallopius, Gabriel. *Observationes Anatomicae*. Paris, 1562.

Fernandez-Galinano, Manuel. *Safo*. Madrid: n.p., 1958.

Finnegan, R. *Oral Poetry: Its Nature, Significance, and Social Context*. Cambridge: Cambridge University Press, 1977.

Fitzhardinge, L. F. *The Spartans*. London: Thames and Hudson, 1980.

Flacelière, Robert. *Histoire littéraire de la Grèce*. Paris: Fayard, 1961.

Foley, Helene P., ed. *Reflections of Women in Antiquity*. New York: Gordon and Breach, 1981.

Forrest, W. G. *A History of Sparta, 950–192 B.C.* New York: Norton, 1968.

Foster, Jeanette. *Sex Variant Women in Literature*. 1956. Reprint, Baltimore: Diana Press, 1975.

Foucault, Michel. *The History of Sexuality*. Vol. 2, *The Use of Pleasure*. New York: Vintage, 1985.

——— . *The History of Sexuality*, Vol. 3: *The Care of the Self*, translated by Robert Hurley. New York: Random House, 1986.

——— . *L'Usage des plaisirs*. Paris: Gallimard, 1984.

——— *La volonté de savoir*. Paris: Gallimard, 1976.

Fränkel, Hermann. *Early Greek Poetry and Philosophy*, translated by Moses Hadas and James Willis. New York: Harcourt, Brace, 1973.

Freeman, Barbara Claire. *The Feminine Sublime: Gender and Excess in Women's Fiction*. Berkeley: University of California Press, 1995.

Frenzel, Elizabeth. *Stoffe der Weltliteratur: Ein Lexikon dichtungsgeschichtlicher Längsschnitte*. Stuttgart: Alfred Kröner, 1963.

Friedman, Susan. "'I go where I love': An Intertextual Study of H.D. and Adrienne Rich." *Signs* 9 (1983) 228–45.

——— . *Psyche Reborn: The Emergence of H.D.* Bloomington: Indiana University Press, 1981.

Friedrich, Paul. *The Meaning of Aphrodite*. Chicago: University of Chicago Press, 1978.

Fuss, Diana. *Essentially Speaking: Feminism, Nature, and Difference*. New York: Routledge, 1989.

Gallavotti, C. "Alcmane, Teocrito, e un'iscrizione laconica." *Quaderni urbinati di cultura classica*, no. 27 (1978) 183–94.

——— . *Saffo ed Alceo: Testimonianze e frammenti*. 3rd rev. ed. Naples: Libreria Scientifica Editrice, 1962.

Gallop, Jane. *Thinking through the Body*. New York: Columbia University Press, 1988.

Gans, Eric. "Naissance du moi lyrique: Du feminin au masculin." *Poetique* 46 (1981) 129–39.

Gardner, Helen. *John Donne: The Elegies and the Songs and Sonnets*. Oxford: Clarendon Press, 1965.

Gentili, Bruno. *Poetry and Its Public in Ancient Greece: From Homer to the Fifth Century*, translated by A. Thomas Cole. Baltimore: Johns Hopkins University Press, 1988.

——— . "La veneranda Saffo." *Quaderni urbinati di cultura classica*, no. 2 (1966) 37–62.

Gerber, Douglas E. *Euterpe: An Anthology of Early Greek Lyric, Elegiac, and Iambic Poetry*. Amsterdam: Hakkert, 1970.

——— . "Studies in Greek Lyric Poetry: 1967–1973." *Classical World* 70 (1976) 65–157.

——— . "Studies in Greek Lyric Poetry: 1975–1985; Part I." *Classical World* 81 (1987) 73–144.

Gernet, Louis. *The Anthropology of Ancient Greece*, translated by John Hamilton and Blaise Nagy. Baltimore: Johns Hopkins University Press, 1981.

Gettone, Evelyn. "Sappho." In *The Encyclopedia of Homosexuality*, edited by Wayne R. Dynes. New York: Garland Press, 1990.

Gilbert, Sandra M., and Susan Gubar. "Ceremonies of the Alphabet." In *The Female Autograph*, edited by Domna Stanton, 23–52. New York: New York Literary Forum, 1984.

——— . *The Madwoman in the Attic: The Woman Writer and the Nineteenth-Century Literary Imagination*. New Haven: Yale University Press, 1979.

Gill, Roma. *"Musa Iocosa Mea:* Thoughts on the *Elegies."* In *John Donne: Essays in Celebration,* edited by A. J. Smith, 47–72. London: Methuen, 1972.

Glei, Reinhold F. " 'Sappho die Lesbierin' im Wandel der Zeiten." In *Liebe und Leidenschaft: Historische Aspekte von Erotik und Sexualität,* edited by Gerhard Binder and Bernd Effe, 145–61. Bochumer Altertumswissenschaftliches Colloquium 12. Trier: Wissenschaftlicher Verlag Trier, 1993.

Goldberg, Jonathan. *Voice Terminal Echo: Postmodernism and English Renaissance Texts.* New York: Methuen, 1986.

Gow, A. S. F., ed. *Theocritus.* 2 vols. Cambridge: Cambridge University Press, 1950.

Gow, A. S. F., and D. L. Page, eds. *The Greek Anthology: Hellenistic Epigrams.* 2 vols. Cambridge: Cambridge University Press, 1965.

Grahn, Judy. *The Highest Apple: Sappho and the Lesbian Poetic Tradition.* San Francisco: Spinsters, Ink, 1985.

Green, Peter. *The Laughter of Aphrodite: A Novel about Sappho of Lesbos.* 1965. Reprint, Berkeley: University of Califonia Press, 1993.

Greenblatt, Stephen. "Fiction and Friction." In *Shakespearean Negotiations: The Circulation of Social Energy in Renaissance England,* 66–93. Berkeley: University of California Press, 1988.

Greene, Ellen. "Apostrophe and Women's Erotics in the Poetry of Sappho." *Transactions of the American Philological Association* 124 (1994) 41–56.

Grierson, Herbert, ed. *The Poems of John Donne.* 2 vols. 1912. Reprint, Oxford: Oxford University Press, 1960.

Griffin, Susan. "Thoughts on Writing: A Diary." In *The Writer on Her Work,* edited by Janet Sternburg, 107–20. New York: Norton, 1980.

Griffiths, Alan. "Alcman's Partheneion: The Morning after the Night Before." *Quaderni urbinati di cultura classica,* no. 14 (1972) 7–30.

Grillparzer, Franz. *Sämtliche Werke.* Vol. 1, *Gedichte—Epigramme—Dramen I,* edited by Peter Frank and Karl Pörnbacher. Munich: Carl Hanser, 1960.

Gronewald, M. "Fragmente aus einem Sappho-Kommentar: Pap. Colon. inv. 5860." *Zeitschrift für Papyrologie und Epigraphik* 14 (1974) 114–18.

Gubar, Susan. "Sapphistries." *Signs* 10 (1984) 43–62. [Citations above are to the version published in this volume.]

Guerlac, Suzanne. "Longinus and the Subject of the Sublime." *New Literary History* 16 (1985) 275–89.

Guest, Barbara. *Herself Defined: The Poet H.D. and Her World.* New York: Doubleday, 1984.

Hadas, Moses. *A History of Greek Literature.* New York: Columbia University Press, 1950.

H.D. *Bid Me to Live (A Madrigal).* New York: Grove Press, 1960.

———. *Collected Poems, 1912–1944,* edited by Louis L. Martz. New York: New Directions, 1983.

———. *The Gift.* New York: New Directions, 1982.

———. *Helen in Egypt.* 1961. Reprint, New York: New Directions, 1974.

———. *Hermetic Definition.* New York: New Directions, 1972.

———. *HERmione.* New York: New Directions, 1981.

———. *Palimpsest.* 1926. Reprint, Carbondale: Southern Illinois University Press, 1968.

———. *Tribute to Freud* (1944–46). New York: McGraw-Hill, 1974.

———. *Trilogy.* 1944–46. New York: New Directions, 1973.

————. "The Wise Sappho." In *Notes on Thought and Vision and The Wise Sappho*, 57–69. San Francisco: City Lights Books, 1982.

Hall, John, trans. *Peri Hypsous, or, Dionysius Longinus on the Height of Eloquence rendered out of the Original*. London, 1652.

Hallett, Judith P. "Female Homoeroticism and the Denial of Roman Reality in Latin Literature." *Yale Journal of Criticism* 3 (1989) 209–27.

————. "Sappho and Her Social Context: Sense and Sensuality." *Signs* 4 (1979) 447–64.

Halperin, David M. "One Hundred Years of Homosexuality." *Diacritics* (1986) 34–45.

————. *One Hundred Years of Homosexuality and Other Essays on Greek Love*. New York: Routledge, 1990.

————. "Why Is Diotima a Woman?" In *One Hundred Years of Homosexuality and Other Essays on Greek Love*, 113–51. New York: Routledge, 1990.

Harmer, J. B. *Victory in Limbo: Imagism, 1908–1917*. New York: St. Martin's Press, 1975.

Harris, Bertha. "The More Profound Nationality of Their Lesbianism: Lesbian Society in Paris in the 1920s." In *Amazon Expedition: A Lesbian Feminist Anthology*, edited by Phyllis Birkby, 77–88. Washington, N.J.: Times Change Press, 1973.

Hartman, Geoffrey. *Beyond Formalism: Literary Essays, 1958–1970*. New Haven: Yale University Press, 1970.

Harvey, Elizabeth D. "Ventriloquizing Sappho: Ovid, Donne, and the Erotics of the Feminine Voice." *Criticism* 31.2 (1989) 115–38.

Hatton, Gwynneth. "Edition of the Unpublished Poems of Christina Rossetti." Master's thesis, Oxford University, 1955.

Heitsch, Ernst. "Sappho 2, 8, und 31, 9 L-P." *Rheinisches Museum* 105 (1962) 284–85.

Henderson, Jeffrey. *The Maculate Muse: Obscene Language in Attic Comedy*. 2nd ed. Oxford: Oxford University Press, 1991.

Henderson, Katherine Usher, and Barbara F. McManus, eds. *Half Humankind: Contexts and Texts of the Controversy about Women in England, 1540–1640*. Urbana: University of Illinois Press, 1985.

Herington, C. John. *Poetry into Drama: Early Tragedy and the Greek Poetic Tradition*. Berkeley: University of California Press, 1985.

Hermann, Gottfried. *Elementa doctrinae metricae*. Leipzig: G. Fleischer Jr., 1816.

Hertz, Neil. "A Reading of Longinus." In *The End of the Line: Essays on Psychoanalysis and the Sublime*, 1–20. New York: Columbia University Press, 1985.

Hewitt, Mary E. *Poems: Sacred, Passionate, and Legendary*. New York: Lamport, Blakeman, and Law, 1854.

————. "Translation of an Ode of Sappho." *The Broadway Journal* 1.24 (14 June 1845) 379.

Holoka, James P. *Gaius Valerius Catullus: A Systematic Bibliography*. New York: Garland Publishing, 1985.

Holstun, James. " 'Will you rent our ancient love asunder?': Lesbian Elegy in Donne, Marvell, and Milton." *ELH* 54 (1987) 835–67.

Hooker, J. T. *The Ancient Spartans*. London: J. M. Dent, 1980.

Huxley, G. L. *Early Sparta*. Cambridge: Harvard University Press, 1962.

Irigaray, Luce. *This Sex Which Is Not One*, translated by Catherine Porter, with Carolyn Burke. Ithaca: Cornell University Press, 1985.

————. *Speculum of the Other Woman*, translated by Gillian C. Gill. Ithaca: Cornell University Press, 1985.

Irwin, E. *Colour Terms in Greek Poetry*. Toronto: University of Toronto Press, 1974.

Itzkowitz, J. B. "On the Last Stanza of Catullus 51." *Latomus* 42 (1983) 129–34.

Jacobs, Carol. "The Monstrosity of Translation." *Modern Language Notes* 90 (1975) 155–66.

Jacobson, Howard. *Ovid's Heroides*. Princeton: Princeton University Press, 1974.

Jaeger, Werner. *Paideia: The Ideals of Greek Culture*, translated by Gilbert Highet. Vol. 1, *Archaic Greece: The Mind of Athens*. Oxford: Blackwell, 1939.

Jagose, Annamarie. *Lesbian Utopics*. New York: Routledge, 1994.

Jardine, Lisa. *Still Harping on Daughters: Women and Drama in the Age of Shakespeare*. Brighton: Harvester Press, 1983.

Jenkyns, Richard. *Three Classical Poets: Sappho, Catullus, and Juvenal*. Cambridge: Harvard University Press, 1982.

——— . *The Victorians and Ancient Greece*. Cambridge: Harvard University Press, 1980.

Johns, Catherine. *Sex or Symbol: Erotic Images of Greece and Rome*. Austin: University of Texas Press, 1982.

Johnson, Barbara. "Les fleurs du mal armé: Some Reflections on Intertexuality." In *Lyric Poetry: Beyond New Criticism*, edited by Chaviva Hosek and Patricia Parker, 264–80. Ithaca: Cornell University Press, 1985.

Johnson, W. R. *The Idea of Lyric*. Berkeley: University of California Press, 1982.

Jonson, Ben. *Complete Poems*, edited by George Parfitt. New Haven: Yale University Press, 1975.

——— . *The Sad Shepherd*. New York: John Day, 1944.

——— . *Timber; or, Discoveries*. Syracuse: Syracuse University Press, 1953.

Joplin, Patricia Klindienst. "The Voice of the Shuttle Is Ours." *Stanford Literature Review* 1 (1984) 25–53.

Kappeler, Susanne. *The Pornography of Representation*. Minneapolis: University of Minnesota Press, 1986.

Kassel, R., and C. Austin. *Poetae Comici Graeci*. 6 vols. to date. Berlin: W. de Gruyter, 1983–.

Kauffman, Linda S. *Discourses of Desire: Gender, Genre, and Epistolary Fiction*. Ithaca: Cornell University Press, 1986.

Kenner, Hugh. "The Muse in Tatters." In *The Pound Era*, 54–75. Berkeley: University of California Press, 1971.

Keuls, Eva. *The Reign of the Phallus: Sexual Politics in Ancient Athens*. Berkeley: University of California Press, 1985.

Keydell, R. "Epithalamium." *Rivista di archeologia cristiana* 5 (1962) 927–43.

Killigrew, Anne. *Poems* (1686), edited by Richard Morton. Gainesville, Fla.: Scholars' Facsimiles and Reprints, 1967.

Kirkwood, G. M. *Early Greek Monody: The History of a Poetic Type*. Ithaca: Cornell University Press, 1974.

Kizer, Carolyn. "Pro Femina." In *Psyche*, edited by Barbara Segnitz and Carol Rainey, 131. New York: Dell, 1973.

Klaich, Dolores. *Woman Plus Woman*. New York: Simon and Schuster, 1974.

Koniaris, George L. "On Sappho Fr. 31 (L.-P.)." *Philologus* 112 (1968) 173–86.

Krafft-Ebing, Richard von. *Psychopathia Sexualis*. Stuttgart: F. Enke, 1888.

Kramarae, Cheris, and Paula A. Treichler. *A Feminist Dictionary*. London: Pandora, 1985.

Kranz, Walter. *Geschichte der griechischen Literatur*. 3rd ed. Bremen: C. Schünemann, 1958.

Kraus, W. "Sappho." In *Der Kleine Pauly*, edited by K. Ziegler and W. Sontheimer, 4:1542–48. Munich: Druckenmüller, 1972.

Kühner, R., and B. Gerth. *Ausführliche Grammatik der griechischen Sprache Satzlehre*. 2 vols. Hanover: Hahn, 1955.

Kurke, Leslie. "The Politics of ἀβροσύνη in Archaic Greece." *Classical Antiquity* (1992) 91–120.

Kuster, Ludolf, ed. *Suidæ Lexicon, Græce Latine*. Cambridge, 1705.

Laidlaw, W. A. "*Otium.*" *Greece and Rome* 15 (1968) 42–52.

Lamartine, Alphonse de. *Œuvres poétiques complètes*, edited by Marius-François Guyard. Bibliothèque de la Pléiade. Paris: Éditions Gallimard, 1963.

Lanata, Giuliana. "Sul linguaggio amoroso di Saffo." *Quaderni urbinati di cultura classica*, no. 2 (1966) 63–79. Lanham, Richard. *The Motives of Eloquence: Literary Rhetoric in the Renaissance*. New Haven: Yale University Press, 1976.

Lanteri-Laura, Georges. *Lecture des perversions: Histoire de leur appropriation médicale*. Paris: Masson, 1979.

Lardinois, André. "Lesbian Sappho and Sappho of Lesbos." In *From Sappho to de Sade: Moments in the History of Sexuality*, edited by Jan Bremmer, 15–35. London: Routledge, 1989.

———. "Subject and Circumstance in Sappho's Poetry." *Transactions of the American Philological Association* 124 (1994) 57–84.

Lasserre, François. "Ornements érotiques dans la poesie lyrique archaique." In *Serta Turyniana: Studies in Greek Literature and Palaeography in Honor of Alexander Turyn*, edited by John L. Heller and J. K. Newman, 5–33. Urbana: University of Illinois Press, 1974.

Latacz, Joachim. "Realität und Imagination: Eine neue Lyrik-Theorie und Sapphos φαίνεταί μοι χῆνος-Lied." *Museum Helveticum* 42 (1985) 67–94.

Latte, K. Review of H. Fränkel, *Dichtung und Philosophie des frühen Griechentums*. *Göttingische Gelehrte Anzeigen* 207 (1953) 30–42.

Lattimore, R. "Sappho 2 and Catullus 51." *Classical Philology* 39 (1944) 184–87.

Laurentius, Andreas. *Historia Anatomica Humani Corporis et singularum eius partium multis*. Paris, 1595.

Le Fèvre, M. [Tanneguy]. *Les Poètes grecs: Première partie*. Saumur: Dan. de Lerpinière et Jean Lesnier, 1664.

Lefkowitz, Mary R. "Critical Stereotypes and the Poetry of Sappho." *Greek, Roman, and Byzantine Studies* 14 (1973) 113–23. [Also reprinted in *Heroines and Hysterics*, 59–68 (London: Duckworth, 1981).]

———. *First-Person Fictions: Pindar's Poetic "I."* Oxford: Oxford University Press, 1991.

———. *The Lives of the Greek Poets*. Baltimore: Johns Hopkins University Press, 1981.

———. "ΤΩ ΚΑΙ ΕΓΩ: The First Person in Pindar." *Harvard Studies in Classical Philology* 67 (1963) 177–253.

Lehnus, Luigi. "Pindaro: Il *Dafneforico* per Agasicle (Fr. 94b Sn-M.)." *Bulletin of the Institute of Classical Studies* 31 (1984) 61–92.

Leighton, Angela. *Victorian Women Poets: Writing against the Heart*. Charlottesville: University Press of Virginia, 1992.

Leishman, J. B. *The Monarch of Wit*. London: Hutchinson, 1959.

Leopardi, Giacomo. *Tutte le Opere*, edited by Walter Binni. 2 vols. Florence: Sansoni, 1969.

Lesky, Albin. *A History of Greek Literature*, translated by James Willis and Cornelius de Herr. New York: Methuen, 1966.

Levi, Peter. *A History of Greek Literature*. Harmondsworth: Penguin, 1985.

Lewis, Philip E. "The Measure of Translation Effects." In *Difference in Translation*, edited by Joseph Graham, 31–62. Ithaca: Cornell University Press, 1985.

Licht, Hans. *See* Brandt, Paul.

Lidov, Joel B. "The Second Stanza of Sappho 31: Another Look." *American Journal of Philology* 114 (1993) 503–35.

Lipking, Lawrence. *Abandoned Women and Poetic Tradition*. Chicago: University of Chicago Press, 1988.

———. "Aristotle's Sister: A Poetics of Abandonment." *Critical Inquiry* 11 (1983) 61–81.

———. "Sappho Descending: Abandonment through the Ages." In *Abandoned Women and Poetic Tradition*, 57–96. Chicago: University of Chicago Press, 1988.

Lobel, Edgar, and Denys Page, eds. *Poetarum Lesbiorum Fragmenta*. Oxford: Oxford University Press, 1955.

Longinus. *On the Sublime*, edited by W. Hamilton Fyfe. Cambridge: Harvard University Press, 1991.

Lowell, Amy. *The Complete Poetical Works of Amy Lowell*. Boston: Houghton Mifflin, 1955.

———. *Tendencies in Modern American Poetry*. New York: Macmillan, 1917.

Lucian. *Affairs of the Heart*, translated by M. D. MacLeod. Cambridge: Harvard University Press, 1979.

Lyly, John. *The Complete Works of John Lyly*, edited by R. Warwick Bond. 3 vols. 1902. Reprint, Oxford: Clarendon Press, 1967.

———. *Sapho and Phao*. In *The Complete Works of John Lyly*, edited by R. Warwick Bond, 2:362–416. 1902. Reprint, Oxford: Oxford University Press, 1967.

Maclean, Ian. *The Renaissance Notion of Woman: A Study in the Fortunes of Scholasticism and Medieval Science in European Intellectual Life*. New York: Cambridge University Press, 1980.

Manley, Delarivier. *New Atalantis*, edited by Rosalind Ballaster. New York: Penguin Books, 1992.

———. *The Royal Mischief*. London, 1696.

Marcovich, M. "Anacreon, 358 PMG." *American Journal of Philology* 104 (1983) 372–83.

———. "Sappho Fr. 31: Anxiety Attack or Love Declaration?" *Classical Quarterly*, n.s. 22 (1972)

Marcus, Jane. "Liberty, Sorority, Misogyny." In *The Representation of Women in Fiction*, edited by Carolyn B. Heilbrun and Margaret R. Higonnet, 60–97. Baltimore: John Hopkins University Press, 1983.

——— *Virginia Woolf and the Languages of Patriarchy*. Bloomington: Indiana University Press, 1987.

Marks, Elaine. "Lesbian Intertextuality." In *Homosexualities and French Literature*, edited by George Stambolian and Elaine Marks, 353–78. Ithaca: Cornell University Press, 1978.

Marquandt, J., et al., eds. *Claudii Galeni Pergameni scripta minora*. 3 vols. Leipzig: Teubner, 1891.

Marzullo, Benedetto. *Frammenti della lirica greca*. Florence: Sansoni, 1965.

Mavor, Elizabeth. *The Ladies of Llangollen: A Study in Romantic Friendship*. London: Penguin Books, 1971.

McEvilley, Thomas. "Sapphic Imagery and Fragment 96." *Hermes* 101 (1973) 257–78.

———. "Sappho, Fragment 31: The Face behind the Mask." *Phoenix* 32 (1978) 1–18.

McIntosh, Mary. "The Homosexual Role." *Social Problems* 16 (1968) 182–92.

Meier, M. H. E. *Histoire de l'amour grec dans l'antiquité.* Paris: Stendhal, 1930.

Merkelbach, Reinhold. "Sappho und ihr Kreis." *Philologus* 101 (1957) 1–29.

Michell, Humfrey. *Sparta.* Cambridge: Cambridge University Press, 1964.

Milgate, W. *John Donne: The Satires, Epigrams, and Verse Letters.* London: Oxford University Press, 1967.

Millay, Edna St. Vincent. "Sappho Crosses the Dark River into Hades." In *Collected Lyrics*, 293–94. New York: Harper and Brothers, 1939.

Miller, Paul Allen. "Sappho 31 and Catullus 51: The Dialogism of Lyric." *Arethusa* 26 (1993) 183–99.

Milton, John. *Complete Poems and Major Prose*, edited by Merritt Y. Hughes. Indianapolis: Odyssey Press, 1957.

Mitchell, Juliet, and Jacqueline Rose. *Feminine Sexuality: Jacques Lacan and the "école freudienne."* New York: Norton, 1982.

Moi, Toril. *Sexual/Textual Politics: Feminist Literary Theory.* London: Methuen, 1985.

Mora, Edith. *Sappho: Histoire d'un poète et traduction intégrale de l'œuvre.* Paris: Flammarion, 1966.

Morgan, Robin. *Monster.* New York: Vintage, 1972.

Morris, Adelaide. "Prospectus for Gender and Genre Session on H.D." Paper presented at the Modern Language Association convention, Los Angeles, December 1982.

Mueller, Janel. "Lesbian Erotics: The Utopian Trope of Donne's 'Sapho to Philaenis.'" In *Homosexuality in Renaissance and Enlightenment England: Literary Representations in Historical Context*, edited by Claude Summers, 103–35. New York: Harrington Park Press, 1992. [Version of "A Letter from Lesbos."]

———. "A Letter from Lesbos: Utopian Homoerotics in Donne's 'Sapho to Philaenis.'" Typescript draft essay, 1989.

———. "Troping Utopia: Donne's Brief for Lesbianism in 'Sapho to Philaenis.'" In *Sexuality and Gender in Early Modern Europe: Institutions, Texts, Images*, edited by James Grantham Turner, 182-207. Cambridge: Cambridge University Press, 1993. [Version of "A Letter from Lesbos."]

Müller, Karl Otfried. *Geschichte der griechischen Literatur bis auf das Zeitalter Alexanders*, edited by Eduard Müller. Vol. 1. Breslau: Josef Max, 1841.

———. *Histoire de la littérature grecque.* 2 vols. Paris: Durand, 1865.

———. *The History and Antiquities of the Doric Race.* 2 vols. Oxford: Collingwood, 1830.

———. *A History of the Literature of Ancient Greece*, translated by John W. Donaldson. 3 vols. 1858. Reprint, Port Washington, N.Y.: Kennikat Press, 1971.

Mure, William. *A Critical History of the Language and Literature of Antient Greece.* 5 vols. London: Longman, 1850–57.

———. "Sappho and the Ideal Love of the Greeks." *Rheinisches Museum* 12 (1857) 564–93.

Murray, Oswyn M., ed. *Sympotica: A Symposium on the Symposion.* Oxford: Oxford University Press, 1990

Muth, R. "'Hymenaios' and 'Epithalamion.'" *Wiener Studien* 67 (1954) 5–45.

Nagy, Gregory. *The Best of the Achaeans: Concepts of the Hero in Archaic Greek Poetry.* Baltimore: Johns Hopkins University Press, 1979.

————. *Comparative Studies in Greek and Indic Meter*. Cambridge: Harvard University Press, 1974.

————. "Phaethon, Sappho's Phaon, and the White Rock of Leukas." *Harvard Studies in Classical Philology* 77 (1973) 137–80.

————. *Pindar's Homer: The Lyric Possession of an Epic Past*. Baltimore: Johns Hopkins University Press, 1990.

Neue, J. Christianus, ed. *Sapphonis Mytilenaeae Fragmenta*. Berlin: G. Nauck, 1827.

Norton, Rictor. *Mother Clap's Molly House: The Gay Subculture in England, 1700–1830*. London: GMP Publishers, 1992.

O'Higgins, Dolores. "Sappho's Splintered Tongue: Silence in Sappho 31 and Catullus 51." *American Journal of Philology* 111 (1990) 156–67. [Citations above are to the version published in this volume.]

Ollier, François. *Le Mirage spartiate: Étude sur l'idéalisation de Sparte dans l'antiquité grecque*. 2 vols. Paris: E. de Boccard, 1933; Societé d'édition Les Belles Lettres, 1943.

Ostriker, Alicia. "The Poet as Heroine: Learning to Read H.D." In *Writing Like a Woman*, 7–41. Ann Arbor: University of Michigan Press, 1983.

Ovid. *Publii Ouidii Nasonis Heroidum epistolae*. [London], 1583.

————. *Tristia*. Cambridge, 1638.

Page, Denys L. *Alcman: The Partheneion*. Oxford: Oxford University Press, 1951.

————. *Sappho and Alcaeus: An Introduction to the Study of Ancient Lesbian Poetry*. Oxford: Oxford University Press, 1955.

————, ed. *Poetae Melici Graeci*. Oxford: Oxford University Press. 1962.

————, ed. *Supplementum Lyricis Graecis*. Oxford: Oxford University Press, 1974.

Paré, Ambroise. *The Workes of that famous Chirurgion Ambrose Parey*, translated by Thomas Johnson. London, 1634.

Park, Katharine. "Hermaphrodites and Lesbians: Sexual Anxiety and French Medicine, 1570–1620." Typescript.

Parke, H. W. *Festivals of the Athenians*. London: Thames and Hudson, 1977.

Parker, Holt N. "Sappho Schoolmistress." *Transactions of the American Philological Association* 123 (1993) 309–51. [Citations above are to the version published in this volume.]

Parker, Patricia. *Literary Fat Ladies: Rhetoric, Gender, Property*. London: Methuen, 1987.

Parry, Milman. "The Traces of the Digamma in Ionic and Lesbian Greek." In *The Making of Homeric Verse*, edited by Adam Parry, 319–403. Oxford: Oxford University Press, 1971.

Passarini, A. "La τρυφή nella storiographia ellenistica." *Studi Italiani di Filologia Classica* 11 (1934) 35–56.

Patterson, Lee. " 'For the Wyves love of Bathe': Feminine Rhetoric and Poetic Resolution in the *Roman de la Rose* and the *Canterbury Tales*." *Speculum* 58 (1983) 656–95.

Patzer, Harald. *Die griechische Knabenliebe*. Wiesbaden: Franz Steiner Verlag, 1982.

Pelliccia, Hayden. "Anacreon 13 (358 *PMG*)." *Classical Philology* 86 (1991) 30–36.

Philips, Ambrose, trans. *The Odes of Anacreon and Sappho*. London, 1711.

Philips, Katherine. "To My Most, Excellent Lucasia: On Our Friendship." In *Poems*, 107. London, 1697.

Plath, Sylvia. *The Collected Poems*, edited by Ted Hughes. New York: Harper and Row, 1981.

Pliny. *The Historie of the World Commonly called, the Naturall Historie of C. Plinius Secundus*, translated by Philemon Holland. London, 1601.

Podlecki, Anthony J. *The Early Greek Poets and Their Times*. Vancouver: University of British Columbia Press, 1984.

Poe, Edgar Allan. "The Philosophy of Composition." In *Selected Prose, Poetry, and "Eureka,"* edited by W. H. Auden, 421–31. New York: Holt, Rinehart, and Winston, 1950.

———. "The Premature Burial." *The Broadway Journal* 1.24 (14 June 1845) 369–73.

Poliakov, Léon. *The Aryan Myth: A History of Racist and Nationalist Ideas in Europe*. New York: Basic Books, 1974.

Pomeroy, Sarah B. *Goddesses, Whores, Wives, and Slaves: Women in Classical Antiquity*. New York: Schocken, 1975.

Pope, Alexander. *The Poems of Alexander Pope*, edited by John Butts. New Haven: Yale University Press, 1963.

Pound, Ezra. *The Cantos*. New York: New Directions, 1986.

———. *Letters*, 1907–1941, edited by D. D. Paige. New York: Harcourt, Brace and Company, 1950.

Praz, Mario. *The Romantic Agony*, translated by Angus Davidson. Oxford: Oxford University Press, 1970.

Prins, Yopie. "Sappho Doubled: Michael Field." *Yale Journal of Criticism* 8.1 (1995) 165–86.

Privitera, G. Aurelio. "Ambiguità antitesi analogia nel fr. 31 L.P. di Saffo." *Quaderni urbinati di cultura classica*, no. 8 (1969) 37–80.

Proust, Marcel. "A propos of Baudelaire." In *Baudelaire: A Collection of Critical Essays*, edited by Henri Peyre, 125–26. Englewood Cliffs, N.J.: Prentice Hall, 1962.

Pucci, P. *Odysseus Polutropos: Intertextual Readings in the "Odyssey" and "Iliad."* Ithaca: Cornell University Press, 1987.

Puelma, M. "Die Selbstbeschreibung des Chores in Alkmans grossem Partheneion-Fragment." *Museum Helveticum* 34 (1977) 1–55.

Quinn, Kenneth, ed. *Catullus: The Poems*. London: Macmillan; New York: St. Martin's Press, 1970.

Quinn, Vincent. *Hilda Doolittle*. New York: Twayne, 1967.

Rayor, Diane, trans. *Sappho's Lyre: Archaic Lyric and Women Poets of Ancient Greece*. Berkeley: University of California Press, 1991.

Read, Alexander. *The Manuall of the Anatomy, or, Dissection of the Body of Man*. London, 1642.

Redfield, James. "The Women of Sparta." *Classical Journal* 73 (1977) 146–61.

Renehan, R. "Anacreon Fragment 13 Page." *Classical Philology* 79 (1984) 28–32.

Reynolds, L. D., et al., eds. *Texts and Transmissions: A Survey of the Latin Classics*. Oxford: Clarendon Press, 1983.

Reynolds, Margaret. " 'I lived for art, I lived for love': The Woman Poet Sings Sappho's Last Song." In *Victorian Women Poets: A Critical Reader*, edited by Angela Leighton. Cambridge, Mass.: Blackwell, 1996.

Rich, Adrienne. Foreword to *Working It Out: Twenty-three Women Writers, Artists, Scientists, and Scholars Talk about Their Lives and Work*, edited by Sara Ruddick and Pamela Daniels, xiv–xxiv. New York: Pantheon, 1977.

———. "Compulsory Heterosexuality and Lesbian Existence." *Signs* 5 (1980) 631–60.

Richter, Gisela M. A. *The Portraits of the Greeks*. 3 vols. London: Phaidon, 1965.

Richter, Johann. *Sappho und Erinna*. Leipzig: Voss, 1833.

Rigolot, François. "Louise Labé et la rédecouverte de Sapho." *Nouvelle revue du seizième siècle* 1 (1983) 19–31.

Rissman, Leah. *Love as War: Homeric Allusion in the Poetry of Sappho.* Beiträge zur klassischen Wissenschaft 157. Konigstein: Hain, 1983.

Rivier, A. "Observations sur Sappho 1, 19 sq." *Revue des études grecques* 80 (1967) 84–92.

Robbins, Elizabeth. *Ancilla's Share.* 1924. Reprint, Westport, Conn.: Hyperion, 1976.

Robbins, Emmet. " 'Every Time I Look at You . . .': Sappho Thirty-One." *Transactions of the American Philological Association* 110 (1980) 255–61.

Roberts, W. Rhys, ed. *Longinus On the Sublime.* 2nd ed. Cambridge: Cambridge University Press, 1907.

Robinson, David M. *Sappho and Her Influence.* Boston: Marshall Jones, 1924.

Rogers, W. G. *Ladies Bountiful.* New York: Harcourt, Brace, and World, 1968.

Rose, H. J. *A Handbook of Greek Literature.* London: Methuen, 1942.

Rösler, Wolfgang. "Homoerotik und Initiation: Über Sappho." In *Homoerotische Lyrik*, 43–54. Vol. 6 of *Kolloquium der Forschungsstelle für europäische Lyrik des Mittelalters an der Universität Mannheim*, edited by Th. Stemmler. Tübingen: Gunter Narr, 1992.

———. "Realitätsbezug und Imagination in Sappho's Gedicht ΦΑΙΝΕΤΑΙ ΜΟΙ ΚΗΝΟΣ." In *Der Übergang von der Mündlichkeit zur Literatur bei den Griechen*, edited by Wolfgang Kullmann and Michael Reichel, 271–87. ScriptOralia 30. Tübingen: Gunter Narr Verlag, 1990.

———. "Über Deixis und einige Aspekte mündlichen und schriftlichen Stils in antiker Lyrik." *Würzburger Jahrbücher* 9 (1983) 7–28.

Rubin, Gayle. Introduction to *A Woman Appeared to Me*, by Renée Vivien. Tallahassee, Fla.: Naiad Press, 1979.

Rüdiger, Horst. *Sappho, Ihr Ruf und Ruhm bei der Nachwelt.* Leipzig: Dieterich, 1933.

Rukeyser, Muriel. "Poem out of Childhood." In *The Collected Poems of Muriel Rukeyser*, 3. New York: McGraw-Hill, 1982.

Russo, Joseph. "Reading the Greek Lyric Poets (Monodists)." *Arion* 1 (1973) 707–30.

Rychlewska, L., ed. *Turpilius: Fragmenta.* Leipzig, 1971.

Saake, Helmut. "Sappho." In *Die Grossen der Weltgeschichte*, 1:306–20. Munich, 1971.

———. *Sapphostudien: Forschungsgeschichtliche, biographische und literarästhetische Untersuchungen.* Munich: Ferdinand Schöningh Verlag, 1972.

———. *Zur Kunst Sapphos: Motiv-analyische und kompositionstechnichische Interpretationen.* Munich: Ferdinand Schöningh Verlag, 1971.

Saltonstall, Wye, trans. *Ovid's Heroicall Epistles.* London, 1636.

———, trans. *Ovids Tristia: Containinge five bookes of mournfull elegies.* London, 1633.

Sappho. *Anacreontis Teii Carmina . . . Subjiciuntur etiam Duo Vetustissimae Poetiae Sapphus Elegantissima Odaria. . . .* London, 1695.

———. *The Poems of Sappho*, translated by Susy Q. Groden. Indianapolis: BobbsMerrill, 1966.

Sarton, May. "My Sisters, O My Sisters." In *Selected Poems of May Sarton*, 192–93. New York: Norton, 1978.

Satan's Harvest Home. 1749. Reprint, New York: Garland Publishing, 1985.

Scarry, Elaine. "Donne: 'But yet the Body is his booke.' " In *Literature and the Body: Essays on Populations and Persons*, edited by Scarry, 70–105. Baltimore: Johns Hopkins University Press, 1988.

Scott, Sarah. *A Description of Millenium Hall.* 1762. Reprint, New York: Garland Publications, 1974.

Schadewaldt, W. *Sappho: Welt und Dichtung, Dasein in der Liebe.* Potsdam: Eduard Stichnote, 1950.

Schlegel, August Wilhelm von. *Vorlesungen über Ästhetik I [1798–1803],* edited by Ernst Behler. Vol. 1 of *Kritische Ausgabe der Vorlesungen,* edited by Ernst Behler and Frank Jolles. Paderborn: Ferdinand Schöningh Verlag, 1989.

Schlegel, Friedrich von. *Geschichte der alten und neuen Litteratur.* Vienna: K. Schaumburg, 1815.

———. *Lectures on the History of Literature, Ancient and Modern,* translated by J. G. Lockhart. 2 vols. Edinburgh: W. Blackwood, 1818.

———. *Studien des Klassischen Altertums,* edited by Ernst Behler. Vol. 1 of *Kritische Friedrich-Schlegel-Ausgabe,* edited by Ernst Behler, Jean-Jacques Anstett, and Hans Eichner. Paderborn: Ferdinand Schöningh Verlag, 1979.

Schmid, W., and O. Stählin. *Geschichte der griechischen Literatur.* Vol. 1. Munich: Beck, 1929.

Schmitt-Pantel, P. "Sacrificial Meal and Symposion: Two Models of Civic Institutions in the Archaic City?" In *Sympotica: A Symposium on the Symposion,* edited by Oswyn M. Murray, 14–33. Oxford: Oxford University Press, 1990.

Scudéry, Madeleine de. *Artamènes, or, The Grand Cyrus: an excellent new romance* (1649–53). London, 1653–55.

Sedgwick, Eve Kosofsky. *Epistemology of the Closet.* Berkeley: University of California Press, 1990.

Segal, Charles. "Catullan Otiosi: The Lover and the Poet." *Greece and Rome* 17 (1970) 25–31.

———. "Eros and Incantation: Sappho and Oral Poetry." *Arethusa* 7 (1974) 139–60.

———. "Otium and Eros: Catullus, Sappho, and Euripides' *Hippolytus.*" *Latomus* 48 (1989) 817–22.

Sergent, Bernard. *L'Homosexualité initiatique dans l'Europe ancienne.* Paris: Payot, 1987.

Sharp, Jane. *The Midwives Book.* 1671. Reprint, New York: Garland Publishing, 1985.

Sherburne, John, trans. *Ovids Heroical Epistles.* London, 1639.

Shockley, Ann Allen. "A Meeting of the Sapphic Daughters." *Sinister Wisdom* 9 (1979) 54–59.

Sitwell, Dame Edith. *Selected Letters, 1919–1964,* edited by John Lehmann and Derek Parker. New York: Vanguard, 1979.

Smyth, H. W. *Greek Grammar.* Cambridge: Harvard University Press, 1920.

Snell, Bruno. *Poetry and Society: The Role of Poetry in Ancient Greece.* Bloomington: Indiana University Press, 1961.

———. "Sapphos Gedicht *phainetai moi kenos.*" *Hermes* 66 (1931) 71–90.

Snyder, Jane McIntosh. "Public Occasion and Private Passion in the Lyrics of Sappho of Lesbos." In *Women's History and Ancient History,* edited by Sarah B. Pomeroy, 1–19. Chapel Hill: University of North Carolina Press, 1990.

———. *The Woman and the Lyre: Women Writers in Classical Greece and Rome.* Carbondale: Southern Illinois University Press, 1989.

Stehle [Stigers], Eva. "Retreat from the Male: Catullus 62 and Sappho's Erotic Flowers." *Ramus* 6 (1977) 83–102.

———. "Romantic Sensuality, Poetic Sense: A Response to Hallett on Sappho." *Signs* 4 (1979) 465–71.

———. "Sappho's Private World." In *Reflections of Women in Antiquity,* edited by Helene P. Foley, 45–61. New York: Gordon and Breach, 1981.

Stein, Gertrude. *The Autobiography of Alice B. Toklas.* 1933. Reprint, New York: Modern Library, 1969.

Stein, Judith. "The Iconography of Sappho, 1775–1875." Ph.D. diss., University of Pennsylvania, 1981.

Stigers, Eva. *See* Stehle, Eva.

Storer, Edward, trans. "Poems and Fragments of Sappho." *Egoist* 2 (1 October 1915) 153–55.

———, trans. *Poems and Fragments of Sappho.* London: Egoist Press, 1915.

Svenbro, Jesper. *Phrasikleia: An Anthropology of Reading in Ancient Greece*, translated by Janet Lloyd. Ithaca: Cornell University Press, 1993.

———. "La tragédie de l'amour: Modèle de la guerre et theorie de l'amour dans la poesie de Sappho." *Quaderni di storia* 19 (1984) 57–79.

Swann, Thomas Burnett. *The Classical World of H.D.* Lincoln: University of Nebraska Press, 1962.

Swetnam, Joseph. *The Arraignment of Lewd, Idle, Froward, and Inconstant Women.* London, 1615.

Swinburne, Algernon Charles. *Selected Poetry and Prose*, edited by John D. Rosenberg. New York: Modern Library, 1968.

———. *The Swinburne Letters*, edited by Cecil Y. Lang. Vol. 4. New Haven: Yale University Press, 1960.

Symonds, John Addington. *A Problem in Greek Ethics, Being an Inquiry into the Phenomenon of Sexual Inversion.* 1901. Reprint, London: Haskell House, 1971.

———. *Studies of the Greek Poets.* London: A. and C. Black, 1900.

Tarditi, Giovanni. *Storia della letteratura greca.* Turin: Loescher Editore, 1973.

Teasdale, Sara. "To Cleis (The Daughter of Sappho)." In *Helen of Troy and Other Poems*, 88–89. New York: Macmillan, 1928.

Theiler, Willy, and Peter von der Muhll. "Das Sapphogedicht auf der Scherbe." *Museum Helveticum* 3 (1946) 22–25.

Timpanaro, Sebastiano. "*Ut vidi, ut perii.*" In *Contributi di filologia e di storia della lingua latina*, 219–87. Ricerche di storia della lingua latina 13. Rome: Edizioni dell'Ateneo e Barigazzi, 1978.

Tobin, J. J. M. "A Note on Dalila as 'Hyaena.'" *Milton Quarterly* 11 (1977) 89–90.

Tomlinson, Sophie. "'My Brain the Stage': Margaret Cavendish and the Fantasy of Female Performance." In *Women, Texts, and Histories, 1575–1760*, edited by Clare Brant and Diane Purkiss, 134–63. London: Routledge, 1992.

Tomory, Peter. "The Fortunes of Sappho: 1770–1850." In *Rediscovering Hellenism: The Hellenic Inheritance and the English Imagination*, edited by G. W. Clarke, 121–35. Cambridge: Cambridge University Press, 1989.

Traub, Valerie. "The Psychomorphology of the Clitoris." *GLQ: A Journal of Lesbian and Gay Studies* 2 (1995) 81–113.

Treu, Max, ed. *Sappho.* 3rd ed. Munich: E. Heimeran, 1963.

Trotter, Catherine. *Agnes de Castro.* London, 1696.

———. *Fatal Friendship.* London, 1698.

Trumbach, Randolph. "Sodomitical Subcultures, Sodomitical Roles, and the Gender Revolution of the Eighteenth Century: The Recent Historiography." In *'Tis Nature's Fault: Unauthorized Sexuality during the Enlightenment*, edited by Robert Purks Maccubbin, 109–21. Cambridge: Cambridge University Press, 1987.

Trumpf, J. "Über das Trinken in der Poesie der Alkaios." *Zeitschrift für Papyrologie und Epigraphik* 12 (1973) 139–60.

Tsagarakis, Odysseus. "Broken Hearts and the Social Circumstances in Sappho's Poetry." *Rheinisches Museum* 129 (1986) 1–17.

———. *Self-Expression in Early Greek Lyric: Elegiac and Iambic Poetry.* Palingenesia 11. Wiesbaden: Franz Steiner Verlag, 1977.

———. "Some Neglected Aspects of Love in Sappho's Fr. 31 LP." *Rheinisches Museum* 122 (1979) 97–118.

Tubach, Sally. "Female Homoeroticism in German Literature and Culture." Ph.D. diss., University of California, Berkeley, 1980.

Turberville, George, trans. *The Heroycall Epistles of the Learned Poet Publius Ovidius Naso.* London, 1567.

Venette, Nicholas. *Conjugal Love; or, The Pleasures of the Marriage Bed.* 1750. Reprint, New York: Garland Publishing, 1984.

Venuti, Lawrence. *The Translator's Invisibility: A History of Translation.* New York: Routledge, 1995.

Verducci, Florence. *Ovid's Toyshop of the Heart: Epistulae Herodium.* Princeton: Princeton University Press, 1985.

Verri, Alessandro. *Le Avventure di Saffo poetessa di Mitilene,* edited by Alfredo Cottignoli. Rome: Salerno Editrice, [1991].

Vessey, Thomson D. W. "Philaenis." *Revue Belge de Philologie et d'Histoire* 54 (1976) 78–83.

Vicinus, Martha. "Lesbian History: All Theory and No Facts or All Facts and No Theory?" *Radical History Review* 60 (1994) 57–75.

Vickers, Nancy. "Diana Described: Scattered Woman and Scattered Rhyme." In *Writing and Sexual Difference,* edited by Elizabeth Abel, 95–109. Chicago: Chicago University Press, 1980.

Vivien, Renée. *Cendres et poussiers.* 1902. Reprint, Paris: Regine Deforges, 1977.

———. *Études et Preludes.* 1904. Reprint, Paris: Regine Desforges, 1976.

———. *The Muse of the Violets,* translated by Margaret Porter and Catherine Kroger. Tallahassee, Fla.: Naiad Press, 1977.

———. *Poèmes de Renée Vivien.* 2 vols. 1923–24. Reprint, New York: Arno, 1975.

———. *A Woman Appeared to Me* (1904), translated by Jeanette H. Foster. Tallahassee, Fla.: Naiad Press, 1979.

Voigt, Eva-Maria, ed. *Sappho et Alcaeus.* Amsterdam: Athenaeum-Polak and van Gennep, 1971.

von der Muhll, Peter. *Ausgewählte Kleine Schriften.* Basel: Friedrich Reinhardt, 1976.

Wagner, Peter. "The Discourse on Sex—or Sex as Discourse: Eighteenth-Century Medical and Paramedical Erotica." In *Sexual Underworlds of the Enlightenment,* edited by G. S. Rousseau and Roy Porter, 46–68. Chapel Hill: University of North Carolina Press, 1988.

Warren, Rosanna. "Sappho: Translation as Elegy." In *The Art of Translation: Voices from the Field,* edited by Warren, 199–216. Boston: Northeastern University Press, 1989.

Watts, Emily Stipes. *The Poetry of American Women from 1632 to 1945.* Austin: University of Texas Press, 1977.

Weeks, Jeffrey. *Sex, Politics, and Society: The Regulation of Sexuality since 1800.* London: Longman, 1981.

————. *Sexuality and Its Discontents: Meanings, Myths, and Modern Sexualities.* London: Routledge, 1985.

Weigall, Arthur. *Sappho of Lesbos: Her Life and Times.* Garden City, N.Y.: Garden City Publishing Company, 1932.

Welcker, F. G. *Sappho von einem herrschenden Vorurtheil befreyt.* In *Kleine Schriften zur Griechischen Litteraturgeschichte,* 2:80–144. Bonn: Eduard Weber, 1845.

————. "Über die beiden Oden der Sappho." *Rheinisches Museum* 11 (1857) 226–59.

West, M. L. "Alcmanica." *Classical Quarterly* 15 (1965) 188–202.

————. "Burning Sappho." *Maia* 22 (1970) 307–30.

————. "Other Early Poetry." In *Ancient Greek Literature,* edited by K. J. Dover, 29–49. Oxford: Oxford University Press, 1980.

————. *Studies in Greek Elegy and Iambus.* Berlin: de Gruyter, 1974.

————, ed. *Iambi et Elegi Graeci.* 2 vols. Oxford: Oxford University Press, 1972.

Wharton, Henry Thornton. *Sappho: Memoir, Text, Selected Renderings, and a Literal Translation.* London: J. Lane, 1885.

Whitford, Margaret. *Luce Irigaray: Philosophy in the Feminine.* London: Routledge, 1991.

Wickes, George. *The Amazon of Letters: The Life and Loves of Natalie Barney.* New York: G. P. Putnam's Sons, 1976.

Wilamowitz-Moellendorf, Ulrich von. "Der Chor der Hagesichora." *Hermes* 32 (1897) 251–63.

————. *Sappho und Simonides: Untersuchungen über griechische Lyriker.* Berlin: Weidmann, 1913.

Wilamowitz-Moellendorf, Ulrich von, et al. *Die griechische und lateinische Literatur und Sprache.* Leipzig: Teubner, 1912.

Williamson, Margaret. *Sappho's Immortal Daughters.* Cambridge: Harvard University Press, 1995.

Wills, Garry. "Sappho 31 and Catullus 51." *Greek, Roman, and Byzantine Studies* 8 (1967) 167–97.

Wilson, G. R. "The Interplay of Perception and Reflection: Mirror Imagery in Donne's Poetry." *Studies in English Literature* 9 (1969) 107–21.

Winckelmann, Johann Joachim. *Histoire de l'art chez les anciens.* Paris: Jansen, 1793. [German ed., 1764–67.]

————. *Recueil des différentes pièces sur les arts.* Paris: Barois, 1786. [German ed., 1763.]

Winkler, John J. *The Constraints of Desire: The Anthropology of Sex and Gender in Ancient Greece.* New York: Routledge, 1990.

————. "Double Consciousness in Sappho's Lyrics." In *The Constraints of Desire: The Anthropology of Sex in Ancient Greece,* 162–87. New York: Routledge, 1990.

————. "Gardens of Nymphs: Public and Private in Sappho's Lyrics." In *Reflections of Women in Antiquity,* edited by Helene P. Foley, 63–90. New York: Gordon and Breach, 1981.

————. "The Laughter of the Oppressed: Demeter and the Gardens of Adonis." in *The Constraints of Desire: The Anthropology of Sex in Ancient Greece,* 188–209. New York: Routledge, 1990.

Winner, Matthias. "Progetti ed esecuzione nella Stanza della Segnatura." In *Raffaello nell'appartamento di Giulio II e Leone X: Monumenti Musei Galerie Pontificie,* 247–91. Milan: Electa, 1993.

Winterson, Jeanette. *Art and Lies: A Piece for Three Voices and a Bawd*. New York: Knopf, 1995.

Wittig, Monique, and Sande Zeig. *Lesbian Peoples: Material for a Dictionary*. New York: Avon, 1979.

Wolle, Francis. *A Moravian Heritage*. Boulder, Colo.: Empire Reproductions, 1972.

Woodbridge, Linda. *Women and the English Renaissance: Literature and the Nature of Womankind*, 1540–1620. Urbana: University of Illinois Press, 1984.

Woolf, Virginia. *A Room of One's Own*. 1929. Reprint, New York: Harcourt, Brace and World, 1957.

————. "A Society." In *The Complete Shorter Fiction of Virginia Woolf*, edited by Susan Dick, 124–36. 2nd ed. New York: Harvest-Harcourt, 1989.

Yates, Frances A. *Giordano Bruno and the Hermetic Tradition*. London: Routledge and Kegan Paul, 1964.

Yourcenar, Marguerite. *Fires* (1963), translated by Dori Katz. New York: Farrar Straus Giroux, 1981.

Zielinski, Th. "Sappho und der leukadische Sprung." *Klio* 23 (1930) 1–19.

Zilboorg, Caroline. "Joint Venture: Richard Aldington, H.D., and the Poets' Translation Series." *Philological Quarterly* 70 (1991) 67–98.

————. *Richard Aldington and H.D.: The Early Years in Letters*. Bloomington: Indiana University Press, 1992.

CONTRIBUTORS

Harriette Andreadis is associate professor of English at Texas A & M University. Among her publications are a critical edition of John Lyly's 1595 play *Mother Bombie* and "The Sapphic-Platonics of Katherine Philips," *Signs* 15 (Autumn 1989). She is currently completing a collection of private writings by nineteenth-century Texas women and a book-length study of same-sex female erotics in early modern England.

Joan DeJean is Trustee Professor of French at the University of Pennsylvania. She is the author, most recently, of *Fictions of Sappho, 1546–1937* (Chicago, 1989) and *Tender Geographies: Women and the Origins of the Novel in France* (New York, 1991).

Ellen Greene, the editor of this volume, is associate professor of classics at the University of Oklahoma. She has published articles on gender and sexuality in the poetry of Sappho, Catullus, Propertius, and Ovid. Her book, *Gender, Power, and the Poetics of Desire: Studies in Latin Love Poetry* (in progress), examines representations of women and the construction of gender in Catullus, Propertius, and Ovid.

Susan Gubar is Distinguished Professor of English and Women's Studies at Indiana University. Among her publications are *The Madwoman in the Attic: The Woman Writer and the Nineteenth Century Literary Imagination*, with Sandra M. Gilbert (New Haven, 1984) and *No Man's Land: The Place of the Woman Writer in the Twentieth Century*, 3 vols., with Sandra M. Gilbert (New Haven, 1988–94). She is the coeditor, with Sandra M. Gilbert, of *Shakespeare's Sisters: Feminist Essays on Women Poets* (Bloomington, 1979); *The Female Imagination and the Modernist Aesthetic* (New York, 1986); and *The Norton Anthology of Literature by Women,* 2nd ed. (New York, 1996). Her forthcoming book is *White Skin, Black Face: Representations of Racechange in Twentieth-Century Culture.*

Elizabeth D. Harvey teaches English and women's studies at the University of Western Ontario. She is the author of *Ventriloquized Voices: Feminist Theory and English Renaissance Texts* (New York, 1992) and coeditor, with Kathleen Okruhlik, of *Women and Reason* (Ann Arbor, 1992) and, with Katharine Maus, of *Soliciting Interpretation: Literary Theory and Seventeenth-Century English Poetry* (Chicago, 1990).

Glenn W. Most is professor of classics at Heidelberg University. He has published on ancient and modern literature and philosophy.

Dolores O'Higgins is associate professor of classics at Bates College in Maine, and she works on ancient poetry, both Greek and Latin. Her current project is a book on women's joking and laughter in ancient Greece.

Holt Parker is associate professor of classics at the University of Cincinnati. Research interests include gender in the classical world, Roman comedy, Latin love poetry, and ancient medicine. He has been the recipient of a Women's Classical Caucus Prize, an NEH fellowship, and the Rome Prize.

Yopie Prins is assistant professor of English and comparative literature at the University of Michigan. She has published various articles on Greek literature, Victorian poetry, and nineteenth-century Hellenism and has a book forthcoming on Sappho's reception in Victorian England, *Victorian Sappho: Declining a Name.*

Erika Rohrbach is a doctoral candidate in English at the Graduate Center, City University of New York. Her research focuses on modernist poetics and the structure of confessional narrative. She has published on Gertrude Stein and Thomas Carlyle.

INDEX

Compositor:	Humanities Typesetting & Graphics, Inc.
Text:	10.5/12.5 Monotype Baskerville
Display:	Monotype Baskerville
Greek:	Ibycus, designed by Silvio Levy
	modified by Pierre A. MacKay
Printer:	Braun-Brumfield, Inc.
Binder:	Braun-Brumfield, Inc.